Programs of
Early Education

Programs of Early Education
The Constructivist View

Rheta DeVries

University of Houston

with

Lawrence Kohlberg

Harvard University

Longman

New York & London

Senior Editor: Naomi Silverman
Production Editor: Halley Gatenby
Text Design: Steven August Krastin
Production Supervisor: Judith Stern
Compositor: Best-set Typesetter Ltd.
Printer and Binder: R. R. Donnelley & Sons Company

Programs of Early Education

Longman Inc.
95 Church Street
White Plains, N.Y. 10601

Associated companies:
Longman Group Ltd., London
Longman Cheshire Pty., Melbourne
Longman Paul Pty., Auckland
Copp Clark Pitman, Toronto
Pitman Publishing Inc., New York

Library of Congress Cataloging-in-Publication Data
DeVries, Rheta.
    Programs of early education.

    Includes bibliographical references and index.
    1. Constructivism (Education) 2. Education,
Preschool—United States. 3. Education, Preschool—
United States—Curricula. I. Kohlberg, Lawrence,
1927–   . II. Title.
LB1140.3.D48 1987   372'.21   86-10318
ISBN 0–582–28301-9

87 88 89 90 9 8 7 6 5 4 3 2 1

Copyright acknowledgments

We gratefully acknowledge permission to quote from the following sources:

Teale, W. & Sulzby, E. (1986). *Emergent literacy: Reading and writing.* Norwood, NJ: Ablex Publishing Corporation.

From *To understand is to invent,* by Jean Piaget. Copyright © Unesco, 1948, 1972. English language translation by George-Anne Roberts. Copyright © 1973 by The Viking Press, Inc. Reprinted by permission of Viking Penguin, Inc.

From *Science of education and the psychology of the child,* by Jean Piaget. Translated from the French by Derek Coltman. Copyright © 1969 by Editions Denoel, Paris. Translation copyright © 1970 by Grossman Publishers, Inc. Reprinted by permission of Viking Penguin, Inc.

From A developmental-interaction approach: Bank Street College of Education, by Barbara Biber. In *The preschool in action* (2nd ed.), ed. M. Day and R. Parker. Boston: Allyn and Bacon, 1977.

Reprinted with permission of the Free Press, a Division of Macmillan, Inc., from *The moral judgment of the child* by Jean Piaget, translated by Marjorie Gabain. New York: The Free Press, 1965.

From *Teacher's guide to accompany early childhood curriculum—A Piaget program,* by Celia Lavatelli. Nashua, NH: Delta Education, Inc., 1970, 1973.

From *Promoting cognitive growth from a developmental-interaction point of view,* by B. Biber, E. Shapiro, and D. Wickens. Copyright © 1971 by the National Association for the Education of Young Children.

We also acknowledge the following sources:

Learning and the development of cognition, by B. Inhelder, H. Sinclair, and M. Bovet. Cambridge, Mass.: Harvard University Press, 1974.

Physical knowledge in preschool education: Implications of Piaget's theory, by C. Kamii and R. DeVries. Englewood Cliffs, N.J.: Prentice-Hall, 1978.

Piaget for early education, by C. Kamii and R. DeVries. In *Preschool in action* (2nd ed.), ed. M. Day and R. Parker. Boston: Allyn and Bacon, 1975/1977.

Literacy before schooling, by E. Ferreiro and A. Teberosky. Portsmouth, N.H.: Heinemann Educational Books, 1979/1982.

Construcción de escrituras a través de la interacción grupal, by A. Teberosky. In *Nuevas perspectivas sobre los procesos de lectura y escritura,* ed. E. Ferreiro and M. Gomez Palacio. Mexico City: Siglo, 1982.

Contents

Part II
Curriculum and Activities Derived from Constructivist Goals

Part III
Traditional School Objectives and Curricula from a Constructivist Perspective

Preface

Our purpose in this book is to present a perspective on early education that is informed by cognitive-developmental and constructivist theory. Through comparison of educational programs and approaches, we raise issues and questions about the relationship between psychological theories of mental development and educational practices.

EMPHASIS ON DEVELOPMENTAL THEORY

Our effort to present a systematic philosophy of educational practice follows the work of John Dewey. Principally, however, our perspective leans on the epistemological and psychological theory of Jean Piaget because his is the most advanced scientific theory we have of mental development. This theory is our centerpiece because its acceptance in child psychology and educational psychology represents what Thomas Kuhn (1962), the historian and philosopher of science, calls a "paradigm shift"—a fundamental change in a scientific community's way of thinking. It is a revolution usually due to an individual's breakthrough rather than the result of slow accumulations of knowledge. In child psychology, the work of Piaget's school represents a paradigm shift because it fundamentally altered our views of the child and the nature of mental development. The central theme of this paradigm is the view of the child as active in constructing not only knowledge but intelligence itself. This paradigm shift has occurred not only in the cognitive domain, but in the sociomoral domain as well. Our book summarizes efforts to extend this paradigm to the field of education, where it is no less revolutionary than in psychology.

Awareness of Piaget's work had by the mid-1960s led some American psychologists and educators to begin developing programs of early education based on it. The theoretical rationale for programs and approaches already in existence (such as Bank Street or other play-oriented or center-based approaches) was re-viewed through the Piagetian lens, and debate began about the educational significance of Genevan research and theory. In this book, we review and compare programs of early education reflecting the cognitive-developmental and constructivist orientation, from the perspective of the general philosophy of educational practice to which this paradigm gives rise.

Our review of programs of early education is limited to programs that (1) clearly define their human development assumptions and (2) start from assumptions broadly compatible with cognitive-developmental and constructivist assumptions. We emphasize the comparison of closely related programs rather than diametrically opposed programs where differences are obvious. It is easy, for example, to see differences between DISTAR and Bank Street programs, but not so easy to see differences between Bank Street and the Kamii-DeVries approach where similar words often have different meanings.

Our analysis and comparison of programs addresses (1) general theoretical base, especially assumptions about the nature of learning, (2) objectives in cognitive, emotional, and sociomoral realms, (3) the teacher's role in each program, and (4) the children's activities. These systematic comparisons lead to conclusions that the Kamii-DeVries approach represents Piaget's theory more completely than other programs. Our purpose is not, however, to evaluate some programs as better than others, but rather to clarify constructivist rationale and practices.

We use the term "cognitive-developmental" to refer to *structural* aspects in cognitive development—particularly the stages of Jean Piaget. This view is "cognitive-developmental" not in the sense that it identifies the intellectual development of the child with the whole development of the child, but in the sense that cognitive organization is present in every area of the child's development where a self thinks about the physical and social world and its own relation to that world. We use the word "constructivist" to refer to the child's *process* of stage change—the reorganization of knowledge and understanding. Our cognitive-developmental and constructivist orientation is informed most notably by the research and theory of Piaget, but also by the work of George Herbert Mead, James Mark Baldwin, and Lev Vygotsky.

EMPHASIS ON LIFE IN THE CLASSROOM

Our aim in this book is to discuss the cognitive-developmental and constructivist view in terms of its practical educational implications. These implications are not obvious, and educators taking child development courses usually find that developmental psychologists for the most part talk in vague generalities about educational issues—when these are addressed at all.

In contrast, we try to go from a general theoretical position to specifics about life in the classroom—about principles of teaching, the role of the teacher, and educational activities. These specifics have been influenced not only by theory but also by the teachers with whom we have worked closely to develop, test, and modify our conceptualizations of practices harmonious with Piaget's theory. Most of all, we seek to take account of the psychological experience of the child and to provide definitions of "constructive" activity that contribute to long-range goals of development to the highest stage of cognitive, sociomoral, and ego development. Our aim is to help teachers develop the ability to think critically about their teaching from the point of view of the child's psychological experience and these long-range goals.

OVERVIEW OF THE BOOK

Part I focuses on the theoretical and philosophical framework of the cognitive-developmental or constructivist view. In the first chapter, the cognitive-developmental view is discussed in relation to two other broad streams of thought in the history of educational philosophy—romantic maturation theory, and the environmental or cultural transmission theory. We argue that development as the aim of education is the most legitimate because it avoids the pitfall of value relativity found in the contrasting "romantic" and "cultural transmission" schools of thought.

In Chapter 2 we review the educational implications of Piaget's research and theory. Since not all of Piaget's work is significant for education, it is necessary to select from the body of Genevan work what is most useful to teachers.

Chapter 3 focuses on three different approaches to translating Piaget's theory into preschool curricula. Kuhn notes that the proliferation of versions of scientific theory is a usual symptom of crisis in science. We believe the proliferation of practical versions of cognitive-developmental and constructivist theory is a sign of crisis in early education that prepares the way for new progress. We therefore undertake an analysis of similarities and differences among three representative versions of such theory in the hope that it may contribute to some resolution of this crisis. The "Piagetian" approaches of Lavatelli, Weikart and his colleagues at the High/Scope Educational Foundation, and Kamii and DeVries are compared. Objectives, principles of teaching, and the role of the teacher are analyzed in terms of the implications presented in Chapter 2.

Part II focuses on curricula and activities derived from constructivist goals. In Chapters 4–6, our own approach is described in further detail. The general goal is to show in very specific and practical terms how we close the gap between Piaget's theory and educational practice. Physical knowledge as a curriculum area is the focus of Chapter 4. Uniquely, the Kamii-DeVries conceptualization is based on Piaget's distinction between different kinds of psychological experience that lead to different kinds of knowledge. This chapter summarizes aims, principles of teaching, and types of activities presented in the book *Physical Knowledge in Preschool Education: Implications of Piaget's Theory* by Kamii and DeVries (1978). It also includes new material from DeVries's subsequent work aimed at a closer integration in this curriculum domain of the structural and functional aspects of Piaget's theory. That is, it describes stages in children's conceptions of shadows and provides description of how teachers use their knowledge of these stages in carrying out shadow activities. Children's active efforts with shadows are presented to illustrate what their reasoning looks like when teachers teach according to constructivist principles.

Group games in the Kamii-DeVries program are discussed in Chapter 5. This chapter summarizes the principles of teaching and types of group games presented in the book *Group Games in Early Education: Implications of Piaget's Theory* by Kamii and DeVries (1980). However, it provides a reformulation of the theoretical rationale, and presents new material on how teachers can evaluate cognitive and sociomoral progress by observing children in games. Stages of development are presented for three games— Marbles, Guess Which Hand the Penny Is In, and Tic-Tac-Toe.

Moral discussion and the classroom meeting are discussed in Chapter 6, by Lawrence Kohlberg and Thomas Lickona. These two program components do not really amount to a "curriculum." Rather, they are contexts for the sustained moral dialogue that has always been central to characterizing the classroom democracy of progressive education. In addition to group games, these contexts involve moral and social dilemma discussion, democratic decision making, interpersonal conflicts, and co-operative projects in a classroom community where the moral atmosphere reflects concern for justice and caring. The unity of the cognitive-developmental perspective is further expressed here in the view of a consistent and positive relationship between the conditions for cognitive growth and the conditions for social and moral growth. Activities advocated represent a progression away from moral education as isolated activity toward an integration of moral and role-taking activity into the flow of everyday events in the classroom.

Part III moves to the constructivist perspective of traditional school objectives and curricula. Number and arithmetic in the Kamii-DeVries approach is the focus of Chapter 7. Piaget's theory of number is reviewed, and some aspects of traditional math education and early efforts to use Piaget's work in preschool education are critiqued. Implications of Genevan work for math education are reviewed, with emphasis on the importance of understanding the nature of children's errors. Constructivist activities and principles of teaching are described, accompanied by accounts of classroom interactions.

Chapter 8 leans heavily on the work of Emilia Ferreiro and Ana Teberosky in the presentation of the constructivist perspective of reading and writing. Their stages in children's psychogenetic progression focus on successive hypotheses about written language. These stages are compared with those described by Elkind and Chall. General practical implications are discussed in terms of 14 principles, and the teacher's role is conceptualized. Classroom interactions illustrate the constructivist perspective on reading and writing.

Part IV is devoted to comparison of programs sharing a cognitive-developmental orientation. Chapter 9 considers the Montessori Method. Broad compatibility with and divergences from the constructivist approach are discussed in terms of basic assumptions about the nature of learning and development. An analytical overview of the Montessori curriculum is provided. Points of divergence are discussed as contrasts: (1) exercise of senses versus exercise of reasoning, (2) self-correcting versus open-ended materials, (3) error-free repetition versus error-filled and error-informed experimentation, (4) work versus play, (5) individual versus collective activity, (6) obedience versus autonomy, and (7) the teacher as "Directress" versus companion/guide.

Chapter 10, on Bank Street theory and practice, is a discussion of the closest relative to the constructivist approach described in Part II. Bank Street is the best-articulated representative of the child-centered nursery school tradition, from which Piagetian programs borrow much. The "developmental-interaction" position that emerged to express Bank Street's common focus on cognitive and affective aspects in interaction is assessed from the cognitive-developmental, constructivist perspective. To illustrate similarities and differences at the level of teacher-child interaction, detailed annotated protocols of making applesauce in Bank Street and constructivist classrooms are presented side by side.

In Chapter 11 we consider the future of cognitive-developmental and constructivist education. First, we take stock of current educational receptivity to this worldview. Then, four core issues are discussed: (1) the development of constructivist teachers, (2) the relation of constructivist education to the teaching of subject matter, (3) the development of applied constructivist theory, and (4) evaluating the effectiveness of cognitive-developmental and constructivist programs.

INTEGRATING DEVELOPMENTAL THEORY AND CLASSROOM PRACTICE

While we believe that developmental psychology can be useful to educational practitioners, we recognize its practical limitations. That is, research and theory in child development cannot be translated directly into child-rearing or teaching principles. Our position is that a developmental psychology useful to practice cannot be created without a conscious concern for educational implications. We also argue that educational practice can be improved neither by research on education as it is nor by basic research on child development. Rather, an experimental education is required that integrates theory and practice. Such an integration must coordinate philosophical objectives with an understanding of the facts of development

While this book is a statement about how education can profit from a developmental psychology and epistemology, we also believe that developmental psychology and epistemology can profit from educators' efforts to give practical definition to their principles. In the final analysis, demonstration of the validity of a theory requires practical application. The truth of a psychological theory must be demonstrated and can be honed in natural "experiments" such as schooling. Constructivist educational experiments can provide a supporting and connecting matrix for the growth of the connective tissue of explanatory psychological theory. Each is interconnected with and dependent on the other for its common definition.

OUR AUDIENCE

This book is meant for professionals and graduate students in child development and in education. It contains more child-development research and theory than customary in a psychology text for education students because we believe that knowledge of the most basic psychological concepts of child development and genetic psychology is essential for the educator. It contains more discussion of education than customary for students of child development because we believe that principles of child development are fully understood only when translated into child-rearing and educational practices. The translation of child-development research and theory into practices reveals the true nature of our understanding of those principles.

For a more detailed review of cognitive-developmental theory and research, we refer readers to a companion volume (*Child Pyschology and Childhood Education* by Kohlberg & Colleagues, 1987). While it is not necessary to read the companion volume before reading this book, we do assume some knowledge of Piaget's theory on the part of the reader—knowledge gained, for example, by reading summary accounts such as those by Ginsburg and Opper (1979), Wadsworth (1978), or Gardner (1982).

We agree with Piaget (1948/1973) that the younger the students, the more difficult the teacher's task. This is why it has been so important for us to think about how *teachers* think about how *children* think. We therefore dedicate this book to all those who take seriously the challenge of early education informed by developmental psychology and genetic epistemology.

Many people have read drafts of various parts of this book, offered reactions, and contributed valuable ideas. We especially want to thank Frank Kessel and Millie Almy for comments on the entire manuscript. Howard Gardner provided useful comments on several chapters. Barbara Biber and Edna Shapiro commented on two drafts of the chapter on Bank Street and entered into a dialogue that greatly enriched our understanding of their views. Others who provided useful comments on that chapter include Greta Fein, Rochelle Mayer, and Gerald Gratch. We also profited from an extensive dialogue with David Weikart on the chapter on Piagetian programs. In addition, we are grateful for reactions to that chapter by Constance Kamii, Hermine Sinclair, Kathryn Saxton, and Roberta Thayer. We thank Emilia Ferreiro and David Yaden for comments on the chapter on reading and writing, and Nancy Rambusch for reactions to an early draft of the chapter on the Montessori Method. In addition, teachers in the Human Development Laboratory School at the University of Houston and students of Rheta DeVries read portions of the book at various stages. We are grateful for all these reactions, which aided us in revision of our ideas and their presentation. In addition, we are especially grateful to the teachers and children with whom we collaborated in classroom experimentation over many years.

Rheta DeVries
Lawrence Kohlberg

An Appreciation

The influence of my co-author Lawrence Kohlberg has been a sustaining presence in my life and work for more than 25 years. First Larry was my professor, then mentor, collaborator, colleague, and friend.

Larry was the professor who invited a beginning graduate student at the University of Chicago to be his research assistant. He was the mentor who took seriously an outlandish proposal to train a cat to wear rabbit and dog masks. He even made weekly trips with me to consult on masks to be used in generic identity interviews. His fascination with new electronic gadgets combined with methodological mentorship in the purchase of the first portable video recorder for that project.

As Larry's student, I often waited two hours past appointed meeting times. I never minded being the last appointment of the day because Larry then gave me all the time I needed, along with a bit of sherry. I grew comfortable with long, preoccupied pauses in conversation, knowing that what came next was always worth waiting for. I learned to read Larry's handwriting.

Collaboration was a colleagueship. As a colleague, Larry provided an intellectual companionship I have found nowhere else. This companionship was a continual source of growth for me. Talking with Larry or hearing his reactions to manuscripts always gave me an enriched or changed perspective that energized revisions. This book took seven years to produce mainly because of the difficulty of writing fairly about theories and programs with which I disagree. Larry was particularly helpful to me in this task. I entered our project a rather rigid Piagetian too harsh in my criticism of others. Sometimes I thought Larry too generous in his attitude toward differences with others. This tension in our views produced many fruitful discussions. If we have succeeded in a balanced and fair perspective, it is largely due to Larry's efforts to help me relate to theories and practices with which I disagree.

Larry was the kind of friend who would travel from Cambridge to Detroit to be with me at a time of medical crisis. As friends, we trusted each other. Our meetings were always affirmations.

For many years, Larry courageously fought a battle with physical pain. In our last telephone conversation, on January 9, 1987, he shared feelings about his increased pain and its debilitating effects. In that phone call, Larry also gave me a gift of renewed affirmation of our friendship.

Larry did not see the final revised manuscript of this book, but he fulfilled his last responsibility to it by traveling to Houston to help me decide how to cut and revise.

Our work together is at an end. I would like to conclude this personal statement of appreciation by echoing inscriptions Larry wrote when he gave me copies of his *Essays on Moral Development:* ''With affection and gratitude for our long friendship'' and ''With love and appreciation for our friendship and colleagueship.'' These feelings are mutual. Larry's influence will always be present for me.

Rheta DeVries
January 31, 1987

PART I

Constructivist Theory

Chapter 1

Education for Development

Education for development is not a new idea. This perspective was created in the United States by John Dewey and has been repopularized in the last decade through the work and influence of Jean Piaget. We advocate the cognitive-developmental view as a convergence of Piaget's constructivism and Dewey's progressivism.

Dewey stated that the fundamental way in which psychology influences educational decisions (consciously or unconsciously) is through shaping educational "worldviews." An educational "worldview" reflects value assumptions about the aims of education and psychological assumptions about the nature of the child and of learning and development. We believe that it is necessary to understand the explicit and implicit psychological assumptions underlying competing educational approaches and to understand as well their related philosophic value assumptions. Such self-conscious analysis is crucial for an informed choice between alternative educational "worldviews."

Development as the aim of education is discussed below in relation to two other broad streams in the history of educational philosophy and practice. Following Piaget, our definition of "development" emphasizes invariant, sequential, and hierarchical stages in mental evolution.

BROAD STREAMS IN EDUCATIONAL THOUGHT

Kohlberg and Mayer (1972) outlined in a classic article three streams in educational thought: romanticism, cultural transmission, and cognitive-developmental or interactional schools of thought. These reflect different educational psychologies having different epistemological components[1] and value systems and lead to different strategies for defining educational objectives and evaluating educational experience.

Romanticism

The Metaphor

Romanticism is an educational worldview reflecting a maturational theory of development. Psychological development is expressed in the metaphor of organic growth in which the environment aids by providing nourishment that triggers the unfolding of innate, prepatterned, predetermined stages. Social-

---

1. *Epistemological components* are assumptions about the nature of knowledge and how it is acquired.

emotional and physical development are both viewed as biological processes not dependent on cognitive growth. Examples of the romantic stream of thought include the theories of Freud (1938) and Gesell (Gesell & Ilg, 1949). To label this ideology "romantic" is not to accuse it of being unscientific. Rather, it is to recognize that the nineteenth-century discovery of the natural development of the child was part of a larger romantic philosophy, an ethic and epistemology involving a discovery of the natural and the inner self. Educational ideology reflecting the romantic stream of thought includes A. S. Neill's Summerhill, "free schools," "deschool," and "open school" movements.

The Epistemological Position

The epistemological position of this stream of educational thought is existential or phenomenological. Knowledge and reality are discussed in terms of immediate, inner experience of the self—truth as self-awareness or self-insight having both emotional and intellectual components. Knowledge beyond the self is achieved through sympathetic understanding of other "selves."

The Value System

Individual freedom is the basis of the value system of romanticism that emphasizes a humanistic ethical concern for the child's rights and happiness. The result is an ethical relativity in which whatever children do and feel naturally is accepted. It assumes that when children are left to themselves without social control, the inner "good" (abilities and social virtues) will unfold and the inner "bad" will come under control, resulting in a state of mental health.

The Strategy for Defining Objectives

Psychiatric theory postulating spontaneity, creativity, and self-confidence as desirable for mental health leads to objectives expressed as a set of traits characterizing an ideal or fully functioning personality. The shortcoming of this approach is that it is vague, arbitrary, and often contradictory. For example, Head Start objectives include both "self-discipline" and "spontaneity," which are arbitrary and contradictory. The problem of value relativity is apparent, for example, in a list of vague virtues including "honesty" and "integrity." As Kohlberg and Mayer (1972) point out, "one person's 'integrity' is another person's 'stubbornness,' one person's 'honesty in expressing your true feelings' is another person's 'insensitivity to the feelings of others' " (p. 479). Kohlberg and Mayer also criticize the "bag of virtues" approach on the grounds that longitudinal research makes questionable the assumption that there are positive childhood personality traits that are adaptive and stable or predictive over time. (See Kohlberg, Ricks, & Snarey, 1984, for a full presentation of this research.)

Cultural Transmission

The Metaphor

The cultural transmission ideology in education is expressed in the metaphor of the machine. The machine may be the wax on which the environment transcribes its markings, it may be the telephone switchboard through which environmental stimulus-energies are transmitted, or it may be the computer in which bits of information from the environment are stored, retrieved, and recombined. In any case, the environment is seen as "input," as information or energy more or less directly transmitted to and accumulated in the organism. The organism in turn emits "output" behavior.

This worldview includes associationistic-learning, information-processing, and environmental-contingency theories of development. It is traceable from John Locke's "blank slate" to Thorndike's laws of learning to B. F. Skinner's laws of stimulus-response learning and Siegfried Engelmann's programming of learning based on conceptual analysis and is currently the major alternative to cognitive-developmental or constructivist theory. It was formulated at the turn of the century by Thorndike, who went to Columbia before the turn of the century to establish a science of education. He thought this science would be based on the experimental establishment of basic laws of learning as learning was influenced by punishment, reward, and practice. This assumption continues in the work of Skinner and Engelmann.

The Epistemological Position

The epistemological position of this view reflects the empiricist tradition that assumes that knowledge results from information coming from outside the individual to the inside through the senses. Although this assumption implies the internality of knowledge, it precludes the necessity for worrying much about internal aspects. What is known is determined primarily by the nature of the external stimulus. In contrast with the romantic epistemology, the cultural transmission approach therefore eliminates references to internal or subjective experience and trait descriptions. It stresses knowledge as it can be inferred from predictable behavior observed in some "objective" way and measured.

The Value System

Thorndikean psychology claims to be value-neutral, defining methods of instruction and measurement relevant or valid for educational practice without specific prior value assumptions. Following Dewey, we would question the neutrality of applying Thorndikean principles to methods of instruction and measurement because these principles imply tacit acceptance of "cultural transmission" or "traditional" educational values.

Attempts to be "value neutral" result in an unintended value premise of social relativity. Social consensus in a society or culture becomes the basis for deciding on educational objectives. As Kohlberg and Mayer (1972) argue, Bereiter and Engelmann (whose work evolved into the curriculum currently known as DISTAR) are an example of aims justified by the social relativistic standard of the American public school.

> In order to use the term cultural deprivation, it is necessary to assume some point of reference. . . . The standards of the American public schools represent one such point of reference. . . . There are standards of knowledge and ability which are consistently held to be valuable in the schools, and any child in the schools who falls short of these standards by reason of his particular cultural background may be said to be culturally deprived. (Bereiter & Engelmann, 1966, p. 24)

In such a view, all values are relative, and there is no ultimate standard of worth for learning and development.

Kohlberg and Mayer discuss the considerable problems in a "value-neutral" position. They argue that no statement of educational goals or prescription for practice can avoid the introduction of value principles. Consider, for example, the advocacy of positive reinforcement. Choices of means, in the last analysis, also imply choices of ends. Concrete, positive reinforcement is not an ethically neutral means. To advise the use of concrete reinforcement is to advise that a certain kind of character, motivated by concrete reinforcement, is the end of education. Skinner equates or derives a value word (good) from a fact word (positive reinforcement). This equation is questionable; we wonder whether obtaining positive reinforcement really is good.

Kohlberg considers Skinner's view as "the psychologist's fallacy," a form of the "naturalistic fallacy." The psychologist's fallacy is to assume that the psychologist's conclusions about human nature, human values, and human desires should be taken by the educator as desirable goals. Kohlberg argues that statements of "ought" are not legitimately derived from statements of "is," and that the conceptions of education and development must be philosophically justified conceptions of the good.

The Strategy for Defining Educational Objectives

The cultural transmission approach is characterized by two strategies for defining educational objectives and evaluating educational experience. The first is to accept the standards of knowledge and behavior found in schools. It defines the long-range objective as eventual power and status in the social system (e.g., income, success).

A second strategy for elaborating aims is what Kohlberg calls the "industrial psychology" approach. Thorndike believed that educational science should be based on the establishment of measures of intelligence and achievement defined by psychometric methods and the normal curve. Value is thus placed on behavior to the extent that it serves as a means to limited but measurable ends, especially to later success that can be empirically predicted from the behavior. Achievement tests are the prime example of attempted prediction of later success in the educational system. The academic contents of these tests have become educational goals of schooling.

This strategy is criticized as a compounding of one type of relativism on another. That is, not only are achievement test items derived by "bootstrapping" from future success in school as it exists; they also include many bits of arbitrary information having no epistemological rationale for their worth. Kohlberg and Mayer question the philosophy of justifying judgments of success on the basis of achievement tests. Not only is much of their content arbitrary, but achievement tests do not, in fact, predict success in life after schooling. Therefore, they cannot be justified as definition of educational goals.

The cultural transmission stream of thought includes not only the achievement-testing movement, but also all approaches emphasizing repetition and reinforcement as a means of teaching. Repetition in drill and practice is pervasive throughout American education. The recent "back to basics" movement reflects the commonsense assumption that if we only give more time to and make more efficient our focus on the cultural transmission of knowledge, educational problems will be solved. The most recent statement of this view comes from Skinner himself, who writes (1984) that "The Shame of American Education" is in its failure to use sufficiently teaching machines and programmed instruction. Yet, despite Skinner's assertion that the cultural transmission view is not taken to its logical conclusion often enough, this school of thought dominates general educational practices in both public and private schools.

Cognitive-Developmental

The Metaphor

The cognitive-developmental ideology is expressed in the metaphor of a dialectic process. In this view, knowledge evolves from an internal psychological core through an interaction or dialogue with the physical and social environment rather than by direct biological maturation or direct learning of external givens from the environment. In contrast to the metaphors of plant and machine, the cognitive-developmental stream of thought emphasizes the child as a philosopher or scientist-poet who progressively reorganizes knowledge on the basis of a personal "reading" of experience.

The dialectical metaphor was first elaborated by Plato, given new meaning by Georg Hegel, and later formed into an educational philosophy by John Dewey. Dewey defined development in terms of ethical and epistemological progress and saw this development as the aim of education. Dewey's vision of cognitive-developmental psychology and its relation to philosophy has an allied flowering in the work of James Mark Baldwin earlier in this century. Neither Dewey's nor Baldwin's theorizing directly inspired a school of American cognitive-developmental, educational, or child psychologists. Dewey by his writing and Baldwin by his personal conversation, however, had a strong influence on a Swiss psychologist and educator, Edouard Claparède, founder of the Jean Jacques Rousseau Institute in Geneva; and Piaget eventually inherited both Claparède's institute and his Dewey-Baldwin theory. Piaget brilliantly enhanced and systematized American cognitive-developmental theory, linked the theory to formal logic and mathematical philosophy, invented methods for exploring the theory empirically, and produced a large body of creative research data to elaborate it, and thus created a "school" in child psychology. Only in the 1960s did cognitive-developmental theory finally come to America.

The Epistemological Position

The epistemological position of this stream of thought is best expressed by Piaget's constructivist theory. Standing in clear contrast to the empiricist assumptions of the cultural transmission stream, Piaget argued that the stimulus is not a stimulus for the individual until he acts on it. Piaget talked about "reading off" reality, which involves interaction of the organism and environmental stimulus ($O \Leftrightarrow S$). In this model, the arrow going toward the stimulus represents assimilation, where the organism acts on the stimulus and interprets it in terms of previous knowledge. The arrow going toward the organism represents accommodation, where previous knowledge is modified. Accommodation occurs in response to incomplete assimilation or contradiction with expectation. In this sense, the stimulus "acts" on the organism, but the action is not in the stimulus—it is in the knower. In contrast to the empiricist $S \rightarrow O$, where the stimulus is conceived as acting on a passive organism, the Piagetian $O \Leftrightarrow S$ puts the organism first and makes the stimulus dependent on the active assimilation-accommodation process within the organism. This epistemological position recognizes the child as an inquiring knower whose knowledge is a product of the process of acting that involves a "reading" of experience and eventually confronting inadequacies and contradictions in this "reading."

The epistemology of the cognitive-developmental stream is often called "interactionist." This means not only a psychological interchange between the individual and the environment but a dynamic interaction *within the individual* of multiple aspects of what is "known," including erroneous ideas that eventually disappear. The epistemology of this educational ideology is expressed as "constructivism"—the view that the knower actively constructs knowledge.

The Value System

The value system of the cognitive-developmental (or progressive) stream of thought focuses on ethical and cognitive universals. Some ethical universals can be justified philosophically, such as Immanuel Kant's principle of respect for persons—"treat others as ends in themselves and not solely as means." Such a philosophical principle cannot be fully stated as an aim of education until it can be stated psychologically or translated into statements about a more adequate stage of development culminating in principled reasoning based on respect for persons. Genetic epistemology and developmental psychology offer descriptions of psychological stages in terms of the evolution of progressively more adequate forms of cognitive and moral reasoning. Examples are Piaget's stages of operational reasoning and Kohlberg's moral stages of justice. Goals based on these values are not arbitrary and relative but are universal across individuals and cultures. In over 40 cultures, for instance, humans are found to go through the same sequence of moral stages (Snarey, 1985).

The Strategy for Defining Educational Objectives

The developmental-philosophic strategy for the cognitive-developmental stream, as opposed to the other two, can deal with the ethical question of having a standard of nonrelative or universal value and with factual questions of prediction. The concept of development, as elaborated by cognitive-developmental theory, implies a standard of adequacy *internal* to and governing the developmental process itself. It is obvious that the notion of development must do more than merely define what comes later in time because it is not necessarily the case that what comes later is better.

Cognitive-developmental theory postulates a formal internal standard of adequacy that is not merely an order of events in time. Cognitive-developmental psychological theory postulates that movement through a sequential progression represents movement from a less adequate to a more adequate psychological state. This formal standard is not itself ultimate, but must be elaborated as a set of ethical and epistemological principles and justified in philosophical and ethical terms. The distinctive feature of the developmental-philosophic approach is that a philosophic conception of adequate principles is coordinated with a psychological theory of development and with the facts of development.

In contrast with "value-free" approaches, the approach suggested by Dewey and Piaget considers questions of value or adequacy at the very start. Piaget begins by establishing epistemological and logical criteria for deciding which thought structures are most adaptive and adequate for coping with complexity. Similarly, our work on ethical stages has taken a philosophic notion of adequate principles of justice (represented especially in the work of Kant and Rawls) as a guide in defining the direction of development. It takes as a hypothesis for empirical confirmation or refutation that development is a movement toward greater epistemological or ethical adequacy as defined by philosophic principles.

The progressives' philosophical method differs from the approaches of philosophers of other persuasions in that the progressive or developmental method is partly empirical rather than purely analytic. Prior notions are revised in light of the facts. This method of "empirical" or "experimental" philosophy is especially central for an educational philosophy prescribing educational aims.

Philosophical principles cannot be stated as ends of education until they can be stated psychologically and assessed empirically. This means translating them into statements about a more adequate stage of development. Otherwise the rationally accepted principles of the philosopher will only be arbitrary concepts and doctrines for the child. Accordingly, to make a genuine statement of an educational end, the educational philosopher must coordinate notions of principles with understanding of the facts of development.

THE DEFINITION OF DEVELOPMENT

The word *stage* is used in a variety of different ways in different theories of development. No wonder it is a "fuzzy concept" in everyday conversation. Parents and teachers frequently say that a child "is just going through a stage," a statement that often means they do not understand or know what to do about a particular behavior and so hope that it will just disappear. A child may also be said to be "going through a stage" in a more positive sense (for example, a love of horses stage or a cowboys and Indians stage). Followers of Gesell (Gesell & Ilg, 1949) speak of stages in terms of what is typical at a particular age. These stages are descriptions of normative behavior that is directly observable, such as the "No's" of "the negative twos." This behavior is believed to be genetic in origin and determined by physiological maturation. A 1-year-old, for example, is expected to be able to climb stairs; a 5-year-old not to be fearful except of such things as bodily harm, dogs, the dark, and that its mother will not return; and a 6-year-old is expected to be very fearful, especially of loud sounds, the supernatural, the elements, and the possibility that someone may be hiding under the bed. This notion of stages is maturational. Parents and teachers are advised that there is nothing they can do except accept the behaviors of a given stage and wait with patience until inevitable bad times and good times pass.

Our advocacy of development as the aim of education involves a specialized definition of development in terms of progression within a sequence of universal stages. Research indicating that reasoning develops through stages provides the evidence for the validity of Piaget's constructivist epistemological position. Review and discussion of research bearing on the issue of stages in various domains of human development are the subject of a companion book (Kohlberg & Colleagues, 1987). Here we assume the general validity of the stage notion demonstrated through that review. However, it is important to acknowledge that Piaget was not the only theorist to talk about stages and that others define them in different ways. Since stage progress is central to the cognitive-developmental aim of education, it is important to clarify the differences among them.

Kohlberg (1984) has made a distinction among three types of stage models that is useful in gaining perspective on various conceptions of stages in development. These are "hard," "soft," and "functional" stage models, briefly defined below.

Hard Stages

The specific criteria for a hard structural stage model are those that have been used to identify Piagetian cognitive stages.

1. *Stages imply a qualitative difference in structures* (modes of thinking) that still serve the same basic function at various points in development (for example, preoperational intelligence and later operational intelligence both refer to the individual's ability to reason about social and object worlds).
2. *These different structures form an invariant sequence in individual development.* While cultural factors may speed up, slow down, or stop development, they do not change its sequence.
3. *Each of these different and sequential modes of thought forms a "structural whole."* A given stage response on a task does not just represent a specific response determined by knowledge and familiarity with that task or tasks similar to it; rather, it represents an underlying thought-organization. The implication is that various aspects of stage structures should appear as a fairly consistent cluster of responses in development. This does not mean that a given child will be at the same level in all domains of reasoning, but that there is a dominant mode of thinking within a given domain. Constructive progress is characterized by a certain lack of synchrony or unevenness across and within content domains. This complicates the notion of the structural wholeness of Piaget's stage concept. Piaget cautions that a given reaction by a child should not be interpreted in a static or absolute way, but should be viewed as one indicator of something that is in fact dynamic. Rather, an entire complex of many reactions can be interpreted as potential for activity. In this respect, Piaget sometimes talked about a "moving equilibrium" to refer to the dynamism of the constructive process that includes fluctuations.
4. *Stages are hierarchical integrations.* As noted, stages form an order of increasingly differentiated and integrated *structures* to fulfill a common function. Accordingly, higher stages displace (or, rather, integrate) the structures found at lower stages. Kohlberg's stages of moral development and Selman's stages of perspective-taking (see Chapter 6 in this volume and Chapter 8 in Kohlberg & Colleagues, 1987) are examples of hard cognitive stages.

Soft Stages

Soft stages focus on the form of development, as do Piagetian stages, but they also include elements of affective and reflective conscious characteristics of persons, characteristics not easily assimilated to the Piagetian paradigm. Of soft structural stage theories, Jane Loevinger's (1976) theory of ego development is the most completely developed. The focus is on the self or ego, viewed as some form of a totality, a system of meaning that confronts the "other" in the world. The unity of the self expressed in soft stages depends on the individual's conscious reflections and insights regarding the self's psychology. Ego development involves the elaboration of a theory about the self that individuals construct. Such reflection is very different from the unconscious "reflective abstraction" in Piaget's theory (discussed in Chapter 2) by which individuals progress in the development of cognitive and sociomoral operations through coordinations of relations. Operations are equilibrated or reversible networks of relations that may be called hard structures.

In contrast to soft stages, hard stages subdivide into discrete content domains, aspects of the totality manifested in soft stages. What hard stages gain by this is precision in the articulation of a structural logic of stages that will transcend the ever-changing growth of psychological knowledge about the self, its functions, and its development. Soft stages may be defined partly in terms of structures having an inner logic, but also partly in terms of functions and motives pertaining to the whole self and its enhancement and defense. The focus of hard structural stages is upon forms of manifest reasoning rather than upon the ego's processes of affirming or defining itself.

Three assumptions are shared by hard and soft structural stage models. First is the shared assumption of a concept of ego. Both perspectives agree that there is a relative unity to personality, an ego that reasons, judges, evaluates, and generally functions to make sense of the world. Second, both perspectives agree on the general requirements of Piaget's hierarchical stage model—(1) that stages represent a structured wholeness, (2) that this develops in an invariant sequence, and (3) that this development proceeds by hierarchical integrations. Third, both perspectives accept the idea that moral judgment and character are major aspects or dimensions of ego development, which contribute to the formation of general ego stages. Developmental assessments are attempts to tap underlying structures, in contrast with traditional psychometric assessments that tap mostly more superficial and often trivial knowledge (see Kohlberg & Colleagues, 1987, for discussion of the differences between Piagetian and psychometric intelligence).

Beyond these similarities, important differences must be noted. Hard and soft structural stage models present different notions of the *nature* of the structured wholeness of stages. While Piaget's notion involves a system of transformational laws that organize and govern reasoning operations, Loevinger's scheme describes structure less as a form of thinking than in terms of fairly stable personality functions and contents. Further, content and structure are confounded in soft structural stage models while they are kept separate in hard stage models.

A second general difference between hard and soft stage models is in the interpretation of the *nature* of hierarchical integration. Progress from one hard stage to another requires transformation of the earlier stage into the later one. Progress from one soft stage to another is cumulative rather than transformative and integrative.

Functional Stages

A functional stage model (for example, that of Erikson, 1963) traces the maturing person through experiences of new sociocultural spheres and roles. Functional stages are representative of differing ego functions in response to different "crises" involving particular and differing tasks over the entire life span. For example, the infant crisis involves the establishment of a basic feeling of trust versus mistrust, the toddler crisis that of autonomy versus shame and doubt, and the 4- to 5-year-old that of initiative versus guilt. In contrast, hard structural stages are described in terms of different structures, or ways of thinking, in response to a single function, such as logical reasoning or moral judgment.

Functional stages rely on psychological accounts, rather than on logical or moral philosophical ones, of the ways in which each stage brings new "strength" or "wisdom" to the individual. As a result, a functional account may be more culturally relative (though not relativistic) than a hard structural account.

Functional stages are also not hierarchically integrated. They are "choices" or uses of new functions by an ego. Earlier functions remain in the background of a new stage, rather than being integrated through transformation.

In conclusion, if teachers aim to promote development in children, it seems essential that they be clearly aware of their assumptions about stages of development and how these influence teaching. If a teacher assumes that stages are hereditary and predetermined, and little influenced by adults, he or she is likely to teach differently from a teacher who assumes that the child's experience is crucial in getting from one stage to the next in a solid and healthy way.

Constructivist education aims at hard structural development, although with a friendly attitude toward those aspects of soft and functional stages that are compatible with or noncontradictory of hard stages. Throughout this book, the reader will find descriptions of hard stages in various domains of knowledge. These form the background of the educational practices proposed.

TRANSLATING PIAGET'S THEORY INTO EDUCATIONAL PRACTICE

Translating a psychological theory of development into "scientific" educational practices is a fourfold task:

1. Overcoming the "psychologist's fallacy" and the "educator's fallacy"
2. Conceptualizing broad implications and objectives

3. Defining classroom practices
4. Demonstrating a relation between educational practices and children's development.

Overcoming the "Psychologist's Fallacy" and the "Practitioner's Fallacy"

Psychologists often assume that educational practices should be deduced directly from research-based psychological theory. This is what one of us (Kohlberg, 1979) calls the "psychologist's fallacy." The "psychologist's fallacy" is the assumption that what the psychologist studies and conceptualizes is what the educator should be concerned about. That is, committing the "psychologist's fallacy" is to assume that the variables important for psychologists to research are the important variables for teachers to think about, or that laws or generalizations that are valid conclusions drawn from research should be the foundation of valid teacher thinking about educational practice. For example, the psychologist's fallacy led to early efforts to foster moral growth by exposing children to reasoning in hypothetical moral dilemmas of children at stages higher than their own (Blatt & Kohlberg, 1975). This effort reflected the fallacy that the relation between psychological theory and teacher practice is a one-way street from the psychologist to the teacher. It was eventually abandoned in favor of a two-way street in which practice emerged from an interaction between teachers and theorists. This, in turn, led the focus away from a formal curriculum to the "hidden curriculum" of children's actual moral experience. The two-way street led to moral education based on action and not just reasoning, to the formation of a participatory democracy or "just community" as the context for moral discussion and moral education. What this means in early education is described in Chapter 6.

To the notion of the "psychologist's fallacy" we add the converse—the "practitioner's fallacy." The "practitioner's fallacy" is the assumption that the teacher should be concerned about "what works" as defined by one's own experience or that of others. The focus is on what the teacher does (principally instruction), and "what works" is defined by short-term assessments of children's accumulation of right answers and "good" behaviors. This fallacy is thus closely related to the cultural transmission stream of educational thought. The criteria for "what works" are determined by the practitioner's values, acknowledged or unacknowledged. These, in turn, reflect implicitly if not explicitly theories about the nature of the child, learning, and development. However, as argued above, value-free teaching is impossible. The effort to ignore theory frequently results in practices full of conceptual contradictions and leaves the child's education at the mercy of the teacher's (or curriculum developer's) individual idiosyncrasy. Psychological theory and research can be of little use when the teacher relies on short-term validation of methods such as worksheets or achievement tests to assess "what works." For example, the practitioner's fallacy has led to the method of drill and practice with flashcards to teach arithmetic computation.

When children succeed in giving right answers, the teacher assumes that the method works. However, when children fail, the practitioner's fallacy leads the teacher to assume that it is the child's fault and to prescribe more practice. This kind of effort reflects the fallacy that the educational relation between the teacher and the child is a one-way street from teaching to learning. The practitioner's fallacy often occurs in association with the "bag of virtues" strategy for defining educational objectives. It results in teaching methods that do not take account of the process of development as this process is illuminated by psychological research and theory.

Constructivist educators have abandoned this view in favor of a two-way street in which the teacher alters teaching methods on the basis of children's understanding (especially the nature of wrong ideas). Making the child do more of what he cannot do is viewed not only as a waste of time but as potentially damaging to children's development. Instead, the teacher tries to understand the child's errors in terms of constructivist research and theory and to base practice on what the child can know and do, creating conditions for the invention of knowledge by the child. What this means in early education is described in Chapters 3–10.

Both the psychologist's fallacy and the practitioner's fallacy must be overcome in order to realize education informed by developmental and genetic psychology.

The work of translating any psychological theory into educational practice is much like the work of translating physiological knowledge into medical practice. Just as medicine relies on facts provided by physiology, education can profit from facts provided by child psychology. Piaget (1948/1973) noted that "The art of education...like the art of medicine...assumes exact and experimental knowledge relating to the human beings on which it is exercised. This is not anatomical and physical knowledge like a doctor's, but psychological" (p. 94). However, he also pointed out (Piaget, 1969/1970) that educational policymakers, unlike medical policymakers, lack the support of a science of educational practice sufficiently developed to provide an empirical basis for decisions. He too contended that such a science of education cannot emerge directly from basic research on child nature and development. The practical results of traveling the two-way street between psychological theory and educational practice are the subject of this book.

Conceptualizing Broad Implications and Objectives

The conceptualization of broad educational implications and objectives emphasizes the theory side of the theory-practice relation. The philosophical and research-based rationale given above for "development" as the aim of education represents one aspect of translating cognitive-developmental theory into educational practice. Further broad implications and objectives are discussed in Chapter 2, and more specifically in Chapters 3–8.

Defining Classroom Practices

Respect for the necessity of traveling the "two-way street" leads to an experimental approach to the specific definition and characterization of classroom practices. Essentially, such an approach involves giving programmatic definition to the theoretical notion of "constructive activity." With a solid understanding of Piaget's theory in mind, the psychologist works with teachers in this phase to conceptualize general classes of classroom experiences in which constructive activity occurs. Classroom experimentation involves teachers who engage children in these types of activities and provides the basis for psychological analysis of children's experiences. The assessment of the quality of children's experiences involves more than observing whether children have a good time, though interest and personal investment are important. It is a psychological analysis of what occupies children's minds and how they reason in a given situation. On the basis of this analysis of individuals and groups, criteria for good educational activities and principles of teaching that are specific to classes of activities are conceptualized. In Chapter 11, we discuss four phases in becoming a constructivist teacher, the final one being autonomy, when a teacher no longer depends on theorists and researchers to guide definition of classroom practices but goes beyond them. Specifics of classroom practice are described in chapters 4–9.

Demonstrating a Relation between
Educational Practices and Children's Development

After the implementation of a program based on conceptual and practical definition of classroom life, a "science of educational practice" demands evaluation of its effectiveness. Formative evaluation occurs as a third phase when teachers and researchers assess the active reasoning of children in classroom activities. Summative evaluation requires the demonstration of a relation between these educational practices and children's "development." Progress in terms of the long-range goal of the highest stage of moral or intellectual reasoning must be shown. Possibilities and problems in such evaluation are discussed in Chapter 11.

SUMMARY

Education for development is the broad aim derived from cognitive-developmental research and theory, most notably that of Jean Piaget. This aim is distinctly different from aims reflecting "romantic" and "cultural transmission" ideologies. "Development" as the aim of education refers to progress in terms of universal stages in intellectual and moral evolution. Steps in translating Piaget's cognitive-developmental theory in educational practice are outlined.

Chapter 2

Piaget's Theory and Education: Forming the Mind, Not Just Furnishing It

NATURE OF THE CHILD'S MIND

We know children construct their knowledge, intelligence, and morality basically because they have so many ideas we never teach them. Piaget's work revealed many surprising ways in which children think. In one of his ingenious, now classic, experimental tasks, young children were shown to believe two balls of clay equal until one was rolled into a cylinder shape; then they believed that it had more quantity or substance (Piaget & Inhelder, 1941/1974). One 5-year-old, for example, when confronted with this task, told us that the cylinder-shaped one had more "Because if you sliced it up, you would get more pieces to chew on." A 7-year-old reasoned similarly when she exclaimed, "It's all slimmed out! You can take bite after bite, like this—chomp, chomp, chomp, chomp, chomp—five bites of nice candy [in the elongated piece], and you could just go chomp [once on the ball], and it'd be all gone." Therefore, when actions modify the shape of a clay ball, the young child views quantity (when he thinks about it at all) as changing along with shape or arrangement. (The reader unfamiliar with the classic Genevan studies of conservation may want to consult Ginsburg & Opper, 1979, or other introductions to Piaget's theory.)

DeVries (1969) further explored Piaget's view (1929/1960) that children's "incorrect" ideas about the world reflect a unique and different subjective experience. The question in this study was whether the phenomenon of nonconservation of properties of inanimate objects had any parallel with the way in which children thought about the characteristics and identity of living creatures. Could a live cat become a real dog? A reluctant but obliging black cat named Maynard was trained to wear a ferocious-looking dog mask and a benign rabbit mask. Children from 3 to 6 years were interviewed about whether the identity changed when the appearance changed. Christopher, a high-IQ boy of 3 years, 8 months, was invited to pet the cat and did so fearlessly and with great affection. Then the cat's head was screened, while Christopher was asked to watch the animal's tail (so he would know that the animal substance was the same). The following then occurred.

(Look, now it has a face like a rabbit. What is this animal now?) Rabbit (smiles, draws feet up onto seat of chair). (How can you tell?) (Laughs) Hi, rabbit. (How can you tell he's a rabbit?) He's a bunny rabbit! Hi! Hi! Hi!... (Is he a real rabbit?) Yes. (What happened?) Make him out a cat—a dog—now. (Could I make him a dog?) Yes.... Make him out a monkey this time! Make him out something else.... Make him out a cat again.... (You know, cats and rabbits have different kinds of insides—different bones and stomachs. What kind of insides does this animal have? Does he have a cat's bones and stomach or a rabbit's bones and stomach?) He has a little baby rabbit into there. When you open him up, you'll see. (Can he hop?) Hop (commanding tone). Hop, rabbit. He don't wants to hop. Hop, please. Hop. Hop for her. He'll hop for you later. (DeVries, 1969, pp. 14–16)

This type of response was given by all the 3-year-olds, 80% of the 4-year-olds, almost 40% of the 5-year-olds, and even 25% of the 6-year-olds.

These studies are only a few of many in which researchers keep coming up with the same general result. No matter what the content domain, young children think in qualitatively different ways from older children and adults. Certainly no one tells the child that quantity or identity changes with a change in appearance. These ideas must, therefore, come from the child—from his or her own effort to make sense out of experience. This is what Piaget meant when he said that the child constructs knowledge. When we take the trouble to find out how children actually think, we find that they *learn*—that is, construct—many things we do not teach.

A central problem in education, we contend, is the failure to adapt teaching to the way children think. From this perspective, many learning disabilities are in fact created by schools. Children beginning school are especially vulnerable when teachers demand they learn what they cannot understand.

EDUCATIONAL AIMS

Although Piaget was not an educator, he reflected on the general educational implications of his research, and during a 10-year period (1929–1939) even attempted to influence educational reform in his capacity as director of the International Bureau of Education. In his autobiography, Piaget explained that he accepted this responsibility because of his hopes for "the official adoption of techniques better adapted to the mind of the child" (Piaget, 1976b, p. 17).[1] In a 1935 document supplemented in 1969[2] and in a 1948 UNESCO publication,[3] he elaborated a rationale growing out of his research, justifying active and social methods of education for the full development of the human personality.

Piaget addressed the problem of how society can best educate by arguing that an individual's right to education should not be limited to acquisition of subject

---

1. All translations from the French are the responsibility of the author.
2. Published in French in 1969, and in English in 1970 as *Science of Education and the Psychology of the Child*.
3. Republished in English as *To Understand Is to Invent* (Piaget, 1972).

matter and reading, writing, and arithmetic skills, but must necessarily extend to nothing less than the totality of intellectual, moral, and affective development. He took the position that society's obligation is not only to instruct, but to provide a formative milieu in which an individual's potential may be developed and not destroyed or smothered. He further argued, "Full development of the personality in its most intellectual aspects is indissoluble from the whole group of emotional, ethical, or social relationships that make up school life" (Piaget, 1948/1973, p. 106). The implications of Piaget's theory for intellectual education must, therefore, be situated within the context of broader developmental aims, and we will discuss the theoretical reasons for this necessary interdependence. Likewise, the emphasis on social and moral development must be considered in a context that incorporates the cognitive, and vice versa.

Piaget's (1970b/1973) work led him to call for educational reforms that take into account the nature of the child's mind and natural laws of mental development.[4] He argued for the need for reform in the following way.

> For traditional education theory has always treated the child, in effect, as a small adult, as a being who reasons and feels just as we do while merely lacking our knowledge and experience. So that, since the child viewed in this way was no more than an ignorant adult, the educator's task was not so much to form its mind as simply to furnish it; the subject matter provided from outside was thought to be exercise enough in itself. But the problem becomes quite different as soon as one begins with the hypothesis of structural variations. If the child's thought is qualitatively different from our own, then the principal aim of education is to form its intellectual and moral reasoning power. And since that power cannot be formed from outside, the question is to find the most suitable methods and environment to help the child constitute it itself, in other words, to achieve coherence and objectivity on the intellectual plane and reciprocity on the moral plane. (Piaget, 1969/1970, pp. 159–160)

He further stated:

> If logic itself is created rather than being inborn, it follows that the first task of education is to form reasoning. The proposition "every person has the right to education"...means, therefore, in the first place, "every human being has the right to be placed in a scholastic environment during his formation which will enable him to build until completion the basic tools of adaptation which are the processes of logic." (Piaget, 1948/1973, pp. 49–50)

EDUCATIONAL PRACTICE: ACTIVE EDUCATION

Piaget's views on educational practice are rooted in his theory of the role of action in development (Piaget, 1972a, b, 1974a). In other words, only by means

---

4. The reforms discussed by Piaget are wide ranging and include issues of teacher education, salaries, parental rights, grading, examinations, methods of guidance, and the role of school psychologists. He also discussed education from preschool through university levels. In this chapter, the discussion is restricted to early education and to programmatic concerns.

of spontaneous activity does the child slowly develop in the direction of a cognitive organization that prepares for logical reasoning characterized by certain mental operations or logical structures. As discussed in Chapter 1, this is in contrast with the psychological assumptions underlying both romantic and cultural transmission views of education. This section addresses the question of what Piaget means by his advocacy of methods appealing to children's spontaneous activity, first by considering why he places action in such a central role, and second, by clarifying his definition of "active methods." The thrust of Piaget's general position as we understand the "most suitable methods and environment," may be summarized in terms of three interdependent characteristics of early education aimed at fostering development.

1. Methods appeal to the child's spontaneous mental activity;
2. The teacher acts as a companion who minimizes the exercise of adult authority and control over children and as a guiding mentor stimulating initiative, play, experimentation, reasoning, and social collaboration;
3. Social life among children offers extensive opportunity for co-operation[5] (including conflict) in situations inspiring children to desire coordination with others.

Let us consider how these characteristics arise from and are expressed in Genevan research and theory.

The Role of Action in Development

The principle that education must be active is based on Piaget's notion that young children develop cognitive structure (that is, become more intelligent) in the course of thinking about physical actions on objects. This is so because for the infant, thought is not possible without action. For the child up to about 7 or 8 years, thought is still closely related to physical action. In one sense, mental development may be described in terms of gradual freeing of thought from action. Piaget's research and theory led him to the conclusion that the source of knowledge and intelligence is in action (Piaget, 1936/1952, 1937/1954). Later, he (Piaget, 1964, 1969/1970, 1970a, 1970c, 1970d/1972, 1970e/1972, 1971/1974) distinguished two distinct types of action by which an individual obtains two kinds of knowledge. These two types of action arise from two basically different types of psychological experience.

The first is *physical experience*, which consists of individual actions on objects and leads to knowledge of the objects themselves. For example, in picking up solids, the child can notice their weight by physical experience. In order to obtain this information, he must focus on this particular aspect of an object and ignore other properties such as color and shape. Piaget refers to this action as

---

5. The various forms of "co-operate" are hyphenated to emphasize Piaget's definition, as operation in relation to another person.

simple or *empirical abstraction*. Other examples include abstracting properties of objects by observing their reactions to being dropped or pushed. Knowledge that has its source mainly in objects is referred to as physical knowledge. This theoretical distinction provides the basis for the elaboration of physical-knowledge activities, discussed in Chapter 4, such as aiming the bob of a pendulum to knock over a stack of blocks.

Logico-mathematical experience, in contrast, consists of actions on objects that introduce characteristics the objects do not have into the individual's ideas about those objects. For example, number is not a property of any group of objects but consists of relationships created by an individual. That is, the "twoness" of two objects does not exist in either object, but is a group of relationships coordinated by the individual who confers on them this characteristic of quantity. Piaget refers to this action as *reflective abstraction*. Reflective abstraction is based not on individual actions but on coordinated actions. For example, *noticing* what happens when a ball is pushed is an *individual* action, while *recognizing a difference* when a ball is pushed more forcefully requires *coordinated actions*—relating two or more actions and reactions. Knowledge that has its source mainly in the knower himself is logico-mathematical knowledge. The distinction between simple and reflective abstraction is especially crucial to the constructivist approach to teaching number and arithmetic, discussed in Chapter 7.

Although Piaget made these important distinctions, he then went on to point out that the different types of experience, action, and knowledge are in reality inseparable. For example, when the child looks at six blue and two yellow blocks[6] and thinks about them as "blue ones and yellow ones," he is focusing on their specific properties on the one hand and also is activating a whole network of cognitive relationships on the other. That is, to think of the blocks as blocks, he must distinguish their similarities and differences in relation to all other objects. In order to think of blueness, he must relate this property to all other colors. These networks of relationships constitute the general framework that enables the child to recognize the blue and yellow blocks.

The two types of experience are actually the two poles of every action. There can be no physical experience without a logico-mathematical framework, and at least for babies and young children, there can be no logico-mathematical experience without objects to put into relationship with one another.

Piaget also discussed a third type of knowledge—social-arbitrary knowledge—which has people as its source. Social-arbitrary knowledge includes arbitrary truths agreed upon by convention (such as the fact that December 25 is Christmas Day) and rules agreed upon by coordination of points of view (such as the rule that cars stay on the right side of the road). Social-arbitrary knowledge is similar to physical knowledge in that it requires specific input from the

---

6. Note that looking at an object is an action on it that is guided by the intelligence. The eye actively focuses and selectively centers on various aspects of the object.

external world. However, this content must also be structured within some logico-mathematical framework. For example, the fact that there is no school on Saturdays and Sundays can have meaning only in relation to every other day of the week, and days thus have to be structured into school days and nonschool days.

Thus, for Piaget, physical action on objects is crucial for the young child's construction of his intelligence as an instrument of knowing. It is the structural aspect of the mind that constitutes the reasoning potential or power to operate mentally on the content of experience—the power to "read" objects and events and thereby furnish the mind with content. From this perspective, the development of knowledge as content proceeds hand in hand with the development of knowledge as intelligence or structure of reasoning.

Piaget demonstrated that reasoning develops in an invariant sequence of qualitatively different stages, each stage having particular structural characteristics that make possible certain forms of reasoning, and (at all but the final stage) that place limits on reasoning possibilities. Let us briefly consider these stages in relation to the role of action and the two types of experience and knowledge.

Knowledge begins in infancy as the child focuses mainly on specific, physical, observable content. In the course of constructing his knowledge of objects by empirical abstraction, he also constructs a logico-mathematical framework by reflective abstraction. The baby's material actions on objects and people have two undifferentiated poles, one in which his attention is oriented toward the specificity of an object's individual reaction (such as the sound of a rattle when he shakes it) and one in which he is oriented toward what is general (such as the way he has to integrate smoothly the different actions of moving toward, grasping, and then shaking the object). The first aspect of the action is physical, and the second is logico-mathematical. During the *sensorimotor period*, the baby constructs objects and his own intelligence by observing what happens when he pushes, pulls, shakes, and drops objects, and by putting into relationship all the variations in the reactions of objects.

During the *preoperational period* (between the approximate ages of 2 and 7 years), the physical-material-observable and logico-mathematical aspects of actions continue to be undifferentiated, with the former still dominating the child's thinking. The observable *result* of actions is the child's main interest, rather than the structured system (including the action that produced the result).

During this period, the child's ability to create and coordinate relationships has progressed but is still limited, and the relationships created are often unstable. For example, in a film entitled "Playing with Rollers: A Preschool Teacher Uses Piaget's Theory" (Kamii, DeVries, Ellis, & Zaritsky, 1975), the unstable nature of 4-year-olds' reasoning is visible as they try to make catapults using rollers and boards. One child, Ricky, manages successfully to make sponges and paper balls fly into the air. He places a board on a wooden roller, puts an object on the end resting on the floor, and jumps on the elevated end.

This reasoning is characterized by a certain system of coordinated relationships, including (1) the raised end is differentiated from the lower end and coordinated with the idea of jumping, and (2) the placement of the object is coordinated with the end opposite the jumping end.[7] The unstable nature of this system of relationships, however, is revealed in one instance when Ricky sets up his catapult and, instead of placing his sponge on the lower end, places it on the raised end. He even goes to the lower end and flexes his knees in preparation to jump before realizing that he has made a mistake. In this instance, when Ricky thinks about making the object fly *up*, he seems to figure that if the object is to go *up*, he has to put it on the end that is *up*. This new relationship is coordinated with the one involving jumping on the end opposite the object, but not with the first relationship involving jumping on the elevated end. He thinks about these relationships separately, but not about all at the same time. Therefore, when he places the sponge on the raised end, he feels no contradiction. It is only in the context of action, when he gets ready to jump, that the first relationship reoccurs to him and he realizes that he has to move the sponge to the lower end.[8]

This example is one of many in the film revealing in a classroom activity the same lack of reversibility, coherence, and stability that Piaget demonstrated to be characteristic of preoperational thought in experiments such as conservation. It also provides a microcosmic illustration of the way in which a system of logico-mathematical relationships becomes gradually coordinated and consolidated in the course of physical experience with objects. Since material action on objects always has two aspects or poles (the physical and the logico-mathematical), the general structure of thought becomes elaborated in the course of constructing specific physical knowledge. Piaget explains this in terms of a gradual interiorization of action, which over several years results in operational systems of relationships. For example, the logic of conservation is characterized by mobility and coherence.

During the period of concrete operations (approximately 7 to 11 years), the logico-mathematical aspect develops into coherent systems, which make possible logical deductions about phenomena involving physical objects. As these systems become more consolidated and powerful, the child becomes able to arrive at deductive conclusions with a feeling of logical necessity. In other words, the logico-mathematical aspect can be said to become partially dissociated from the physical aspect during this period. By means of this deductive power the child can reason beyond the limitations of perceptual or

---

7. The system includes other relationships as well, but they are irrelevant to this example: (1) the raised position of one end of the board is coordinated with the position of the roller underneath; (2) the placement of the roller is in the process of being coordinated with the proportional distance from the fulcrum to the two ends and the force of the catapult (how high up an object flies); (3) the characteristics of the fulcrum (especially diameter) are in the process of being put into relationship with the catapult's force or the effect on objects; and (4) the characteristics of objects (weight, size, shape) are being put into relationship with the degree of dramatic effect.
8. See Chapter 5 in Kamii and DeVries (1978) for a written account of this activity.

figurative knowing (of states but not transformations) and figure out, for example, that a quantity is conserved despite a change in form. Operational systems appear first with respect to contents that offer less resistance and are easy to structure. Thus, the conservation of elementary number appears before the conservation of amount and weight of clay.

During the period of *formal operations* (beginning at about 11 or 12 years), the logico-mathematical aspect develops into coherent systems that make possible logical deductions about hypotheses. With the attainment of formal operations during adolescence, the logico-mathematical pole becomes independent of content (as can be seen in "pure" mathematics), and the further elaboration of all aspects of knowledge becomes more dependent on logico-mathematical structuring.

The basic law of development for Piaget, then, is that the child constructs his intelligence and knowledge—which in the beginning is undifferentiated from action but which becomes gradually more and more differentiated from and therefore less dependent on physical action. Piaget therefore emphasized that "constructivism...obviously leads to placing all educational stress on the spontaneous aspects of the child's activity" (1948/1973, p. 11). And it is important to note that while Piaget's definition of what is active includes the common meaning in terms of physical movement and manipulation of concrete objects, he situates these within the framework of their significance in relation to the child's self-regulating intelligence.

Methods Appealing to Children's Spontaneous Activity

The aim of forming the mind and not just furnishing it led Piaget to several general ideas about the nature of active education. Not all so-called "active" methods are effectively active in the sense of fostering constructive *mental* (and not just physical) activity. Active methods presuppose the child's interest, include play, involve genuine experimentation with all its necessary groping and error, and imply co-operation between adults and children and among children themselves. Let us consider why each of these characteristics is implied by Piaget's work.

Interest

Piaget (1954/1981, 1969/1970) referred to the element of interest as the "fuel" of the constructive process. Adults, whose interests are generally differentiated, coordinated, and unified, are often capable of constructive activity even when their interest is at a low level and they feel the pressure of some kind of coercion. Even for adults, however, the absence of interest can prevent effective effort. Certainly, when our interest is thoroughly engaged, our efforts are most productive. This condition is even more necessary for young children whose personalities are relatively undifferentiated. According to Piaget, interest is central to the spontaneous actions of empirical and reflective abstraction by which the child constructs knowledge and intelligence. Thus, in Piaget's view, the affective aspect that intervenes constantly in intellectual functioning is the element of interest. And without interest, the child would never make the constructive effort to make sense out of experience (that is, no assimilation to existing structures would occur). Without interest in what is new, the child would never modify the instrument of reasoning (that is, would make no accommodation of existing structures). Interest performs a regulatory function, freeing up or stopping the investment of energy in an object, person, or event. Thus, methods aimed at promoting this constructive process must arouse the child's spontaneous interest, which is inherent in the child's activity.

Just what these methods might be, however, is not obvious, and Piaget (1948/1973) notes, "There is nothing more difficult for the adult than to know how to appeal to the spontaneous and real activity of the child or adolescent" (p. 105). In a general way, he indicated that the challenge is to identify content that intrigues children and arouses in them a need and desire to figure something out. As we shall see in Chapter 3, some educators have used the ingenious Genevan experimental tasks that provided the data leading to the theory as situations to stimulate children's cognitive development. However, although Piaget and his colleagues did stimulate children's reasoning with their tasks, it is clear in the following that for Piaget these experimental situations do *not* define the best active methods.

> The child can certainly be interested in seriating for the sake of seriating, and classifying for the sake of classifying, etc., when the occasion presents itself. However, on the whole it is when he has events or phenomena to explain or goals to reach in an intriguing situation that operations are the most exercised. (Piaget & Garcia, 1971, p. 26)

In general, "intriguing situations" for young children do not include lectures, repetition in drills, programmed instruction, or audio-visual or teacher demonstrations. Piaget has criticized such approaches as not active enough.[9] Similarly,

9. Piaget did not deny that some learning may result from these methods. However, he suggested that the specific content learned may be more limited than anticipated by adherants of these approaches, and that they fail to develop the structure of operational intelligence as effectively as more active methods. For example, Piaget (1948/1973) said:

> Programmed instruction is indeed conducive to learning, but by no means to inventing, unless, following S. Papert's experiment, the child is made to do the programming himself. The same goes for audio-visual methods in general. Too many educators have sung their praises, whereas in fact they may lead to a kind of verbalization of images, if they only foster associations without giving rise to genuine activities. (pp. 7–8)

Piaget also discussed the Cuisenaire method of teaching number relationships with sticks in lengths representing numbers 1, 2, 3, etc. This method and Piaget's view are discussed in Chapter 7. He argued that audio-visual methods and other types of teacher demonstrations that make a figurative copy of reality (and thereby give the result of possible operations) are "totally inadequate for developing the child's operative activity" (Piaget, 1969/1970, p. 72). As will be seen later in this chapter, such methods also may be criticized for their limitation of autonomy necessary to the constructive process.

"experiments" in which children follow prescribed procedures do not offer the best opportunity for them to exercise their reasoning through experimentation.

Consideration of the child's interest makes it possible for teachers to distinguish between "tasks" and "activities." We define *tasks* as situations where the child does something solely because of the *teacher's* interest, just to oblige the adult. *Activities*, in contrast, are situations where the *child's* interest is dominant. The purpose may come entirely from the child, or a child may take an adult's suggestion and make it her own purpose, investing her own initiative in its pursuit.

The role of interest in affective and personality development is discussed later in this chapter.

Play

Some of the activities appealing to children's spontaneous interests are often referred to as play. Piaget (1969/1970) commented, "Play is a typical case of the forms of behavior neglected by the traditional school because it appears to them to be devoid of functional significance" (p. 155). Piaget (1945/1962) distinguished four categories of play.

The first is a primitive "exercise play" that is the only form of play in infants at the sensorimotor level. Piaget and Inhelder (1966b/1969) described it as follows.

> Exercise play...consists in repeating, for the pleasure of it, activities acquired elsewhere in the course of adaptation. For example, the child, having discovered by chance the possibility of swinging a suspended object, at first repeats the action in order to adapt to it and understand it, which is not play. Then, having done this, he uses this behavior pattern for simple "functional pleasure" (K. Buhler) or for the pleasure of causing an effect and of confirming his newly acquired skill (something the adult does, too, say, with a new car or a new television set. (p. 59)

The second category of play is "symbolic play" or pretense which has a special significance for the development of representational thought. Piaget (1945/1962) traced the origins of pretense to imitation in infancy and argued that its appearance marks an important intellectual advance, serving as a transition from representation in action to representation in thought. An early precursor form occurs in delayed imitation when the child in the second year of life imitates an absent model detached from its context. The symbol becomes freed as an instrument of thought, and serves as a transition to mental imagery and internal thought. Between the ages of about 2 and 7 years, pretense plays a particularly important role in the life of the child because the intelligence is not yet capable of logical reasoning. Symbolic thought is a real form of thought or "language" for the child. Piaget described instances of pretense in which his children pretended to be a church steeple (by standing stiff and still and imitating the sound of the bells), and a plucked, dead duck (by lying motionless with arms pressed against the body and legs bent). He commented:

> In order to think of a church steeple or a dead duck, or to re-live a scene which took place because one wouldn't eat one's soup, would it not suffice to use interior speech, i.e., verbal and conceptual thought? Why imitate the church steeple, lie motionless to mime a duck, make one's doll drink imaginary soup, scolding or encouraging it the while? The answer is obvious: the child's interior thought is not as yet sufficiently precise and mobile, his logico-verbal thought is still too inadequate and vague, while the symbol concretizes and animates everything. But this means that the symbol is not to be explained by pre-exercise: it is the very structure of the child's thought. (Piaget, 1945/1962, pp. 154–155)

Pretense is thus for Piaget a special "language" the child uses to express feelings and thoughts he cannot express otherwise.

> The essential instrument of social adaptation is language, which is not invented by the child but transmitted to him in ready-made, compulsory, and collective forms. These are not suited to expressing the child's needs or his living experience of himself. The child, therefore, needs a means of self-expression, that is, a system of signifiers constructed by him and capable of being bent to his wishes. Such is the system of symbols characteristic of symbolic play. (Piaget & Inhelder, 1966b/1969, p. 58)

In contrast with exercise play, symbolic play functions as affective compensation, wish-fulfillment, or liquidation of conflicts. Rather than just reproducing reality for pleasure, the child "corrects" it. A forbidden action may be done in make-believe. A frightening situation may be reenacted to neutralize the fear or provide a catharsis by doing in play what would not be dared in reality. A difficult or unpleasant situation may be assimilated and accepted by reliving it. Possible consequences may be anticipated and "thought through" in pretend play.

Piaget and Inhelder (1966b/1969) argued that symbolic play fulfills an important function in the child's life.

> Obliged to adapt himself constantly to a social world of elders whose interests and rules remain external to him, and to a physical world which he understands only slightly, the child does not succeed as we adults do in satisfying the affective and even intellectual needs of his personality through these adaptations. It is indispensable to his affective and intellectual equilibrium, therefore, that he have available to him an area of activity whose motivation is not adaptation to reality but, on the contrary, assimilation of reality to the self, without coercions or sanctions. Such an area is play. (pp. 57–58)

The third category of play that Piaget distinguished is games with rules such as Marbles, Hop-scotch, and Hide-and-Seek. The ability to play games with rules indicates cognitive and sociomoral advance. This will be discussed in Chapter 5.

Many educators, including Montessori, see the development of pretend or symbolic play as an alternative to the development of the capacity to work. Obviously, a central goal of education is to increase children's ability to work. Erikson, for instance, takes the development of "industry" as a central task of the early school-age child. For Piaget, the capacity to work is not something opposed to play and imposed on the child by adult instruction, but is something that develops out of the play interest. In contrast with Montessori (see Chapter 9), Piaget (1945/1962) saw symbolic play becoming more and more reflective of reality, developing "in the direction of constructive activity or work" (p. 112). For example, a child who pretends that a piece of wood is a boat may later really make a boat replica. Thus, out of symbolic play emerges the fourth category of play, "games of construction." Piaget and Inhelder (1966b/1969) noted that these "are initially imbued with play symbolism but tend later to constitute genuine adaptations (mechanical constructions, etc.) or solutions to problems and intelligent creations" (p. 59). Piaget (1945/1962) explained:

> When the child...really makes a boat by hollowing out the wood, putting in masts, sails and seats, the "signifier" merges into the "signified," and the symbolic game into a real imitation of the boat. The question then is, whether this construction is a game, imitation or spontaneous work. This problem is not specific to such cases, but arises generally with regard to drawing, modelling and all the techniques of representation using materials. Similarly, when a game with "parts" becomes part of a play or a whole drama, we are leaving the realm of play for that of imitation and work.... Constructional games...occupy...a position half-way between play and intelligent work, or between play and imitation. (p. 113)

Addressing the educational issue directly, Piaget (1969/1970) wrote:

> In the course of its own internal development, the play of small children is gradually transformed into adapted constructions requiring an ever-increasing amount of what is in effect work, to such an extent that in the infant classes of an active school every kind of spontaneous transition may be observed between play and work. (p. 157)

In summary, the constructivist view leads to educational methods for young children that include a large component of play.[10] It is important to note that in his advocacy of play, Piaget did not suggest that children be given complete freedom. He criticized such a view in the following way.

> A few years ago the main trend, especially owing to the widespread influence of psychoanalysis, was carefully to avoid frustrating the developing child in any way. This led to an excess of unsupervised liberty which ended in generalized play without much educational benefit. (Piaget, 1948/1973, pp. 6–7)

Experimentation

For Piaget, genuine experimentation and "authentic work" are salient character-istics of active education. He noted:

10. The interested reader may refer to Chapters 11 and 13 in Kohlberg and Colleagues (1987) for a more in-depth discussion of issues concerning the role of play in a child's development. The view of play elaborated there is different from the emphasis on "creativity" and "self-expression" in the child-centered tradition in education.

> When the active school requires that the student's effort should come from the student himself instead of being imposed, and that his intelligence should undertake authentic work instead of accepting pre-digested knowledge from outside, it is therefore simply asking that the laws of all intelligence should be respected. (Piaget, 1969/1970, p. 159)

He further emphasized:

> Active methods...give broad scope to the spontaneous research of the child or adolescent and require that every new truth to be learned be rediscovered or at least reconstructed by the student and not simply imparted to him. (Piaget, 1948/1973, pp. 15–16)

Methods permitting rediscovery or reconstruction, according to Piaget, are very different from methods focused upon transmitting a body of correct knowledge. By definition, experimentation inevitably involves many efforts that do not succeed in attaining "truth" as adults interpret it.

A central and revolutionary aspect of Piaget's thought on education is the view that children's "erroneous" ideas are necessary to their construction of knowledge and intelligence. This view is critical because the stages of intellectual development identified through Genevan research demonstrate unquestionably that the child's thought is characterized by particular kinds of errors in reasoning. As Piaget (1948/1973) noted:

> In order to understand certain basic phenomena through the combination of deductive reasoning and the data of experience, the child must pass through a certain number of stages characterized by ideas which will later be judged erroneous but which appear necessary in order to reach the final correct solution. (p. 21)

Such valuing of "erroneous ideas" is revolutionary because it is counter to commonsense intuition and the classic approach to teaching "correct" facts and values through social transmission. Piaget elaborates this idea in the following way:

> Only this (spontaneous) activity, oriented and constantly stimulated by the teacher, but remaining free in its attempts, its tentative efforts,[11] and even its errors, can lead to intellectual independence.[12] It is not by knowing the Pythagorean theorem that free exercise of personal reasoning power is assured; it is in having rediscovered its existence and usage. The goal of intellectual education is not to know how to repeat or retain ready-made truths (a truth that is parroted is only a half-truth). It is in learning to master the truth by oneself at the risk of losing a lot of time and of going through all the roundabout ways that are inherent in real activity. (Piaget, 1948/1973, pp. 105–106)

Piaget summarized this general point of view in the title of his 1948/1973 book on education: *To Understand Is to Invent.*

11. "Gropings" may be a better translation of *tâtonnements* than "tentative efforts."
12. "Autonomy" is a better translation of *l'autonomie* than "independence."

An important additional idea is that experimentation, for Piaget, is a matter of individual work, but thrives best in a particular kind of social context, discussed next, and has a pervasive and general impact on all aspects of development.

Co-operation

The social context Piaget advocates is characterized by co-operative relationships among children and between teachers and children. By "co-operation" Piaget did not mean submissive compliance or superficial good-naturedness. For Piaget, co-operaton is a *method* of social relations, and includes conflict. Mutual respect creates the basic dynamic in which individuals want and try to co-operate, that is, to operate in terms of one another's desires and ideas. To understand how Piaget came to this view and more specifically what he means, it is necessary to consider his research and theory concerning the development of reasoning, moral and social judgment, and affect and personality.

REASONING. Essentially, Piaget's research convinced him that young children are unable to co-operate because their thought is egocentric. This does not mean that children are selfish and do not *wish* to consider others' desires, but that they *cannot*. They cannot because immobility in the structure of their reasoning prevents the coordination of different points of view. Take the example of a 2-year-old who takes a toy from another child. Neither can be conscious of the other's feeling or thought. Both experience the event in terms of the toy—getting or losing it. By age 4 or 5, mutual interest in a toy can lead to co-operative play, and with adult support conflicts can be negotiated.

Recent research suggests that there are different kinds of egocentrism, some of which disappear earlier than others. We hypothesize that egocentric notions most amenable to intervention are those involving what is observable to the child (as seen, for example, when a 3-year-old takes a tissue to a crying child). This is the reason we emphasize materials and activities that provide something observable for the child to think about.

Piaget (1967) characterized egocentric thought in terms of a centering on single aspects or points of view without relating them to one another. The child may center on what in a situation is most salient to her and remain unaware of other perspectives (or be aware but fail to relate them). For example, in a board game, a 4-year-old may know about taking turns, yet roll the dice several times without giving anyone else a turn. The developmental task is therefore for the child to become able to decenter and thereby move from subjectivity to objectivity by coordinating a variety of perspectives.

Piaget (1928b/1964, 1932/1965, 1933/1976, 1948/1973, 1954/1981; Piaget and Inhelder, 1966b/1969) repeatedly argued that decentering is most importantly prompted by contact with the desires and ideas of other minds, and that an individual is not able to attain reason independent of progressive social relations. He stated, "Social life is a necessary condition for the development of logic" (Piaget, 1928a/1976, p. 80), and argued (1932/1965, p. 165) that when the child has the experience of others who react to what he says, he begins to feel that truth is important. In contrast, the egocentric child sees nothing wrong with untruths that conform better to what he desires. Piaget (1932/1965) spoke about "a long reciprocal education of the children by each other" (p. 318), and noted that social relations stimulate the intelligence and create the conditions in which mutual accommodation can flourish. This favors the development of a critical sense and desire for evidence about what is true (Piaget, 1948/1973, p. 108).

For Piaget, therefore, the social context offers possibilities for children to become aware of differences in perspectives and offers special motivation to coordinate these. The significance of such coordinations goes beyond the specific situation because these are reflective abstractions by which the structure of reasoning itself becomes more and more differentiated and mobile. Piaget thus recommended co-operation as the method by which the child is led out of egocentrism or subjectivity in thought to reciprocity and objectivity. For Piaget, however, co-operation implies a social relation characterized by a certain feeling, attitude, and style that can best be understood by considering his work on moral and social judgment.

MORAL AND SOCIAL JUDGMENT.   The intellectual egocentrism characteristic of children's logic about objects has a parallel in reasoning about social relations. Just as young children are unable to decenter in their reasoning about objects, they also cannot take a variety of social perspectives into account. Piaget raised the question of how the child who is so "shut up in his own ego" becomes liberated from these egocentric limitations and able to consider other points of view. He accounts for the decline of egocentrism in terms of a passage from unilateral to mutual respect through co-operation.

Unilateral respect arises from the fact that relations to adults are necessarily and largely heteronomous. That is, for reasons of health and safety, as well as reasons stemming from practical and psychological pressures on the adult, parents must regulate infants and toddlers externally in many ways. The child is forced to submit to a whole set of rules whose reasons are incomprehensible to him. The obligations to eat certain foods at certain times, to have a bath before bed, not to touch certain delicate or important objects, etc., can only be felt as external, since the necessity to carry out these obligations cannot be felt from within. Such adult constraint tends to consolidate instead of to correct the natural egocentric tendencies of the child. When governed continually by the values, beliefs, and ideas of others, the child practices a submission that can lead to mindless conformity in both moral and intellectual spheres. That is, so long as adults keep the child preoccupied with learning what adults want him to do and with obeying their rules, he will not be motivated to question, analyze, or examine his own convictions and construct his own reasons for following rules. In Piaget's view, *following the rules of others through a morality of obedience will never lead to the kind of reflection necessary for commitment to a set of internal or autonomous principles of moral judgment.* In contrast, a relation of mutual respect gives a child the possibility to exercise his will by elaborating his own moral rules.

Piaget pointed out that moral rules are always too general to give rise to a uniform application in all particular situations. The problem is how to adapt the general rule in each new situation. Such adaptation is not mere application of the rule because the moral issue must be confronted. Personal rules must be created that are somewhat different in each situation. Piaget refers to the capacity to create rules as *autonomy*. To the extent that the *will* of an individual is active in the elaboration of personal rules, the accent is shifted from external, observable, material bases for judgments, to internal factors such as intentions. Obedience of others is transformed into self-regulation—adherence to self-constructed rules.

In contrast with relations of co-operation, Piaget viewed constraint or coercion as having the unfortunate effect of perpetuating the child's global, undifferentiated, egocentric comprehensions—not just in the moral domain, but in affective and other intellectual and social domains as well. While the young child's life is in many respects dominated by heteronomous relationships, these are never completely heteronomous. To the extent that heteronomy is mixed with reciprocity, the child has possibilities for overcoming egocentrism and becoming intellectually and morally autonomous.

Piaget pointed out the roots of mutual respect existing from the beginning of the child's life in spontaneous mutual affection, reciprocal esteem, and valuation. Egocentrism is gradually overcome to the extent that the adult reduces the pressure of constraint on the child and practices co-operation. Piaget (1932/1965) said:

> In so far as the adult can cooperate with the child, that is to say, can discuss things on an equal footing and collaborate with him in finding things out, it goes without saying that his influence will lead to analysis. But in so far as his words are spoken with authority, in so far, especially, as verbal instruction outweighs experiment in common, it is obvious that the adult will consolidate childish verbalism. Unfortunately it is the second alternative that is most often realized in the teaching given in schools and even in the home. The prestige of the spoken word triumphs over any amount of active experiment and free discussion. Schools have been held responsible for the verbalism of children. This is not quite correct, as verbalism arises out of certain spontaneous tendencies in the child. But the school, instead of creating an atmosphere favourable to the diminution of these tendencies, does base its teaching upon them and consolidates them by making use of them. (p. 195)

In pointing out the way in which adult constraint combines with childish egocentrism, Piaget emphasized the parallelism between moral and intellectual development. Essentially, he focused on the psychological dynamic necessary for a loosening of the child's heteronomous attitude—for a lessening of the conviction that what is good is to conform to rules given by others, for a decentering that dislodges unanalytic belief in subjective experience. This will be discussed in more detail in the sections below devoted to the particular contributions of relationships with adults and with peers.

AFFECT AND PERSONALITY.   Piaget's (1954/1981, 1963/1976, 1965/1977, 1976a) view of affective and personality development is integrated with his theory of intellectual development. He spoke about affectivity in a broad sense as the energetic source on which the functioning of intelligence depends, drawing the analogy of affectivity as the fuel that makes the motor of intelligence go. The fuel of affectivity does not, however, modify the structure of the motor (intelligence). Piaget suggested that affectivity can stimulate or perturb intellectual operations, causing acceleration or retardation, but that it cannot cause intellectual development. To the extent that affect and intellect may be dissociated, Piaget (1954/1981) stated that "Comprehension is more the cause of emotion than emotion is the cause of comprehension" (p. 23). He noted in this regard that an emotion implies a differentiation among objects and meanings, and that this is an intellectual activity. However, Piaget insisted on a constant interaction and dialectic between affectivity and intelligence that transforms these as a function of the child's own progressive organization of behavior.

In a more specific sense, Piaget took the position that every scheme has both cognitive and affective elements, and that these are thus indissociable. He argued that feelings are structured along with the structuring of knowledge. This is illustrated by his discussion of the infant's development of affectivity through six stages toward object permanence. For Piaget, objects are simultaneously cognitive and affective. An object disappearing behind a screen is at the same time an object of knowledge and a source of interest, amusement, satisfaction, or disappointment. Affectivity is present from birth in feelings linked to action of the reflexes and to perceptual actions. Differentiation of needs and interests arises from feelings of pleasure, pain, disappointment, etc., associated with satisfaction or failure to satisfy certain needs. When the infant differentiates means from ends (for example, by pulling a cover to get an object on top of it) and becomes able to coordinate means toward an end previously set, these new differentiations lead to new coordinations of interests (as when an object becomes interesting because of its relation to others already valued) and to a beginning hierarchy of values. Decentration of affect begins when feelings begin to be directed to others as distinct from the baby's body. Interest thus changes from interest in the action that gives pleasure to interest in the source of pleasure. This occurs with construction of the person of another as a permanent object and the differentiation of cause and effect.

We have already discussed the importance of interest for the constructive process in general and now turn to the role of interest in affective and personality development. As the infant and young child pursue interests in objects and people, they differentiate these interests in the course of constructing knowledge about properties and characteristics of the physical and social worlds. This differentiation presupposes a decentering that is simultaneously cognitive and affective. The affective decentration is interest in a series of new sources of impressions, sources of interest, pleasure, joy, sadness. Some objects or aspects are more interesting than others, some are interesting for similar reasons, and the child begins to coordinate interests and thus to construct a hierarchy of personal values—likes and dislikes. With the construction of the persons of others as independent objects, permanent and autonomous, the relations with others begin to become relations of real exchange between the self and the other. The values attributed to others become the point of departure for new feelings, in particular sympathies and antipathies and moral feelings of respect. At about the same time the child constructs the permanent object, he begins to represent objects and events in thought. This ability to think about persons and objects not present makes possible conservation of feelings, the permanence of values, and the eventual elaboration of a coherent system of moral values.

The core of affective and personality development, for Piaget, is social reciprocity. As noted in the foregoing section, from the very beginning of the child's life, there exists a spontaneous reciprocity in relations with caretakers. This reciprocity is a sort of spontaneous mutual engagement, mutual valuing, and the beginning of interindividual feelings. In the exchange of gestures, smiles, mimicking, and reciprocal imitation there is a sketch of reciprocity. Spontaneous reciprocities, however, are variable and fluctuating, as in the case of reciprocal imitation and the first social feelings. Permanence in values and duration of feelings is made possible only when thought becomes representational. Affect then can persist in the absence, for example, of a person loved. Feeling is conserved in schemes of reaction which, taken all together at a later point in development, constitute the individual's character or permanent modes of reactions.

A system of permanent feelings or values is regulated by what Piaget calls "will." In the case of a conflict between values (such as feeling tempted to leave a writing task to go out on a nice day), it is by an affective decentering or will that one revives in oneself the various feelings and values attached to the work. The reconstitution of the feeling can transform the strengths of the conflicting tendencies and subordinate them to the values that are permanent and stable. By decentering, the field of comparison is enlarged, and the less stable desire or tendency becomes weaker. Piaget then defined will as the power of conservation of values, noting that an individual without will is unstable, believing in certain values at certain moments and forgetting them at other moments. Just as operations serve as regulators of the intelligence, enabling the mind to achieve logical coherence, will serves as affective regulator, enabling the individual to achieve stability and coherence in personality and in social relations. Piaget pointed out the necessity of educating the will as a regulator of feelings or values.

The progressive differentiation of interests, feelings, and values, and the increasing stability and coherence of affectivity are bound up with intellectual development, and both depend on social relations of reciprocity. Piaget (1947/1966) pointed out that the process of coordinating different points of view and co-operating with others includes all aspects of development. For example, he found that a child of 4 or 5 is often not aware that he is the brother or sister of his brother or sister. This lack of reciprocity in perspective affects both this logic and his awareness of self. Also, to the degree that the child fails to distinguish between internal and external, subjective and objective, he is undifferentiated as a self and as a personality, unable to situate himself in relations of co-operation with others. For Piaget, self and personality development proceed hand in hand with the decline of intellectual egocentrism that results from interaction with others. He pointed out that the child cannot penetrate behind the surface of behavior (that is, what is observable to her). She can therefore only interpret the behavior of others from her own point of view, and cannot take into account such factors as others' intentions or feelings. This egocentrism is broken down through the gradual rise of reciprocity—that is, the consciousness of others as psychological creatures. Consciousness of self accompanies the rise of consciousness of others. This is the substance of personality development, the evolution of stable characteristics (Piaget, 1969/1970, pp. 175–176).

Piaget (1932/1965, pp. 93–96, 393–394) emphasized that ego development necessitates liberation from the thought and will of others. Lack of this liberation results in inability to co-operate. How does this liberation come about? For Piaget, it is through the child's experience of being respected by the adult who offers to co-operate with the child. Learning to understand others begins as others show that they understand the child's inner feelings and ideas. In this way, Piaget noted that co-operation is a factor in the creation of personality as a stable ego. Personality is for Piaget the result of continuous interaction with others—comparison, opposition, and mutual adjustment. For affective and personality development, as in the development of reasoning and moral judgment, Piaget argued that heteronomous relationships are counterproductive, and that co-operative relationships are necessary. For Piaget, therefore, co-operation is an essential characteristic of developmentally oriented education not simply because it is a culturally valued virtue, but because of its psychodynamic developmental significance.

The Teacher as Companion/Guide

The challenge to create intellectually and socially active methods of educating calls for a particular combination of functions in the role of the teacher. In Piaget's view, the teacher must be an evaluator, organizer, stimulator, and collaborator. As an evaluator, the teacher must have solid psychological knowledge of the child and mental development in order to understand and assess children's spontaneous procedures, which otherwise might appear a waste of time. Then, the implementation of a program in accordance with this psychological knowledge requires not only skills in selecting and organizing activities, and in intervening to stimulate children's reasoning, but also the ability to establish an egalitarian relationship with children and to be a companion as well as a guiding mentor. This fourfold conception of the teacher's role contrasts with the cultural transmission version of the teacher as transmitter of information and values to the child. It also contrasts with the romantic image of the teacher as permissively or passively observing facilitator of the child's growth and creativity. Let us consider in more detail Piaget's expressed ideas about the teacher's role.

Piaget (1948/1973) strongly believed that the teacher, in order to organize and intervene effectively, "should know not only his own science but also be well versed in the details of the development of the child's or adolescent's mind" (pp. 16–17). He drew an analogy between medicine and education, noting that just as the physician's art cannot be practiced without exact and experimental knowledge of the human being, the art of education cannot be practiced without exact and experimental knowledge, especially regarding the formation of the mind.

For Piaget (1978), the broad contribution of his theory to education is "to know how a child reasons and what kinds of new constructions he is capable of when we encourage his spontaneity to a maximum" (p. vii). He noted:

> The double advantage which can be obtained is: (1) from the standpoint of psychological diagnosis, to foresee in part the progress the child will be able to make later; and (2) from the pedagogical point of view, to reinforce his constructivity and thus find a method of teaching in accordance with "constructivism" which is the fundamental principle of our interpretation of intellectual development. (p. vii)

In emphasizing the child's *construction* and de-emphasizing the teacher's *instruction*, Piaget made it clear, however, that teaching in accordance with constructivism should not be mistaken to imply that the teacher has no role to play or that children should be left with unlimited freedom to work or play on their own.

> It is important that teachers present children with materials and situations and occasions that allow them to move forward. It is not a matter of just allowing children to do anything. It is a matter of presenting to the children situations which offer new problems, problems that follow on from one another. You need a mixture of direction and freedom. (Quoted in Evans, 1973, p. 53)

Piaget (1948/1973, p. 16) emphasized that the teacher must organize materials and situations that will provide useful problems for the child.

Piaget also viewed the teacher's role in terms of active intervention. He commented on his visit to Susan Isaacs' Malting House School in England (probably in the 1930s) in which teachers were guided by the belief that if children are left alone with rich materials, they will be led by virtue of a hereditary mental structure to record reality. In this school, Piaget observed that teachers did refrain from intervention, and that children were learning to observe and reason as they engaged with great interest in manipulation and experimentation. However, he felt that "some form of systematization applied by the adult would perhaps not have been wholly harmful to the pupils" (Piaget, 1969/1970, p. 169). A glimpse of the kind of intervention envisioned by Piaget may be found in the following remark that the teacher:

is needed to provide counter-examples that compel reflection and reconsideration of over-hasty solutions. What is desired is that the teacher cease being a lecturer, satisfied with transmitting ready-made solutions; his role should rather be that of a mentor stimulating initiative and research. (Piaget, 1948/1973, p. 16)

Piaget went on to suggest that in order to facilitate the development of reasoning capable of rational, deductive experimentation, children need a social context characterized not only by co-operation with other children, but also co-operation with adults. The crucial role of co-operation for the constructive process was discussed above in contrast with the role of constraint. *Co-operation* and *constraint*, or *autonomy* and *heteronomy*, characterize two types of adult-child relationships, one that that tends to promote and one that tends to retard the child's construction of knowledge or morality. Essentially, the difference between these two types of adult-child relationships is a difference in the exercise of power. Piaget (1948/1973) commented:

> In reality, education constitutes an indissoluble whole, and it is not possible to create independent personalities in the ethical area if the individual is also subjected to intellectual constraint to such an extent that he must restrict himself to learning by rote without discovering the truth for himself. If he is intellectually passive, he will not know how to be free ethically. Conversely, if his ethics consist exclusively in submission to adult authority, and if the only social exchanges that make up the life of the class are those that bind each student individually to a master holding all power, he will not know how to be intellectually active. (p. 107)

In a relationship of co-operation characterized by mutual respect, the adult minimizes his authority in relation to the child and gives him as much opportunity as possible to practice governing his behavior on the basis of his interests and judgments. By exercising his ability to govern his own beliefs and actions the child gradually constructs internally coherent knowledge, morality, and personality. Piaget (1932/1965) stated simply that "a 'priest' is the last thing a schoolmaster should be: he should be an elder collaborator, and, if he has it in him, a simple comrade to the children" (p. 364).

The relationship Piaget described is not one in which the adult abdicates responsibility, nor is it one in which the adult hopes to eliminate all heteronomy. For health and safety reasons, at least, the adult sometimes must give commands that will be incomprehensible to the child's mind, and the child's acceptance of such mysterious commands is necessarily heteronomous. However, Piaget suggested taking care not to impose duties unnecessarily on children and instead making every effort to base necessary but incomprehensible regulations on mutual sympathy and children's desire to please, rather than to obey. In addition, Piaget (1932/1965) recommended the adult's acknowledgment of obligations and mistakes.

> One must place oneself on the child's own level, and give him a feeling of equality by laying stress on one's own obligations and one's own deficiencies. In the sphere

of clumsiness and of untidiness in general (putting away toys, personal cleanliness, etc.), in short in all the multifarious obligations that are so secondary for moral theory but so all-important in daily life (perhaps nine-tenths of the commands given to children relate to these material questions) it is quite easy to draw attention to one's own needs, one's own difficulties, even one's own blunders, and to point out their consequences, thus creating an atmosphere of mutual help and under-standing. In this way the child will find himself in the presence, not of a system of commands requiring ritualistic and external obedience, but of a system of social relations such that everyone does his best to obey the same obligations, and does so out of mutual respect. (pp. 137–138)

The teacher who attempts to employ active methods must therefore be concerned not only about materials and interventions designed to promote experimentation and reasoning. In order to achieve these goals, the teacher must also be concerned about the psychological dynamic of the adult-child relationship, especially with regard to control and affection. This will be discussed further with specific focus on social and moral development in Chapter 6. It is crucial to emphasize that for Piaget this socioemotional dynamic is of central importance for cognitive development, as well as social and moral development.

Mutual respect between adult and child frees the child to exercise and develop autonomy. Adult-child relations, however, have a history of heteronomy that may be difficult to overcome. Piaget (1954/1981) was optimistic about the possibility, although he pointed out its difficulty.

It [mutual respect] is a feeling that exists in relation with all sorts of partners and which is even possible between the child and the adult although it may not be easy to make the child forget, at least in the early years, the superiority he attributes to the adult.

But in a liberal education, in relations without the characteristic of constraint between parents and children, it is clear that one can introduce more and more, with development, the mutual respect that ends by overcoming, and overcoming greatly, unilateral respect. Only in the domain of relations between children and adults, it is extremely difficult to make the child forget that in the background there is always an authority who could reappear, even if one does one's utmost to make him forget. There is always a basic unilateral respect because there is in fact an inequality that goes without saying. (Piaget, 1932/1965, p. 135)

Piaget's concern with co-operation as an educational factor extended to peer relations. For him, a vital part of the teacher's role is to foster co-operative peer interaction.

Social Life among Children

Contact with the desires and ideas of other minds facilitates the decentering and coordination of perspectives. Part of the teacher's role therefore is to establish an environment in which social life among children is characterized by growing consciousness of others and by a need and desire to coordinate with others. The "long reciprocal education of the children by each other" is, according to Piaget, just as necessary as the relationship with the teacher for the child's development of autonomy.

Piaget's studies of the development of children's mutual respect in the collective game of Marbles and in their attitudes toward obedience of various adult rules (such as not to lie) led him to the conviction that the greater equality among children of the same age is of special importance for overcoming unilateral respect. He continued the passage quoted above:

> On the contrary, in the relations of children to children, we find the whole gamut of feelings in question; we find unilateral respect in the relations of younger to older, when the younger themselves choose the company of certain older children who have prestige in their eyes, whom they seek to imitate, to equal. This respect of the elder is less strong in certain cases, stronger in others, than for the adult, but we find it typical.
>
> We find on the other hand among children of the same age a mutual respect by which it will then be possible, in societies of children, to dissociate the effects due to unilateral respect. (Piaget, 1932/1965, p. 135)

Piaget's (1951/1976, 1963/1976, 1963/1976) view was that children develop the intellectual coordination that eventually makes possible logical and moral reasoning through continual efforts to adapt to one another and to collaborate in creating "rules" governing their relating. The problem for the educator, of course, is that the young child is not yet capable of collaborating precisely because he lacks the necessary intellectual instrument that makes coordination with others possible. Nevertheless, Piaget argued that social life among children themselves has the necessary ingredients for this development. Referring to experiments by Dewey and Decroly, Piaget especially emphasized the importance of self-government and collaborative work in groups on intellectual research. He also mentioned the advantages of children's real moral dilemmas in their lives, pretend play, group games, and constructive activities such as model building. Piaget pointed out the importance of capitalizing on the special understanding existing among children and fostering a feeling of solidarity in a group of children. For Piaget, too, the method of co-operation includes conflict situations as excellent instances in which children are especially challenged to coordinate with others and to engage in mutual adaptation.

THE CONSTRUCTION OF CONSTRUCTIVIST EDUCATION

"Piagetian" programs can be Piagetian only in part, since the theory does not encompass all aspects of development and since it is not a theory of educational practice. The problem, then, is how we can develop educational practice informed by such a psychological and epistemological theory. Bridging this gap between theory and practice requires what in the first chapter we called a "two-way street" between teachers and researchers with theoretical convictions. One form of the psychologist's fallacy is described as a one-way relationship between theory and practice in which psychologists design an educational program only on the basis of a particular theory.

Piaget was cognizant of the danger of committing the psychologist's fallacy. He expressed this awareness in at least two ways. First, he refrained from making specific educational recommendations. While he criticized some educational practices (such as teaching his tasks and using Cuisenaire rods and Montessori's materials), his recommendations for education remained for the most part general. Piaget's convictions about the development of children's knowledge did not lead him to conclusions about educational practice in its specific concerns about what and how to teach. His co-workers Inhelder, Sinclair, and Bovet (1974) concluded their research on learning in the context of general cognitive structures such as conservation and class inclusion by stating:

> Piaget's theory and the extensive experimentation attached to it can be applied to educational practice only in a very indirect way, as many educators have been forced to admit. Although learning studies certainly do not close the gap between cognitive psychology and classroom practice, they constitute a link in the chain that may eventually unite the two. (p. 30)

Sinclair (1971) earlier commented on education in relation to number and measurement:

> Educational applications of Piaget's experimental procedures and theoretical principles will have to be very indirect—and he himself has given hardly any indication of how one could go about it. His experiments cannot be modified into specific teaching methods for specific problems, and his principles should not be used simply to set the general tone of an instructional program. (p. 2)

The second way Piaget indicated the importance of avoiding the psychologist's fallacy was to caution against the mere surface application of psychological knowledge to education. He urged, instead, research in the classroom by teachers and educational psychologists, to find out whether the practical implications of psychological research are of any demonstrable value. His two-way-street notion of the relation between research psychology and experimental teaching is best expressed in the last paragraph of an early book, *The Moral Judgment of the Child.*

> But pedagogy is very far from being a mere application of psychological knowl-edge. Apart from the question of the aims of education, it is obvious that even with regard to technical methods it is for experiment alone and not deduction to show us whether methods such as that of work in groups and of self-government are of any real value. For, after all, it is one thing to prove that cooperation in the play and spontaneous social life of children brings about certain moral effects, and another to establish the fact that this cooperation can be universally applied as a method of

education. This last point is one which only experimental education can settle. Educational experiment, on condition that it be scientifically controlled, is certainly more instructive for psychology than any amount of laboratory experiments, and because of this experimental pedagogy might perhaps be incorporated into the body of the psycho-sociological disciplines. But the type of experiment which such research would require can only be conducted by teachers or by the combined efforts of practical workers and educational psychologists. And it is not in our power to deduce the results to which this would lead. (Piaget, 1932/1965, p. 406).

SUMMARY

Piaget's research showed that the mind of the child is qualitatively different from that of older children and adults. This fact led him to argue that the aim of education should be not only to instruct, but to provide a formative milieu for the child's indissociable intellectual, moral, and affective development—not just to furnish the mind, but to help form its reasoning power. Piaget's research led him to conclude that the source of knowledge, intelligence, and morality is in action. Two types of psychological experience are characterized by two types of action and lead to two kinds of knowledge—physical knowledge and logico-mathematical knowledge. Physical knowledge and logico-mathematical knowledge are not distinguished by educators who teach everything as if it were a third type—social-arbitrary or conventional knowledge. Affectivity is bound up with intellectual development, where the differentiation of interests, feelings, and values and the exercise of will are an integral part of developing thought about physical and social worlds.

Piaget's research and theory on the role of action in development led him to emphasize the necessity for educators to develop methods appealing to children's spontaneous activity. The essential characteristics of active methods are that they inspire children's interest, play, experimentation, and co-operation. Two types of adult-child relationships are described: heteronomous relations that retard children's development, and autonomous or co-operative relations that promote development.

Chapter 3

Translating Piaget's Theory into Curriculum: Three Approaches

Before the early 1960s, Piaget's work was unfamiliar to most educators and psychologists in the United States. By 1965, however, interest was beginning to be widespread, due in part to the appearance of a book by Flavell (1963) and American research replicating or extending Piaget's work (for example, Elkind, 1961a, 1961b; Bruner, 1960, 1964; Kohlberg, 1966). This interest happened to coincide with the focus of national concern and federal resources on early cognitive education of "deprived" or "disadvantaged" children from poor families. It is thus not surprising that among those who responded to the challenge to develop preschool programs were psychologists and educators impressed with Piaget's work as the best available, research-based theory of cognitive development. They sought to develop a theory of educational practice based on this theory of development.

Early Piagetians concerned with education faced two challenges. The first was to understand Piaget's epistemological orientation—that is, his particular perspective on the basic question of how knowledge develops. This meant becoming conversant with a large body of work already amassed by Piaget and his collaborators since the early 1920s. This task was complicated by the fact that the prevailing views in American education and psychology were behavioristic, psychoanalytic, and normative, in sharp contrast to the Piagetian constructivist, interactionist, and universalist emphases. Old ways of thinking about human behavior, the mind of the child, and the nature of developmental change influenced the assimilation of Piaget's work and often resulted in its distortion. This problem was further exacerbated by the fact that each part of the theory could be properly understood only in the context of the whole that was still being elaborated. Moreover, for those not reading French, efforts to follow Piaget's epistemological search were slowed by the lag in English publication of Genevan work.

The second challenge faced by early Piagetian educators was to derive the practical significance of Piaget's work. As noted in Chapter 2, his theory is not a theory of teaching, and its educational significance is not obvious. Piaget was concerned with the questions "What is knowledge?" and "How does knowledge (intelligence) develop?" while educators ask "How do we facilitate the development of knowledge and intelligence?" The latter question encompasses the former but requires going further, and—as we have seen—Piaget himself provided only general indications of an answer to the educational question.

Preschool educators struggled with their double challenge, proceeding during the 1960s and 1970s with program development reflecting in various ways the Genevan influence. It was surely inevitable that these early efforts to put the theory into practice would reflect premature closure, and that a well-elaborated and internally consistent theory-practice view would emerge only over a long period of time. Indeed, such coherence is still only partly achieved.

This chapter examines the nature of the connection between theory and practice in three representative Piagetian preschool programs—Lavatelli's (1970a/1973, 1970b/1973) *Early Childhood Curriculum: A Piaget Program*; the High/Scope *Cognitively Oriented Curriculum* of Weikart and his collaborators (Weikart, Rogers, Adcock, & McClelland, 1971; Hohmann, Banet, & Weikart, 1979); and the Kamii-DeVries approach (Kamii & DeVries, 1975/1977, 1976, 1978, 1980, DeVries, 1978). These are selected for special focus both because they are representative of such efforts and because they all remain influential in early education. Several other important books have appeared that also use Piaget's theory as inspiration for recommendations to teachers and that provide interesting classroom activities to promote cognitive development (Forman & Hill, 1980; Forman & Kuschner, 1977; Copple, Sigel, & Saunders, 1979). Much of what they propose is closer to the Kamii-DeVries approach than the Lavatelli or High/Scope programs. For the sake of brevity, this chapter does not attempt to review these books.

In this chapter, we concentrate on a systematic comparison of similarities and differences among three programs. In the course of this comparison, there will be some suggestion that the Kamii-DeVries program is a more adequate representative of Piaget's theory than are the other two. Our primary purpose, however, is not to characterize some early education programs as better than others. Rather, it is to prepare the reader for rationales involved in succeeding chapters of the book on physical-knowledge activities, group games, moral discussion and class meeting, number and arithmetic, and reading and writing. These chapters are written from the perspective employed in the Kamii-DeVries approach, a perspective that will become clearer by this discussion of similarities and differences among Piaget-based programs.

In Chapter 2 we discussed Piaget's insistence that education should stress the spontaneous aspects of the child's activity. The central issue is: What is spontaneous activity? For Piaget, its central meaning involves the kinds of psychological experiences that lead to operational intelligence. These are not easy to define. Piaget (1948/1973) noted that "there is nothing more difficult for the adult than to know how to appeal to the spontaneous and real activity of the child or adolescent" (p. 105). *This difficulty is responsible for most differences among Piagetian educators.* All agree on the fundamental importance of action as the child's means of constructing knowledge and intelligence. However, they disagree on *what* action to encourage and *how* to foster it. In other words, there is no consensus regarding a definition of "constructive activity." Let us begin with a glimpse of the three programs—three bits of classroom interaction in which teachers in the different programs try to foster children's ability to classify.

LAVATELLI

(Gives child miniature brown dogs and cats, black cats, and a white dog)
    Make a group of all the dogs.... Now make a group of cats.... Now make a group of animals.... Which made the bigger group, a group of white dogs or a group of dogs? Why? (Lavatelli, 1970b/1973, p. 22)

HIGH/SCOPE

An adult is watching Erica cut out and glue wrapping-paper squares on a piece of paper. "This is a wipe-mat for my Mom and I'm going to give it to her." The adult picks up on Erica's interest and talks about similarities at the same time. "When you give this to your Mommy are you going to show her anything that's the same?" Erica proceeds to point out and talk about all the parts of her picture that are the same. (Hohmann, Banet, & Weikart, 1979, pp. 202–203)

KAMII-DEVRIES.   Three children play a card game called Making Families, in which they try to make sets of four sheep (cows, etc.), each of a different color. After the teacher introduces the rules, players take turns asking one another for particular cards.

Looking at his cards (a yellow fish and three cows) Emanuel asked, "Eron, do you have the yellow fish (the same card as the one on top of those he was holding)?"
    Laughing, Eron, pointed out, "No, you have it yourself. Look there." Eron forcefully touched Emanuel's top card to show it to him. Emanuel looked serious, not embarrassed or amused. He continued to address Eron by saying, "Then a bl–red fish."
    Eron replied, "No."
    Emanuel went on asking Eron, "The blue fish."
    Maurice piped up, "It's me that have it!" (Kamii & DeVries, 1978, p. 180)

In these examples, children have very different psychological experiences with classification. Table 3.1 summarizes the main similarities and differences we see in these programs. These are discussed below.

THREE TYPES OF TRANSLATION OF PIAGET'S THEORY INTO EDUCATIONAL PRACTICE

Different Piagetian approaches may be viewed from the perspective of a distinction among three types of educational translations of Piaget's theory. These types can be viewed as analogous to three ways of translating one language into another—global translation, literal translation, and free translation. In a global translation, the interpretation is a general vague summary, lacking the detail necessary for precise meaning. A literal translation is a word-by-word interpretation that ignores the context and fails to take account of word

TABLE 3.1
Characteristics of Piaget-Based Programs

	Program		
	Lavatelli	High/Scope	Kamii-DeVries
Type of translation			
Global	x	x	x
Literal	X	X	
Free		x	X
Relation between Piaget's theory and children's spontaneous activity			
Unintegrated-Juxtaposed	X		
Inserted		X	
Integrated			X
Emphasis on Structural aspects of Piaget's theory	X	x	x
Emphasis on Constructivist aspects of Piaget's theory		x	X

Note: x = somewhat characteristic; X = very characteristic

combinations having idiomatic meanings; literal translations often make little sense. A free translation respects idiomatic meaning and interprets precise ideas rather than individual words.

Each of these types of translation of Piaget's theory into educational terms raises problems for the elaboration of a coherent theory of educational practice. These three translations do not correspond precisely to our three Piagetian programs to be discussed, but we will show how each approach can be viewed in these terms.

Global Translation

Global translation of Piaget's work into educational language is a simplification into vague generalities—certain very general aspects of the theory are loosely matched with certain educational objectives or practices. For example, Piaget's work is cited as justification or inspiration for humanistic objectives such as full development of the human personality, autonomy, mastery, a sense of competence or positive self-image, social co-operation, imagination, and creativity. Or, Piaget's emphasis on action is offered as justification for methods referred to as "hands-on experiences," "learning by doing," or "play."

Such translations are correct at this level of generality. No doubt all Piagetian translators would agree that these words express their educational goals. The shortcoming of global translation, however, is that with only these kinds of generalities in mind, it fails to provide guidelines for discriminating the relative value of specific activities and ways of teaching. More importantly, global translations do not specify the nature of the child's experience that programs aim to foster.

Unfortunately, this kind of imprecise translation has led to many instances of pasting a "Piaget" label on practices that are inconsistent with the theory. Vague generalities can be used indiscriminantly to justify almost any practice. This type of translation is not so much a translation of Piaget's theory into practice, as a translation into another theory—a diluted version in which generalities do disservice to the research-based theoretical precision Piaget sought, and which he achieved to such a remarkable degree.

In Table 3.1 we attribute global translation to all three Piagetian programs discussed in this chapter.

Literal Translation

Literal translation of Piaget's work into educational language is a direct transfer or *application* of parts of his research and theory to teaching. Translation by transfer is problematic when an isolated part selected for classroom application contradicts the general practical implications of constructivism. That is, not all Piaget's research issues and experiments, findings, and theory transfer equally well to classroom concerns or to a theory of educational practice.[1] It is thus important to relate any such transfers to a coherent, consistent theory of practice. For example, transfers from Piaget's research on group games and moral discussion are justified in a broad context of theory-based cognitive and sociomoral objectives (Chapters 5 and 6). In our view, some other transfers are not as defensible. The principal example of indefensible transfers include literal translations that emphasize the structural aspects of the theory—that is, the stages, and the tasks with which stages were demonstrated.

Preoccupation with Piaget's stages led to the frequent preschool objective of moving children from the preoperational level to the stage of concrete operations. Some educational efforts centered on teaching children the Genevan tasks—for example, teaching children to say that when one of two equal-sized balls of clay is flattened, it still has the same amount as the unflattened ball

---

1. If a catalog existed of Piagetian theoretical constructs and experimental situations, we could systematically discuss what is of educational significance and what merits transfer to the classroom. Such an exhaustive task is beyond our scope here. We will make reference to relevant constructs in appropriate contexts throughout the book. For example, Piaget's notion of figurative knowing is useful in justifying the game Pin the Part on the Pig in Chapter 5 and, later in this chapter, his study of the role of pretend play in formation of the symbol is useful in justifying the encouragement of pretense in preschool.

(conservation of substance). Without teaching tasks specifically, other educational efforts centered on trying to teach the "mechanics" of concrete operational reasoning such as seriation.

This kind of translation by transfer is problematic because even such a rich description of stages as Piaget's has at least three limitations from the educational perspective. First, a sequence in cognitive structures is not a sequence in underlying formative functions. That is, structural stages do not give a description of *how* a child gets from one stage to the next. Second, the description of stages presents a picture of changes that occur so gradually over several years that it is difficult to see how these insights should inform teaching at a particular moment. Third, although the Genevan task situations were useful in demonstrating stages, most do not meet criteria for good educational activities based on constructivist aspects of the theory. Exceptions are those that are amenable to experimentation, making it possible for children to observe different reactions to different actions on objects. For example, children can observe whether objects float or sink, and can experiment with changes in shadows due to variations in arrangement of light, object, and screen. When Piagetian tasks do provide a source of activities in which children are interested, the constructivist teacher, in contrast to Lavatelli, does not teach tasks didactically.

If the child constructs knowledge by abstracting from her experience meaning as she interprets it, it makes no sense to try to teach ideas that are inaccessible to her. Conservation of substance, for example, is inaccessible to the nonconserver because there is no way for the child to make the invariance conclusion through her own observation and physical action on objects. That is, conservation is a logico-mathematical deduction that requires going beyond what is knowable through physical experience.

The inadequacy of the literal approach to educational translation is, therefore, that the transfer of research tasks and structural stages to objectives, activities, and methods of teaching contradicts the constructivist aspect of Piaget's theory. Of the three Piagetian programs discussed below, Lavatelli's best fits the literal model, although in their early work Kamii and High/Scope writers also took this approach. Their later efforts shifted the emphasis away from *application* of these isolated parts. Instead, broader *implications* of the theory as a whole were sought. As we shall see, later High/Scope writers made efforts to avoid a literal approach, but were only partially successful.

Free Translation

Free translation of Piaget's theory into educational language is a process of elaborating practices that preserve the spirit of the theory's constructivism. The planning of classroom experimentation is guided by *implications* (in contrast with *applications*) derived from the theory, and the evaluation of materials and methods is guided by psychological analysis of children's activity in the classroom. In other words, free translation travels a two-way street between theory and practice.

In contrast to literal translation, free translation represents a shift in emphasis from Piagetian stages to constructivism—that is, to the processes underlying stage change. This shift reflects the realization that, for Piaget, the significance of the stages lay not in the structures themselves, but in their functional implications for developmental processes. As noted above, the demonstration of stages indicated in part that that children make their own sense out of their experience—and construct many "wrong" ideas on the way to knowledge adults consider correct. That is, a focus on stages emphasizes the *result* of development and misses the principal theme of the theory—constructivism, the *process* of development. Free translation emphasizing the constructivist aspects of Piaget's theory has led to objectives stated not in terms of stages, but in terms of the exercise of moral and intellectual autonomy, decentering and coordination of perspectives, and the exercise of initiative in purposeful activities that inspire new constructions (Kamii & DeVries, 1975/1977, 1978, 1980).

The ways in which each set of program developers tried to retain the spirit of Piaget's constructivism in a free translation are discussed below. We let program developers speak for themselves in the presentations that follow, and we lay out comparisons to make differences clear.

The disadvantage of free translation is that it presents three difficulties that threaten a breakdown or short circuit of free translation. The first difficulty is the relation of Piaget's theory to freely translated educational objectives (of autonomy, decentering, and new constructions). This is problematic because although these objectives are rooted in precise and complex ways in Piaget's theory of autonomous reasoning arising from action, they are susceptible to the same danger noted for global translations of Piaget's work. That is, if autonomy, decentering and the like are not understood in the context of Piaget's theory, objectives may be reduced to additional vague generalities resulting from global translation—thus a breakdown of free translation. Out of context, these objectives could just as well have come from Dewey or Montessori. And they could just as easily lead to the project method, the Montessori Method, or the Bank Street or High/Scope or Kamii-DeVries program. Many different avenues may be paved with the same rhetoric. Thus, *the generality of constructivst objectives has led to a lack of consensus about the practical definition of constructive activity.*

The second difficulty that creates a short circuit is the heart of free translation—teaching in terms of children's actual experience. No teacher finds it easy to teach in terms of how children are making sense of their experience. This means understanding the qualitative ways in which children think differently from older children and adults. Certainly, all Piagetian programs to be discussed reflect this basic lesson from Piaget's research. However, the place specifically given to preoperational thought and reasoning, for example, certainly varies. In free translation, teachers plan for it, are on the lookout for it, and teach in terms of it. This is in contrast with other translations in which preoperational thought may not be apparent, may not be acknowledged, and may even be suppressed—thus short-circuiting a free translation. When teachers do not realize the importance of children's spontaneous but often wrong ideas, they (with the best of intentions) often dedicate their efforts to getting children to give right answers to their questions. When children's efforts are preoccupied with trying to please the teacher, there is little opportunity for their honest reasoning. At the practical level, teaching in terms of preoperational thought means teaching according to a child's present reasoning, not according to future concrete operations. Teaching in terms of how children make sense of their experience is aided by understanding the kinds of psychological experience distinguished by Piaget, and the corresponding kinds of mental action and resultant knowledge (see Chapter 2).

The third area of difficulty for free translation is the integration of structural stages with constructivist educational implications. In the focus on constructivism, structural stages may seem to have been abandonned—thus short-circuiting a free translation. Indeed, as we argue below, stages based on Genevan tasks are for the most part not directly useful to teachers because the content is inaccessible to young children. We do not mean to say, however, that stages are never useful. The challenge is to identify stages in content with which a constructivist teacher is concerned. In Chapters 4, 5, and 6 we show how structural stages in physical-knowledge activities, group games, and moral development aid the constructivist teacher.

INTEGRATION OF THEORETICAL AIMS WITH CHILDREN'S SPONTANEOUS ACTIVITY

Another difference among Piagetian programs is the degree to which theoretical aims are integrated with children's spontaneous activity. Of the three programs, Lavatelli's exercises reflect the least integration—classification tasks based on Piagetian experiments are simply added to the nursery school tradition of free play. Spontaneous action in play remains juxtaposed to structured training on the tasks. The High/Scope excerpt reflects a partial integration of theoretical aims with children's interest and activity—the teacher inserts tasklike questions about classification that are outside the child's purposes in making a collage. In the Kamii-DeVries excerpt, the focus of the child's interest is fully integrated with the teacher's theoretical aim—the teacher's comments and questions about classes and their relations coincide with the child's own interests in making sets of animals. Thus, Lavatelli *juxtaposes* theory and practice, High/Scope *inserts* theory into practice, and Kamii-DeVries *integrates* theory and practice.

STAGES AND CONSTRUCTIVISM

A further difference among Piagetian programs, already discussed briefly in the section on types of translation, merits further elaboration. This is a diffence in balance between two aspects of Piaget's work—structural stages and functional constructivism. The *functional* aspect of Piaget's theory is constructivism—the process part of the account of cognitive and sociomoral development where action plays such an important role, as detailed in Chapter 2. The *structural* aspect is the invariant sequence of qualitatively different stages—the successive forms of reasoning that result from the constructive process. We tried to show in Chapter 2 the interdependent relationship in Piaget's thinking between these two aspects, especially at the level of the child's experience. Despite this inseparability, the conceptual distinction between structural and functional aspects is useful because it throws into relief the tendency among many Piagetian educators to overemphasize the structural stages. This tendency is due in part to Piaget's own emphasis on stage structures. For Piaget, however, the stages simply signified the mental structures that show that knowledge, especially logic, is neither innate nor learned by simple social transmission, but develops little by little in an error-filled course. To assert the existence of stages means to say that the thought of the 1-year-old is qualitatively different from that of the 4-year-old whose thought is qualitatively different from that of the 9-year-old whose thought is qualitatively different from that of the 15-year-old. Piaget's genius was in conceptualizing the nature of these differences within specific content domains.

Since the stages are a description of discontinuous organizations, or milestones, in development of operational structures, they do not, in themselves, enlighten us about how one gets from one stage to the next. In describing structural stages, Piaget always pointed out functional or dynamic processes, but only in his later work did he elaborate the functional or constructivist aspect of the theory. As a result, it was perhaps inevitable that early efforts to put his theory into practice would reflect preoccupation with the structural *stages*, with the research *tasks* revealing structural development of certain epistemologically important notions in children's reasoning, and with the *domains of knowledge* in which Piaget identified stages. These preoccupations had the effect of reducing the theory to its structural aspects and in reducing the broad developmental stages to stages of performance on the tasks. Overemphasis on structural stages identified in Piaget's research also tended to reduce the educational significance of the theory to task content—that is, to scientific knowledge, and even to isolated operations.[2]

None of the three Piagetian programs to be discussed in this chapter focuses solely on either the structural or the functional aspects of Piaget's work; all draw from both in some way. However, the three approaches do differ significantly with respect to their emphasis and balance of these.

---

2. See DeVries (1978) for further discussion of educational reductiveness to narrow structural and content aims, and DeVries (1984) and DeVries and Smith (1982) for discussion of legitimate uses of stages in education.

COMPARISONS OF PIAGETIAN PROGRAMS

Four general points of agreement may be noted among advocates of the three programs to be discussed:

1. All contend that a basic objective to be drawn from Piaget's work is to foster structural change in children's reasoning in the direction of operational thought.
2. All emphasize the fundamental importance of the child's action for learning and development.
3. All borrow ideas from the child-development tradition in early education for materials, equipment, and activities that permit children to be active (for example, painting and other art activities, blockbuilding, pretend play, singing, and sand and water play) (Kamii & DeVries, 1973).
4. None of the three Piagetian programs is *just* "Piagetian." Each recognizes certain limitations in using Piaget's theory alone as a basis for educational practice.

To the casual observer of classroom activity in the three programs, general similarities may mask differences. Despite the similarities that distinguish Piagetian programs from others (especially those with academic emphases such as DISTAR), important distinctions exist as well. As we shall see, the broad similarities listed above give way to differences when the programs are articulated in detail and especially when they are translated into specific practices. One perspective on these is to consider what is kept in sharpest focus—(1) stages, tasks and domains of knowledge, or (2) constructive processes (such as children's spontaneous activity arising from interest in particular phenomena or events, and purposeful experimentation to reach a goal). Also, the reader may keep the following questions in mind.

- How is action conceptualized? How is it encouraged?
- To what extent is the basic goal logic in language, and to what extent is it exercise of the reasoning of practical intelligence apart from language?
- What is the program's relation to the child-development tradition in early education? What modifications are made in this tradition?
- How are the limitations in the educational usefulness of Piaget's theory viewed?
- To what extent are interest, experimentation, and co-operation fostered?

In what follows, we shall show the differences in what the three programs try to do (objectives), and how they try to do it (practice).

THEORY IN OBJECTIVES

In their beginnings, all three Piagetian programs emphasized similar aims that reflected the structural aspects of Piaget's work. Emerging differences can be viewed in terms of the degree to which they moved away from narrow *application* of structure-content aspects of Genevan work to broader *implications* of the functional or constructivist aspects. Differences can also be viewed in terms of the degree to which the translations of theory into practice moved from global or literal translation to free translation.

More specifically, three kinds of objectives are found. The first type specifies objectives in terms of reasoning underlying the operations necessary for success in Piagetian tasks (such as class inclusion and conservation). The second type reflects what the authors see as a breakdown of operations into elements or precursors (for example, one-to-one correspondence, recognizing complementary classes such as red trucks and not-red trucks, and grouping objects according to physical attributes and use). These first two types of objectives are usually accompanied by the specification of corresponding language to be learned (such as naming attributes of objects and their similarities and differences, and negatives to express complementary classes).

The third type of objective embeds structurally described aims within a more broadly constructivist framework. These broader aims emphasize the child's spontaneous activity and certain individual and group dynamics, including interest, attitudes of mutual respect, autonomy, and co-operation. Structural aims are secondary to constructivist aims. To the extent that a program emphasizes this third objective, it may be characterized as a free translation of constructivist implications of Piaget's research and theory.

Now let us examine the objectives of selected Piagetian programs with these conceptualizations in mind.

LAVATELLI

Lavatelli's objectives include the first two types described above. Her *Early Childhood Curriculum: A Piaget Program* (1970b–1973) represents the view that the general aim is to move children from the preoperational to the concrete operational stage of reasoning. For her, this implied specific objectives of training children to think logically through practice in 20-minute sessions with Genevan tasks in order to promote "development of intellectual skills or operations in classification, number, space and measurement, and seriation" (1970b/1973, p. 1). More specifically, the objectives included what Lavatelli called "mental operations" such as one-to-one correspondence, intersection of classes (visualizing an object as having simultaneous membership in two classes at once), complementary classes (sorting objects into classes and subclasses, and recognizing complementary classes such as red trucks and not-red trucks), seriation, transitivity, and conservation of number, area, length, and liquid. Lavatelli also specified many language goals related to operations (for example, conditional "if-then" statements, and disjoint comparatives such as "This one is shorter, but that one is lighter"). Aims thus reflect a literal translation of Piaget's work; his theory is applied by taking specific operations and performance on experimental tasks as educational goals.[3]

It should be noted that Lavatelli's Piagetian objectives do not describe all her aims for an educational program. She had long been associated with the child-development tradition in nursery school education, and continued to advocate its emphasis on social and emotional objectives. While she justified some traditional activities in terms of her Piagetian cognitive objectives, Lavatelli (1970a/1973) did not present an integrated set of program objectives. We reserve the discussion of Lavatelli's connection of her Piagetian objectives with child-development activities for the later section on classroom practice.

HIGH/SCOPE

In an effort to respond to the challenge of educating disadvantaged children, Weikart and his early collaborators felt more strongly than Lavatelli the need for a new cognitively oriented classroom program. Their High/Scope program was described in a 1971 publication entitled *The Cognitively-Oriented Curriculum* by Weikart, Rogers, Adcock, and McClelland. A second publication in 1979 entitled *Young Children in Action*, by Hohmann, Banet, and Weikart, describes the High/Scope program after it evolved and changed. The early objectives of Weikart and his collaborators differed somewhat from their later aims, but the consistent aim throughout their effort has been to build "the links to traditional academic exercises in reading and mathematics" (Hohmann, Banet, & Weikart, 1979, p. 6). Academic success in public schools was and is the most general objective.

The first conceptualization of objectives by Weikart, Adcock, Rogers, and McClelland was of the second type described above, emphasizing precursors or elements of operations. Like Lavatelli, the High/Scope group took Piaget's work literally as a direct source of objectives. Their aim in 1971 was to teach "Piagetian skills." However, unlike Lavatelli's aims, those of High/Scope did not include the achievement of operational thought (in conservation, class inclusion, etc.) Objectives were introduced as having the focus on the *process* of learning rather than on facts or subject matter. Goals were specified in terms of four Genevan research topics taken as curriculum content areas—classification, seriation, temporal relations, and spatial relations. Specific skills in these areas included sorting objects, ordering four different-sized objects, verbalizing relations such as in/out and near/far, and ordering events in time (first, second, last, and soon). Specific goals for each content area were supposed to reflect sequences from simple to complex and concrete to abstract, and from motoric to verbal levels of operations. High/Scope authors had their own definition of

---

3. Had Lavatelli lived longer (she died in the mid 1970s), her work might have evolved in the same constructivist direction as the other Piagetian programs we discuss here.

operations as "representational acts," in contrast to Piaget's definition in terms of a network of coordinated mental actions underlying specific knowledge and reasoning. In addition, Piaget's discussion of the signifiers index, symbol, and sign was interpreted by High/Scope authors as a description of levels of representation that could serve as goals within each of the four content areas. The signifiers (indices, symbols, and signs) were misconceived as describing progress to preoperational, concrete operational, and formal operational stages, respectively. In fact, indices, symbols, and signs become signifiers for the child by the age of about 18–24 months.[4] This erroneous interpretation resulted in definition of "operational" goals as verbal and written words. "Concrete operational" goals also included object permanence[5] and representation of objects in symbols such as pictures and models. By 1979 this theoretical equation of operational-stage development with levels of representation had disappeared.

High/Scope aims in 1971 were literal applications of the structural aspects of Piaget's theory with the content of Genevan tasks and domains of knowledge studied by Piaget. However, by 1979 High/Scope authors had evolved away from an emphasis on teaching specific Piagetian tasks. Instead, they emphasized the child as constructor of knowledge (Hohmann et al., 1979, pp. xv–xvi).

The general High/Scope objective in 1979 remained cognitive. It was called the "Cognitively Oriented Curriculum" until recently, when it was renamed the "High/Scope Preschool Curriculum." Specific objectives, called "Key Experiences of Cognitive Development," are organized in seven chapters: "Language," "Experiencing and Representing," "Classification," "Seriation," "Number," "Spatial Relations," and "Time." These objectives are essentially the same as those in 1971. However, a chapter "Active Learning" is added, and the High/Scope authors stress that their intention is to present objectives of the third type mentioned above—that is, to embed the structural objectives within the context of the child's action. This change was a significant shift in the direction of constructivism. The ways in which High/Scope teachers are encouraged to view and plan active learning will be discussed in the section on classroom practice.

Another change noted from 1971 to 1979 is that number objectives are separated from seriation and are elaborated to include one-to-one correspondence, counting beyond five, and numerical comparison. To the spatial relations list are added fitting things together and taking them apart, rearranging and

---

4. Piaget (1945/1962) used the term "index" to refer to the signal of an object by a part or an aspect (for example, a dog's bark or a fire engine's siren). He distinguished the index from the symbol, which depends on resemblance between the object signified and its signifier (for example, a picture or mental image of an object). The sign is an arbitrary socially determined signifier (for example, the name of an object). Rather than referring to stages through adolescence as High/Scope authors say, index, symbol, and sign all appear during the sensorimotor period (up to 24 months).

5. Recognizing that object permanence is well established before 2 years of age, High/Scope authors eliminated this inappropriate objective from 1979 goals. However, the 1971 book is still on the market, and readers may still be misled by these inaccuracies.

reshaping objects, and observing and describing things from different spatial viewpoints. Temporal aims are broadened to include seasonal and clock time. While language continues to be heavily emphasized, language objectives are broadened to stress communication.

The High/Scope position with regard to socioemotional objectives should be noted. No discussion of this goal appeared in 1971. However, in 1979 the authors noted that socioemotional development is also being fostered. A brief statement (Hohmann et al., 1979, pp. 1–2) explains that teachers provide a positive, supportive relationship and acceptance of children's language and culture. Priorities include promoting feelings of self-worth through giving children responsibility and control over what happens to them. High/Scope authors feel that it is more productive, for example, for teachers to focus directly on helping children plan a sequence of activities and classify objects than on group dynamics and interpreting fantasies. While High/Scope teachers are thus expected to be sensitive to children's social and emotional needs, these objectives are not linked with Piaget and are not integrated theoretically with cognitively oriented efforts.

The High/Scope conceptualization of objectives is thus still of the second type—organized according to the domains of Piaget's interests and emphasizing elements and precursors of operations. In this respect, High/Scope objectives still reflect a literal translation of Piaget's work. However, the third type of objective also seems to be expressed in the stated emphasis on the child's action. The emotional objectives mentioned seem to resemble the emphasis of the third type of objective on autonomy and mutual respect, although group dynamics are not included. This movement toward constructivism leads us to ask whether the 1979 High/Scope program may be a free translation rather than a literal translation. The answer is not clear in the statements of objectives. We must look for the answer in the ways objectives are interpreted in classroom practice.

KAMII AND DEVRIES

During 1967–1970 Kamii developed a program having objectives similar to those of Weikart and his High/Scope group, with the general aim of enabling disadvantaged children to succeed in school (Kamii & Radin, 1967). This similarity is due to the fact that Kamii and Radin had been active in program development at High/Scope. Like the early (1971) High/Scope objectives, Kamii's also emphasized elements or precursors of operations (a kind of accumulation of elements), with an emphasis on representation and structural stages in classification, seriation, and number. Kamii later criticized the objectives of trying to help children go from one stage to the next in each task (Denis-Prinzhorn, Kamii, & Mounoud, 1972).

In contrast with High/Scope (and Lavatelli), Kamii and Radin did not expect operations before about age 7, and operations were not confused with representation. Kamii and Radin did, however, aim to teach identity despite changes in appearance, in order to enable children to conserve later. In effect, this was an effort to promote conservation. This mistake was later recognized, and neither identity nor conservation was included in 1970 objectives. Also in contrast to High/Scope, Kamii and Radin stated language objectives separately from aims related to Piagetian categories. They emphasized language for communication, not for labeling object attributes or teaching spatial relationships. For example, specific words in a two-week goal plan were pronouns with prepositions, polars with objects, and verbs (Kamii, Derman, Sonquist, & Anderson, 1967).

As socioemotional objectives, Kamii and Radin included inner control, but they did not draw this aim from Piaget's work. As the reader will see later, when Piaget's theory was mined for its socioemotional implications, socioemotional objectives changed.

For Kamii, the shift toward constructivism was set in motion in 1969 during a consultation visit by Professor Hermina Sinclair, one of Piaget's collaborators. Sinclair pointed out that Piaget never intended his tasks as instructional models and that teaching tasks or even specific task skills is like trying to enrich an entire field by applying some handfuls of soil from a fertile field (Sinclair, 1971). Sinclair also called attention to Piaget's important distinction between physical and logico-mathematical experience. This proved to be a turning point in Kamii's perspective. During the remaining year of the Ypsilanti project, she began to think about physical-knowledge activities focused on the child's construction of knowledge about the nature of matter, through actions on objects and observation of their reactions. In 1970 the category of physical knowledge appeared for the first time in the list of objectives (Kamii & Radin, 1970), marking the first significant difference between Kamii and other Piagetian program developers.

Nevertheless, Kamii's objectives still emphasized precursors of operations, with the expectation that teaching these would make operational thought possible by age 7. The general aim was to move the child beyond prelogical reasoning to a transitional stage where logic is coherent to a point. Although concrete operations were disclaimed as specific preschool aims, concrete operations seemed to be a long-range goal.

In 1971 the distinction between logico-mathematical and physical knowledge foreshadowed the later clear shift to constructivist aims, but Kamii's emphasis was still focused on the accumulation of correct structural elements such as classification and seriation. Physical-knowledge aims were limited to knowledge of properties of objects and development of a repertoire of actions with which to explore objects. (Later physical-knowledge aims described in Chapter 4 emphasize reasoning about causes and effects in physical phenomena such as movement and changes in objects.)

The shift away from emphasizing structural aspects of Piaget's theory was elaborated in collaboration with DeVries, beginning in 1970. By 1973 the old statements of objectives had given way to objectives emphasizing constructivism —that is, the child's feelings and actions. Cognitive objectives were stated simply: for the child to come up with interesting ideas, problems, and questions, and for the child to put things into relationships and notice similarities and differences (Kamii & DeVries, 1975/1977). Reading Piaget's (1932/1965) book *The Moral Judgment of the Child* led to conceptualizing socioemotional aims as necessary for realizing cognitive objectives. Socioemotional aims were for the child to feel secure in a noncoercive relationship with adults, to respect the feelings and rights of others and begin to coordinate different points of view (decentering and co-operating), to be independent, alert, and curious, to use initiative in pursuing curiosities, to have confidence in his ability to figure things out for himself, and to speak his mind with conviction (Kamii & DeVries, 1975/1977). Concern with interpersonal and group dynamics took on new significance, and the role of social interaction was emphasized.

Two retrospective comments on earlier conceptualizations of objectives are worth noting:

> The previous conceptualizations no longer make sense to us for two reasons. First, . . . they confused the development seen on Piagetian tasks with the development of the child in the everyday world. Second, they compartmentalized the objectives into classification, seriation, numerical reasoning, spatial reasoning, etc. This juxtaposition of cognitive abilities as if they were separate mechanisms . . . was an assimilation of Piaget's theory into a mechanistic notion of intelligence. (Kamii & DeVries, 1975/1977, p. 394)

> Trying to teach Piagetian tasks is like trying to make the child more intelligent by teaching him to give correct answers on the Stanford-Binet Intelligence Scale. Even if we successfully teach the tasks to a child, he does not thereby attain the same general intellectual level as a child who solves them without specific training. When a child solves a task without instruction, his performance reflects a structure which consists of a whole network of interrelated actions. Learning a task is not the same as developing this entire network. Therefore, although earlier efforts by the senior author [Kamii, 1971, 1972a, 1972b, 1973a, 1973b, Kamii and Radin, 1967, 1970; Sonquist and Kamii, 1967; Sonquist, Kamii, and Derman, 1970] to apply Piaget's theory were conceptualized around each domain delineated by him, we now view such objectives as a misapplication of the theory.
>
> While it is certainly desirable for children eventually to reach the stage of formal operations, and they inevitably pass through the stage of concrete operations on the way, this does not mean that we should aim to rush four-year-olds into concrete operations. Trying to move children to the stage of concrete operations reflects a confusion between the *results* of development and the *process* of development. The stages describe only in general terms the results of an underlying constructive process. It is this constructive process which is the most crucial aspect of Piaget's theory for educators. (Kamii & DeVries, 1978, pp. 39–40)

Thus, the earlier aim of preparing children for academic success in school had given way to the aim of development. Ultimately it became clear to Kamii and

DeVries that constructivist aims are antithetical to many school objectives—though not to aims of literacy and knowledge of subject matter.

Socioemotional and cognitive aims were viewed as inseparable in practice and were later stated in an integrated way that, however, omitted some important details (Kamii & DeVries, 1980; DeVries, 1981, 1983). C. Kamii (1984a) distilled aims even further into the single aim of autonomy. This evolution was a process of circling around and closing in on an essential goal characterizing all constructivist considerations. Autonomy is thus conceived as an objective inclusive of all other objectives. None of the other Piagetian approaches focused on autonomy as a central consideration in their objectives.

Although the distillation of objectives into autonomy is useful in understanding an essential difference among programs, it introduces the difficulty of understanding differences in objectives at less rarified levels of concern. In our earlier discussion of the weaknesses of the free approach to translation, we noted that constructivist objectives are susceptible to the danger of becoming vague generalities. This is the case when objectives are reduced to autonomy. In our view, reduction of aims to autonomy is too one-sided, omitting what the notion of structural stages contributes to educational planning. In fact, when one looks closely at Kamii-DeVries rationales for particular activities, one finds reference to structural considerations such as classification and spatial relations. Thus, in a sense, the contrast of the later Kamii-DeVries objectives with those of High/Scope and Lavatelli may be somewhat misleading. Kamii and DeVries *do* have operational reasoning as a long-range goal, but the ways in which this goal influences educational practice are what is important.

In the revised objectives, the educational implications of Piaget's theory were no longer limited to cognitive development but extended to social, moral, and personality development. Piaget's constructivism was understood to mean that no experience involves or impacts on any single aspect of development in an isolated way. A narrow emphasis on cognitive development was viewed as dangerous because a neglect of other aspects inevitably leads to contradictions with the basic assumptions of constructivism that include broad concerns with motivation, personality, and unconscious factors.

In comparison with 1971 aims, 1975 aims were dramatically different, especially with regard to the teacher-child relationship and sociomoral development. In 1971 the objective was for the child to internalize adult rules and want to follow them. In 1975 the aim was for children to be self-regulating or autonomous in constructing their own moral rules. Kamii and DeVries took great pains to make it clear that socioemotional objectives were their first priority and that this conclusion was based on Piaget's discussion (especially in *The Moral Judgment of the Child*) of the importance of increasing autonomy (self-regulation) for the construction of moral ideas and values, personality, intelligence, and knowledge.

The expansion of goals to constructivist aims that included all aspects of development was not the only change. Structural aims were also drastically modified. Instead of specifying precursors of operations, structural aims were defined more generally as the construction of relationships—including erroneous or illogical relationships that occur to children. It is a bit ironic that the question of the educational significance of Piaget's stages finally led to the conclusion that the stages offer little that is specifically useful in helping teachers know what to *do*. The extreme form of this conclusion was expressed as follows:

> Let us first mention two objectives often given by others which are *not* aims in this book:
>
> 1. We do not aim to teach Piagetian tasks.
> 2. We do not aim to move children to the stage of concrete operations. (Kamii & DeVries, 1975/1977, p. 390; see also Kamii & DeVries, 1978, p. 39)

The denial of operations as aims was not intended to be a denial of the importance of operational development. In fact, the Kamii-DeVries approach strongly emphasized the kind of intellectual activity in which progressive coordinations are expected to lead eventually to operational thought. These coordinations are described and justified in terms of an analysis of the structure of specific content children are motivated to think about. For example, in the card game Making Families (excerpts presented above and later in this chapter) children have the possibility for intellectual exercise related to classification, and the rationale for and evaluation of its educational value includes classification. Structural objectives related to classification, however, are subordinated to constructivist concerns with autonomy and social reciprocity.

In part, the reason Kamii-DeVries disclaim the aim of children acquiring concrete operations was a desire to talk about objectives at the level of everyday planning and teaching. To the teacher of children whose thought is typically preoperational, the aim of concrete operations is of little direct help. At a broad conceptual level, certainly the aim is to foster the kind of thought that leads to operations. At the time of the disclaimer of concrete operations as an aim, it seemed necessary to shift the educational focus away from a narrow emphasis on stages, away from direct *applications* to drawing broader *implications* of the theory as a whole.

THEORY IN PRACTICE

Comparing the aims of programs having so much in common is a risky business. Differences among verbalized objectives of programs are elusive because what one set of authors presents as a priority, others may mention casually in passing. The question then arises as to the differences among the programs in actual practice. Are the theoretical differences we see merely pedantic "splitting of hairs"? To answer this question, we must know how each program interprets its objectives in practical terms. What do teachers do? How do they do it? Finally, for us, the most meaningful comparison of approaches and programs is at the level of the child's psychological experience.

Within our presentation of each program's practical reality, we focus on several topics. First, we acknowledge that all Piagetian programs are eclectic in their reliance not only on Piaget but other sources of curriculum as well. All are eclectic also in the sense that they have not created an entirely new approach to early education. All have drawn from the child-centered tradition in nursery school education its emphasis on play and other activities that appeal to children. However, by emphasizing cognitive objectives, each Piagetian program developer modifies the child-development tradition in particular ways.

Next, we elaborate the sketch given at the beginning of the chapter of how each program approaches the teaching of classification. Then we comment on the degree to which interest, experimentation, and co-operation (discussed in Chapter 2 as characteristics of what Piaget called "active education") are found in each program. In addition, we outline the role of the teacher. Finally, we consider the role of preoperational thought in the development of operational reasoning.

Lavatelli

Eclecticism and the Child-Development Tradition in Early Education

Lavatelli saw Piagetian tasks as valuable cognitive supplements to the traditional child-development or child-centered nursery school with which she was closely identified during most of her career (see, for example, Gans, Stendler,[6] & Almy, 1952). "The objective is not to change drastically those preschool practices which have stood the test of time, but to provide a cognitive underpinning that will make the preschool more intellectually challenging" (Lavatelli, 1970b/1973, p. 1). Lavatelli developed kits of materials like those used in Genevan experiments and wrote lessons for teachers to conduct with children. In her eclecticism, Piaget's theory was treated as a useful cognitive accessory to psychodynamic theory, which she viewed as the basis for practices promoting children's social and emotional development. Since Lavatelli felt that most nursery school teachers had not been trained to appreciate and foster cognitive development in play, the solution she proposed was to use part of the school day for 20-minute training sessions on Piagetian tasks and the rest of the day for relatively free activities. Thus, Lavatelli did not intend her Piagetian program as major curriculum reform. On one hand, Lavatelli's answer to the question of the sufficiency of Piaget's theory as a basis of curriculum was that it provided the source for a complete instructional program for cognitive development. However, on the other hand she sometimes also viewed her program as a modest supplement to a traditional child-development nursery school. This tension in her stance was never resolved.

Lavatelli's efforts to bring Piaget's work into educational practices are

6. Stendler was Lavatelli's name at that time.

therefore paradoxical. On the one hand, she glimpsed the possibilities for integration of the theory's implications when she argued that Piaget's theory provides justification for forms of play found in the child-development classroom. On the other hand, she did not follow up this general idea with a critical review and specific recommendations for classroom practice. She felt that if teachers understood the logical processes necessary to do her exercises, "they will find innumerable occasions in the course of the day to reinforce the learning developed in the small group sessions" (Lavatelli, 1970b/1973, p. 4). Her Piagetian translation with respect to the child-centered nursery school tradition thus fits our definition of global translation. In her translation of Genevan tasks into lessons, however, she ended up with a literal application of Piaget's work and a juxtaposition of Genevan tasks alongside the child's spontaneous activity in a traditional child-centered program.

The Teaching of Classification

As noted earlier, Lavatelli's general objective to train children to think logically emphasized operational language as well as reasoning. Her literal translation of Piaget's work led her to recommend classification exercises. In these, the teacher uses objects such as beads and miniature planes, trucks, or animals to teach children to identify common properties of objects, make groupings of complementary classes, do multiple classification matrices, and compare a superordinate class with its subclasses. For example, to teach children to identify properties of objects, children are shown a red bead and asked to string all the red ones on a string. Then they are asked to string all those that are blue, yellow, round, square, large, and small, and are told that each bead has size, shape, and color attributes. The teacher makes model strings of beads whose properties vary, and children are asked to copy them.

Lavatelli's (1970b/1973) lesson on complementary classes requires children to separate vehicles into two piles. The teacher is instructed to conduct the lesson as follows.

T: "Tell me what each object is." (The children name planes, trucks, car.) "I want you to put the trucks in one dish, and the things not trucks in the other dish. You must put everything in one dish or the other."

T: (As the children proceed) "Tell me what you are doing. What are you putting in one dish?" (Have the children say, "I'm putting a truck in the dish.") "And what are you putting in the other dish?" (If child says, "a plane," ask why a plane.)

T: For the child who needs help, ask, "What did I ask you to put in that dish?" Remind the child, if he cannot answer, "Things-not-trucks."

As each child finishes, the teacher gives him another car and asks whether it could be put in a particular dish. Later, the teacher asks children to shift the basis for classification and divide all the objects into just two groups.

In the lesson on class inclusion, the teacher gives each child 8 brown dogs, 1 white dog, 4 brown cats, 4 black cats, and a green square to represent a field. The teacher's instructions are as follows.

> Say, "Today, we're going to make some groups of animals. First, I'd like to have you make a group of all the dogs. Put the group of dogs on the field." As the children work, say to each in turn:
>
> T: "Tell me what you are doing." (Model the correct response for the children who need it.) "If you make a group out of all of the dogs, will you use this one (the white dog)? Why (or why not)?" (If a child gives the wrong answer, ask, "What are you putting on the field? Is this also a dog? Then should it go on the field?" Say, "Now I'd like you to make a group of *animals*." Repeat the same directions as for dogs, substituting "animals" for "dog."

To get children to take a class apart to find subclasses, Lavatelli advocates the following.

> T: "Now I'd like to have you make a group of *brown* dogs. Find the brown dogs to put on the field." Have the children make groups, in turn, of the white dogs, then the black cats and the brown cats. Repeat the questions used above for each group.

To make comparisons of "all" and "some," the teacher is instructed as follows.

> T: As each child finishes, ask: "Which made the bigger group, a group of white dogs or a group of dogs? Why?" "Which made the bigger group, a group of animals or a group of dogs? Why?" "If we take all the dogs away, will there be any animals left? Why?" "If we take all the animals away, will there be any dogs left? Why?" (Have the children perform the action in each case to demonstrate correctness of response or to discover incorrectness of response, as the case may be. For example, say to the children, "I'd like you to take all the *animals* and put them in your lap. Now look at the table. Are there any dogs left? Are there any cats left? Why not?" (Lavatelli, 1970b/1973, pp. 22–23)

Lavatelli gave only a few examples to indicate how she thought teachers could encourage classification in the classroom. She did recommend the following.

> As the children put the toys away in the doll corner after playing, set up categories and check to see if the children can keep a particular class in mind in finding all the items belonging to that category: for example, "things-to-clean-house-with"; "food"; "things-to-cook-with"; "clothing."
>
> Use cooking experiences to extend class concepts. If the children are making oatmeal, for example, tell them that oatmeal is also a cereal and ask for the names of other cereals.
>
> Have the children search old magazines for pictures of objects that go together in some way. Have them cut out the pictures and tell you what the pictures have in common. Do not supply the name of a class. For example, don't tell the children to find pictures of vehicles; let them find a common property in a number of objects, name the class and extend it. When they have correctly set up a class, have them paste the pictures on a sheet of paper. Then print the name of the class on the paper. (Lavatelli, 1970b/1973, p. 27)

In summary, with the exception of these classroom recommendations, Lavatelli's approach—as illustrated in the excerpts above—is to teach according to Piaget's tasks and structural stages in sessions outside the classroom. Spontaneous activity is reserved for the classroom, and it is in this sense that we say that Lavatelli's literal translation is a *juxtaposition* of the child's spontaneous activity with Piaget's work, as indicated in Table 3.1. Such juxtaposition reflects a fragmented theory-practice relation, and in turn, leads to a fragmented psychological experience for the child.

Interest

Lavatelli used colorful objects such as beads and miniature dogs and cats to interest children in practicing Genevan tasks. She was influenced, no doubt, by the success of Piaget and his collaborators in obtaining children's responses to their experiments. While a good experimenter (or a good teacher) can arouse a child's interest in classifying objects, such interest is likely to be short-lived and may simply be at best a good-natured accommodation of the adult's request rather than reflecting a personal concern. Piaget was quoted in Chapter 2 as indicating that the interest observed in Genevan tasks is not what he had in mind for active education.

While children may be more or less interested in doing what Lavatelli's teacher tells them to do, it is the teacher's interests and goals that are central to the activity, not the child's. It is striking to note in Lavatelli's (1971a, 1971b) filmstrip of a classification activity that the children exhibit little energy in their responses. In comparison to children playing cards, they appear passive and uninterested. How can we expect a child to be interested and spontaneously active for very long when what is demanded makes little sense to him? When the child is asked to reason beyond his developmental level, his resources for initiative are limited.

Experimentation

Lavatelli did not develop experimentation in her curriculum. None of her lessons gives children problems in which they can find out through acting on objects whether their expectations are correct. All of Lavatelli's lessons involve logico-mathematical knowledge that cannot be verified physically. In physical-knowledge activities, in contrast, children's preoperational expectations are usually contradicted by an object's reaction. Such confrontations more easily result in consciousness of contradiction than in logico-mathematical knowledge where the contradiction among schemes must become conscious. Although Lavatelli's teacher tries to help children see logical contradictions, we are not persuaded that children really correct their reasoning through such lessons.

Co-operation

Lavatelli makes no mention of co-operation, although one might infer from her advocacy of the child-development tradition that she favored social interaction of a co-operative sort.

High/Scope

Eclecticism and the Child-Development Tradition in Early Education

Weikart and his collaborators made much more extensive use than did Lavatelli of Piagetian theory in developing a total program. In both 1971 and 1979, they conceptualized classroom activities in terms of the domains of knowledge studied by Piaget—classification, number, spatial relations, time, and language —and representation of these domains. In 1971 each activity was carefully planned with a single Piagetian concept as the cognitive goal. Although this single-minded approach was abandoned by 1979, it is clear that theory was and is a crucial source of curriculum.

While the High/Scope authors saw Piaget's theory as the basis of the Cognitively Oriented Curriculum in 1971, other writers were also cited. For example, in part, the encouragement of pretend play was based on Smilansky's work, and classification activities were based on research by Sigel and others on object sorting. Later, the strong emphasis on language was indirectly based on work by Chomsky and Cazden (Hohmann et al., 1979, p. 2). In addition to these acknowledgments, High/Scope authors concluded in 1971, "On the whole, however, the curriculum can be seen as based upon the theoretical work and experiments of Piaget" (Weikart et al., 1971, pp. viii–ix). High/Scope's early eclecticism was not limited to drawing on a variety of theoretical sources for curriculum development. It extended to the modification of Piaget's theory to make it more usable by teachers:

> It is important to note, however, that no matter how sophisticated a theory may be, in a practical classroom program it is but a tool. It should be employed only as long as it seems to do the job, and it may be altered to meet differing situations when it seems advisable. This approach to theory leads into trouble very easily, because it permits a flexibility which may circumvent the theory. For example, Piagetian child development theory does not use some of the terms of processes employed in this guide. In addition, the guide alters some of the terms such as "operations" to mesh with the recommended teaching patterns which have worked well. Yet, the basic thrust of the theory is present. Therefore, while there is a growing congregation of "high church" Piagetians in preschool education, I would classify this curriculum as the product of "store front" Piagetian theory utilization. (Weikart et al, 1971, p. ix)

As a base for their program in 1979, High/Scope authors still rely on Piaget's work for their general orientation, but retain the early skepticism regarding the possibility of deriving from it educational practices.

> What we can do at best is to take a theory such as Piaget's and use it to generate hypotheses about the kinds of experiences that would be most relevant to the goal of supporting the rapidly growing cognitive systems of the normal child. . . .
>
> We urge that this not be viewed as a narrowly Piagetian curriculum but as a general framework for an approach to education that stresses problem-solving and decision-making by both child and adult. (Hohmann et al., 1979, pp. 2, vi)

Thus, it is clear that when Weikart and his collaborators tried to use Piaget's work as a basis for curriculum, they found it insufficient. To Piaget's theory they added the rationales and practices that made sense to them.

High/Scope authors clearly acknowledge their reliance on the child-development tradition. In the foreword to their 1979 book, they note that Piaget's theory determined the content of their program, but that the format of the day and the general method of teacher-child interaction were "rooted in the suggestions of Smilansky and traditional nursery-school programming" (Hohmann et al., 1979, p. xiv). They credit the influence of this tradition as partly responsible for the fact that they did not make the mistake of creating kits to "teach" classification, or whatever, or of diagnosing children by means of Piagetian developmental tests so as to guide remedial teaching. Nevertheless, the cognitive emphasis in the High/Scope program makes it different from the traditional nursery school. Although the High/Scope collaborators viewed their program as more serious in its focus on cognitive objectives, much of their classroom practice does not differ from child-development traditions. Classroom arrangement and equipment are basically the same, and High/Scope children engage in classic nursery school activities such as painting and other art activities, pretend play, block play, puzzles, carpentry, sand and water play, cooking, modeling clay and Play-Doh, and listening to stories. Such experiences have long been trademarks of the child-development approach (for example, High/Scope authors cite Leeper, Dales, Skipper, & Witherspoon, 1968; Nimnicht, McAfee, & Meier, 1969; Spodek, 1972; Hess & Croft, 1975; Read, 1966). These nursery school texts have also emphasized sensory experiences and specified classification, seriation, and spatial and temporal relationships and language in much the same way as High/Scope.

Two significant differences with child-development practices are worth noting. The first is that High/Scope has emphasized children's conscious planning-doing-recalling of activities. Before children begin their "work time," they meet in small groups and are asked to decide what they are going to do, and teachers help them elaborate their ideas. After "work time," the small groups are reconvened for children to tell what they did and to represent what they did (for example, by drawing). An objective is for children to make more complete initial plans for the entire work time. The rationale for planning and recall is for children to see themselves as responsible for making and carrying out decisions and as having some control over what they do. Planning is viewed as valuable for the development of representation and for the practical purpose of thinking about how to carry out a plan. Recall occurs throughout work time when a child completes a planned activity. Before planning the next, the child must review what was done first. High/Scope authors note that children may go through the plan-do-review process a number of times before the recall time in the small group.

The second difference between High/Scope and the traditional child-development tradition is that High/Scope focuses on cognitive objectives in a more exclusive way, with little emphasis on the social and emotional objectives that are so central to programs like Bank Street (discussed in Chapter 11).

The Teaching of Classification

The early High/Scope examples of how to teach classification are much like Lavatelli's, except for their conduct inside, rather than outside, the classroom (Weikart et al., 1971; Weikart & Hohmann, 1973). Activities reflected a strong emphasis on sorting and verbalizing category names of objects as well as similarities and differences among groups of objects. Recommendations include having children sort beads according to size or plastic pieces according to shape. Children verbalize the similarities and differences, or the teacher labels the groupings.

High/Scope authors in 1979 criticized their early focus on teaching Piagetian tasks. The new constructivist orientation is reflected in efforts to integrate the pursuit of theoretical objectives with children's spontaneous interests. Instead of having children sort for the sake of sorting, they emphasized sorting within the context of children's interests (for example, art or pretense). However, like 1971 objectives, 1979 classification goals emphasize describing attributes of objects, their similarities and differences, matching and sorting, negations (recognizing an attribute an object does not have, or class it does not belong to), using "some" and "all," and keeping more than one attribute in mind at a time (Hohmann et al., 1979, p. 195).

Many examples are given in the High/Scope manual that reflect the priority of the aim of classification, and especially classification language. Since no single, long protocol is given of children's reasoning about classes and relations, we have selected examples of activities recommended by High/Scope authors to reflect these goals. We group them into the following categories, as activities in which one finds:

1. Children's spontaneous thought about attributes of objects and similarities and differences
2. Teachers' insertion into children's spontaneous activities of commentary and questions aimed at inspiring thought about attributes of objects, similarities and differences, and classes and relations
3. Games

High/Scope examples emphasize the logical or structural elements of classification (in contrast with emphasis on the "illogical" constructive action of preoperational thought).

CHILDREN'S SPONTANEOUS THOUGHT. Like Lavatelli and Kamii and DeVries, High/Scope authors recognize the significance for the development of classificatory operations of children's spontaneous grouping of similarities and differences. For example, children putting on boots may remark that they are the same and comment on similar attributes such as color. Teachers are described as responding to children's spontaneous thoughts about similarities and differences in an affirmative way. In this category of examples, the child's spontaneous groupings are simply observed or supported.

INSERTION OF COMMENTARY AND QUESTIONS INTO CHILDREN'S SPONTANEOUS ACTIVITY. The interventions we term "insertions" are of two types—one that seems to flow into children's spontaneous activity in a nonintrusive way, and the other that is far from children's preoccupations.

In nonintrusive insertions, the teacher picks up on children's ideas and suggests an extension that may provoke their interest in a new challenge. For example, one teacher observed that a child had rolled playdough into balls of similar size and suggested making some of different size. Cleanup offers an important context for this type of intervention. In one example, a High/Scope teacher noticed that children had discovered that some blocks roll, and suggested rolling or spinning blocks across a table into a container.

In these examples, it is easier to find primary justification in terms of the advantages of physical-knowledge activities than in terms of classification. Children are encouraged to think about attributes in the context of physical actions on objects where the reactions of objects provide the basis for observation of similarities and differences. High/Scope teachers also suggest categories of object reaction (for example, suggesting that a child put away all the instruments that make a noise when shaken). This kind of suggestion is likely to appeal to a child's spontaneous interest and result in active searching based on object attributes.

In other examples of nonintrusive intervention, High/Scope teachers verbalize category names, negations, and adjectives describing attributes. For example, "Lois, you're stringing the beads that are in the box, and Tillie is stringing the beads that are not in the box" (Hohmann et al., 1979, p. 211).

In these examples, teachers succeeded in integrating Piaget's theory about classification with teaching in the context of children's interests and activity. Commentary is inserted as an accompaniment to children's activity. These interventions may be viewed in terms of teaching children the vocabulary of classes.

Now we turn to examples of teacher intervention that seem to introduce the teacher's preoccupation with classification intrusively into the flow of children's reasoning. Chiefly, these interventions are questions asked in the context of activities in which the child has a focus different from classification:

- When a child glues squares on a piece of paper to make a "wipe-mat" for her mother, the teacher says, "When you give this to your Mommy are you going to show her anything that's the same?" (Hohmann et al., 1979, pp. 202–203)

- When a child pretends to give toys to a doll, the teacher asks whether he can show the baby what is the same about all the toys he has for her (Hohmann et al., 1979, p. 215)
- When children play store, the teacher buys milk, and says, "Can you find me two cartons in your store that are not the same?... When you were looking for them on the shelf, how could you tell they were not the same?... You're not sure? Well, one way I bet you could tell they were not the same, Mr. Grocery Store Man, is that this carton has a cow on it and this one doesn't." (Hohmann et al., 1979, pp. 210–211)
- When a child constructs a building the teacher comments that it is made out of all red plastic pieces, and asks what else she can add that is red and plastic. (Hohmann et al., 1979, p. 213)
- When a child gathers a bunch of leaves, the teacher comments that they are all green and long, and asks whether he can add something else green and long.
- When elementary school children make caramel apples for Halloween, the teacher has them separate all the materials into things bought at the store (caramels and sticks) and things found at school (such as pot, cinnamon, and waxed paper). Apples brought by the teacher do not fit in either category, and the teacher suggests they sort all the things again into two groups that will include the apples (things to eat and things not to eat). (Hohmann et al., 1979, p. 193)
- When Lisa built tunnels, the teacher asked what is the same about her four tunnels. (Hohmann et al., 1979, p. 202)

In these examples, the necessity to use classificatory reasoning is not intrinsic to the child's purposes. For example, sorting and resorting apple-making materials is not necessary to making caramel apples and does not arise from children's feeling of necessity to engage in classificatory thought except to please the teacher. In many situations described by High/Scope authors, insertion of a theoretical concern outside a child's interest results in a lost opportunity to discover and build on a child's purpose.

When a High/Scope teacher finds that a child cannot respond to questioning, she describes similarities and differences for the child. For example, "Lynette, you've put all the carpet pieces together and all the red blocks together in your building. You're putting things that are the same together" (Hohmann et al., 1979, p. 84). The fact that the child arranged the objects by similarities shows she had them in mind, and the most the teacher may accomplish by this intervention is to provide verbal labels (which could better be taught in other situations: color in painting activities and "same" in Lotto games). Whether these examples of interventions based on program goals are actually intrusive depends on the child's reaction. Some children just ignore what the teacher says and go on with the pursuit of their purposes. This would seem to be more easily done in the case of accompaniment commentary, but is less easy in the situations in which the teacher asks the child for a verbal response.

GAMES. While children *may* respond to a teacher's question by actively thinking about attributes, similarities and differences, or classes and relations, they more likely invest energy in doing so when classificatory reasoning is intrinsic to their own purposes. Certain group games offer such a context. Citing DeVries and Kamii's (1975) early paper on group games in their chapter on active learning, High/Scope authors elsewhere recommend three games to promote classification, including Red Rover in which the teacher says, for example, "Red rover, red rover, let everyone wearing pants the same color as Harvey's come over" (Hohmann et al., 1979, p. 204). Other games mentioned are races in which the teacher asks how children could race but not run, and following commands such as "If you're not wearing red, touch your head" (Hohmann et al., 1979, p. 197).

Games like these offer children possibilities for using classificatory thinking in the context of their interest in figuring out how to play and thus make a good integration of theory with spontaneous activity. These examples of encouraging classificatory thinking in the context of group games are very similar to examples given by Kamii and DeVries. However, the High/Scope treatment of games is to mention just a few in relation to discrete cognitive goals, while Kamii and DeVries make group games a central part of their program in relation not only to cognitive goals, but to sociomoral and affective goals as well.

A small proportion of activities included in High/Scope's 1979 manual do integrate Piaget's theory with children's spontaneous activity. When the child's personal need to think about categories is present, the teacher's intervention is likely to flow into and extend the child's thought. When the child responds with personal interest in following suggestions from the teacher, what is spontaneous in activity is precisely the exercise of classificatory reasoning. Thought about classes is integral with the child's spontaneous and personal purposes. This kind of activity seems much more likely to result in continued classificatory reasoning than that in which the concern with classification is more the teacher's than the child's.

Interest

In contrast with Lavatelli, High/Scope authors did not leave Piaget's theory outside the classroom. The 1979 guide describes activities that aim to capitalize on children's personal interests and goals. Considerable opportunity for initiative is present. The child's interest and initiative are stressed as key to education (Hohmann et al., pp. vi, 130). Our only reservation on this point is that to the extent that teachers interrupt children to insert tasklike questions and comments, we wonder if children's reasoning is fostered.

Experimentation

Although the organization of High/Scope classrooms in 1971 certainly included materials that could be used in experimental ways, no mention was made of experimentation. The 1979 guide, however, specifically suggests that teachers provide materials that encourage active exploration. However, exploration seems to mean simply becoming familiar with many objects in the world. For example, High/Scope authors describe the various actions (dropping, crawling under, smelling, and so on) by which a child learns what an object is. Very little experimentation of the type described in Chapter 4 is suggested. For the most part, the object of High/Scope exploration is to become conscious of sensory aspects of experience[7] and to practice corresponding language (for example, how playdough feels and smells); to master the use of tools (for example, opening glue bottles and cutting fruit); and to have "active experiences" outside the classroom (for example, collecting leaves, and helping a grocery clerk fill bags).

High/Scope authors extend their notion of exploration by talking about the discovery of relations through direct experience. The relations to which High/Scope authors refer are those expressed by prepositions such as "big/little, over/under, heavy/light, inside/outside" (Hohmann et al., 1979, p. 135). In addition, High/Scope authors refer to other spatial relations such as "trying to find a block to span the gap between two other blocks" (p. 136). They emphasize that "whether the child finds the right block isn't nearly so important as the fact that he or she is discovering relations through direct experience" (p. 136). An excellent recommendation made by High/Scope authors in relation to experimentation is that the teacher should ask for action—should ask the child what can be done with a material (such as playdough). Examples of this kind of question, however, are difficult to find in the High/Scope guide. In short, although High/Scope authors agree with the principle of experimentation, the kind of experimentation they seem to have in mind does not go very far, at least in what they have written about what they do.

Co-operation

Weikart and his High/Scope collaborators briefly mention their encouragement of interaction and co-operation among children in the service of language objectives and representation in pretend play.

Kamii and DeVries

Eclecticism and the Child-Development Tradition in Early Education

Kamii's early curriculum was largely cognitive and was attributed solely to Piaget. Socioemotional and perceptual-motor concerns, although included, were

---

7. Of course, to the extent that "sensory" activities are of interest to the child and lead to experimentation, they can be justified with a constructivist rationale. Too often, however, activities for the sake of the senses provide little opportunity for reasoning. This point is discussed more fully in Chapter 10 in relation to Montessori's notion that knowledge is the result of sensory absorption.

not justified by reference to Piaget, but suggested other, unspecified sources. Later, Kamii and DeVries found Piaget's work more sufficient as a basis for varied aspects of curriculum than either Lavatelli or Weikart. This is primarily because they drew from Piaget's work more broadly, not limiting themselves to its structural or cognitive aspects. They found in Piaget's work educational implications for moral, social, and affective, as well as cognitive development.

Even though Kamii and DeVries drew comprehensive educational implications from Piaget's work, they too recognized that this alone could not provide a complete basis for their program, which rests in part on child-development practices including sensitivity to fantasy and emotion. Similar to the High/Scope statement, Kamii and DeVries wrote, "The curriculum we derive from Piaget's theory has much in common with the child-development curriculum exemplified by the Bank Street model (Biber, Shapiro, and Wickens, 1971) and by Read's classic text" (Kamii & DeVries, 1975/1977, p. 396). Like High/Scope authors, Kamii and DeVries also recommend pretend play, blockbuilding, art activities, songs and stories, and puzzles. However, Kamii and DeVries (1975/1977) critiqued the advantages and disadvantages in specific typical nursery school activities. Going beyond global justifications, they analyzed the cognitive possibilities of such activities from the point of view of Piaget's distinction among physical knowledge, logico-mathematical knowledge, spatio-temporal knowledge, and arbitrary social knowledge, as well as representation. For example, art activities with paste involve physical knowledge when the child is still figuring out that paste can make things stick together and that there are disadvantages in using too much or too little. Spatial reasoning is involved when the child is still figuring out where to put the paste to get particular results. For example, most children at some point have to find out what happens when the paste is put on the side intended to show! At the same time the child is realizing that some substances have the property of making things stick together and stay together, but others (such as water) don't—or they make things stick for a while but then come apart again. Such thinking involves constructing classificatory schemes that are eventually elaborated into operational classification. This kind of analysis led to more powerful justifications of many activities than previously given.

Piaget's theory thus provides for Kamii and DeVries a basis for selecting from curricula already developed by intuitive teachers. It also provides a basis on which to modify or eliminate certain practices. For example, many science aims and activities in preschool texts (such as teaching that air is all around us) do not meet criteria based on Piaget's theory for good physical-knowledge activities. They are thus eliminated because the phenomena (such as the extinction of a flame when a glass is put over a lighted candle) are beyond the child's access through action and observation. Other kinds of activities dropped from the traditional program include some specifically valued for their cognitive content (in addition to science, group lessons on color and shape names). Content added to the traditional program includes group games such as Tag, Hide and Seek, Chutes and Ladders, and Rummy, and physical-knowledge activities that go beyond nursery school activities involving actions on objects (Kamii & DeVries, 1975/1977, 1976, 1978, 1980).

To a great extent, the affinity of the child-development tradition to the educational implications of Piaget's work is due to the psychodynamic emphasis in traditional programs on the internal nature of social and emotional development, on play as the best context for fostering these aspects of development, and on the teacher's role as facilitator. Cognitive objectives in the child-development tradition, however, have reflected assumptions about the nature of intellectual development contradictory both to constructivist and psychodynamic emphasis on internal emotional structuring. That is, typical nursery school texts assert that children learn through their senses and by being given information and verbal concepts. The sensory model led to activities to develop or "reinforce" sensory skills. These were usually linked to language goals that led teachers to try to reinforce and extend the child's "foundation for concepts" by comments and descriptive words (Read, 1976, pp. 227–236).

For Kamii and DeVries, Piaget's theory provided the basis for an integrated view of all aspects of development and methods of teaching that reflected a comprehensive, coherent theory. The integration of Piaget's theory with the child-development tradition in early education requires careful selection from this tradition. Some practices are eliminated, some are modified, and others are added.

The Teaching of Classification

The first thing to point out in the Kamii-DeVries approach to classification is that there are no classification activities as such. Unlike Lavatelli and High/Scope authors, Kamii and DeVries do not view classification as the most important goal in activities justified (partly) in terms of classification. They would agree that it is important for children to observe the attributes of objects and to note similarities and differences. They would not agree, however, that these actions are yet at the level of classification; rather, they are simply the exercise of classificatory schemes which only later will become elaborated into operational classification (reasoning about hierarchical, inclusive classes).

Kamii and DeVries prefer situations in which operational classification is possible though not necessary to the child's pursuit of his objectives. That is, children can pursue their objectives by reasoning with classificatory schemes that are still illogical or incomplete. However, in their efforts to achieve their purposes, children are motivated to do more than consider similarities and differences. The nature of their purpose leads them to compare subclasses and classes. In our view, such a context is a ripe setting for the eventual elaboration of schemes into operations.

Although Kamii and DeVries do not recommend classification activities as such, they note how teachers can encourage children's classificatory reasoning. Let us focus now on the kinds of activities they advocate for the development of classificatory reasoning—though not for this aspect of development alone. Three examples are presented below.

A PHYSICAL-KNOWLEDGE ACTIVITY INVOLVING MOVING OBJECTS. In physical-knowledge activities (the focus of Chapter 4), the purpose is for children to act on objects to see how they react or try to produce particular effects, and to structure observations of reactions. The following excerpt from a blowing activity illustrates the typical way in which opportunities occur to promote classificatory reasoning within the context of objectives pertaining to general cognitive development, and alongside other specific objectives.

> In a blowing activity, for example, if the child tries to move a straw across the floor by blowing it with another straw, he finds out that he has to blow in the middle at a right angle to make it go straight. As a function of where one blows relative to the center of the straw, it turns more or less to the right or to the left, sometimes turning a complete 360 degrees. As the child sees how the straw reacts to different actions, he structures spatial and logical relationships. How this happens can be seen more clearly in the following description of a blowing activity. After giving each child a straw, Ms. Ellis showed them a box containing several of each of the following items: Kleenex, round Tinker Toys, popsicle sticks, straws, empty cans (frozen orange juice and one-pound coffee cans), marbles, and small blocks. She said, "Can you find something that you can blow across the floor?" This question prompted the children to look at objects with their "blowability" in mind and to think, at some vague, intuitive level, about considerations such as the following: Is the object's weight relevant? Is its shape important? Are both important? How can we find out?
>
> These questions illustrate the logico-mathematical structuring that takes place during a physical-knowledge activity. The child constructs logico-mathematical structures in the course of structuring specific contents. In this blowing activity, the child has an opportunity to create at least three categories—"things that *never* move" (a block), "things that *always* move" (a Kleenex, marble, straw, and popsicle stick), and "things that *sometimes* move" (an orange juice can and tinker toy which move only when they are in a certain position). In addition, the child may observe that certain objects move by sliding, certain objects move by rolling, and still others (such as a straw) move in both ways. A classificatory scheme becomes also necessary to put into correspondence the result of blowing in the middle and the results of blowing on other parts of the straw. With this classificatory scheme the child can conclude that the only way to make the straw go straight is by blowing in the middle. (Kamii & DeVries, 1978, pp. 6–7)

In this example, it should be noted that what children are structuring into classificatory schemes are their actions on objects and the objects' reactions. This is quite a different experience from one in which the child is trying to answer the teacher's questions about attributes.

GROUPTIME DISCUSSION: COLLECTING PARENT PERMISSION SLIPS. At grouptime, the primary objective is to promote children's feeling of community with others in the group. This includes decentering to recognize and value the feelings and ideas of others and to experience the desirability of social reciprocity. One way teachers try to do this is to involve children in projects of mutual interest such as planning a field trip. At grouptime, the teacher consults with children and shares responsibility for preparations. Capitalizing on their natural investment in making the trip, the teacher can take advantage of possibilities for classificatory reasoning by asking such questions as "Do we have all the slips we need? How many brought the slip back today?[8] It should be emphasized that these questions are only asked in a context in which children have developed an active concern and feeling of personal participation in preparing for the trip. The goal is not for children to answer questions because the teacher wants them to do so, but for children to be motivated to think about the questions out of their own concern for the answers.

When children become active in figuring out how many slips are yet needed in order to be ready for the trip, they have the possibility for thinking about and putting into relation the following categories:

- all the slips needed and those that are missing;
- children who returned slips and those who did not return them.

In order to think about the first question, children may be inspired to compare the whole class (all the slips) with a subclass (slips missing or slips in hand). Similarly, the second question may prompt thinking about the whole class (children who got slips) in relation to a subclass (those who brought slips back), and perhaps to the complementary class (those who did not return slips). These and other questions focused on the problem (and not just on the question of class inclusion for its own sake) thus give children a personal reason for trying to compare a whole class with its subclasses. The class inclusion question itself (Are there more slips or more signed slips?) is not one that arises or fits into children's personal interests. However, the issue gives children the opportunity to think, insofar as they are able, about class relationships. When children think about the fact that there are "not enough slips" this implies awareness of the whole and at least a subclass of missing slips. The fact may be comprehended at a variety of levels from a global consciousness of some slips that are missing to a fully quantified system of class inclusion. Since a child will perhaps most likely think rather quickly about his own slip, the situation seems especially conducive to thinking about the relation of an individual member of a category to fellow members of the same class and to nonmembers of this category (and perhaps to their grouping into the complementary class). In this activity where the teacher's main objective is developing children's feeling of community in the group, classificatory reasoning is integrated with social and moral activity. This is also seen in the following example.

8. Other questions may be found in Kamii and DeVries (1976).

A CARD GAME: MAKING FAMILIES. For Kamii and DeVries, central objectives of group games are to promote social decentering and co-operation in the context of rules and reasoning about strategies (discussed in Chapter 7). Analysis of particular cognitive advantages of group games often reveals the possibility for classificatory reasoning, as in many card games involving making sets of two, three, or four cards that are alike in some way. The systematic comparison of each card with every other card in one's hand involves continuous consideration of the question "Same or different?" and inspires children to isolate class membership criteria.

Let us consider a detailed and extended example of how one teacher used the game "Making Families" to promote classificatory thinking. In this game the teacher selected 20 cards from a larger set including five families (duck, sheep, fish, cow, man) of four cards each. The four members of each family were in four colors (red, blue, yellow, and white). The rule is that players take turns asking others to give them a particular card. When a player asks another for a yellow sheep, for example, it must be surrendered if held. As long as a player is successful in getting cards he asks for, he can continue asking. When he fails to receive the card he requests, the turn passes to the person from whom it was requested. Play continues until all cards have been put down in groups of four, and the person who makes the most families is the winner. In the particular instance quoted below, the teacher spread out the cards in a random arrangement and began by asking a question.

> The first question the teacher asked was: "Do you see any families that you can make with these cards?"
>
> Eron immediately answered, "I see a family of yellow cards." Maurice followed with "I see a family of blue ones," and Emanuel with "I see white ones."
>
> "Can we make other families?" the teacher asked, hoping that this question might get the children to shift from grouping by color to grouping by object as they had done the week before.
>
> Emanuel responded immediately, "Yes, I see a family of red ones."
>
> As she pointed to an example of each color, the teacher said, "Yes, the red ones, the yellow ones, the blue ones, and the white ones." She felt that summarizing this grouping by color was the best way to get children to go beyond this criterion.
>
> The children joined her in this description.
>
> "But can't we make any other families?" the teacher continued.
>
> "Yes, I will have to think," said Eron thoughtfully.
>
> "What other families do you think we can make?" the teacher asked again.
>
> Emanuel began a sentence without knowing how to finish it. "We can put...mmmmm...": he slowly picked up a white fish, looked at it, and finished the sentence, "all the fish together."
>
> Eron immediately got the idea of saying, "Then *I* feel like picking up all the sheep."
>
> Turning to Maurice, the teacher asked, "What do you feel like picking up?"
>
> "Me? All the men," replied Maurice.

"Go ahead," the teacher encouraged

Each player collected his own cards quickly. Eron then asked, as he picked up two cows, "Then who is going to take all the cows?"

"Me, I'll take them!" exclaimed Maurice as he picked up a third cow.

Without a word, Emanuel took a cow, too, and added it to his collection.

Eron meanwhile objected to Maurice by saying, "Oh, no. It's me. It's mine."

Maurice let Eron grab the cow from his hand and, seeing the four ducks, which were the only cards left on the floor, he announced, "I'll take all the ducks then."

The teacher asked Eron, "What families do you have?"

Eron answered, "Cows and sheep."

"Can you put them down so we call all look at them?" the teacher requested, knowing that Eron had only three cows.

Eron made a line of seven cards, separating the three cows from the four sheep and saying, "I have only three."

"Is that a family when you have only three?" the teacher inquired.

The other children also spread out their cards. . . . Eron did not say anything, but Maurice responded, "I have four," and Emanuel echoed, "Me, too. I have four."

Turning to Emanuel, the teacher asked, "Can you make a family with your cow all by itself ?"

Maurice answered, "No," for Emanuel.

"What are you going to do then?" the teacher continued.

Eron declared as he picked up Emanuel's cow, "I think you should give it to me." Emanuel did not protest.

The teacher pointed to each family, getting the children to name each one as she went around in a circle saying, "Then we have a family of ?"

"Fish."

"And the family of?"

"Ducks."

"And the family of ?"

"Men."

"And the family of ?"

"Sheep."

"And the family of ?"

"Cows."

Note: The teacher's purpose in going over the name of each family was not to teach words but to ascertain that the children would use the same words in playing the game. For example, a man could have been considered a boy by some children, in which case a child holding a man could have said he did not have any men when, in fact, he did.

Satisfied that the children were all using the same terms as the week before and that they remembered that each family consisted of four cards, the teacher said, "Now, we have to mix all the cards. . . . Let's make sure we all remember how to play this game. First, I'll distribute the cards, and the object of the game is to make families. For example, you can try to put together all the sheep, remember?" She said this as she picked up four cards showing sheep. She then arranged five cards. . . and demonstrated. "If you get these cards, for example, you try to make a family of all the sheep. . .or all the. . .?"

"Ducks."

"Yes, or all the...?"

"Men."

"Yes. Do you all remember?"

Everybody nodded with certainty, saying yes.

As she held all the cards in her hand, the teacher asked, "Who wants to distribute them?"... She said, "We begin by asking someone for the card we want, don't we?"

All the players held their cards in a way that prevented others from looking.

Emanuel began by asking, "Eron, do you have a duck?" (Emanuel did not have any ducks in his hand.)

Eron in turn asked, "A duck of what color?"

Emanuel hesitated and added, "Wait. Let me see if I have a duck." He looked through his cards and found none. Changing his mind, he went on. "No, the cow."

Eron inquired, "The cow of what color?"

Up to now, everybody had been looking only at his own cards, but now Maurice took a long, intent look at Emanuel's hand. Emanuel did not notice this inspection....

Emanuel was deep in thought. After a long moment, he replied, "The yellow cow (which he had in his hand)."

Eron said, "No." (Kamii & DeVries, 1980, pp. 174–177)

When Emanuel asks for a card he is holding, the natural consequence is always the same. He will never get a card identical to one he is holding. Other players will from time to time point out that of course he does not have the card Emanuel requested because Emanuel already has it. The week before, Emanuel had engaged in the same kind of behavior but in an even more extreme form. He kept asking for the red sheep, which he already had in his hand. He asked the three other players, one by one, for the red sheep, and was told each time that that person did not have it. Finally, the entire group got into a discussion about where the red sheep was and ended up explaining with the teacher that nobody else could possibly have the red sheep because Emanuel had it. Emanuel listened to the explanation with a puzzled look, and when his next turn came, he again asked for the red sheep! Even when children are not aware of their contradictory, inconsistent behavior, possibilities for the emergence of such awareness are inherent in the nature of the game.

The teacher wondered whether or not she should say that it was unnecessary to specify the color of the card one was looking for. Like the previous week, the children made their own rule that made the game much harder than the one she had in mind. She decided not to say anything because it seemed best not to interfere with the rule that all the children seemed to be accepting.

The teacher also considered Emanuel's tendency to ask for the cards he was holding in his hand, as if he did not know that there was only one of each. [By analyzing the videotape later, she observed that Emanuel had asked for "*a* duck," "*the* cow," and "*a* red cow," and that he had said, "I have *a* blue, yellow, and red one." The use of the indefinite article ("a" red cow rather than "the" red cow) indicates that he did not know or remember that there was only one red cow.] She decided not to say anything to Emanuel, recalling that correction by the entire group the week before did not do any good.

Turning to Eron, the teacher told him, "It's your turn to ask for a card."

Eron asked, "Maurice, do you have the duck that's yellow?"

Maurice gladly replied, "Yes," and gave the card to Eron.

Eron accepted the card saying, "Thank you."

The teacher explained, "You can go on asking for another card. As long as somebody gives you the card, you can continue asking for another one."

Making a row of three ducks in front of himself, Eron told everybody, "Look at what I've got."

The teacher asked, "Is that a family?"

Eron answered, "No, there has to be another one."

Continuing to address Eron, the teacher said, "Then you'll have to look for it."

Instead of trying to complete the family of ducks, Eron turned to Emanuel saying, "Emanuel, do you have the sheep?" Maurice interrupted Eron at this point, announcing, "I've got the blue duck."

Eron hesitated for a few seconds, smirking, and said sheepishly to Maurice, "Maurice, do you have the blue duck?"

Delighted, Maurice replied, "Yes," and threw the card on the row of three ducks.

"There, I've got four," Eron said, beaming and straightening up the row of four ducks.... (Kamii & DeVries, 1980, pp. 177–180)[9]

The children playing Making Families saw nothing contradictory in trying to make as many families as possible while at the same time distributing cards face up, openly looking at others' cards, and letting others know the cards held. Emanuel saw nothing contradictory about asking for the red sheep he already held, even after asking everyone for it, finding out no other player had one, and hearing a discussion of the fact that no one else could have it because Emanuel himself had it. Correction clearly does not produce correct reasoning. Because Emanuel had not constructed the system of relations, being told that he was the only one having a red sheep did not lead to the deduction that no one could give him another one. He was, for the most part, limited to thinking about the observable class members, and had difficulty thinking of the absent ones.

Viewed within the Kamii-DeVries framework, this excerpt illustrates the value of the child's spontaneous exercise of classificatory schemes—an example of spontaneous activity. Such schemes are not yet coordinated into the operational structures necessary for class inclusion, but out of such exercise these can arise. While the possibility for hierarchical classification exists in the Making Families game, this by no means suggests that the educational value depends on operational reasoning. By not insisting on logical or objective thinking about classes and their relations, the teacher fosters the kind of sustained thought that will eventually result in operational reasoning. That is, in

---

9. See Kamii and DeVries (1980) for the complete description of the game and for further analyses of the game's possibilities for reasoning.

the course of reasoning in preoperational ways, the child sooner or later becomes conscious of contradictions in what he thinks. The emphasis is therefore not on trying to get children to think about inclusive classes but on creating a situation in which children categorize similarities and differences and reason using these categories in order to pursue their own interests. In such situations there are greater opportunities for the child's construction of classification than in situations in which children are asked to focus in a brief and limited way on attributes, similarities, and differences.

With experience in playing the game, children will also have the opportunity to observe their feelings at the end of the game when they sometimes have more and sometimes fewer families. With the consolidation of a desire to collect as many as possible, they can begin to feel the contradiction between this desire and the desire to help others get cards. A feeling of necessity eventually results with regard to distributing cards face down, concealing one's cards, and to playing fairly by rules that imply a mutual agreement not to look at one another's cards.

In summary, these examples from the Kamii-DeVries approach illustrate how teachers design and carry out activities in which the inherent appeal to children's initiative is inseparable from Piagetian theoretical interests in classification as the organization of relations among classes. Children reason about the relations among classes out of their personal interest, not because a teacher inserts a question into preoccupations that are elsewhere. Classificatory reasoning is intrinsic to the activities themselves and not artificially imposed. Children use classificatory reasoning in order to have the fun of producing the exciting result of making an object roll or slide, collecting a family of cards, or out of desire to complete arrangements in order to go on a special trip.

These activities offer opportunities for realizing theoretical objectives not only in these particular instances of teaching. That is, if children are spontaneously interested in making sets while playing cards, they are likely to be motivated to play repeatedly. This kind of sustained activity provides a further integration of theory with action in that intrinsic interest breeds continued exercise of reasoning and the possibility for evolution in the structure of thought.

Regarding the possibility for evolution, we emphasize that the Kamii-DeVries activities describe the possibility for real classification. Collecting permission slips and playing cards are not limited to a focus on the elements of classification (attributes, and similarities and differences) or to activities of sorting and matching.

Interest

For Kamii and DeVries, the focus of the child's interest is inseparable from the teacher's theoretical aim. The inherent appeal to the child's interest coincides with Piagetian theoretical concerns. For example, in the card game children have their own reasons for thinking about classes and their relations.

Experimentation

Two kinds of experimentation with physical objects are emphasized by Kamii and DeVries. The first is similar to the High/Scope recommendation that the teacher ask the child what can be done with a material. "See whatever you can think of to do with these things" is one way to introduce a physical-knowledge activity. This is not just a passing question, but is used when the teacher has put out materials to which children will spontaneously gravitate, and when she expects children to have their own ideas right away of how to use them. For example, with rollers (wooden dowels about 16 inches long and of varying diameters), and boards and boxes, some children make a "skateboard" ( ), try to balance on it, and vary the number and size of rollers used. Other children make a catapult ( ), propel objects in the air by jumping on the high end, and experiment not only with different kinds of objects to catapult but also with different objects and different numbers of objects as the fulcrum.[10] These are only two examples of many ideas children want to try.

The second kind of experimentation with physical objects occurs when the teacher says, "Can you . . . ?" The teacher suggests an idea when the materials used are familiar to children and when she expects children to respond enthusiastically, taking up the idea as their preoccupation. Children in the blowing activity described above eagerly pursued the teacher's suggestion and found out, for example, that cotton and Kleenex reacted differently than wooden blocks, and that an orange juice can rolled in one positon, but did not roll in another. In another instance, the teacher provided a pendulum (with a block as the bob), put a doll on the floor and asked, "Can you make the doll fall over?" Children then experimented by putting the doll in many different places, and aiming with the bob from different positions. The Kamii-DeVries emphasis on experimentation will be discussed further in Chapter 5.

Co-operation

For Kamii and DeVries co-operation is a central method by which teachers aim to promote the child's cognitive and affective decentering. We shall return to this issue in the discussion of the role of the teacher.

THE ROLE OF THE TEACHER

We turn from the consideration of the child's experiences to the consideration of the teacher's experience. In the examples of activities involving classification, the teachers in each of the three approaches intervene in very different ways.

10. This activity may be found in film form, "Playing with Rollers" (Kamii et al., 1975) and in written form (Kamii & DeVries, 1978, Chapter 4).

Lavatelli

Lavatelli's intention was that her lessons would provide children opportunities to modify their reasoning by their own actions, not by teacher correction.

> The teacher's role is to stimulate and guide, not to teach specific responses, not to tell the child the right answer, nor even to tell him that he is wrong. The teacher must have confidence in the child's ability to learn *on his own*. When he is wrong, she may ask questions or call attention to cues that he has missed so that he has more data to assimilate, but giving him the right answer will not convince the child. *He* must be convinced by *his own* actions. (Lavatelli, 1970a/1973, p. 48)

Lavatelli recognized that children do not simply accumulate ideas that are correct from the adult point of view, but that they construct their knowledge by assimilations that often result in a series of "wrong" ideas. She recognized the importance of accepting children's "wrong" answers. Nevertheless, throughout her lessons, one finds that the teacher should not be satisfied with the child's wrong answers. Many procedures are given for what the teacher can do to get the child to correct himself. These are summarized below from her *Teacher's Guide* (Lavatelli, 1970b/1973).

1. *Ask leading questions.* If a child chooses a figure other than the green square in the classification task, the teacher should ask, "Is that a green square?" with emphasis on the word for the property the child has missed. (p. 30)
2. *Give a verbal rule.* In a number, measurement, and space activity, the teacher is told to add and take away from a group of cubes, repeating the verbal formula each time, "Adding makes things have more; taking one away makes things have less." (p. 44)
3. *Demonstrate actions the child should perform.* Children are to make as many different pairs as they can with three types of cars. If they do not use a system of starting with one car and combining that car with each of the other two, then starting with the next car, and so on, the teacher is told to say, "Would it help if we used a system like this?" and to demonstrate the system. (p. 35)
4. *Provide figurative material.* If a child does not conserve number, the teacher is told to move the shorter line of pennies slowly back into one-to-one correspondence with the other line.
5. *Direct the child's action.* In the classification activity quoted in the foregoing section, the child's efforts are closely and continuously regulated by the teacher.
6. *Model logical thought and language.* Lavatelli (1970b/1973) emphasized language training as an important feature of her program, and advocated modeling language as a support to developing operations. Instructions call for the teacher or aide to say, over and over again, "Tell me what you are doing," to model for the child what he is to say, and to have the child repeat what the teacher has modeled. (p. 5)

Lavatelli's recommendations to teachers make clear how much she was committed to the idea that teachers could make children conscious of ways of using the mind to solve problems. She therefore advocated that teachers carefully guide children to practice operational thought. These principles of teaching reflect the assumption that the development of logic can be fostered by presenting logical contradictions to the child. The problem is that logic is necessary for recognition of the logical contradiction. In logico-mathematical knowledge, contradictions are between the child's schemes, and must arise from an internal sense of contradiction (Piaget, 1974b/1980). This is in contrast with contradictions in physical knowledge that arise from observation of unanticipated reactions of objects, and therefore are more accessible to children's consciousness.

The role of Lavatelli's teacher is heteronomous. The child has little opportunity for self-regulation when the teacher follows Lavatelli's principles of teaching. Problems for the child to consider are given by the teacher, who directs the child's actions, models logical thought and correct language, and reinforces correct responses. Moreover, the teacher asks leading questions containing hints, gives verbal rules, and demonstrates actions the child should perform. Little opportunity exists for the exercise of initiative, and social "reciprocity" consists in the child's doing what the teacher says.

High/Scope

In 1971 Weikart and his collaborators advocated that teachers focus on only one concept in any given activity, order the sequence of what the child is to learn, reinforce concepts, and bombard the child with language. By 1979 these principles of teaching had been replaced. Especially with regard to the changed role of the teacher High/Scope authors note the influence of Piaget's constructivist ideas. They describe a shift from viewing the child as a receiver of teaching to viewing the child as partly responsible for initiating learning experiences. Of particular interest to us is their comment that "the teachers stopped asking questions of the children to which they [the teachers] knew the answers and began asking children to talk about what they were doing, thinking, intending..." (Hohmann et al., 1979, p. xv).

The High/Scope description of the teacher's role is in some respects no different from the Kamii-DeVries description that follows. For example, both have in mind the ideal teacher who enters into children's activities without disrupting their flow, who is able to take direction from children's ideas, who avoids telling children they are wrong and instead encourages new ideas, and who refers children to one another. Especially congruent is the following excerpt.

> Allow children to make mistakes and learn from them without saying, "That's wrong." Remember that the *processes* involved in any solution are where the learning occurs, even if the solution itself isn't particularly satisfactory. For

example, a child trying to hold a book together with bits of clay learns something about the physical limits of clay and the requirements of objects that open and shut. With this experience, the child is ready to look for a more effective binding material. The clay didn't work, but it wasn't "wrong" either, because it led the child to try something else. Had an adult said, "Don't use clay, it won't work," the child's first idea would've been rejected, and he might have been afraid to suggest another, preferring instead the safety of waiting for an adult to tell him the "right thing." (Hohmann et al., 1979, p. 293)

While the High/Scope conception of the teacher's role is similar in many respects to the Kamii-DeVries conception, their descriptions of the teacher's actual role (as found in examples above) often differ. In our view, many High/Scope examples of teacher-child interaction contradict their stated principles of teaching. The teacher often seems intrusive rather than unobtrusive. Children's required verbal planning sometimes seems coerced and thus contradictory to the principle of autonomy.[11] Children's mistakes often seem to be something to avoid rather than encourage. Preoccupation with language often seems to interfere with fostering reasoning and the exercise of autonomy. The effort to get children to say what they're doing seems to interrupt the doing, and trying to get children to answer questions seems to interfere with reasoning and the exercise of initiative.

No theoretical discussion of the issue of heteronomy versus autonomy in teacher-child relationships is included in the High/Scope guide. However, the importance of choice for children is emphasized as necessary for active learning. Insofar as this suggests the fostering of autonomy, it seems contradicted by the many instance throughout the book (some relating to classification were quoted above) where the important focus is the teacher's choice. The child's interest only provides the context in which the teacher can manipulate the focus in the direction of the teacher's interest. Despite their contrary intention, High/Scope teachers sometimes pursue their theoretical objectives by *inserting* tasklike questions and comments that do not reflect children's concerns. Instead of identifying and extending children's interests, these teachers interrupt and impose their own preoccupations. These kinds of interventions fall short of the kind of theory-practice integration Kamii and DeVries advocate, as exemplified in their approach to classification described above.

Kamii and DeVries

In specifying the role of the teacher and principles of teaching, Kamii and DeVries assume that the teacher is child-centered, relates well to children, knows how to manage a classroom smoothly and how to provide traditional

---

11. Weikart (personal communication to author) objects to this statement since he does not intend the plan-do-review cycle to be coercive.

nursery school activities. The principles of teaching they describe are therefore additions to or, in some cases, modifications of traditional practices. The following general statement of the teacher's role is reflected in descriptions of classroom interaction above and elsewhere in this book.

1. *To create an environment and an atmosphere conducive to learning.* In the final analysis, it is the quality of the environment the teacher creates, including teacher-child and child-child relationships, that either promotes or retards development. An atmosphere conducive to development is one in which the child is independent, uses his own initiative in pursuing his interests, says exactly what he thinks, asks questions, experiments, and comes up with a variety of ideas.

2. *To provide materials, suggest activities, and assess what is going on inside the child's head from moment to moment.* When the teacher puts out materials, she encourages children to do everything they can with them and observes what they do (what schemes they apply to the objects). When the children have exhausted their own ideas, she models or suggests an activity in such a way that it flows into their play in a natural way. In general, the teacher tunes in and picks up on children's reactions and ideas rather than trying to impose her own predetermined goals. (She proposes ideas rather than imposes them.) Proposals focus on action rather than on verbal answers to questions. Assessment is a continuous process. By watching what the child does and says, the teacher who is well acquainted with the child and with Piaget's theory can gain many insights into what the child is thinking. These insights help her decide what to do next.

3. *To respond to children in terms of the kind of knowledge involved.* With regard to social-arbitrary knowledge, the teacher tells the right answer and reinforces it. In physical knowledge, the teacher encourages the child to find the answer directly from objects. In logico-mathematical knowledge, the teacher refrains from telling the right answer or reinforcing it and, instead, encourages reflecting abstraction. In general, the Piagetian teacher, like any good child-development teacher, shares in the child's pleasure, frustration, and disappointment—when the child wants to include the teacher in his activity. She encourages children to construct their own preoperational knowledge and to go through many different ways of being "wrong."

4. *To help the child extend his ideas.* Without intruding or interrupting, the Piagetian teacher interacts with children in such a way as to encourage them to extend their own ideas. (Kamii & DeVries, 1975/1977, p. 410)

In a global way, much of this description of the teacher's role resembles the High/Scope description. Beyond the stated ideal, however, classroom protocols reveal differences in the ways the teacher's role is actually practiced.

PREOPERATIONAL STRUCTURING

We raise, finally, the issue of the role of preoperational thought in the development of concrete operations, first because it is a central issue for all constructivist curricula, and second because it underscores the principal differences among the three approaches discussed in this chapter. All Piagetians express proper respect for the phenomena of preoperational thought. Most have verified for themselves (either by informal observation or systematic research) such phenomena as nonconservation and inability to reason about hierarchical and inclusive classes. However, after acknowledging the persuasive evidence for qualitative differences between child and adult thought, many educators seem to be uncomfortable about what to do with preoperational thought in the classroom. The ambivalence has been, on the one hand, to place preoperational thought on a pedestal, and even to find respectful amusement in the "cute" things children say and do. On the other hand, in many efforts to educate young children, the implicit—if not explicit—practical attitude has been at best to ignore it, and at worst to suppress it or get it out of the way as quickly as possible.

Such ambivalance toward preoperational thought seems to arise from failure to distinguish the *diagnostic* significance of preoperational thought from its *educational* significance. For example, after diagnosing children's reasoning as preoperational, Lavatelli tried to teach children to correct preoperational errors. This approach seems inconsistent with even Piaget's description of stages. That is, his stages are not just descriptions of increasingly logical reasoning, but also descriptions of sequences of "illogical" ideas. It would therefore be just as sensible to teach the sorts of "illogical" ideas that occur to children along the path to operational thought. No one, of course, has tried to do this! Just because children go through a stage in reasoning, for example, when they say (if asked) that there are more girls than children in a class, this does not imply that we should teach such incorrect ideas to children. However, it seems equally clear to us that we should not try to teach the correct statement that there are more children than girls in the world. In other words, preoperational thought is a period leading to adult-type thought that cannot be skipped.

If preoperational thought cannot be avoided, what is its educational significance? What is it like in the classroom, and what should teachers do with it?

In protocols such as Making Families (as well as protocols in other chapters in this book), we try to show the importance of preoperational thought for the development of operational thought. In a nutshell, our view is that when children reason preoperationally, they are usually unable at that moment to correct themselves or to understand correction by others. We also take the position that operational thought evolves out of preoperational thought as the child becomes more and more conscious of new aspects to think about in situations in which interests motivate thinking.

In the protocols taken from various Piagetian programs, different ways of handling preoperational thought were presented. Lavatelli's approach may be described as correcting it. The 1971 High/Scope approach seemed oriented to preventing its occurrence; their 1979 response is more accepting and supportive. In contrast, Kamii and DeVries's teachers may be described as valuing preoperational thought, planning for it, and teaching in terms of it.

SUMMARY

In order to clarify the constructivist perspective we have in mind, we examined in this chapter different ways in which Piaget's work has been interpreted in education. Differences among Piagetian preschool programs may be understood as balancing in different ways the two broad aspects of Piaget's work—structural stages and functional constructivism. Differences among programs may also be understood in terms of three ways of translating Piaget's theory into educational practices—analogous to three ways of translating one language into another (global, literal, and free translation). Various ways of defining the relation between Piaget's theory and children's spontaneous activity include Lavatelli's juxtaposition, High/Scope's insertion, and Kamii-DeVries's integration.

Three Piagetian programs—Lavatelli, High/Scope, and Kamii-DeVries—are discussed in terms of their similarities and differences. All emphasize the important role of action in children's development of reasoning and borrow extensively from the child-development tradition in early education for materials, equipment, and activities. Commonalities and differences in objectives are considered. By 1979 both the High/Scope and Kamii-DeVries approaches characterized themselves in terms of a commitment to Piaget's constructivist emphases on the child's action; as a result, theoretical differences that had previously separated them were reduced. Lavatelli, too, emphasized the importance of action, but this was not reflected in her cognitive objectives that were derived from the structural aspects of Piaget's work. In this respect, Lavatelli's "Piaget Program" is different from both High/Scope and Kamii-DeVries approaches. However, differences in statements of objectives remain between these latter two approaches. The High/Scope program, despite its evolution in a constructivist direction between 1971 and 1979, remains closer to concerns with stages and tasks than Kamii and DeVries. High/Scope authors emphasize cognitive objectives based on Piaget's writing on classification, seriation, spatial and temporal relations, number, language, and representation. In contrast, Kamii and DeVries emphasize integrated objectives reflecting both socioemotional and cognitive aspects of Piaget's constructivism, drawn from his writing on the role of interest, autonomy, and social interaction in the child's cognitive, sociomoral, and affective development.

These differences in objectives are more pronounced when translated into classroom practices. Practices are compared in terms of how each of the three program advocates view their use of Piaget's theory, the degree to which each has integrated the theory with the child's spontaneous activity in the context of the child-development tradition, how each specifically teaches classification, and how it provides for interest, experimentation, and co-operation. Finally, the three programs are discussed in terms of the different perspectives on the role of preoperational structuring in the development of operational reasoning. Lavatelli tries to correct preoperational thought, High/Scope accepts and supports it, and Kamii and DeVries value it, plan for it, and teach in terms of it.

Children have different psychological experiences in the three programs, as illustrated by the discussion of activities involving classification. We hypothesize that these differences in psychological experience are significant in terms of promoting the child's development of intelligence, morality, and personality.

PART II

Curriculum and Activities
Derived from Constructivist Goals

Chapter 4

Physical-Knowledge Activities

Two kinds of action distinguished by Piaget—simple or empirical abstraction and reflective abstraction—were discussed in Chapter 2 in relation to the construction of two kinds of knowledge—physical and logico-mathematical knowledge. This distinction led to the definition of physical-knowledge activities that are recommended because they offer the child possibilities for the kinds of action on objects by which such knowledge is formed. This chapter provides an introduction to this part of our constructivist program. (For a more extensive discussion of these activities, see *Physical Knowledge in Preschool Education: Implications of Piaget's Theory* by Kamii & DeVries, 1978). In this chapter we review the definition, rationale, objectives, types, and criteria of good physical-knowledge activities, and principles of teaching. In addition, the issue of evaluation is addressed with a case study of physical knowledge involving shadows. Recent research is presented on stages in children's conceptions of shadow phenomena followed by discussion and examples of how these can inform teaching practice and illuminate observation and evaluation of children's actions in activities involving shadows.

DEFINITION, RATIONALE, AND OBJECTIVES

Physical-knowledge activities involve the child's action on and observation of the reactions of objects in the physical world. Actions on objects may derive from the child's desire to see what will happen (as when children push a pendulum for the first time), from desire to verify an anticipation of what will happen (as when children try to hit a target that is out of range of the pendulum by aiming the bob), from systematic experimentation that is a combination of these (as when a child pushes the pendulum harder, steps closer to the target, and lengthens the string). In the course of such actions, children have the possibility to construct relations of correspondence between actions and reactions, and these very gradually evolve over many years into causal, explanatory relations.

The rationale for physical-knowledge activities is rooted in Piaget's emphasis on the role of action in the development not only of knowledge of the physical world but of intelligence itself in a more general sense. The logico-mathematical construction and coordination of relations at the heart of this theory may be thought of as a process with two poles of action. One end of this pole is content-oriented in relation to the external world of objects. The other is form-oriented (or structure-oriented) in relation to the child's capacity for organizing experience. Although both refer to something in the mind of the child, the former pertains to specific knowledge of particular objects, and the latter to what is general in the child's organizing of this specific content. What is general is the logico-mathematical structuring. Thus, the objectives of physical-knowledge activities are not just for the construction of knowledge of the world of objects, but for logico-mathematical structure as well.

For babies, thought and action are completely interdependent, as Piaget (1936/1952, 1937/1954) demonstrated in his books on sensorimotor intelligence. According to Piaget, cognitive development progresses with gradual interiorization of action making possible thought without overt action. Since the thought of preschool children still is closely linked to physical action, activities to promote the development of thought must appeal to children's interest in figuring out how to do things—that is, in physical-knowledge activities.

The reader will find that the phenomena of many physical-knowledge activities are not unique to the constructivist approach. Intuitive teachers in the child-development tradition have long advocated some of the activities that fall within our definition of physical knowledge. The reader will also find, however, that in our constructivist approach, these activities are often modified and taught in ways that are significantly different. To the extent that physical-knowledge activities are unique to the constructivist approach, it is in the close focus on observing and facilitating the child's efforts to produce and understand particular physical phenomena. We begin the discussion of this focus with criteria of good physical-knowledge activities.

CRITERIA OF GOOD PHYSICAL-KNOWLEDGE ACTIVITIES

The constructivist rationale and objectives emphasizing action lead to four criteria for good physical-knowledge activites. These were conceptualized with activities in mind that involve the movement of objects.

1. *The child must be able to produce the phenomenon by his own action.* As stated above, the essence of physical-knowledge activities is the child's action on objects and his observation of the object's reaction. The phenomenon selected must therefore be something the child can produce by his own action. The movement of a piece of Kleenex in reaction to the child's blowing or sucking on it through a straw meets this criterion. The movement of objects caused by a magnet, on the other hand, is an example of a phenomenon that is produced only indirectly by the child's action and primarily by magnetic attraction. This does not imply that magnets should be omitted from a classroom. It does imply that we should recognize the educational limitations of experimenting with magnets.

2. *The child must be able to vary his action.* When the variations in the child's action result in corresponding variations of the object's reaction, the child has the opportunity to structure these regularities. In a pool game, for example, if the child misses the target by hitting a ball too far to the left, he can adjust the

next attempt accordingly. In a pinball-type game, by contrast, the child's action is limited to pulling a lever, and there is very little variation possible in how he releases the lever. The child thus cannot significantly affect the outcome. Without a direct correspondence between the variations in actions and reactions, a phenomenon offers little opportunity for structuring.

3. *The reaction of the object must be observable.* If the child cannot observe a reaction to his actions on objects, there is no content for him to structure. For example, an opaque tube in waterplay prevents observation of the water inside, and provides less material for structuring than a transparent tube.

4. *The reaction of the object must be immediate.* Correspondences are much easier to establish when the object's reaction is immediate. For example, when a child rolls a ball toward a target, she can immediately observe whether the target is hit or not, and if so, how it specifically reacts. In contrast, the reaction of a plant to water is not immediately observable, and its action on the water is only indirectly the result of the child's action. This does not imply that growing plants should be omitted from the classroom. In light of the immediacy criterion, sprouting beans on wet paper towels is a better activity to promote such understanding than watering a houseplant.

TYPES OF PHYSICAL-KNOWLEDGE ACTIVITIES

Two principal types of physical-knowledge activities are those that involve the *movement* of objects and those that involve *changes* in objects.

The Movement of Objects

Activities involving the movement of objects meet the foregoing criteria in especially satisfactory ways. Actions that can be performed on objects to make them move include pulling, pushing, rolling, kicking, jumping, blowing, sucking, throwing, swinging, twirling, balancing, and dropping. All activities in this category offer the advantage of being good for the structuring of space and logico-mathematical knowledge, in addition to physical knowledge. We described a physical-knowledge activity involving moving objects across the floor by blowing on them through a straw in the section in Chapter 3 on the Kamii-DeVries approach to teaching classification. In addition to promoting classificatory reasoning, this blowing activity has other cognitive possibilities. It also provides the opportunity to construct serial correspondences. The child can put into correspondence the differences in weight of the objects and differences in their movability. He can also relate the variations in blowing hard or softly to the speed of the object's motion. As he varies the distance between his straw and the object, he may note that, although it is generally better to get close to the object, it is not possible to establish a simple correspondence between distance and movability. A particularly interesting problem is making the coffee can roll. Finding this task at first quite impossible, some children vary the position and direction of the airstream. By watching the object's reaction, they discover that the best place to blow is across the top. When the can finally moves, it rolls away a little bit but then rolls back toward the child, and then away again! By coordinating his action with the can's movement and blowing only when it is rolling away from him, the child can succeed in blowing the object across the floor (in a way similar to rocking a car back and forth to get it out of snow). There is a serial correspondence between the can's rolling in one direction and its rolling in the opposite direction. Each successive movement is greater than the previous one, and the more it rolls forward, the more it rolls backward— until it builds up enough momentum to sail steadily forward.

Kamii and DeVries (1978) give detailed examples of how teachers planned, tried, and evaluated this and other physical-knowledge activities, with separate chapters on rollers (wooden dowels and other objects), target ball, inclines, the pendulum, and water play with flowing in tubes and draining. Another chapter on how to develop physical-knowledge activities provides guidelines and suggestions for creating activies from the repertoire of actions the child can perform on objects, the games and sports of older children and adults, toys that can be bought or made, and children's own spontaneous uses of materials. In addition, strategies are discussed for selecting and modifying activities from education textbooks on art, music, outdoor play, and science, and for integrating physical knowledge into an ongoing program.

Changes in Objects

In the activities discussed above, objects move, but they do not change. A second type of physical-knowledge activity involves changes in the objects themselves. Examples include cooking (see Chapter 11 for detailed description of making applesauce), mixing paints or paint powder and water, drying paint, making pottery, melting wax and making candles, and freezing and thawing water. In this type of activity, the child's action plays a role, but a less directly causal one than in producing an object's movement. That is, the cause of changes in objects is due more to the interaction of the objects themselves than to the nature of the child's action.

Like the objective of activities involving movement, the objective of activities involving changes is for children to observe and structure regularities. For example, when hot water is added to Jello, the powder disappears and the water becomes colored and flavored. Understanding at the level of explanation is usually not possible for preschool children, and causal relations will not be completed. It is therefore particularly important to analyze the kinds of action and observation that are possible in activities involving changes in objects.

Activities between the Two Categories

Between the two categories of movement and changes in objects are many other activities which cannot be categorized as neatly. Examples are:

Finding out whether an object sinks or floats
Sifting
Playing with mirrors
Producing echoes
Looking through a magnifying glass
Touching various objects with a magnet
Shadow play

These activities share elements with the other two categories but cannot be placed in either of them. The child's actions clearly do not produce a change in the objects themselves; on the other hand, any movement that results from the action is caused more by the properties of the object than by the child's action. These activities meet the four criteria of good activities presented above. All encourage the child to produce a phenomenon, to vary his action, and to observe the object's immediate reaction.

In addition to these types of physical-knowledge activities, there are countless incidental situations throughout the day when the child elaborates his physical knowledge. These, too, can be evaluated according to the same criteria. Examples that do not meet these criteria are why there are four seasons in the year, why flowers are beginning to bloom, how the room is heated, and how hot water comes to the bathroom. On the other hand, experiences that the teacher will do well to capitalize on include drying wet mittens, hanging up paintings to dry, pasting things together, noticing that ice cubes always float, watching ice and snow melt into a mess, and spilling and mopping up various substances.

PRINCIPLES OF TEACHING
PHYSICAL-KNOWLEDGE ACTIVITIES

Constructivist principles of teaching flow from the definition, rationale, objectives, criteria, and types of good physical-knowledge activities. Briefly, let us consider how the teacher can plan, introduce, conduct, and follow up activities.

Planning an Activity

The criteria for good physical-knowledge activities are useful in selecting phenomena for children's experimentation. It is also useful to keep in mind the following four ways, or levels, of acting on objects, each of which suggests a form of physical-knowledge activity.

1. *Acting on objects and seeing how they react.* Babies put objects in their mouths, shake them, turn them over, and squeeze them, engaging in increasingly more finely tuned exploration. The first actions on objects are thus without any intention to produce a desired effect. Young children, too, act on objects without any particular effect in mind. This way of acting on

objects suggests physical-knowledge activities of the sort in which children go through their repertoire of actions on objects new to them.

2. *Acting on objects to produce a desired effect.* By 10 to 12 months of age, babies begin to show intentions to produce an at least partly foreseen effect. When intentions appear, the exploratory behavior discussed above does not disappear, but a new way of acting on objects appears in addition—intentional behavior. At this time, for example, babies bang a spoon on the table *in order to* make a noise and throw things out of the playpen *in order to* see them go outside. This way of acting on objects is also important for older children. It suggests physical-knowledge activities of the sort in which the teacher encourages purposeful experimentation by asking, "Can you do *X* (such as blowing an object across the floor, or knocking a doll down by releasing a pendulum)?"

3. *Becoming aware of how one produced the desired effect.* By the time they are 4 or 5 years of age, children can do many things at the level of practical intelligence, but they are often not aware of *how* they produced the desired result. When children have become successful in producing certain physical phenomena, the teacher may plan interventions to help them become more conscious of what they are doing and to experiment more consciously by deliberately varying their action.

4. *Explaining causes.* Correct description is often not possible until many years after the production of a desired effect. Explanation is even more difficult. Explanations of most phenomena are, in fact, impossible for preschool children. They cannot possibly understand many "explanations" recommended in elementary science education, such as why rain comes out of the sky. Asking young children for an explanation is generally fruitless and produces answers of the type "The water came down because it wanted to."

Piaget's theory of the role of action in cognitive development leads to the conclusion that the best activities for preschool children involve the first two types of actions—acting on objects and seeing how they react, and acting on objects to produce a desired effect. To illustrate how thinking about the different kinds of actions can be helpful in planning, consider what one teacher did with a blowing activity. The teacher, Ms. Fineberg, dismissed the first way of acting on objects because it would be boring to her 4- and 5-year-olds to blow on things without a clear purpose. She decided on the second type of action and chose the effect of blowing things across water in the water table. She selected a variety of junk objects on the basis of their potential for reacting in different ways, including:

Straws	Mirror
Ping-Pong balls	Unit block
Paper boat	Nerf ball
Cotton balls	Rubber band
4 different spoons	Plastic top to can

Paper cup	Plastic bowl
Pine cone	Wadded paper towel
Gourd	Styrofoam packing bits
Orange juice can	Crayon
Scissors	Round Tinkertoy
Chestnut	Cork
Paper punch	Checker
Ivory soap	

The teacher planned to give a straw to each child and to suggest that he or she find the things that could be blown with it to the other side of the water table. She also planned the following two possibilities to suggest, depending on how the activity went:

1. A race (by asking children to find the object that would get across the fastest);
2. A kind of hockey game in which two children on opposite sides of a water table blow on a Ping-Pong ball, each trying to make it touch the other side.

Such planning has built-in flexibility that prepares the teacher to conduct the activity by responding to children's initiatives and intervening in ways that will promote children's experimentation.

Beginning the Activity

Principle I: Introduce the activity in a way that maximizes children's initiative. Three ways to introduce an activity are: (1) by putting out material to which children will naturally gravitate, (2) by presenting new materials and saying, "See whatever you can think of to do with these things," and (3) by proposing a specific problem with familiar materials (such as in the blowing activity just described) by saying, "Can you...?"

Principle II: Begin with parallel play. Although interaction and co-operation among children are important objectives, it is better to begin physical-knowledge activities by providing each child with her own materials and encouraging parallel play. In these activities, young children want to *do* things with objects, and this initiative is exactly what we want to encourage. If children have to take turns, they become restless and their initiative is thwarted.

Beginning with parallel play does not mean that objectives of interaction and co-operation are abandoned. They are only temporarily set aside in the interest of encouraging children's initiative with objects. In fact, interaction and co-operation evolve more easily out of parallel play than out of "co-operation" imposed by the teacher from the beginning. In the blowing activity, children began by doing their own thing but soon showed off their feats, imitated each other, compared discoveries, and offered advice to one another. Another way to state this principle is: Introduce the activity in such a way that co-operation is possible but not necessary.

Continuing the Activity

Once the activity has begun, three principles may be kept in mind in continuing it.

Principle I: Figure out what the child is thinking and respond sparingly in his terms. If children build their physical and logico-mathematical knowledge by constructing it from within, it follows that the teacher must interact with children in terms of how *they* are thinking. Figuring out what a child is thinking is the most challenging aspect of constructivist teaching. It is not always possible to know, but careful observation can lead the teacher to educated guesses. For example, if a child blows harder and harder through a straw, trying to make an object move by blowing on it from the top, the teacher might hypothesize that, in this child's mind, force is what counts—not the direction of the airstream. Based on this guess, he or she might say, "What happens when you blow on things from the top?" or, "Can you think of another way to blow to make it move?"

The kinds of questions to ask children are suggested by the four ways of acting on objects.

1. "Acting on objects and seeing how they react" suggests questions that involve predictions, such as, "What do you think will happen if you do X?"
2. "Acting on objects to produce a desired effect" suggests questions of the type, "Can you do X?" and, "Can you find anything else that you can do X with?"
3. "Becoming aware of how one produced the desired effect" suggests questions such as, "How did you do X?" The teacher can also encourage comparisons by raising questions such as, "Which way works better (or is easier)?" "How is (another child) doing X differently?" and, "Does it make any difference if you do X?"
4. "Explaining causes" suggests asking, "Why does X happen?" or saying, "I wonder why X happened."

If the teacher decides to ask a question, it should be timed to serve the child's construction of knowledge. Often, when teachers are too centered on their own ideas, they interrupt the child's thought with an intrusive barrage of questions which are far removed from the child's thought. Such intrusions usually stop a child's experimentation and often cause him to lose interest in the activity completely.

The best questions for young children are the first three of the above four types because they connect well with natural interests in action. The constructivist teacher will probably use all three types of questions in a given activity. The fourth "why" type is best not asked, unless the teacher's purpose is to call the child's attention to something or to find out what he thinks.

In addition to verbal interventions, nonverbal interventions tend to be particularly effective because children are more interested in action than in words. Three examples are the following.

1. *Help the child with practical problems to facilitate experimentation and observation.* As children think of more and more things to do with materials, they sometimes invent ideas they cannot carry out alone. At such times, the teacher's help is necessary to enable a child to continue a line of experimentation. For example, in an activity with the movement of water in tubes, the teacher held tubes and bottles in place to facilitate the child's observation of the effects of their creation.
2. *Offer materials to facilitate comparisons.* As children experiment, the teacher can foster logico-mathematical comparison through offering an untried object. For example, in a catapult activity, the teacher offered a large cardboard roller to a child who was experimenting with varying the fulcrum of his catapult.
3. *Model new possibilities.* When children's play becomes repetitive, or interest begins to lag, the teacher can often revitalize experimentation by simply modeling a new idea. For example, in a rollers activity when children were drumming away on boxes for a long time, the teacher quietly modeled a kneeling ride on a board across a track of rollers (see Chapter 4 in Kamii & DeVries, 1978, for a full description of this activity).

All interventions on the part of the teacher should be used sparingly to encourage the child's initiative. An ill-chosen or ill-timed action may be difficult for the child to ignore, and the teacher should be sensitive to the possibility of disrupting children's play. For example, in one water activity, the teacher thought she might open a new possibility by taking the cap off the funnel a child was using to pour water. The effect in this instance was to frustrate the child and stop her play.

When the child takes initiative, it is important to follow her train of thought and not interrupt. However, it is equally important for the teacher to be ready with ideas and possibilities to suggest when the child's initiative lags. Part of the teacher's job, after all, is to provide intriguing problems that children have not thought about before.

Principle II: Encourage children to interact with other children. When parallel play is well under way, the next goal for the teacher is to increase interindividual coordination and co-operation. The four types of questions listed above are also helpful in following this principle.

1. *Prediction* ("What will happen if...?"). Certain questions of this type are particularly good because they elicit uncertainty and different predictions from different children.
2. *Producing a desired effect* ("Can you...?"). Children often do not need adult encouragement to imitate others. At times, however, they do not notice a feat worth emulating, and the teacher does well to call it to their attention by saying, "Look at what (particular child) is doing. Can anybody else do that, too?" Some desired effects require more than one child, and these are ideal situations in which to promote children's efforts to co-operate, that is, to decenter and operate in terms of one another.

3. *Becoming aware of how one produced a desired effect* ("How did you do that?"). Piaget (1974d, 1978) pointed out that children often succeed in doing something at a practical level with little consciousness of just what they are doing. For example, he found that most 4-year-olds could swing a ball on a string in a circular motion parallel to the floor and then let it go to make it land in a box several feet away. Although they let go of the string at the position of 9 o'clock in a clockwise revolution (or 3 o'clock in a counter-clockwise revolution), they described their action otherwise. Four- and 5-year-olds said they let it go right in front of themselves, at the 6 o'clock position—the same point from which they would have thrown the ball into the box. Children 7 to 9 years old also said they let it go in front of themselves, but at the 12 o'clock position. It was not until 9 to 10 years of age that children were able to describe accurately what they did so successfully.

To foster children's consciousness and reflection on what they do, it is useful to encourage children successful in producing some effect to tell others how to do it. The process of telling others how to do something often results in more awareness of the process. This kind of interaction is, therefore, good both for the child who is shown how to do something and the one who shows how to produce a desired effect. The teacher can foster interaction by making remarks such as "I think Suzy wants you to show her how to blow to make the Popsicle stick jump," or, to a child having difficulty, "Why don't you ask Jeff to show you?"

4. *Explaining causes* ("Why...?"). Although most explanations are too hard for young children, an occasional "Why" question can stimulate discussion and reflection.

In encouraging interaction among children by asking these types of questions, it is important for the teacher to keep in mind that the objective is to foster an experimental attitude in a community of children and to encourage exchange of ideas and observations—not to arrive at the correct answer or even to reach a consensus. Such attitudes are fostered by the general atmosphere of a classroom, which is greatly influenced by the kind of interaction the teacher strives to promote.

Group games involving physical phenomena can create a context that enhances not only social interactions but also the quality of children's play with objects. For example, Marbles quickly becomes boring when the object is only to aim one at a pile of others. However, incorporated into a game this activity acquires more purpose, challenge, and interest. Other advantages of group games are discussed in Chapter 6.

Principle III: Integrate all aspects of development in physical-knowledge activities. In physical-knowledge activities, situations involving social and moral issues arise continuously, and language and symbolization are exercised, as well as logico-mathematical sorting and comparison of objects. Physical-knowledge activities are thus never just physical-knowledge activities, and constructivist teaching requires sensitivity to all aspects of a situation in which children are structuring their experience in its many different aspects.

After an Activity

During an activity, teacher-initiated verbalization and discussion should be kept brief. Afterward, however, it is desirable for children to reflect upon what they did, what they found out, and how they produced a desired effect. This may be done at snack time or large grouptime. The first and third types of questions are especially useful in promoting discussions. Examples are: "What happened when you blew through two straws instead of one?" "What did you have to do to make the straw go straight?" "What happened when the string (of a pendulum) broke?" "What do you want to try next time?"

What is important is for children to think honestly about what they did, what they observed, what other children noticed, and how they felt—not that they try to come up with the "right" answer for the adult. The focus here is on fostering children's awareness of their actions on objects and their alertness to how objects react.

PHYSICAL KNOWLEDGE AND SCIENCE EDUCATION

It is important to keep in mind that the objective of physical-knowledge activities is not to teach scientific concepts, principles, or explanations. It is, rather, to provide opportunities for the child to act on objects, observe the reactions, and construct and coordinate specific relations, in order to build the foundation for physics and chemistry.

Physical-knowledge activities may be contrasted with "science education" typically found in early education. Many phenomena selected for "science education" do not meet our criteria for good physical-knowledge activities, and objectives and ways of teaching often differ significantly. Consider the following examples.

Phenomena Selected

Some physical phenomena offer better possibilities than others for structuring. In making playdough, for example, variation of the amount of water results in a predictable variation in texture. In contrast, consider the following outline of the study of evaporation and condensation of water from an early-education text.

Experience	*Related concepts*
Notice early morning fog.	A cloud moves down onto the earth and is called *fog* by the people in it.
Make fog by boiling water under a pan of ice water.	When air is cooled, it cannot hold so much water vapor.

See the fog on a cold window pane.
Put ice into a glass of water; set it
aside until water condenses on the
glass.
While having a hot bath, notice
mirrors and windows. Feel their
coldness and dampness. (Use
flannelboard and pictures to show
this at school.)

On the cold surface, see the water
that came out of the air.

Water comes out of the air when the
air touches a cold surface.

(Todd & Heffernan, 1970, p. 319)

The only actions recommended in this activity consist of boiling water under a
pan of ice water and of putting ice into a glass of water. These actions are
dictated by the teacher and do not offer the motivation that a cooking activity,
for example, affords. From the standpoint of the observability of the
phenomena, too, this activity must be questioned. Air and the water in it are
both unobservable, and no amount of explanation with a flannelboard and
pictures will help young children make sense out of the teacher's attempts to
teach.

For the same reasons of unobservability and incomprehensibility, the
following content is also questionable though it is recommended in the science
chapters of other early-education texts.

Electricity

> . . . Dry cell batteries can be used to ring bells and to light bulbs. Children can learn
> to complete the circuit to make it work. Show the children the electric element on
> the hot plate or electric frying pan used for cooking projects. They can learn such
> words as battery, circuit, outlets, plugs, bulbs, and switches. (Hildebrand, 1971,
> pp. 157–158)

Experimenting with batteries and bulbs may be a good activity for older children
who can make hypotheses and systematically vary the connections among parts
in order to isolate relevant variables. In such experimentation, negation plays an
important role. That is, the lack of reaction to particular actions is valuable
information that can be meaningfully structured. However, Piaget (1974b/1980)
pointed out that young children tend not to be interested in negations, but
intrigued with positive reactions to actions. Since the action of connecting
batteries, wires, and bulbs is not intrinsically interesting, preschool children lose
interest when nothing happens as a result of their actions. It is important to
select phenomena in which the child's action is interesting and informative even
when unsuccessful. For example, when a child rolls a ball but misses a target, he
can observe where the ball went and use this information as a basis for modifying
his action. In contrast, when they cannot operate in a systematic way by making
hypotheses and drawing deductions, information gained from an unsuccessful
connection with batteries and bulbs does not help. A fortuitous successful
connection is likely to be regarded as magical.

Objectives and Ways of Teaching

Constructivist education may also be contrasted with "science education" by presenting two different sets of objectives and two different ways of teaching the same content—crystals. The first, quoted from a text on preschool education, is an example of the "science education" approach that focuses principally on subject matter.

Theme: Crystals

Behavioral objective:

At the end of the experience, the child will be able to:

1. Pick out crystals when shown a variety of things.
2. Define what a crystal is.
3. Discuss the steps in making crystals at school.

Learning activities:

The teacher will show the children different crystals and rocks. She will explain what a crystal is and what things are crystals (sand, sugar, salt, etc.). Then she will show some crystals she made previously. The children are given materials...so they can make crystals to take home. A magnifying glass is used so the children can examine the crystals.

Method 1: Mix 1/2 cup each of salt, bluing, water, and 1 T (tablespoon) ammonia. Pour over crumpled paper towels. In 1 hour crystals begin to form. They reach a peak in about 4 hours and last for a couple of days. (Taylor, 1964, pp. 80–81)

Maureen Ellis, a teacher colleague, read the above lesson, modified it into a physical-knowledge activity, and wrote the following account of her teaching with crystals:

While looking through an early-education text, I found the "recipe" for making crystals. I decided to try it, but not as a science project... we used it like a cooking activity. I told them that we didn't know why it happened, but they got the idea that when some things mix together, sometimes something extraordinary happens. The activity was such a success that for days individual children were showing others how to make crystals, and some made their "own" to take home.

This experiment inspired other experiments and a whole atmosphere of experimentation. One boy, during cleanup, decided to pour the grease from the popcorn pan into a cup with water and food coloring. He put it on the windowsill until the next day. He was sure "something" would happen and was surprised when nothing much did. Another child said she knew an experiment with salt, soap, and pepper (which she had seen on television). She demonstrated for those who were interested. A third child was inspired by the soap experiment to fill a cup with water and put a bar of soap in. She was astonished by the change in water level and then tested other things in the water—a pair of scissors, chalk, crayon, and her hand to see the change in water level.

The next day, one child brought a cup filled with beans, blue water, styrofoam packing materials, and a Q-Tip. "This is my experiment. Cook it," he said. So I asked what he thought would happen to each of the things in the cup. He made a few predictions, and I told him we could cook it the next day. (I wanted to experiment first to see if there might be anything dangerous involved.) At group time, he told everyone about his experiment, and the group made predictions which I wrote on the blackboard. Among these were: "The whole thing will get hot," "The water will change color," "The beans will get cooked, and you can eat them," and "The beans will grow." When I asked, "Will anything melt?" the children predicted that the styrofoam would not melt, but that the Q-Tip would. The next day, the child did his cooking experiment, and wrote down the results with my help. Many of his predictions were found to be true, but there were some surprises: It smelled terrible, the Q-Tip did not melt, and the whole thing bubbled. (Kamii & DeVries, 1978, p. 4)

In the "science education" approach above, the teacher's objective is for the child to learn about crystals. More specifically, the objectives are to get children to become able to *recognize* and *define* crystals, and to *describe* how they can be made. In this content-centered approach, children listen to explanations, look at what the teacher shows, and do what he or she planned.

In the "physical-knowledge" approach, by contrast, the teacher's objective is for children to pursue the problems and questions *they* come up with. The purpose of making crystals is thus not to teach about crystals per se, but to stimulate various ideas within a total atmosphere of experimentation. In the situation reported above, the making of crystals inspired four children in four different ways. It also stimulated other children to think about many possible outcomes and encouraged decentering through exchange of ideas about what might happen. The physical-knowledge approach thus emphasizes children's initiative, their actions on objects, their observation of the feedback from objects, and social interaction.

COGNITIVE PROGRESS IN PHYSICAL-KNOWLEDGE ACTIVITIES: CASE STUDY OF CHILDREN'S CONCEPTIONS OF SHADOW PHENOMENA

In Chapters 2 and 3 we pointed out that literal translation of Piaget's theory into educational language focused on structural stages, and free translation focused on constructivism. While we advocate free translation, we also conclude that the next step in the development of constructivist education is a return to the structural stages. However, rather than literal translation, we advocate research to identify stages in children's thought about phenomena that are the content of constructivist activities. In this section, the focus is an example of how the structural and constructivist aspects of Piaget's theory may be integrated in physical-knowledge activities involving shadows. First, the nature of shadow phenomena is explored in relation to the types of physical-knowledge activities outlined above. A study by DeVries is then summarized in a description of four stages in children's construction of spatio-causal relations with regard to shadows. Finally, classroom activities with shadows are discussed, including how teachers can plan activities and evaluate children's progress with reference to the structural levels.

Shadows as Physical-Knowledge Phenomena

Shadows constitute an aspect of the physical world but are not physical objects in the material sense. Observable in the physical world, they are nevertheless an "object" of knowledge for the child's adapting intelligence. Shadows were selected for study because, unlike Piaget's conservation and class inclusion tasks, for example, children spontaneously think about shadow phenomena (Piaget, 1927/1960; 1945/1962). Further, shadow phenomena meet the criteria for good physical-knowledge activities. That is, they are observable by the child, producible (at least in part) by his actions, variable in reaction to varied actions, and immediate in reaction to actions of a particular sort.

Understanding the phenomena that shadows present involves spatial reasoning, causality, and inferences about the nature of light. These phenomena may usefully be compared with the two categories of physical phenomena involving the movement of objects and changes in objects since shadows are unique in some ways although they share elements of both these categories. Like phenomena of basic mechanics, shadows do obey some laws related to their movement. However, these are not "actions on the shadow-as-object" in the strict sense, and the same action (from the child's perspective) does not always lead to the same result. That is, the action of pushing a ball always gives the child the same result to observe each time. However, walking up to one wall may produce a shadow while walking up to another (or even the same one) may not.

Like phenomena involving changes in objects, shadows themselves change in some respects (in size, shape, density). However, unlike, for example, the transformation of dry paint or flour when liquid is added, these are not changes in the "substance" of shadows. In mixing flour and water, it is the direct interaction of the objects most responsible for observable reactions. However, with shadows, interactions among the objects involved are not direct, but occur over a distance.

Stages in Children's Conceptions of Shadows

In order to identify structural stages that may be observed by teachers in classroom activities, an Active Interview was designed to have some of the characteristics of an activity, as well as those of a task. (The difference between tasks and activities was discussed in Chapter 2.) This interview was an activity in the sense that the situation offered the possibility of engaging the child's spontaneous activity in pursuing purposes adopted freely as personal preoccupations. Yet, the interview was a task in the sense that the child was asked to co-operate with the experimenter's preoccupations by answering certain questions and trying certain things that may or may not appeal to interest at the moment. Although the possibility for experimentation was not as free as it can be in the classroom where activity may be continued over many days and weeks, the research situation seemed a satisfactory compromise between the desirability of naturalistic study and the demands for collection of comparable data across individuals.

The principal procedures of the Active Interview with 151 children aged 2–9 years (see DeVries, 1986, for further details) were as follows. Children were brought one at a time to a room lit by a single goosenecked floor lamp, placed so that a strong shadow was cast on a wall when one stood in front of it. The child was immediately engaged with his own shadow and asked what it is, how it gets there, and what makes it dark. Each was asked to predict whether he will see the shadow of a toy horse when it is held behind and in front of him as he faces the lighted wall. The prediction was tested, and of course no shadow could be observed. Then, with the toy horse held in front and back, the experimenter asked, "Is the shadow of the horse still there, even though you can't see it?" This question on the existence of an unseen shadow was also asked when the experimenter merged her shadow with the child's and when both stood behind the lamp. It was also asked in conjunction with questions about what happens to shadows at night when one goes to bed, turns off all the lights, and gets under the covers. To observe whether the child could organize the light and object to make a shadow on a new screen, the child was asked to make his shadow on the dark wall opposite the lighted one, and on the other side of himself when sitting on the floor. To further explore the child's understanding of spatial relations, pictures of shadows in front and in back of children were shown. The question was, "Why is it that sometimes shadows are in front, and sometimes they are in back?" Finally, children were asked to show where to hold a hand in relation to a flashlight in order to make shadows on the four walls, floor, and ceiling.

The analysis of children's reasoning about shadows is aided by the diagram in Figure 4.1, which represents the spatio-causal relations constructed by children in their efforts to understand and explain shadow phenomena. Children may think about these relations singly or in coordination. Development of conceptions about shadow phenomena seems to be constituted by the progressive coordination of these relations.

Level 1A. Figural Correspondence of Well-Defined Shadows with Special Objects: The Object-Shadow Relation of Resemblance

Level 1A (ages 2–3 years) is characterized by limited recognition of the figural correspondence between objects (the self and special objects). It is often difficult to get children at this level to notice shadows because they are more interested in the objects themselves. The object-shadow relation of resemblance has no

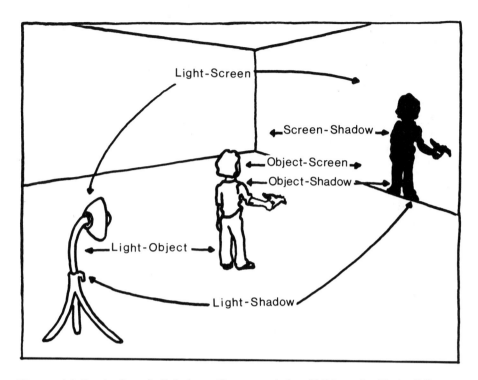

Figure 4.1 Spatio-Causal Relations Constructed by Children in Their Efforts to Understand and Explain Shadow Phenomena.

spatial component, and children are oblivious to the presence of light. Shadows seem to be experienced simply as sometimes present and sometimes absent. For example, Alan (age 2) identifies his shadow as "Alan," but when asked to put his finger on the horse's shadow and his own shadow head and shadow hands, he touches the objects and does not even look at the shadows.

Although the shadow of the self is recognized at this level, physical separateness seems to give rise at times to reference and behavior suggesting that some children experience it as an "other." For example, Michael, a 2-year-old, said of his shadow, "There he is!" Katinka, another 2-year-old, enjoyed playing peek-a-boo with her shadow, and was amused and somewhat surprised to see that it disappeared and reappeared as she stooped and stood in front of the wall.

Having recognized their shadows in the interview, children may be able, when taken behind the lamp where no shadow is visible, to "find" their shadow again by returning to the place where they stood before. The behavior of going back to where he was when he saw his shadow before is reminiscent of behaviors at a much earlier level when babies search for a covered object by looking in the place where they found it last.

Level 1B. Coordination of the Object-Shadow and Object-Screen Relations into a Causal Relation of Proximity

The Level 1A correspondence becomes well consolidated at Level 1B (ages 2–5 years) when children can recognize the figural similarity between shadows and the objects that cast them. The child's experience in observing shadows leads to the primitive spatial notion that shadows are "always" near their object, regardless of the light. Shadows are thus often expected in impossible places or impossible conditions. It is then a small step to another false inference—that shadows may be created in a certain place by actions of the object—such as walking or leaning toward the place where one wants to see a shadow. For example, Jason (age 4) tries to make his shadow in front by leaning forward until he almost falls. Danielle (age 5) says pictured shadows are in front and behind "'Cause one's looking in back and one's looking in front." Many children expect to make a shadow on a dark wall simply by walking up to it. Thus, the object is believed to cause the shadow. The absence of consideration of the light was especially clear in the interview with one 4-year-old who accidentally backed into the lamp and asked in irritation, "What's *this* for?"

Level 2A: Light as a Third Term in the Object-Shadow and Object-Screen Relations

At this level (ages 3 to 6 years) the direct link between the shadow and its object remains strong, and children continue to expect proximity of object and screen and/or the action of the object to be effective factors in the formation of shadows. What is new at this level is that children introduce a third term—the light—though not a precise relation. That is, the child recognizes that the presence of light is a factor in the appearance of shadows. Simple abstraction from their experience leads children at this level to be conscious of the ever-present light, but it is viewed as merely a kind of accompaniment to the shadow. It is simply added to, but not coordinated in a precise way with the object-shadow and object-screen relations. For example, Erin (age 3) can go no further than saying, "When you stand in the sun, you see your shadow." Matt (age 4) says "The sun helps it [the shadow]," but cannot say how. At Level 2A, we find a continuation of the ideas of 1B. Proximity remains the causal notion, and children remain unsuccessful in creating shadows on new screens when movement of the lamp is necessary. The emergence of awareness of the light source will be elaborated at Level 2B as directional and at Level 2C as active.

Level 2B. Light as Specific Illumination and the Search for Spatial Solution to Practical Problems: Coordination of Object-Screen and Light-Screen Relations and Introduction of a Limited Light-Object Relation

What is new at Level 2B (ages 3 to 9 years) is:

1. A shift from thinking about light as general illumination of a room to the specific illumination of the screen on which the shadow falls;
2. A search for spatial solution to practical problems through trial-and-error experimentation.

The nature of the constructive process from 2A to 2B thus has as its principal hallmark progress from a lack of consciousness of the role of the lamp's orientation to a dawning consciousness that the direction the lamp faces is a factor in where shadows appear. Children at this level can think of moving the lamp to make a shadow on a new wall, and through trial and error they sometimes succeed. However, they fail in some aspect of the interview dealing with the spatial arrangement of light, object, and screen. Their feeling of necessity about the light's direction may be fragile, occurring at certain moments and not at others.

Level 2C. Light as Active in the Formation of Shadows

Level 2C (ages 5 to 9 years) differs from 2B only in that children at 2C are beginning to think at least sometimes of light as active in the formation of shadows. For example, children say that the light "goes down," "can't get on me (when E stands behind child and shadow is merged)," "hits your body," "bounces off," and so on. This is notable because it is an inference (by reflective abstraction) that goes beyond the observable—beyond "reading" of reality by simple or empirical abstraction. Although children continue to have great difficulty thinking about what happens in the space between the object and the shadow, progress to Level 2C is marked by clear reference to an active process occurring between the light source and the object or screen. This may occur alongside continued reference to general illumination as well. It is also marked by increased efforts to coordinate the light-object relation with the light-screen and object-screen relations. At Level 2C, children are becoming more conscious of the paradox that the light makes a dark shadow. However, this paradox remains unresolved. Furthermore, like children at 2B, they continue to give explanations unrelated to the spatial law or contradictory to it.

Level 3A. The Law of Spatial Relations: Equilibrated Coordination of Relations at the Level of Practical Intelligence

At Level 3A (appearing for a small number of children at ages 7 to 9 years), the search for the law culminates in its equilibration at the level of practical intelligence. That is, children have discovered the law of spatial relations among light source, object, and screen. They have the "know-how" to arrange the lamp and object so as to produce a shadow on any particular screen. Children's mechanical "know-how" generally still depends on actual physical manipulation and does not immediately lead to causal explanation—that is, to the idea of light blocked by the object. "Explanations" of why the spatial relations are necessary remain the same as at earlier levels and are unrelated to the law or even contradictory to it.

Level 3B. Conceptual Explanation of Spatial Relations

At Level 3B (appearing at age 8 for a small number of children), "knowing how" is elaborated into "knowing why." This level is characterized by a conceptual notion of blocked light. The idea of blocking as a resistance of the object to the action of the light is seen at this level in children's reasoning that the light cannot go through the object and that the object thus prevents light from reaching the screen. This idea is a deduction that goes beyond what is observable, and children at this level usually do not need to manipulate physical objects in order to bring understanding to consciousness. For example, Jess (age 9 years) explains that her shadow is on the wall " 'Cause I'm in the way of the light, and the light can't get there." Chris (age 9) says that "The light goes on and your body blocks the light from hitting that spot." Despite this significant advance in conceptualization, children at this level have not taken this idea to its logical conclusion of the definition of a shadow as the absence of light, although its fragile beginnings appear. Like children at all earlier levels, they continue to believe that the unseen shadow is still there at night or when merged.

Level 4. Deduction of Transitoriness

Level 4 (beginning to appear among a very small number of 8-year-olds) children are distinguished by their insistence that unseen shadows are not there at all. They no longer view shadows as having any material properties of objects, and their deduction of transitoriness has a feeling of logical necessity that this must be so. Delilah (age 8) expounds the imperative that "If you see it, it's there, and if you don't, it's not." At earlier levels, children believe that the shadow is there in the darkness and you need light simply to illuminate it. At Level 4, children believe that you must have light to see a shadow because there *is* no shadow if there's no light.

Beliefs Spanning Several Levels

Alongside emergent correct beliefs represented by these stages are a number of incorrect beliefs spanning two or more levels. In general, these incorrect ideas may be understood as constructions that are by-products of the absence of constructions represented in the stage progression. Children from Stages 1 through 2C express the idea that a shadow is a physical emanation from the object. For example, some children believe that their unseen shadow goes inside them. Children also refer to God, magic, the wind, or other mystical or irrelevant causal factors from Levels 1 through 3B. Correct description of spatial relations was given by children as early as Level 2B, though these were not well consolidated (consistent) until Level 3A. Hypotheses about the disappearance of objects at all levels up through Level 3B included postulation (1) that the shadow is independent of its object, (2) that it remains somewhere nearby, (3) that it goes into the darkness, (4) that it goes inside the object or onto its surface, and (5) that a merged shadow is covered or mixed with another.

This study confirms the phenomena observed by Piaget (1927/1960) but does not confirm his description of stages. Piaget claimed that during the first three of four stages children understand shadows as emanation. In the DeVries study, only 11% of the children expressed emanation beliefs, and there is no systematic relation between this belief and the levels described above.

SHADOW ACTIVITIES TO PROMOTE DEVELOPMENT

Throughout the developmental levels in children's reasoning about shadows, children's errors are apparent. It is thus clear that the constructive process is full of many erroneous conceptions that are, in fact, intelligent and that eventually lead to the kinds of contradictions in children's minds that result in accurate knowledge. This is a very long process, incomplete even at age 9 for most children. What does this mean for teachers? Does it mean that we should avoid shadow activities, since children are incapable of the coordination of relations necessary for correct thinking? On the contrary! Because shadows are full of possibilities for contradicting children's anticipations, and thus surprising them, they are an excellent source of activities.

With respect to educational concerns, the most important result of the foregoing research is that some children made progress in their consciousness of and reasoning about shadows in the course of the Active Interview. For example, a number of children tried to make a shadow on a dark wall simply by illuminating it. Only when they saw no shadow did they think of putting themselves between the lamp and the lighted wall. All children found some phenomena intriguing and experimented to try out their ideas. When children are encouraged to experiment, shadows seem to offer a context that has potential for children's development. That is, through experimenting with shadows, children can modify and elaborate their knowledge and reasoning.

Good shadow activities also provide a dynamic context in which teachers can assess children's reasoning. With such formative evaluation in mind, the teacher can intervene to facilitate further reasoning and can plan new activities that may inspire new efforts on the part of children.

Shadows as Educational "Materials" in the Classroom

Constructivist "teaching" is not a didactic presentation of facts to children. It requires the provision of materials and suggestions that inspire children's real interest, pursuit of curiosities, and efforts to figure something out. For preschool children, "figuring out" does not usually mean figuring out "why" but figuring out "how to." Piaget (1974d/1978) has emphasized that success must precede understanding of phenomena whose causal explanations cannot be observed directly and must therefore be invented. The challenge for the teacher is to promote children's own purposes in observing and experimenting with shadows.

Constructivist "teaching" is also not the same as interviewing children in the study described above. While the research situation did elicit children's observation and some experimentation, children were asked to think about many aspects of shadows, and we moved rapidly from one to the next. Thus, opportunity for experimentation was limited. In the classroom, the study of shadows can be richer and more relaxed, extending over many weeks and years. Let us begin our consideration of classroom possibilities with a few principles of teaching similar to constructivist principles of teaching discussed in other chapters of this book.

Principles of Teaching

1. *Begin with shadows of objects having a unique shape.* This fosters the observation of correspondences between objects and their shadows. Children's
   interest in their own shadows can be capitalized upon.
2. *Foster children's interest and attitude of curiosity and experimentation.* This
   can be done in a variety of ways. A child's spontaneous remark about
   shadows may be repeated to another, and his idea may be encouraged. An
   especially intriguing observation may be repeated at grouptime, and
   discussion fostered. Stories involving shadows may provide a take-off point
   for discussion. For example, *Peter Pan* (Barrie, 1911) has his shadow caught
   in a window, and Mrs. Darling puts it away in a drawer. Children may want to
   discuss whether that can happen, and many may believe it possible! Surely
   Peter's concern over finding his shadow will elevate the importance of
   shadows. Other good books to read and discuss with children are *Dark as a
   Shadow* (Lowery, 1969), *Mr. Wink and his shadow, Ned* (Gachenbach,
   1983), and *Nothing Sticks Like a Shadow* (Tompert, 1984).

   An important part of fostering children's interest is for the teacher to
   express interest and wonder about shadows. The "know-it-all authority" will
   not succeed, but the companion-guide who wonders aloud, asks children's
   opinions, and consults with children will succeed in supporting and extending
   children's active and spontaneous discoveries.
3. *Create a forum in which children can share their discoveries with others.* At
   grouptime, the teacher can encourage children to report their observations
   and experiments, and some can even be conducted in the large group.
   Children may enjoy seeing their own "Shadow Book" grow as the teacher
   records the results of their observations and investigations.
4. *Encourage children to figure out how to make shadows "behave" in particular
   ways.* Intriguing problems for children include how to create a sharp shadow

of an object on a wall, how to make it "dance" or move, how to make a shadow longer, shorter, bigger, smaller, and how to make it fall on a particular side or on the ceiling. Other ideas are suggested below.

5. *Accept children's wrong ideas.* Incorrect anticipations are just as important as correct ones, and the teacher should feel successful when children are invested in actively thinking, "What will happen if. . .?" After expectations are formulated, children should be encouraged to "Try it and see what happens." Sometimes, of course, children will not verbalize their anticipation but will simply act. What is important is to recognize the significance of wrong ideas and puzzlement for a child's progress. The child who wonders about the fact that shadows are sometimes in front and sometimes in back is ahead of the child who has not yet noticed this fact. Similarly, the child who expects a shadow to appear in front when he leans forward is more advanced than the child who has no anticipations.

Wrong ideas that cannot be tested should be especially respected. If a child believes that a merged shadow is still there (and all children between 4 and 7 years believe this), there is no proof that will really convince him or her that this idea is wrong. While it may be useful casually to raise the question of whether an unseen shadow is still there or not, the preschool and early elementary teacher should not expect children to "learn" that shadows are transitory. Many children will say the shadow is not there, but what they mean is, "I can't see it." When asked, "Is the shadow still there, even though you can't see it?" all except 3 of the children in the study at least sometimes believed it was still there. When a child expresses an opinion that the unseen shadow is not there (even though this may be the right idea for the "wrong" reason), its repetition may contribute to planting a seed of doubt in some children's minds. It is useful to say, "Deborah thinks the shadow is not still there," without pronouncing whether this is right or wrong.

Classroom Projects

Although lists of activity ideas have some usefulness, it is perhaps more useful to know the ways in which particular teachers have worked with shadows. I would therefore like to summarize the experiences of two teachers in Geneva, Switzerland.

Marie-Claire Bernasconi

Taking at first a diagnostic approach, Marie-Claire tried in informal ways to learn what children already knew about shadows. At grouptime, she asked children to say what they noticed on the rug. When one child finally mentioned a shadow, she was able to observe which children understood the word and its referent. She noticed that some children saw the shadow but could not put their finger on it because it disappeared in their own shadow when they approached it. Children who understood what shadows are took their comrades around the room to show them shadows. At grouptime on another day, Marie-Claire put a small vase on the carpet and moved it to various positions as children pointed to the shadow. When one child noted that she couldn't see the small shadow very well and the teacher asked what to do, children suggested getting bigger objects. Other questions and observations that arose, either from children or the teacher, over a five-week period included the following.

- If the light in the room is turned off, will there be shadows?
- If three lamps shine from different directions, how many shadows will there be?
- If one of the lamps is turned off, which shadow will disappear? Children put their finger on the shadow they expected to stay, and observed the result when the lamp was turned off.
- When you stand up, you can't see the shadow of your feet. When you stand with feet apart, there are two shadows, but when you put both feet together, there is just one.
- A white paper under an object makes the shadow get better; a brown paper makes the shadow dim.
- If you move a flashlight, the shadow moves.
- When you move the flashlight far away from the object, the shadow gets big and you can't see it very well; it is light in color; but when you move the flashlight close, the shadow gets small and dark.
- When you hold the flashlight high and slanting down, the shadow gets short and fat; when you hold it low, the shadow gets long and skinny.
- A transparent glass doesn't make a very good shadow.
- The profile shadow is an astonishing "trick."
- Making one's own shadow "behave" raises a lot of problems and brings a lot of suggestions; you cannot make a profile shadow and see it at the same time!
- Paper cutouts are hard to see if your hand shadow is visible; adding a stick makes it better.
- Cutting holes in cutouts makes the identity more evident.
- Pantomiming actions (such as washing hands) is an interesting guessing game.

G. Pralong

In her class, G. Pralong encountered many of the same reactions Marie-Claire observed. In addition, her children discovered that:

- When the playground is empty, there are no shadows.
- You can't catch your shadow or pass it.
- You don't see a little shadow under a big shadow.

- The shadow of the birch tree on the playground is lighter than the children's shadows.
- When I face the sun, the shadow is in front of me; when I have my back to the sun, it is behind me. (Not all "observations" are correct!)
- The higher I jump, the longer my shadow.
- Flashlights with different-shaped reflectors produce different-shaped shadows.
- The closer the flashlight to the wall, the clearer and brighter the spot, and the more it shrinks.
- If the flashlight with a round reflector is tilted, the spot becomes oval; a rectangular reflector's spot is deformed.

In the Human Development Laboratory in Houston

In classrooms in the Human Development Laboratory our experiences include the following ideas. Some of these ideas were contributed by Karen Von Gonten, Ruth Dickey, Rama Ramanadhan, Laura LeRoy, and Kathy McCrary, and by Claire Smith (former teacher in the Merrill-Palmer Child Care Center).

- Telling the shadow story of "Billy Goats Gruff" presents an interesting problem if the goat cut-outs are all the same size; using a tape-recorded story helps children remember what to do next.
- The cut-out eyes, nose, and mouth of a pumpkin can be made to "disappear" if you put your hand over them on the object. They also disappear when you put your hand halfway between the pumpkin and the wall—but then the nose or eye appears on your hand!
- A sheet hung from the ceiling makes a good screen for "Shadow Charades," and children enjoy using hats, purses, and other props to give their shadow a unique identity.
- When children have not had experience with the sheet arrangement, it is best to give them a few days for free experimentation before introducing a game or other activity.
- Children may expect the shadow to appear on the sheet when they go on the side without the projector!
- When an object is made to lean toward the light, the shadow eventually disappears from one side and appears on the side near the light.
- The shape of a shadow changes when you turn the object. It's not so easy to keep it in profile!
- You can sometimes make your shadow "walk" around the corner from one wall to another, but not always.
- Candles make shadows, too!
- There are no shadows when there's a thunderstorm.
- A shadow is never smaller than its object.
- Young children may experience their shadow as an "other," and enjoy

playing peek-a-boo by squatting and standing in front of a wall.
- Shadows of some alphabet letters are reversed, but some are not.
- Children like to figure out whether drawings of shadows are possible or not.
- If you go very close to the light, the shadow disappears, and the whole wall is dark.
- You don't have to climb up to the ceiling to make a shadow there.

Pseudoscientific Verbalism

In recommending shadow phenomena to educators, it must be cautioned that activities oriented more to *instruction* than to the child's *construction* are likely to be "unconstructive," if not damaging, to children's development. Several children in the DeVries study exhibited the adverse results of teachers' efforts to teach scientific principles before children had assimilatory structures adequate to make such teaching productive.

In the excerpt below, Joe calls upon his memories of what he has been told about electricity, movements of the sun and moon, eclipses, space, and using color to paint a picture of fire. Joe refers to a science lesson in which the teacher demonstrated the movements of sun, moon, and earth. What he remembers is something vague about the movements of the sun and moon. He omits the earth from this relation, and retains only the imprecise notion that the moon moves to make a shadow. The effort to give a scientific explanation prevents Joe from investing his full energy in trying to think about the phenomena at hand. Alongside his pseudoscientific verbalism we also find the same kinds of ideas offered by other children. Unconvinced by his own efforts to give the kind of physical explanation he thinks the adult wants, Joe's honest reasoning focuses principally on the relation between the light and the object, and we see what is really "understood" beneath the "scientific" explanations. For all Joe's serious effort to use what he has been taught, his structure for understanding is inadequate, and he, too, believes a merged shadow is still there, and that unseen shadows go to a dark corner. One cannot help but wonder whether Joe's *instruction* about shadows has not, in fact, interfered with his *construction*.

Joe, 8 years

What makes a shadow? The light.

How does that work? This light comes from electricity and it comes up into the lamp or light bulb, and when you turn it on, it shines here and if you stand here, you see your shadow—cause it's like the moon going behind the sun. Say this is the sun (area of lighted wall). This moon (his fist) is going right

So this is the sun and the moon, and that's all that matters?

there (moves fist across wall so shadow of fist appears), and it goes like this, and it makes a shadow. Yeah, the shadow, sun—I'm not sure. I keep on getting mixed up. Wait! Do you think space might have to do with this stuff?

Maybe. What do you mean?

You know how space is dark, and like when the sun—no—can't—well, maybe—like when the sun in space, you know. You know space is dark. Well, somewhere there's a sun and lots of rays coming out. It sometimes goes into the darkness. It'll turn to yellow or something like that.

What does?

The sun's rays when it comes into the dark. It turns into light. The black's gone, you know, but the stars and stuff like that are still in there, but prob'ly change their color.

The rays of the sun change color?

Yeah—Oh, I get it! I think— no—well, that's just like if this is the sun (lamp) and like I'm the moon and I'm standing here and make the shadow—just like the sun and the moon.

So if that's (wall) the sun and you're the moon—let's see—and the sun is shining on the moon—

It'll make the shadow, but it'd be dark. That's the hard part. How does it get—become dark? Oh, yeah, I know! The earth has all kinds of colors on it, but the sun just has yellow and it comes here, you know. When you make the shadow, it sort of copies. It turns black. Like the sun, it's yellow—all yellow—nothing else, just gases. The black of the shadow is—oh, I keep on getting confused. I forget where I am and I get confused and I go back to start.

Joe goes on to explain that he got his sun and moon idea from what he observed in the classroom. His description of black and white circles glued to a stick is very confused, and helps him not at all in understanding how his shadow gets on the wall. Later in the interview:

If the shadow is made out of light, how come the shadow is dark?

That's the hardest question I ever had. (More long-winded verbalism about circles and sticks.) It somehow turns black. This is just like a mystery, you know. You can't find a answer to it. Prob'ly nobody has.

More research to identify developmental stages in constructivist classroom activities will help teachers avoid the kind of untimely teaching that produces such confusion and uncertainty.

SUMMARY

Physical-knowledge activities involving movement of objects or changes in objects are discussed as a means for children to construct specific knowledge of the physical world and general structures of reasoning. Adaptation to the physical world of objects involves experiences that lead eventually to knowledge of the properties of objects, to notions of causality, and to feelings of logical necessity about many truths pertaining to physical reality.

Good physical-knowledge activities must be observable and producible by the child, variable in reaction to varying actions, and immediate in reaction to the child's action. Principles of teaching are discussed, and physical-knowledge activities are contrasted with phenomena typically recommended as science education for preschoolers. To illustrate how cognitive progress may be assessed by the constructivist teacher, a case study involving shadows is presented. Developmental levels are described, and recommendations offered for using shadows as educational "materials" in the classroom.

Chapter 5

Group Games

In Chapter 4, the focus was on activities to promote the child's adaptation to the physical world of objects. This chapter and the next focus on activities to promote children's adaptation to the social world. The difference between the child's adaptation to the world of objects and to the world of people is discussed in Chapter 2. Our discussion emphasizes both the cognitive and affective aspects of this adaptation. This chapter reviews some of the material in the book *Group Games in Early Education* (Kamii & DeVries, 1980). However, it provides further elaboration of rationale and objectives, and describes stages in children's ways of thinking and playing games. We begin our consideration of group games with their definition and prior role in early education. Then we present the rationale and objectives of group games in constructivist education, and stages in playing three games. Following this is discussion of the development of role-taking and cognitive and moral judgment in group games. Criteria of good group games, types of group games, and principles of teaching provide further practical guidelines for using group games to promote children's development.

DEFINITION OF GROUP GAMES

The word "games" is commonly used to refer broadly to activities that are "fun," such as individual play at pretense or blockbuilding, and group activities like singing and dancing. However, the group games discussed here have a more restricted definition as those in which children play together according to conventional rules specifying (1) some preestablished climax (or series of climaxes) to be achieved, and (2) what players should try to do in roles which are *interdependent, opposed, and collaborative*. In the game of "Hide and Seek," for example, the preestablished climax is finding/being-found or not-finding/not-being-found. The child who hides is supposed to try to avoid being found, and the child who seeks is supposed to try to find the hidden players. These arbitrary rules are fixed by convention and consensus. The hider and finder roles are *interdependent* because neither can exist without the other. "Hiding" implies "hiding *from* someone who will seek," and "seeking" implies "looking *for* someone who has hidden." These roles are *opposed* because the intentions of the hider and seeker are to prevent what the other is aiming to do. This implies the possibility of using strategy. Finally, these roles are *collaborative* because the game cannot occur unless players mutually agree on the rules and co-operate by following them and accepting their consequences.

This definition of group games excludes certain valuable activities often referred to as games. For example, although dancing and singing songs with others involve conventional rules and complementary roles, no opposed intentions exist. Other good group activities also excluded are co-operative block building and pretend play because of the absence of conventional rules. In all these activities, there is no clear, specific, predetermined end result to be accomplished that can be judged a success or a failure. In addition, the restricted definition also excludes many so-called "games" in education which are simply didactic lessons in disguise.

THE PRIOR ROLE OF GAMES IN EDUCATION

The constructivist view of the unique educational advantages of group games is in contrast with the opinion found in early education texts in the child-development tradition. Many authors (such as Taylor, 1964) simply make no mention of group games in their otherwise detailed curricula. Other authors refer to group games only to discourage their use. For example, Kellogg (1949) states emphatically that group games "are seldom found in a good nursery school" (p. 156). The widely accepted view has been that group games are inappropriate for 4-year-olds because such games "are too complicated" (Hildebrand, 1971, p. 253). Leeper, Witherspoon, and Day (1984) express a similar attitude in their statement that "Nursery school children are usually not ready for organized games, and only very simple games are appropriate for the kindergarten" (p. 532). They do recommend three group games, Tag, Musical Chairs, and Simon Says, along with rituals like Mulberry Bush because these have few rules and do not involve competition. In this rare case when group games are included in a curriculum in a limited way, they are not distinguished from ritual activities, and no unique justification is given.

The consensus in early education texts is that group games at best offer little of particular value. The use of group games is thus an addition to the child-development tradition in early education. As noted in Chapter 4, other Piagetian programs either have not included games at all or have included them in only a limited way without the special emphasis and rationale described here.

For older, elementary-aged children, group games have long been accepted and justified in terms of physical and social development. Specific reasons sometimes given are energy release (a need resulting from inactive periods spent sitting), muscular exercise, entertainment, or a motivational ruse to teach a particular body of information. Certainly children benefit in physical ways from the activity of many group games. However, the cognitive and sociomoral rationales presented below go beyond and provide more specific justifications for group games with preschoolers as well as elementary-school children.

RATIONALE AND OBJECTIVES

The rationale for group games in constructivist education addresses the general objectives of sociomoral, intellectual, and personality development. More specifically, the objectives of autonomy and co-operation are twin aspects of each of these dimensions of development. Let us consider the special ways in which games contribute to development.

Sociomoral Development

The sociomoral objective of constructivist teaching is long-term progress in the structure or stage of moral reasoning, not just in the specific content of moral rules or even behavior conforming to moral rules. That is, as Kohlberg has argued, our aim should focus not in an isolated way just on teaching moral rules or moral *behaviors* but on facilitating the construction of inner moral convictions about what is good and necessary in one's relations with others. If one focuses only on conformity to heteronomous rules given ready-made to children, conforming behavior may reflect only superficial knowledge of social expectation without personal commitment to the moral value itself.

The broad constructivist sociomoral goal is for children to develop autonomous feelings of obligation (or moral necessity) about relations with others that are not just dictates accepted from adults. Rather, a feeling of moral necessity reflects an internal system of personal convictions. Such a personal system is autonomous in so far as it leads to beliefs and behavior that are self-regulated rather than other-regulated. It is co-operative insofar as it reflects a view of the self as part of a system of reciprocal social relations.

From the point of view of promoting children's autonomy, group games contribute by providing a context in which children can voluntarily accept and submit themselves to rules. Children are free to exercise their autonomy by choosing to play and choosing to follow rules. Rules in games are different from the set of obligations adults must impose in daily living (such as eating certain foods, going to bed at a certain time, and not playing with certain delicate objects). Rules in everyday living are fully formed and given to the child ready-made. The child usually cannot understand the reasons for these rules and thus can only abide by them out of obedience to the authority of adults. That is, he cannot follow them out of an internal feeling of commitment to their necessity.

Autonomous adoption of sociomoral rules is prevented to the extent that the child is bound by a heteronomous attitude. That is, when the child thinks and acts in terms of what he perceives to be the requirements of others, he is not likely to submit these to the reflection that leads to understood and self-accepted values. The loosening of the heteronomous attitude requires experiences in which children can exercise autonomy by choosing to follow or not follow rules, reflecting on the consequences, and gradually growing to understand the reasons for rules that are rooted in maintaining desired relations with others.

In a group game, the adult authority and system of rules is temporarily suspended. Players can practice co-operation among equals when adult authority is put aside in favor of rules to which adults, too, must conform. When the adult participates as one player among others, adult authority can be more easily suspended in the minds of children, and this opportunity for interacting with the adult on a more equal basis is particularly good for the loosening of children's heteronomous attitudes. In daily living, it is difficult for the adult to tolerate a child's breaking a rule. In games, however, rules are not so sacred. In games, adult authority can decrease while children's power increases. When power is equalized, coercion ceases to be the regulating force, and autonomous co-operation can begin.

In games, therefore, the child finds conditions in which he can willingly adapt to society. Children thus have the opportunity to exercise autonomy in freely regulating their actions with others in relation to rules. They experience the consequences of failing to follow a rule when others protest and the game comes to a halt. They can then decide whether to change their behavior or, with the teacher's help at first, change the rule. This leads to dawning awareness of the necessity of collective agreement to the continuation of a mutually satisfying experience. In a game, the child thus has the possibility of creating in part the rules and values by which he regulates his behavior.

It should be noted that it is possible to learn a rule without autonomy. That is, when a child follows a rule merely out of obedience to external authority, autonomy is not exercised. It is perhaps useful to think of a continuum from heteronomy to autonomy. To the degree that a rule is followed out of willingness and understanding, the behavior falls more on the autonomous end. To the degree that it is followed out of conformity to an adult, the behavior falls more on the heteronomous end.

In a game with rules, society intervenes in the experience of the individual, offering a situation in which the child can adapt to external social rules and construct feelings of obligation to them. From the point of view of promoting children's co-operation, group games contribute by providing a context—a mini-society—in which children can autonomously relate to others according to rules. Interest in the game leads to interest in others. Interest in playing with others according to the rules leads to efforts to coordinate individual actions with those of others. Self-regulation thus evolves into mutual adaptation—that is, the mutual accommodation, mutual adjustment, of co-operation. Interest in the end (playing the game) brings an interest in the means (co-operation) by which to have fun in the game.

Games uniquely promote attitudes of reciprocity that lead to feelings of moral necessity—the core of sociomoral development. These feelings of obligation arise, not out of obedience, but out of a feeling of personal necessity. Feelings of moral necessity about relations with others develop in games as children confront issues of fairness, individual rights, and the reasons for rules. They can practice mutual respect which is a defining characteristic of co-operation and democratic principles.

A competitive game is especially conducive to moral development because opposed intentions must be coordinated within a broader context of co-operation. That is, competition can only exist when players co-operate in agreeing on the rules, enforcing them, abiding by them, and accepting their consequences even when unfavorable to themselves. The game cannot occur unless players co-operate by coordinating their points of view. When players have different conceptions of how a game should be played, the game may stop, and this creates a situation in which children have the opportunity to confront the different perspective of someone else, decenter, and to negotiate an agreement. Seen in this light, the competitive aspect is in fact, subordinate to the co-operative aspect. Following mutually agreed-upon rules puts everyone on an equal basis in a social system regulated by players themselves. Playing a group game is thus a useful point of departure for promoting children's sociomoral progress.

Intellectual Development

The broad constructivist cognitive goal is for the child to move toward feelings of logical necessity that reflect operational reasoning about the physical as well as the social world. Sociomoral development has an important cognitive component (the decentered substitution of points of view), and moral and intellectual objectives are thus interdependent.

Operational reasoning, like moral reasoning, is autonomous in that it is not just a set of truths accepted as given by others, but reflects an internal system of personal and logical convictions. It is "co-operative," too, in that it is not egocentric but decentered. That is, moral reasoning involves overcoming the limitations of one perspective to consider multiple perspectives. Similarly, reasoning about the physical world involves overcoming a limited perspective to consider and coordinate the relations among all aspects of material phenomena.

The cognitive advantages of group games vary, depending on the type of game, its idiosyncratic characteristics, and the ways in which children use it. Some games involve physical knowledge and thus carry all the advantages of physical-knowledge activities considered in Chapter 4. Cognitive advantages of various types of group games are discussed elsewhere (Kamii & DeVries, 1980).

Personality Development

The broad, constructivist goal of personality or character development is, in part, for children to elaborate a stable sense of self and will (reflecting a hierarchy of personal values, discussed in Chapter 2) as a regulator of feelings. In discussing the relations between cognitive and affective development, Piaget (1954/1981) talked about "schemes of social reaction." These include attitudes and behaviors toward others and interpretations of others' behaviors that are constructed by the child in the course of social experiences. Schemes of social reaction are not just patterns but active instruments with which the child "reads" and reacts to social material. Young children are thus elaborating the very social-cognitive instrument that is necessary for later development.

The interests and values of young children are unstable and fluctuating.

Development of self and will is, in part, a matter of becoming less fluctuating in interests and values. These obviously involve discriminations that are cognitive, as well as feelings of liking and disliking. Piaget pointed out that the attribution of value to other persons is the point of departure for moral feelings. Insofar as the child feels that the partner is valuable, she will practice mutual respect by acting to affirm and not devalue (disrespect) the partner. Personality development thus involves the construction of more or less stable systems (of interests, values, attitudes, typical ways of interpreting and responding to the social world) and is thus interdependent with sociomoral and cognitive development.

Piaget pointed out that while values, interests, and other personality characteristics become conserved, these will never be as stable or coherent as systems of logical reasoning (as in, for example, conservation of substance or number). Nevertheless, these systems determine the energy the child invests in action and are crucial to the process of sociomoral and cognitive development. An important aspect of personality is the degree to which a person is conscious of the relativity of individual perspective (decentering) and puts this relativity into a system or group of various perspectives. The long-range goal of coordinating individuality with the perspectives of others is well expressed by Kohlberg's postconventional stages (see Chapter 6).

Consciousness of an autonomous self develops along with and partly as a result of growing consciousness of others. This involves both affective and cognitive decentering as the child becomes aware of similarities and differences among selves first in their physical and behavioral aspects and, finally, in their psychological aspects.

Group games contribute to personality development by providing a context in which children can exercise and differentiate their will and schemes of social reaction, and consolidate interests in coordination with others. Volition is exercised when the child submits his will to external rules because he wants to for his own reasons and not because adults want him to obey. Will, along with schemes of social reaction, is elaborated and refined in the course of interaction with others. Habits and attitudes of co-operation with others can become established in social interchanges (including conflicts) in which children confront the necessity for working out mutual agreements. Through efforts to coordinate with others in games, the child can progress in overcoming egocentrism. Affective decentration can occur as players begin to take the other's desires into account and make progress toward reciprocity in feelings about others.

With these preceding ideas in mind, the objectives of group games may be summarized as follows:

1. Players exercise autonomy in voluntarily submitting themselves to a system of rules governing their relations to others;
2. Players practice mutual respect and co-operation among equals through regulating the legislation of common rules, following and enforcing rules, and deciding issues of fairness;

3. Players exercise role-taking or decentering to recognize others' points of view and figure out how to play and how to win.

THE DEVELOPMENT OF ROLE-TAKING, AND COGNITIVE AND MORAL JUDGMENT IN GROUP GAMES

We have thus far given a very general and theoretical rationale for the use of group games. In order to make this rationale clear, we shall now describe research-defined levels and stages in playing three games: Marbles, Guess Which Hand the Penny Is In, and Tic-Tac-Toe. These descriptions of levels will not only allow the reader to understand the usefulness of group games for the development of social and logical reasoning, but will help the educator to assess individual children's progress in playing these games.

Marbles

One of the ways Piaget (1932/1965) approached the study of moral judgment was to establish the nature of the child's respect for rules in the game of Marbles. Raising the question of how the mind comes to feel an obligation to a system of rules, he focused his attention on the practice and consciousness of rules in this game that was so popular in the spontaneous "street play" of Swiss boys. Pretending not to remember the rules, Piaget and his collaborators asked about 100 children ranging in age from 4 to 13 years to show them how to play. His study was restricted to boys in Switzerland because in the 1920s only boys played Marbles. After establishing the facts of a child's *practice* of rules, Piaget probed their *consciousness* of rules by asking, for example, whether the child could invent a new rule, and whether rules could be changed. Piaget then identified four types of behavior in relation to rules and four corresponding types of rules. These he referred to as "stages," although these do not reflect the same sort of hard stage analysis of logical operations as his later stages. He found four stages or levels in the practice of rules.

Motor and Individual Play (Below 2 Years)

At the first stage of playing with marbles, the child's rules are motor and individual. The attitude of the baby and very young child toward rules is asocial, and the "rules" are individual motor rules. These are really rituals or habits whose regularity is based on intrigue with the action itself or its result. The child at this stage is not conscious of any rules and feels no social obligation or external necessity to submit to rules. For example, Piaget's daughter played with marbles by dropping them on the carpet, putting them in the hollow of an armchair, throwing them, piling them in a pyramid, bouncing them, and "cooking" them in a toy saucepan. She did not regulate these actions by any rules, but simply sought to understand the nature of the objects by acting on them in a variety of ways to observe their reactions, and to use them in the service of her symbolic play. Over several days, some of these actions became rituals, repeated without any new experimentation or elaboration. Such rituals are motivated by intrigue with the action itself or its result. This regulation is guided by an individual rule that is *asocial*, in contrast with a collective rule accepted as given by others. Although one may observe in such motor play some consciousness of the regularity, Piaget pointed out the absence of the feeling of obligation that distinguishes a rule from mere regularity. At this stage, "rules" are individual rather than social since they do not involve the submission to something outside the self that is characteristic of rule following.

Egocentric Play (Ages 2–5 Years)

Egocentric behavior in relation to rules, in contrast, is definitely social. The child learns (or tries to learn) other people's rules and submits himself to their authority. However, the social character of play lies more in the child's intention than in actuality. That is, the child at this stage practices rules according to his egocentric assimilation—without realizing when his conception of the rule is different from that of those from whom he "learned" it. In Marbles, for example, young children may play without drawing a square, may sometimes keep the marbles they knock out and sometimes replace them in the square, and may take aim many times and even at the same time as the partner. They thus imitate the observable features of the play of others in a global way that is schematically correct but incorrect in detail. Play is social only in a superficial sense. Children at this stage may even play alone or with others but without trying to win. No real competition exists at this stage, and "winning" means simply following some rules or having fun, not getting the better of others. Although children may play side by side, they often do not bother to watch each other and do not unify their respective rules (often playing by different rules without realizing it or without caring). Nevertheless, egocentric rules are social in that the child accepts them as coming from a higher authority and therefore *feels* constrained to (try to) follow them. This stage is thus characterized by a *heteronomous attitude*, since the child submits to regulation by others and by a rule whose reason is external to her understanding.

Piaget describes one example of egocentric play between two boys (one 6 and the other 7 years of age) who declare they play Marbles frequently together. Nevertheless, when alone with Piaget, they give different accounts of how they play. One says they decide who is to begin by having one throw his shooter and the other trying to hit it with his (he begins first if successful). The other child says he does not know what to do to begin, and when the procedure described by his friend is then mentioned, says he knows nothing about it. One makes a pyramid of marbles as the initial target, but the other does not. One simply rolls the shooter, and the other flicks it with his thumb. When successful in knocking a marble out of the square, one child puts it in his pocket, and the other puts it back in the square and arbitrarily decides to take out a marble every third shot (but not necessarily a marble he has hit). Together, these children do not feel a need to unify their perspectives and do not play according to a common set of rules. Each follows his own notion of the rules, but sometimes these are not even consistent. When one knocks out four marbles, he announces that he can have four turns, and the other seems to accept this innovation as quite natural. Each shoots from wherever he likes, with no feeling of necessity to agree on a common minimum distance. Each shoots as many times in a row as he likes, and often they shoot at the same time.

This example illustrates how, at this level, play is social only in a superficial sense. Each child plays his own game, and it is clear that the contact with the other player is not what is important. Piaget notes the dual and somewhat contradictory attitude of the child at this stage in relation to others. On the one hand, the attitude is a desire to play like other children, especially those older (and thus is social in intention). On the other hand, the attitude toward the partner is rather indifferent with no felt need to take much account of or coordinate play with the partner. Thus, while play at this stage is social in intention, it is not truly social in action.

Incipient Co-operation (Begins at 7–8 Years)

At the third stage, each player tries to win and is concerned with mutual regulation by rules commonly agreed upon. Co-operative behavior differs from egocentric behavior with regard to the type of respect for rules and the nature of the rule. Co-operation with rules is characterized by mutual respect. That is, the rule rests on mutual agreement and reciprocity. Such a relation to others is autonomous, since the child submits to the regulation of an internal rule whose necessity is based on mutual agreement with others.

Somewhat paradoxically, the criterion for the stage of co-operation is competition. That is, at this level the child tries to contend with other players *while observing common rules*. Children no longer say they have won when they have simply followed rules or succeeded in hitting marbles out of the square. Winning is now defined in relation to what others have done. Pleasure in the game is now truly social because play involves mutual evaluation according to mutually accepted rules. Mere competition is not the primary motive. Rather, the motive is to regulate the game with a whole set of systematic rules which will guarantee the most complete reciprocity in contending on an equal basis. This level is not the final stage, however, as children do not know all the rules, and their incomplete rule system results in a simplified game.

Piaget describes an example of this stage in the play of two boys (one 10 and one 11 years of age) who both play marbles a great deal. They agree that a square is necessary and that a player may keep a marble he dislodges, but they express different ideas about almost every other aspect of the game. When interviewed separately, they are like children at the egocentric stage who lack a common system of rules. However, they differ in their general attitude of desiring to discover what are the fixed and common rules and recognize some need to play by common rules. One boy, for example, tolerates more than one possible method of shooting, but insists that "everyone must play the same" (Piaget, 1932/1965, p. 43). Children at this stage still have personal and incomplete rule systems, and agreement on rules tends to be limited to momentary collective coordinations during a particular game. They are unable to legislate rules covering all cases that may arise, and co-operation thus still exists to a great extent in intention only. Nevertheless, toward the end of this stage, the child understands the necessity of rules as the basis for agreement on how to play. For example, when asked why there are rules in the game of Marbles, one 11-year-old answered, "So as not to be always quarrelling you must have rules, and then play properly [=stick to them]" (Piaget, 1932/1965, pp. 66, 71). Thus, the feeling of obligation to obey rules is motivated not by external coercion as in the second stage, but by self-regulated co-operation.

Codification of Rules (Begins at 11–12 Years)

At the fourth stage, children are not only interested in co-operation but in anticipating all possible instances of conflict of interest and providing a codified set of rules to regulate play. The game is elaborated in a very complex way, and when disagreements arise about rules, players know how to come to agreement. One 13-year-old acknowledged that people sometimes play differently, but said that when there are conflicting ideas, "you ask each other what you want to do." Asked what happens if they can't agree, he said, "We scrap for a bit and then we fix things up" (p. 49). At this stage, the relation to others is no longer *heteronomous* but *autonomous*, since the regulation by rules is mutual self-regulation.

Guess Which Hand the Penny Is In

Piaget's study of the game of Marbles focused primarily on development of children's orientation to rules, which he thought of in terms of the development of moral judgment. Equally central to social development in the guessing game is the development of role-taking or what Selman (1980) calls perspective-taking. Selman has done extensive research and theoretical analysis of levels of perspective-taking in school-age children and adolescents. In Selman's analysis each new level of perspective-taking is defined by a new differentiation of perspective of self and other, a new movement away from egocentricity and a new kind of coordination between perspectives of self and other. This analysis is discussed in our next chapter with illustrations of the levels. Selman's levels, however, are primarily descriptive of development after the preschool years, and our presentation in the next chapter of these levels does not focus on group games. Accordingly, our description of the development of role-taking through group games will focus on children's play of a guessing game and the game of Tic-Tac-Toe.

The levels of development of role-taking in the guessing game were studied by DeVries (1970) in 223 boys and girls 3 to 7 years of age. This game is one of strategy in that each partner is attempting to outwit the other. Each child was invited to make a series of guesses about which of two closed fists held a penny. After each guess, the experimenter put her hands behind her back in order to present a situation of uncertainty (she actually had a penny in each hand to insure the child's success on the first series of guesses).

This game differs from Marbles in terms of the type of relation between players. In Marbles, players occupy parallel roles. Guess Which Hand the Penny Is In involves complementary roles in which players have opposed intentions and try to do different things. Analysis of children's behaviors resulted in description of levels as follows.

Level 0
No Uncertainty
O. No imitation of observable actions

Level 1
Egocentric Imitation of Observable Behaviors
1A. Effort to imitate hider's role
1B. When hiding, imitates changing location of penny at least once
1C. When hiding, imitates changing location of penny more than once
1D. Imitates concealing penny at least once
1E. Imitates variation in guessing different hands at least once
1F. Imitates variation in guessing different hand more than once
1G. Almost always conceals penny when hiding

Level 2
Deceptive Intention
2A. Wants to prevent guesser from finding penny

Level 3
Coordination of Perspectives
3A. Follows strategy of shifting penny from one hand to another in irregular sequence
3B. Follows strategy of shifting guesses from one hand to another in irregular sequence

Level 0. No Uncertainty

The child at this level seems to construe the game as one in which no uncertainty exists. Although she may enjoy picking one hand or the other when asked to find the penny, she has no idea what to do when asked to hide it. She always guesses the same hand, and the penny is thus conceived as continuously occupying the same place. The *object* of guessing for the child at this level is simply to uncover the penny. Children at this level are like those at Piaget's motor or individual stage of play. For them, the situation is one in which to enjoy a pleasant interchange with an adult and have the fun of uncovering a penny.

Level 1. Egocentric Imitation of Observable Behaviors

Children at the beginning of this level are like those at Level 0 except that they make some effort to hide the penny when asked to do so. Hiding, if attempted at all, is characterized by a total lack of recognition of a need for secrecy and deceptiveness. The child may simply offer the penny when asked to hide or hold out only the fist with the penny. His assimilation is that he is supposed to let the other take the penny. This is the barest suggestion of a rule.

In Level 1, the subtypes 1B–1F reflect improved overt guessing and hiding behavior, due to increased imitative skill. Deceptive intent is absent, and the game is still conceived as involving little uncertainty. The players are believed obliged to follow a regular alternation rule in changing the location of the penny.

Until the end of this stage, the method of hiding contains flaws. For example, the penny fist may be extended suggestively, or the empty hand may not be fisted. Failure to appreciate the competitive nature of the game is revealed by desire for the other to find the penny. For example, if the guesser picks the empty fist, the child at this stage may correct him by saying, "No, pick *this* one" (the one with the penny). Or he may try to avoid a mistake on the other's part by telling him which hand to guess before a choice is made. No strong positive or negative affect is shown during either guessing or hiding, except for some disappointment if the penny is not found. The child is aware of a perspective in the game different from her own with regard to *behavioral roles*. However, she is not aware of different *motivational perspectives*. That is, players' goals are viewed as identical, rather than opposed. Both are thought to want the guesser always to be successful.

Correct hiding at Level 1F requires that the child put both hands behind her back, then bring both fists forward without revealing the penny or holding out either hand suggestively to the guesser. Consistent correct hiding can appear as a result of effective imitation (Level 1), or it can appear at Level 2 where it is a result of careful maneuvering in order to present the guesser with a highly uncertain situation.

Level 2: Deceptive Intention

Deceptive hiding occurs when the child keeps his knowledge of the penny's location distinct from fulfilling the role of the hider who must present the guesser with an uncertain situation. The hider is the nonneutral deceiver and the executor of a neutrally presented choice. While she knows where the penny is, the deceptive hider acts in a manner so as not to provide the guesser with a clue to the whereabouts of the penny. She may even act deliberately to give the guesser a false clue.

In describing Marbles, we pointed out that a competitive attitude is embedded in a co-operative attitude to the game. At this third stage we find the competitive attitude in the guessing game. The child recognizes the opposed goals of the players. She often expresses strong chagrin when the opponent guesses correctly and gleeful triumph when the opponent fails to guess correctly. For example, she may say, "Ha-ha, I tricked you," "I'm too sneaky for you, aren't I" "How did you know where it was that time?" "I'm winning lots of times." Cheating may even occur at this stage, though usually in a joking fashion. That is, the guesser may be told he is wrong when he is actually right, but then the child will laugh and show where the penny is. Similarly, she may leave the penny behind her on the chair, but will then show the guesser that both hands were empty and laugh about her "trick." At this level cheating is not seen as violating the rules of co-operation in the game.

While there is an important advance at this level in understanding the players' opposed desires when the child hides, the child at this stage is unable to realize that the other is thinking out a guessing strategy to try to outwit *her*. She still uses a transparent and easily predictable regular alternation strategy (left, right, left, right, left, and so on). It thus seems unlikely that she is actively taking the other's point of view, thinking what the other might be thinking and then deliberately putting the penny in the opposite hand. Players at this level tend to spend little time thinking when their hands are behind them, in contrast with shift-hiders at Level 3 who squint thoughtfully at the opponent and seem to undergo a conscious decision process before presenting their fists to the guesser.

Level 3: Coordination of Perspectives

This level is characterized by what Piaget calls co-operative play. The competitive attitude may serve as the mechanism by which children realize that they must present the guesser with an unpredictable choice situation. That is, the child at this level recognizes the need to be unpredictable in order to achieve the goal of fooling the guesser into selecting the empty fist. Players at this level begin to shift the location of the penny in an irregular pattern as they engage in recursive reasoning to try to think where the other may expect the penny to be next. That is, their thinking is of the order "He may think I am going to put the penny in a *different* hand than last time, so I will put it in the *same* hand," or "He probably thinks I think he thinks the penny will be in a *different* hand and that I will put it in the *same* hand, so I will put it in the *other* hand." The deceptive intention of shift-hiders is usually clearly indicated behaviorally as players take great pleasure in outwitting the guesser and express disappointment when the guesser outwits her.

The use of an irregular shifting pattern appears in hiding before it appears in guessing. This suggests that the child is able to take account of the other's perspective before he is able to take account of *the-other's-taking-account-of* the child's perspective. At the most advanced level, the child uses a shifting strategy in guessing as well as in hiding. She is able to consider the opponent's probable strategy and modify her guessing behavior accordingly. It is often clear that the shift guessers are actively figuring out the hider's plan. Their decision time is longer, they may search the opponent's face as they consider which hand to choose, and they frequently verbalize the recognition of the opponent's intent by saying, "You tricked me that time," "You can't fool me," or "I *thought* you would have it in that hand because *you* thought I'd pick this other hand." At this level, the child not only takes account of the other's role, but she knows the other is taking account of her perspective. She modifies her behavior appropriately on the basis of a prediction about the other's behavioral modification that is in turn based on a prediction of the child's prediction. With this full recognition of situational complexity, there is real appreciation for the nature of the continual uncertainty that is never really resolved in this guessing game.

The findings of this study suggest the fruitfulness of analyzing individual games in terms of the specific ways they provoke players to co-operate, that is, to operate in terms of one another.

Tic-Tac-Toe (TTT)

Tic-Tac-Toe (also called "Noughts and Crosses") is a well-known game played on a 3-×-3 board. One player uses *X*s and the other uses *O*s. They take turns putting an *X* or an *O* in one of the spaces, and try to win by being the first to complete a row, column, or diagonal sequence of three in a line. Players' roles are parallel in the sense that they are both trying to do the same thing. Roles are also complementary in the sense that each player also tries to prevent the other from making three in a line. That is, sophisticated players use both offensive and defensive strategies in order to win and keep the other from winning.

TTT involves spatial reasoning for thinking about the various ways in which a line can be made on the board. Constructing the notion of the line itself, especially the diagonal, is a challenge for younger children. TTT also involves temporal reasoning for thinking about the serial order of turns, thinking ahead to consider future moves, and to construct the notion that the first line wins (the latter being unexpectedly difficult). Social decentering is necessary for awareness of players' opposed intentions, and for thinking about what the other player may do next. Reasoning about strategies involves constructing offensive and defensive awareness, including blocking and two-way win setups. It also involves thinking flexibly about the different options for play as they develop in the dynamic, interactive context.

Fernie and DeVries (1984) studied the play of Tic-Tac-Toe (using plastic *X*s and *O*s placed on a heavy paper board) among 102 children 3–9 years of age.

One at a time, children played 16 TTT games with Fernie while an observer made diagrams of the sequence of play and videotaped the session. The child was allowed to win the first six games and the last, but the Experimenter (E) tried to win the other 9 games. On another day, each child was interviewed about certain aspects of the game. For example, children were asked, "When you play TTT, what do you try to do?" and "What is the best move?" in hypothetical game situations introduced as "games other kids played."

An important part of the analysis of children's conceptions of TTT was a detailed study of the sequence of play in each of the 16 games to determine, for example, how many times the child blocked, failed to block, set up two-way wins, and failed to make a winning line when this was possible. Levels were constructed representing progressive emergence of new aspects of reasoning in TTT.

Level 0: Motor and Individual Play

At this level, children simply explore the physical properties of the game materials. *X*s and *O*s are stacked, arranged, thrown, and used as props for pretense. The game itself has no meaning for the child at this level, who is not aware of rules, of the goal of making three in a line, of players' opposed intentions, and certainly not of strategies. For example, one 3-year-old when told that it is his turn to be first, puts all his *O*s on the board without giving E a turn. When asked where he is going to put his first *O*, he says, "Right there, right there...," and points to each space on the board.

Level 1A: Egocentric Play: Schematic Imitation of Some Aspects of the Game

At this level, children begin to accept the rule that the goal of the game is to make a straight line. However, the spatial idea of three in a line is fragile, and the child sometimes says a crooked sequence is a line. Turntaking is not considered important, and children at this level may even feel the game is spoiled when the opponent blocks their completion of a line. One 4-year-old responded to a block by suggesting, "Why don't you put your *O*s down here [horizontal across bottom of board], and I'll put my *X*s up here [horizontal across top of board]." Such a solution makes sense to the child at this level who feels no necessity to take turns, is only beginning to accept the rule that a straight line "wins," and does not have a competitive attitude.

The child at this level views players as nonopposed in parallel efforts to make three in a line. She often keeps playing after the opponent completes a line, and insists that both have won. Egocentric play such as this is an advance over Level 0 in that the child tries to follow a few "rules" that are imitations of observable behavior. However, rules are understood only in a superficial, schematic way. While the child believes she is playing the game, in reality, she is "following" the rules in ways that are continual violations.

Level 1B: Egocentric Play: Takes Turns Regularly

At this level, turntaking becomes established, though its competitive implications are far from fully realized. That is, children are not aware that turntaking leads to the logical conclusion that only the player who makes the first line can win. Like children at 1A, children at 1B often continue to play after E wins, completing their own line and then claiming they win. They deny that it matters who wins first. At Level 1B, once the pieces are played, it is as though the temporal order of their play no longer can be considered.

Level 1C: Egocentric Play: Knows the Goal of the Game Is Straight Line

At this level, children recognize that pieces must be arranged in a straight line to make a win and never claim a win for a crooked line. However, they continue to be noncompetitive, insisting that both players can win. Wins are not always recognized, and blocking never occurs.

Taken together, advances by the end of Level 1 create more common procedures between the child and the sophisticated player. To the observer, it may appear that they share a mutual view of the game. However, there is no counterpoint of continuous mutual opposition. Play is still noncompetitive. Some players actually remove the opponents' pieces when they are in the way! Level 1 play of TTT is well described by Piaget's (1932/1965) characterization of egocentric marble play: "Though the child imitates what he observes, and believes in perfect good faith that he is playing like the others, the child...plays in an individualistic manner with material that is social. Such is egocentrism" (p. 37).

Level 2A: Co-operative Play: Emergence of Competitive Attitude

Level 2 players want to win, and express glee when they do win and disappointment when they lose. They are aware of the possibility of blocking, but seldom do. Their competitiveness is not expressed in logical strategies aimed at winning. Instead, it may take the form of momentary misleading behaviors that, in fact, do not mislead the opponent at all. For example, one 7-year-old views it as tricky to start to put his marker in one space, but then put it in another.

Level 2B: Co-operation: The Strategy of Blocking

The emergence of a competitive attitude is the mechanism by which children are motivated to figure out better means to the end of winning. Without the competitive attitude, TTT is a parallel exercise in making lines of Xs and Os in different locations. The breakthrough advance tied to the competitive attitude is the emergence of blocking. A repertoire of offensive and defensive "good moves" develops. However, it is difficult for children to determine a best move suited to situations. Faced with a hypothetical game situation where blocking is the only way to avoid loss, Level 2 children nevertheless regard the block as only one of several good moves for that situation. Children lack the flexibility of thought to consider and decide whether blocking or offensive play is best in particular situations.

Players at this level are aware of the opponent's effort to block. In the interview following the games, one 5-year-old explains, "You block, and try to keep people from going your way." Despite this aim, children at this stage frequently do not see the opponent's possible win on a next move and fail to block. Also, despite an implicit awareness of temporal order in the blocking strategy, children at this level still say both players win once two lines are created.

Level 3A: Consolidation of Defensive with Simple Offensive Strategies—Blocks at Least Two-Thirds of the Time When Necessary

Whereas Level 2 players focus in an isolated way on offense or defense, Level 3 players consider both simultaneously, then choose the appropriate strategy to fit the situation. They are able to think at least one move ahead—that is, to reflect on the present move in relation to the opponent's possible next moves. They then decide whether to build a line toward three in a row or to block. Awareness of the necessity for blocking is better consolidated at this level as players block at least two-thirds of the time when necessary and talk more about blocking. However, the newness of the idea of blocking leads players at this level to be so preoccupied with it that they sometimes fail to take an opportunity to win and block instead.

Level 3B: Consolidation of Defensive with Simple Offensive Strategies: Knows that First Line Wins

At this level, children rarely keep playing after E has won, and if by oversight they fail to see the opponent's win, they immediately acknowledge it when it is pointed out. Unlike players at Level 2, they never say that both win. At this level, children's decision times are faster, and they block not only more consistently but more quickly. Offensive play is not sophisticated, and two-way set-ups (described below) are viewed as a matter of luck rather than planning.

Level 4A: Coordination of Advanced Offensive and Defensive Strategies—Use of Two-Way Set-Ups

Although some children at Level 3 know about two-way set-ups, players at Level 4A employ them more regularly. This expansion of offensive strategy is an effort to guarantee a win by setting up the situation so that the possibility to make three in a line exists in two directions at the same time. Once set up, this is a foolproof strategy, since the opponent can only block one way on the next turn, and a win is thus assured on the following play. Conscious use of two-ways shows that Level 4 players think at least two plays ahead to anticipate their inevitable win. Common forms of this strategy include playing in three corners, or the middle and two corners.

When children first invent the two-way stragegy, they often use this powerful offense at times when it is not strategic to do so. For example, although one 7-year-old knows very well the necessity to block when the opponent threatens with two in a line, he sometimes fails to notice the threat as he puts his energy into thinking out how to set up a two-way. In his preoccupation with figuring out a two-way, he thus loses two games by failing to block the opponent. Inflexible use of two-ways is also accompanied by failure to recognize and defend against the opponent's use of two-ways. Nevertheless, the player at this level tries to integrate defensive and offensive strategies. Although the network of offensive and defensive relations is not well consolidated, he consciously tries to take both offense and defense into account. When asked the best way to play, the 7-year-old referred to above says, "Try to block the other person from winning, and try to win." Awareness of and efforts to win with two-way strategies prepares the way for the last advance.

Level 4B: Coordination of Advanced Offensive and Defensive Strategies—Shifts When Necessary between Two-Ways and Blocking

At this level, two-way strategies are put in their proper place as one possibility within a player's repertoire. The more selective use of two-way set-ups adds a powerful offensive tool. Thus, the major accomplishment of 4B is to refrain from using two-ways in the interest of defensive necessity. After winning several games using various two-way set-ups, a 9-year-old is confronted with a choice either to make a necessary block or to set up a new two-way. With marker in hand, she jumps it back and forth between the two possibilities, then blocks and laughs. In response to E's question, "Why did you go there?" she says, " 'Cause you could have gotten it there [winning space]." She thus plans and searches to take advantage of two-way offenses only when this is safe. When E forces her on the defensive in another game, she complains of a lost opportunity for a two-way: "Yuk! I could have gone there, and then I could have gone there [a diagonal win] or there [a vertical win]." However, she yet has room to progress within Level 4B. She is not yet fully equilibrated in her integration of offensive and defensive reasoning, since she twice fails to block as she concentrates on two-ways. Nevertheless, in contrast with laborious efforts of children at level 4A, her otherwise consistent consideration of both offensive possibilities and defensive necessities is more mobile and aware.

CRITERIA OF GOOD GROUP GAMES

Not all group games are educationally valuable. To be educationally useful, a group game should meet several general criteria involving both affective and cognitive considerations. These are presented below as questions the teacher can ask in the process of deciding whether to try or continue a particular game.

Is There Something Interesting and Challenging for Children to Figure Out How to Do?

The teacher's thinking about this criterion begins at the level of what the experience is likely to be from the child's point of view. By taking the child's perspective, the teacher can evaluate the degree to which a particular game might or does inspire children's reasoning and efforts to co-operate with others. In assessing whether a game meets this criterion, the content should first be analyzed in terms of what the child has the possibility to do and to think about. For example, in Drop the Clothespins (aiming clothespins at containers), the challenge of figuring out how and where to let go of the clothespin inspires a wide range of mental activity in most preschool children. After a miss, the child may decide to hold the clothespin closer to the container or in a more perpendicular position, to stand so as to look directly down at the target, to get a container with a larger opening, or to use a smaller object. If this becomes too easy or boring, he may decide to hold the clothespin at nose level or arm's length, to stand on a chair, to use a container with a smaller opening, or to take a larger object. Children 5 years old and older who are experienced with games may be able to figure out how to organize themselves to take turns and to regulate the play according to the rules they decide upon. Three- and 4-year-old children may be more interested when everyone has his own container and pins (in which case it is valuable as a physical-knowledge activity rather than a group game). Interest in the basic actions can motivate them, with the support of the teacher, to think about such problems as how to distribute the pins fairly, what to do when people's pins get mixed up, and how to compare one's success with someone else's at the end by counting the pins in the containers.

Theoretical analysis of cognitive advantages will also be useful to the teacher in assessing the potential value of group games. For example, Drop the Clothespins involves spatial reasoning, physical knowledge, logico-mathematical relations of correspondence, and the construction of number.

Some games cannot be individual activities and succeed only if children can collaborate in following the rules. The educational value of some games therefore depends on the child's level of development and thus must be judged with consideration of how the child uses the game. The different ways in which two different groups of children played the game Tom, Tom, Run for Your Supper may be cited as an example. In this game, "It" walks around a circle formed by other players. He stops and extends an arm between two players, saying, "Tom, Tom, run for your supper." The two players run in opposite directions around the circle, away from It, and then back to touch It's arm. The first player to touch It's arm becomes the next It.

Only some 4-year-olds observed in this game knew which way to run when It stopped beside them. After the teacher got them going in the right direction, most did not know where to stop running, and failed to touch It's arm. Some had difficulty knowing what to do when they met face to face halfway around the circle. Often, upon meeting, they stopped in surprised puzzlement, clearly unable to anticipate this event. Usually, one player reversed direction, and the two ended up in a parallel race back to It.

This game did not elicit reasoning in these 4-year-olds because the basic rules were so difficult that children had no way of figuring out what to do on their own. The teacher ended up literally pushing them around, telling them constantly when to run, which way to go, where to stop, and what goal to touch. As a result, children seemed to feel confused and incompetent. Because she could not think of any satisfactory modification, the teacher simply abandoned the game. This decision was made *not* because children were unable to play the game correctly, but because their particular difficulties made it impossible for them to play without substantial teacher regulation. These children tended to act because the teacher pushed them or told them what to do, and the teacher's corrections did not seem to lead them to know what to do later. They had little idea of why they were running a particular way, and their action was a mindless response to teacher direction, even after several opportunities to play the game.

In contrast, when the same difficulties arose in a group of 5-year-olds experienced in playing games, they were not as helpless. When someone started to run in the wrong direction, other players excitedly yelled to tell them to go the other way and afterwards tried hard to explain how they were supposed to play. Children who did not understand the game simply did not do what they were told. Confronted by other children's protests and explanations, they felt a need to think about what they did and try to figure out how to play differently. Thus, these problems provided the 5-year-olds with an excellent context for spatio-temporal reasoning and co-operating in mutual regulation.

The criterion that a good game provides children with "something interesting to figure out how to do" does not imply that a good game is necessarily one that children can master. Nevertheless, there is a limit to which children can profit from a game they only partially understand.

Can Children Themselves Judge Their Success?

If children cannot judge for themselves the success of what they are trying to do, their possibilities for reasoning about how to revise their efforts will be severely curtailed. Moreover, if children must depend on others to tell them whether they are successful or not, they are apt to become insecure about their own ability to figure things out. In Drop the Clothespins the child knows for sure when he hits or misses the target. In contrast is the game of Bull's-eye, in which children try to hit a paper wall-target with a ball. Since the ball touches the target for only an instant and makes no lasting trace for the child to see, even the adult finds it difficult to judge exactly where the ball hit. To modify this game to meet the criterion, the teacher, for example, might use a board with a large hole so that children can see for sure whether or not the ball went where they wanted it to go.

Do All Players Participate Actively Throughout the Game?

When a player has nothing to do in a game, his mental activity is not inspired. Whether a child finds something to do depends on developmental level and idiosyncratic interest. For young children, this usually means physical activity because thought has not been completely differentiated from action. The possibility for mental activity thus relates closely to the possibility for physical activity. For example, in the game Musical Chairs 3- and 4-year-old children who are put out when they don't get a chair usually lose interest. This is not the case for children 6 years and older who are intrigued to think of the decreasing size of the group and who are excited about cheering on the remaining players. The game can be modified for younger children by allowing the player who does not get a chair to join the march again afterwards.

These criteria make it clear that it is not particularly important whether children play a game strictly according to the rules. The educational value depends on whether a game proves to be a stimulating context for children's mental activity and their efforts to co-operate with one another.

TYPES OF GROUP GAMES

In order to use the first criterion of good group games (something interesting and challenging for children to figure out how to do), it is useful to think about types of group games from the point of view of what children do. Thinking about the ways in which they can be mentally and physically active led to the following categorization of group games.

1. Aiming games
2. Races
3. Chasing games
4. Hiding games
5. Guessing games
6. Games involving verbal commands

In addition, two other types of games are categorized on the basis of types of materials:

7. Card games
8. Board games.

The reader should consult Kamii and DeVries (1980) for an extensive discussion and examples of each type.

PRINCIPLES OF TEACHING

General principles of teaching group games are based on theory as presented in Chapter 2.

Reduce the Use of Adult Authority, and Encourage Children to Regulate the Game

A certain danger in recommending group games is that if a teacher takes the correct playing of the game as an end in itself, games may be used in ways that contradict the advantages discussed above. We have observed teachers who force children to play according to the rules and generally run games in an authoritarian manner, leaving children little room for self-regulation and mutual adjustment. However, games offer the teacher a unique opportunity to reduce the exercise of adult authority and promote children's autonomy.

1. *Present rules as coming from authority beyond the teacher.* When the teacher calls children's attention to the need to consult written rules, she communicates that she is submitting herself to a higher authority, along with children. This does not mean that the teacher must always teach a game by referring to written rules. In general, however, it is a good idea to prepare written rules or use those provided with commercial games.
2. *Participate as a player in the game.* Participating as a player in a game creates a more equal psychological relationship between teacher and child. When the higher authority is not the teacher but the rules in the game, children can exercise more autonomy by willingly submitting themselves to the rules and regulating the game accordingly. Moreover, as a player, the teacher can help children become more conscious of the possibilities in the game through talking aloud about her play and modeling the use of strategies and ways of handling difficult feelings upon losing. Also, the teacher may protest when rules are not followed and initiate discussions of what is fair. Such actions have a less heteronomous effect when the teacher is upholding her rights as a player than when she is simply an observer.
3. *When conflicts arise, support and help children discuss rules and reach mutual agreement about how to play and what is fair.* The teacher's role in conflict situations is crucial to helping children be conscious of other's views and find a way out of their difficulty. Conflicts should not be smoothed over in order to get back to the game. They deserve time and effort because it is in such situations that children learn *methods* of co-operating. These methods include negotiating, compromising, and proposing new rules to get everyone's agreement on how to play.

4. *When children ask the teacher what to do, refrain from telling and turn the decision making back to children.* It is easier simply to tell children what to do, but this reinforces their heteronomous dependence on the adult. It is therefore better to respond by saying, "That is a problem. What can we do?" If children really have no ideas, the teacher may propose one or more solutions, but should consult children about whether they want to take up these ideas.

5. *Encourage children to invent games.* Children who are experienced with games will be able to make up their own games. To encourage this, the teacher can provide blank game boards and a variety of materials such as dice, spinners, paper, and pens, and suggest that they make up games. He can be available to help children discuss and write their rules.

Modify the Game in Terms of How Children Think, So They Have Something They Want to Try to Figure Out

This consideration is important in selecting and planning games to introduce to children, and it is also important in the course of play. The following principles should be kept in mind.

1. *Let children play according to their understanding of rules.* Children assimilate rules in their own way, and this is often not in the way presented by the teacher. While the teacher may repeat a rule she thinks children have simply forgotten, he should guard against insisting on rules to such an extent that children lose their autonomy. If children in an aiming game do not stand behind the line and nobody objects, the teacher should not insist on this rule. He may, however, call attention to his own behavior when he takes a turn, in the hope that children will want to take up this rule as their own. For example, he may say, "I'm going to stand behind the line because it's more fun to try when it's kind of hard. The rule said to stand behind the line." When a child breaks a rule, the teacher may try to help the child become conscious of it. He might, for example, simply remark, "Josh decided not to stand behind the line." Or, he might suggest, "Do you want to change the rule that says to stay behind the line, or do you want to keep that rule?" When a child breaks a rule, it is often best not to correct. Other children may, however, protest, and when they do, the situation is ripe for discussion and collaboration in deciding what to do. Children experience correction by other children differently than correction by the teacher. The decision as to when to insist on the rules and when to refrain from insisting is a matter of considering what is going on in the mind of an individual child.

2. *Do not insist on competition.* Although competitive games are recommended for constructivist programs, the teacher should not push competition if children play in a noncompetitive manner. For young children, it is often challenge enough to figure out how to follow the rules that say what to do. As

noted above, the emergence of awareness of players' opposed intentions is in itself a sign of developmental progress, and is one of the goals of playing group games with children.

3. *Evaluate a game in terms of how mentally active children are.* A general principle of constructivist teaching is to "Figure out what is going on in children's minds from moment to moment." In group games, this includes observing the sense children make of the rules, assessing whether or not they have a competitive attitude, and observing the strategies or lack of strategies they invent. Other principles of teaching group games may be found in Kamii and DeVries (1980).

SUMMARY

Group games are advocated because they contribute in unique ways to children's sociomoral, intellectual, and personality development. When the teacher adopts an attitude that respects children's autonomy, children have the opportunity to exercise intelligence and perspective-taking by figuring out how to play and strategies to win. They have an opportunity to exercise moral reasoning by legislating and enforcing rules in co-operation with others and discussing issues of fairness. They have the opportunity to exercise will as a regulator of feelings, and schemes of social reaction that are central components of self. These aspects of development operate and develop in interdependence as the child engages in group games.

Rules in games are significantly different from other rules in the child's life, which are generally given ready-made. In games, children can relate to rules more autonomously, by voluntarily submitting to them, experiencing in a "safe" context the consequences of breaking them, negotiating with others the establishment and enforcement of rules, and generally acting on growing feelings of necessity about rules.

Levels of development are described for three group games, Marbles, Guess Which Hand the Penny Is In, and Tic-Tac-Toe. These illustrate the cognitive and sociomoral value of playing such games and provide guidelines for evaluating the play of individual children. Criteria and types of good group games are presented, and specific principles of teaching are suggested.

Chapter 6

Moral Discussion and the Class Meeting

Lawrence Kohlberg
Thomas Lickona

One of the most common objections to cognitive-developmental theory, especially Piagetian theory, is that it ignores the social-emotional side of the child. This objection is, however, superficial, resting on a confused or incomplete notion of what the theory means by "cognitive" and stemming from the fact that Piaget was more interested in concentrating on the study of cognitive development than in continuing his earlier work (1932/1965) on moral development. In fact, the cognitive-developmental and constructivist perspective includes a unique emphasis on the importance of the social and moral atmosphere in a classroom. This atmosphere is viewed as crucial for optimal cognitive as well as sociomoral and affective development.

In Chapter 2, the way in which cognitive-structural development is in reality intertwined with the development and experience of emotions is discussed. In this chapter, we discuss the implications of developmental stages for the social and moral education of children in the context of a continuing concern for cognitive development. It is easy to maintain this link with cognition because cognitive-developmental theory provides a view of the "whole child." It does so not in the vague sense but in the sense that its theory and findings specify the way in which the conditions for cognitive growth and the conditions for social and moral growth relate to each other in a consistent and positive fashion. Put another way, cognitive-developmental theory helps us understand the way in which cognitive development and social development go hand in hand.

In Chapter 2, Piaget's view of the necessary role of social life in the development of intelligence is sketched. In this view, the intellectual egocentrism characteristic of the child's logic has a parallel in reasoning about social relations. Elsewhere (Kohlberg, 1984), two propositions of cognitive-developmental theories are explained and documented.

The first proposition is that there are parallel structures or stages in the domains of physical reasoning and of social and moral reasoning. The second proposition is that attainment of a given stage of physical reasoning is necessary but not sufficient for attainment of the parallel stage of social, and thus of moral, reasoning.

Cognitive-developmental theory thus tells us that the activities discussed in the previous chapters on cognitive aspects of Piagetian programs can make important, even if indirect, contributions to the child's social and moral development. First, the cognitive activities proposed in Chapters 5, 7, and 8 enhance the child's ego autonomy in logico-mathematical domains. Second, the cognitive activities proposed in Chapter 4 stimulate advance in stage of reasoning about the physical world. Such advance contributes in an indirect but important way to social and moral development. In the preceding chapter, the cognitive-developmental approach to group games as stimulating the development of social reasoning is also discussed. In that chapter, however, the discussion is limited to games, that is, to activities that have a strong play component. As Piaget pointed out, games like Marbles have a rules component that is in a sense moral in that they involve attitudes of respect for rules and authorities. As Turiel (1983) observes, the rules of the game are matters of arbitrary convention rather than matters of morality or justice, except where deliberate cheating is involved. The advice to teachers in Chapter 5 was therefore based on avoiding moral labeling of children's violation of rules. A central part of constructivist early education, however, has to deal with the resolution of conflicts between the claims and needs of children. The constructivist educator should help children clarify and resolve these conflicts in a way that will stimulate moral and social development.

In this chapter we outline stages of moral discussion and decision methods that promote social and moral reasoning in its application to real life situations. Our approach takes two forms. The first was developed by Robert Selman and Lawrence Kohlberg (1972a, 1972b) and by Selman, Kohlberg, and Byrne (1974a, 1974b). It uses hypothetical filmstrip dilemmas to stimulate moral reasoning and reasoning about the viewpoints of the various characters involved in a social problem situation (social role-taking). This approach, like the Lavatelli cognitive curriculum discussed earlier, sets aside a classroom period for a special exercise.

The second approach takes as its "curriculum" the social life of the classroom. It aims to make the classroom a democratic "just community." Social and moral issues discussed are those that arise from the interactions among the children and between teachers and children. Kohlberg and his colleagues have systematically developed and studied this approach with high school groups, and Lickona has worked with preschool and elementary groups. In their work with preschoolers, Kamii and DeVries have also incorporated this general approach less formally into their recommendation that teachers develop a "feeling of community" among children and capitalize on naturally arising conflicts and other situations in which to promote social role-taking and reasoning about social and moral issues.

THE DILEMMA APPROACH

The dilemma approach grew out of theory and research surrounding Kohlberg's moral stages described in Table 6.1. The stages summarized in Table 6.1 and the research findings on these stages are reviewed at length in Kohlberg and Colleagues (1987). The filmstrip program in stimulating young children to debate dilemmas had its origins in earlier extensive work in discussing dilemmas with junior high and high school students (Blatt & Kohlberg, 1975). The first step in Blatt's program was to pretest all of the children in the various classes. The pretests showed that the children in these classes ranged from Stage 2 to Stage 4. During the 12-week program the members of the class discussed and argued a series of moral dilemmas different from those used in the pretest. Since the children were not all functioning at the same stage, the arguments they used with each other were on different levels. In the course of these discussions among the students, the teacher supported and clarified those arguments that were one stage above the majority of the children. When it seemed that the students understood these arguments, the teacher then challenged that stage (through discussion of new situations) and clarified the arguments one stage above the previous one.

At the end of the 12 weeks all of the children were retested to assess the immediate effects of the discussions; a year later the children were tested once again to determine the long-term effects of the program. Twenty to 40% of the children in the various classes had moved ahead almost one full stage. Those who had advanced after the 12 weeks retained the advance one year later, compared to controls.

These procedures did serve to stimulate persisting developmental change. The measured changes in stages represented genuine stimulation of development rather than the memorization of a set of new moral statements. The children who showed change were able to apply these judgments to situations that were different from those used in the classroom. In addition, development always occurred in stepwise fashion. Although all of the children were exposed to the same discussions, changes were relative to the child's stage. Children at Stage 2 changed to some Stage 3 thinking; Stage 3 children showed more Stage 4 thinking.

This initial work of Blatt's has been quite consistently replicated by more than a dozen dissertations exploring varying curricula for moral discussion (Lockwood, 1978; Mosher, 1980). One major replication was the Stone Foundation project (Colby, Kohlberg, Fenton, & Speicher-Dubin, 1977). The Stone project not only replicated the Blatt effect in twenty schools, but it also demonstrated the significance of the three central elements of the Blatt approach to moral education. Any approach to education involves defining variables in curriculum, in student and classroom composition and characteristics, and in teacher instructional behavior. The essential curriculum element of the Blatt approach was controversial moral dilemmas in areas that would arouse disagreement between students or "cognitive conflict" in choice. The essential variable in classroom composition is the presence of children at more than one stage. The central element in teacher behavior was an open but challenging position of Socratic probing.

The Stone project indicated that each of these characteristics had to be

TABLE 6.1
Kohlberg's Six Moral Stages

Level and Stage	Content of Stage		Social Perspective of Stage
	What Is Right	Reasons for Doing Right	
Level I—Preconventional Stage 1—Heteronomous Morality	To avoid breaking rules backed by punishment, obedience for its own sake, and avoiding physical damage to persons and property.	Avoidance of punishment, and the superior power of authorities.	*Egocentric point of view.* Doesn't consider the interests of others or recognize that they differ from the actor's; doesn't relate two points of view. Actions are considered physically rather than in terms of psychological interests of others. Confusion of authority's perspective with one's own.
Stage 2—Individualism, Instrumental Purpose, and Exchange	Following rules only when it is to someone's immediate interest; acting to meet one's own interests and needs and letting others do the same. **Right is also what's fair,** what's an equal exchange, a deal, an agreement.	To serve one's own needs or interests in a world where you have to recognize that other people have their interests, too.	*Concrete individualistic perspective.* Aware that everybody has his own interest to pursue and these conflict, so that right is relative (in the concrete individualistic sense).
Level II—Conventional Stage 3—Mutual Interpersonal Expectations, Relationships, and Interpersonal Conformity	Living up to what is expected by people close to you or what people generally expect of people in your role as son, brother, friend, etc. "Being good" is important and means having good motives, showing concern about others. It also means keeping mutual relationships, such as trust, loyalty, respect and gratitude.	The need to be a good person in your own eyes and those of others. Your caring for others. Belief in the Golden Rule. Desire to maintain rules and authority which support stereotypical good behavior.	*Perspective of the individual in relationships with other individuals.* Aware of shared feelings, agreements, and expectations which take primacy over individual interests. Relates points of view through the concrete Golden Rule, putting yourself in the other guy's shoes. Does not yet consider generalized system perspective.
Stage 4—Social System and Conscience	Fulfilling the actual duties to which you have agreed. Laws are	To keep the institution going as a whole, to avoid the break-	*Differentiates social point of view from interpersonal agreement or motives.* Takes

146

	What Is Right	Reasons for Doing Right	Social Perspective of Stage
	to be upheld except in extreme cases where they conflict with other fixed social duties. Right is also contributing to society, the group, or institution.	down in system "if everyone did it," or the imperative of conscience to meet one's defined obligations (Easily confused with Stage 3 belief in rules and authority; see text.)	the point of view of the system that defines roles and rules. Considers individual relations in terms of place in the system.
Level III—Postconventional, or Principled	Being aware that people hold a variety of values and opinions, that most values and rules are relative to your group. These relative rules should usually be upheld, however, in the interest of impartiality and because they are the social contract. Some nonrelative values and rights like *life* and *liberty*, however, must be upheld in any society and regardless of majority opinion.	A sense of obligation to law because of one's social contract to make and abide by laws for the welfare of all and for the protection of all people's rights. A feeling of contractual commitment, freely entered upon, to family, friendship, trust, and work obligations. Concern that laws and duties be based on rational calculation of overall utility, "the greatest good for the greatest number."	*Prior-to-society perspective.* Perspective of a rational individual aware of values and rights prior to social attachments and contracts. Integrates perspectives by formal mechanisms of agreement, contract, objective impartiality, and due process. Considers moral and legal points of view; recognizes that they sometimes conflict and finds it difficult to integrate them.
Stage 5—Social Contract or Utility and Individual Rights			
Stage 6—Universal Ethical Principles	Following self-chosen ethical principles. Particular laws or social agreements are usually valid because they rest on such principles. When laws violate these principles, one acts in accordance with the principle. Principles are universal principles of justice: the equality of human rights and respect for the dignity of human beings as individual persons.	The belief as a rational person in the validity of universal moral principles, and a sense of personal commitment to them.	*Perspective of a moral point of view* from which social arrangements derive. Perspective is that of any rational individual recognizing the nature of morality or the fact that persons are ends in themselves and must be treated as such.

Source: Kohlberg, 1984, pp. 174–176.

present if any change were to occur. With regard to curriculum, the Stone project demonstrated the necessity of controversial dilemmas. In the control classes without dilemmas, no change occurred. In the experimental classes with dilemmas, more change occurred in the classes that discussed twenty dilemmas than in those that discussed only ten.

With regard to student and classroom characteristics, the Stone project comparison of "change" and "no-change" experimental classrooms indicated one significant difference. The "change" classes all had mixtures of students at two and usually three stages; the "no-change" classes did not.

With regard to teacher instructional behavior, the Stone project indicated one significant difference between teacher behavior in "change" and in "no-change" classrooms. All teachers in the classrooms in which students had changed used extensive or Socratic probes of reasoning: they asked for "Why's." Most of the "no-change" class teachers did not. This difference in the use of Socratic probes was the only item in a 100-item observation schedule of teacher behavior that differentiated the "change" and "no-change" classes at a statistically significant level. Socratic probing, then, was central to teacher behavior in cognitive-developmental moral interaction.

In summary, both the Blatt and the Stone students demonstrated the following assumptions of cognitive-developmental moral education:

1. Moral education is best conceived of as a natural process of dialogue among peers rather than as a process of didactic instruction or preaching.
2. The teacher and the curriculum are best conceived of as facilitators of this dialogue through presenting challenging dilemmas or situations, through probing for student reasoning and listening to reasons, and through presenting reasoning at a higher stage.
3. While no change occurs without any one of these elements in the discussion, the teacher may not be required to supply any of these conditions if the students themselves supply them.

Dilemmas for Young Children

When Selman and Kohlberg commenced work with young children, they assumed the principles elaborated by the research with adolescents. We had, however, two basic questions as to applicability to younger children. First, were hypothetical moral dilemmas meaningful, challenging, or thought-provoking to younger children? Second, was a process of free moral discussion by young children in a group meaningful and interesting? To answer these questions we first developed a set of dilemmas more appropriate for children from 4 to 8 years old than those we had previously used. Second, we analyzed responses to these dilemmas to clarify stages of moral reasoning in younger children. Third, we engaged children from kindergarten to second grade in discussing these dilemmas in both small groups and in whole classrooms. Somewhat to our surprise, and that of the teachers, young children really became involved in these discussions and would enthusiastically discuss a single dilemma for up to half an hour. Apart from their specifically moral nature, the dilemmas presented very concrete situations about which children could take sides, disagree, and discuss. Most children enjoyed the process. For many of the teachers, it was a new experience to hear their children engaged in sustained, spontaneous group discussion and disagreement in the classroom.

In terms of relevance to younger children, the following moral issues were selected and two dilemmas constructed for each issue:

1. Truth-telling
2. Taking turns or reciprocity
3. Promise-keeping
4. Property rights
5. Rules

In constructing the dilemmas, we had the following criteria in mind:

1. They present dramatic stories which are enjoyable and involving for children of this age to watch.
2. They present a conflict between two or more values understood by children of this age.
3. They are open—children of this age disagree about what is right and have difficulty making up their minds.
4. Without giving "right answers" they present reasons above the level of most of the children in the class that may help stimulate the child to make his own level of reasoning more adequate.

With regard to the last point, in most of the filmstrips we had the participants in the drama engage in some discussion as to what to do. They presented arguments on both sides of the dilemma at Stages 1, 2, and 3. We did this with two objectives. The first was to help clarify the notion of a moral reason and to help discussion get going. The second was to make sure the children had some exposure to the next stage of reasoning above their own.

These objectives made sense in terms of previous experimental research with adolescents (Rest, 1973) which found, (1) that children comprehend their own stage and all lower stages; (2) they sometimes comprehend the next stage up but not more than one stage up; (3) when they do comprehend reasoning at the next stage up, they prefer it to all lower stages, including their own, and (4) when children are exposed to reasoning at various stages they essentially assimilate or increase their usage only of the next stage up.

A Sample Dilemma: Holly's Dilemma

An example of our filmstrip dilemmas is that of Holly, a girl who likes to climb trees. After falling from a tree she was climbing, she promises her father not to climb trees any more. Subsequently she comes upon some friends, one of whom owns a kitten that is up in a tree and can't get down. None of the other children is a good enough climber to get up to the kitten, so they ask Holly to climb the tree and rescue it. Should she break her promise to save the kitten? Here are the arguments pro and con which the children in the filmstrip present:

Jennifer: Yeah, Holly, you're always supposed to keep a promise. Besides, your Dad is right, you could get hurt if you climb up that high. (Stage 1, literal obedience to rules or authority backed by concern about punishment or injury.)

Barry: Holly, you don't always have to keep a promise if you have a good reason for breaking it. Saving a kitten is a good enough reason to break a promise. (Stage 2, awareness of having a sensible purpose or intention, which may justify disobedience to rules.)

Holly: I'd like to climb the tree and save your kitten, but I just don't know if I should. After all, my father would feel like I let him down. If I don't keep my word, then he won't be able to trust me ever again. (Stage 3, awareness of disappointed feelings and shared expectations and of promise as maintaining a trust relationship, rather than simply "something you're supposed to do.")

Barry: But how is your father going to find out? Besides, I think he would understand if you broke your promise this time, this is an emergency. (Stage 2, realistic view of punishment and expectation that people are aware of each other's purposes.)

Holly: I just don't know if I should keep my promise or save the kitten. I don't know what to do.

A Filmstrip Discussion

After the filmstrip is shown, the teacher starts a moral discussion. Typically, after starting the discussion in the class, the teacher will divide the children into smaller groups of four or five. After the small groups, the children are sometimes reconvened to have a "debate" before the whole class. Let us present an excerpt from one such discussion, conducted by Jean Gill, a New Jersey primary school librarian.

After getting some first opinions, Jean broke the class into small groups. Each group contained some children who thought Holly should climb the tree and some who thought she should not. Jean moved from group to group, asking the children to give reasons for their position and asking them to listen to each others' reasons. One group had the following dialogue:

Harold: It's all right if she's gonna break her promise—at least she's, um, saving the kitten's life, and...

Kathy: But it isn't hers.

Nicole: So what, she's gonna get in trouble.

Harold: No, she won't because...she's saving a kitten's life.

Kathy: The cat isn't hers, and she shouldn't worry about it. It's not her problem.

Harold: Then she'll feel real bad in her mind because she hurt somebody else's feelings.

Kathy: No, if she doesn't climb the tree, she won't be thinking—thinking of it.

Harold: What if it stays up the tree and nobody lets it down. It'll die up in the tree.

Nicole: Okay, Kathy, whatcha gonna say about that? Which side are you on?

Harold: Well, we're on the side that you should break the promise.

Jean Gill: But how is her father going to feel if she breaks her promise?

Nicole: But how is the father going to know?

Harold: She's not really breaking a promise exactly, because she's saving a kitten's life.

Jean Gill: But why did Holly's father make her promise not to climb trees?

Harold: Because she might get hurt.

Nicole: But if she's Catholic, God will help her.

Kathy: I'm not Catholic. God always helps me.

Nicole: Well, if you're Jewish, you won't get help.

Harold: Well, I'm Jewish...naah, and that's the truth!

Let's interpret the dialogue developmentally. Harold says, "It's all right if she's going to break her promise. Well, she's not really breaking a promise because she's saving a kitten's life. It's a lot better than just the word promise." Without hearing more from Harold we don't know if his reasoning is Stage 2 or 3. Clearly he has been through Stage 1 and rejects it. At Stage 1, labels like stealing or breaking promises are magical no-no's. Stages 2 and 3 know that sticks and stones can break your bones but in themselves words like "stealer" or "promise-breaker" can never hurt you. "Promise," says Harold, is just a word and words aren't as good as kittens.

Nicole doesn't quite follow Harold's reasoning. She doesn't agree that Holly should climb the tree. Why? She answers, "So what, Harold. She's gonna get in trouble." Nicole's response is Stage 1 in moral reasoning. *What* is right for Nicole is obedience to authority, the father. The *reason why* something is right is punishment. "She's gonna get in trouble." Nicole has faith not only in the authority of Holly's father but of her heavenly father. She says, "But if she's Catholic, God will help her. If she isn't, if you're Jewish, you won't get help."

After Stage 1 is Stage 2, illustrated by Kathy. Stage 2 is not very impressed by the Stage 1 need for obedience and avoiding punishment. Punishment and disapproval are just consequences to be instrumentally calculated. And the basis of calculation is pretty much the self, one's own welfare. One is responsible for consequences to the self, not to others.

Kathy, whose thinking is Stage 2, doesn't agree with Harold that Holly should climb the tree. She says, "But Harold, the cat isn't hers and she shouldn't worry about it. It's not her problem."

After Stage 2 comes Stage 3. We said that Harold's thinking a live kitten is better than the word "promise" was a rejection of a lower stage, Stage 1 thinking. But we couldn't tell what stage Harold's own positive thinking was. Some things he says later help. They allow us to judge that he is at the third moral stage, the goodness stage of concern about others' feelings and expectations. Harold says, "If she doesn't help the kitten and the friend, she'll be hurting someone else's feelings. And her father would understand." Harold is concerned about the consequences of actions to others' feelings and has an empathic concern for the kitten's life.

Harold's Stage 3 centering of moral judgment on empathy means he judges and expects others to judge the intention behind the action. The father should be empathic, too, so the prospect of disobedience and punishment is not frightening. Harold's Stage 3 thinking understands and refutes Nicole's Stage 1 thinking. It also can deal with Kathy's Stage 2 thinking. Kathy says, "The cat isn't hers and she shouldn't worry about it. It's not her problem." Harold answers, "But she'll feel real bad in her mind because she hurt her friend's feelings."

The filmstrip thus suggests why moral dilemma discussion can lead to moral development even in young children: first, because dilemmas and disagreement arouse conflict and rethinking; second, because exposure to the reasoning of other children at a higher stage leads to some assimilaton. Exposure to the dilemma and to Harold's Stage 2 and 3 thinking helps Nicole to move from Stage 1 to Stage 2. When Harold says, "What if it stays up in the tree, it'll die." Nicole comments, "Okay, Kathy, what are you gonna say about that?" Nicole has picked up some of Harold's Stage 2 and 3 concern about value consequences to the cat and changes her mind.

Research Evaluation of Filmstrip Discussions

Research suggests that discussions like Jean Gill's do lead to moral development, development not found in elementary classrooms without this focus (Selman & Lieberman, 1974). In the fall of 1974, Selman ran a brief workshop for Cambridge, Massachusetts, second-grade teachers and then asked them to present filmstrip dilemmas to their classes and to lead discussions of them as Jean Gill did. There were 10 periods of filmstrip discussions over a period of 5 weeks. Some of the teachers were sufficiently excited by the moral discussions that they continued them for the remainder of the year, bringing in their own dilemmas or having the students bring theirs. The children in the three experimental classes were interviewed just before the discussions. They were interviewed about the dilemmas they would later discuss as well as some test dilemmas. At the end of the year they were reinterviewed. These interviews were used to define the the children's stage before and after the discussion experiment. Before the discussions almost all the children in all three classes were at our first stage of moral reasoning. After the discussions, one-third of the children in the experimental classes had moved ahead one stage to our second stage. Selman picked as controls two additional classrooms where the children had no moral discussion during the year. In these control classes, all the children were still Stage 1 at the end of the year. No one in the control group had moved a stage, as had one-third of the experimental children.

Filmstrip Dilemmas for Social Reasoning

We have discussed at some length the processes of filmstrip discussion to stimulate moral reasoning. Selman, Kohlberg, and Byrne (1972) also developed a complementary film-strip series to stimulate social reasoning or social perspective-taking. The series are complementary in the sense that there are stages of social perspective-taking parallel to the moral stages. Social perspective stages are more general than moral stages, and attainment of a given level of perspective-taking is necessary but not sufficient for attainment of the parallel moral stage. For these reasons and others, a program for developing social reasoning is a parallel necessary prerequisite for a program aimed at developing moral reasoning.

The filmstrip program for social reasoning broke the domain into the following aspects, with two filmstrip situations for each aspect:

1. *Problem-solving prediction of the behavior of the other ("How do you know what others will do?")*—Situation 1: Two children have lost one another— how should the search behavior of each take into account that of the other? Situation 2: A pet parrot is released from its cage and disappears. Which person might have had the intention to let it go?
2. *Affective perspective-taking ("How would you feel?")*—Situation 1: How would a friend feel if he's given a puppy to replace a lost dog? Situation 2: How would an old friend feel if the protagonist goes to an exhibition with a new friend at the time when the old friend wants to meet with her?
3. *Decisions of fairness ("How do you know what's fair?")*—Two peer moral dilemmas similar to those already discussed.
4. *Persuasion and communication ("How can you work things out?")*—Situation 1: persuading a new boy in the neighborhood to join a hockey team. Situation 2: A girl goes to a rodeo at the last minute after telling a friend she is not going. She meets her friend at the rodeo and seems to be caught in a lie. How can she explain it to her friend?

Each of these situations was designed to elicit the Selman (1980) levels of perspective-taking found in children aged 3 to 9.

A Sample Dilemma: Greg's Dilemma

To illustrate, we shall present the first of the two filmstrip dilemmas involving affective role-taking, Greg's dilemma. Tom and Greg try to figure out what to get their friend Mike for his birthday. Greg has already bought some checkers for Mike, but Tom cannot decide whether to get Mike a football or a little toy truck. The boys see Mike across the street and decide to try to find out what he would like for his birthday.

Greg and Tom ask Mike about trucks and football, but nothing seems to interest him. He is very sad because his dog, Pepper, has been lost for two weeks. Mike's family has put an advertisement in the paper for Pepper, but there seems to be no chance of getting him back. When Greg suggests that Mike could get a new dog, Mike says it wouldn't be the same as having Pepper. He says he does not even like to look at other dogs because they make him miss Pepper so much. Nearly crying, he leaves to go home.

Tom still does not know what to buy Mike. On their way to the toy store, Tom and Greg pass a store with a sign in the window, "Puppies for Sale." There are only two dogs left and both are cute. Should Tom get Mike a puppy for his birthday? Greg remembers what Mike said about not liking to even look at other dogs, but Tom thinks he would be happy with the puppy because it would be his. Greg thinks that getting a puppy might make Mike sad and spoil his birthday. The filmstrip ends as Tom says, "I know what I'll do."

Discussing the Filmstrip

A somewhat simplified version of the Selman perspective-taking levels in relation to the puppy dilemma is as follows:

Selman's Stages of Perspective Taking

- Level One: *Egocentric perspective taking (about ages four to six).* The child has difficulty distinguishing between his view and those of others. He reasons that his point of view is the true perspective, not because he is right and others are wrong, but because he is unaware that others may have a different perspective. He may say in response to the puppy dilemma, "Tom should give Mike a puppy. I like puppies. Puppies are fun." He does not consider the possibility that Mike may not want a puppy.
- Level Two: *Informational perspective taking (about ages six to eight).* The child sees himself and other people as having possibly different interpretations of the same social situation, depending upon how much information each has. However, he cannot put himself in another's place because he does not realize that another person can think about what he is thinking. A child at this level may respond to the puppy story like this. "Mike said he doesn't want a puppy. Tom likes puppies, but he shouldn't get one for Mike."
- Level Three: *Self-reflective perspective taking (about ages eight to ten).* The child becomes aware that people think or feel differently from one another, not only because they have different information, but also because they have different values. The child can put himself in other people's shoes, and, in doing this, he can see himself through their eyes. He understands that one person can think about another's views. A child at this level may answer, "If I were Mike, I'd want a puppy. Maybe Mike just doesn't know how he would feel if he had a new dog."
- Level Four: *Mutual perspective taking (about ages ten to twelve).* The child realizes that both he and other people are thinking about each other's views at

the same time. The child can view his own interactions with people as if he were a bystander. A child at the level of mutual perspective taking may say, "Well, if Tom gets Mike a puppy and Mike doesn't like it, Tom still knows Mike will understand that he was only trying to make him happy." At this level the child understands that people can be simultaneously and mutually aware of their own and others' motivations. (Selman, Byrne, & Kohlberg, 1974, p. 8)

To illustrate the levels we reproduce an edited discussion conducted by Shirley Ponman, a New York City public school teacher, with her second grade class.

Shirley Ponman: "Okay, arrange your discussion groups into circles so that you can see each other. You can talk to each other better that way. Now try and think what you think Tom decided to do. Did he buy Mike the puppy or not?"

Donna: "Well, I think that the boy shouldn't buy the dog because he might hurt his feelings, and then he'd think of his other dog, and then he might cry."

Arthur: "I don't think he should buy it either, 'cause if you buy something for the other person that he doesn't like, he might get mad at you or something and not be your friend."

Beth: "But imagine if you were Mike and you lost a dog—would you feel happy if you got another one? Or one of its relatives or something? Besides, I think he should be glad because at least he got another dog."

Donna thinks that a new puppy would not be a good gift because Mike will be sad. She accepts Mike's comments at face value, which is characteristic of level two. She doesn't consider that Mike might realize that Tom had good intentions or that Mike's own feelings might change over a period of time.

Arthur also thinks that Tom will not give Mike the puppy. But he considers not only Mike's feelings about the puppy but his possible reaction to Tom as well. This ability is indicative of level three. He agrees with Donna but his opinion is based on a higher level of social reasoning.

Like Arthur, Beth is able to reflect on her reactions in someone else's shoes, a level-three ability, but this leads her to suggest buying the puppy for Mike, the opposite of Arthur's suggestion.

Children can be at the same level, like Arthur and Beth, and disagree as to what they think will happen. Or they can agree, like Donna and Arthur, but for different reasons. This promotes discussion.

The teacher may also try to encourage children to relate the problems presented in the filmstrip to events that they have experienced in their own lives.

Michele: "We had to give away our dog, and then we got a new one."

Jean: "How did you feel?"

Michele: "Well, at first I wasn't so happy about it. But then I forgot all about the other dog, and now the dog we have, I feel pretty good about it. So sometimes you're going to feel bad in the beginning and then later on you're going to feel real good about it."

Michael: "One time I had a dog and he ran away. And he never came back. My father went and bought me a new dog but I wasn't really sure I wanted him. But then after a while I started getting used to the dog that my father bought me and it sort of took the place of the other dog. But I still didn't like him as much as the other one because I wanted the other one back."

Besides using questions to keep the discussion going and to relate the dilemma to children's experiences, the teacher sometimes asks the children to role-play endings they have proposed. This helps them understand how they would feel if they were one of the characters in the dilemma.

James: "I don't think Tom should get Mike the puppy; it'll just make him feel worse."

Melanie: "Yeah, but I bet Mike would like it after a while. Little puppies are so cute."

Shirley Ponman: "Okay, Melanie, why don't you be Tom and pretend you get Mike the puppy. All right, James, now you be Mike and see how you would feel."

Melanie: "Happy birthday, Mike. Here's your present."

James: "Oh, it's a puppy."

Melanie: "I thought a new dog might make you feel better."

James: "I didn't say I wanted a new dog. I want Pepper back."

Melanie: "Yeah, but don't you think the puppy's cute?"

James: "Well, yeah, he is, kind of. I guess I'm glad to have a dog, even if it isn't Pepper."

Melanie: "You mean you like him? You're not mad?"

James: "No. He's kind of a cute puppy."

Melanie: "Hey, James, how come you changed your mind? You said Mike wouldn't want a dog and he'd be mad at Tom?"

James: "Well, I just felt different when I was pretending to be Mike."

James, then, has moved from Selman's Level 2 to Level 3 "seeing himself through the other's eyes" on the puppy story through role-playing.

A BROADER APPROACH TO SOCIAL-MORAL EDUCATION: CREATING A JUST COMMUNITY IN THE CLASSROOM

Why is it not enough for a teacher to do hypothetical social-moral[1] dilemma discussions and group games? Obviously, these are limited approaches, each

---

1. In other chapters, we have used the term *sociomoral* to cover the general relation of thought and action in relation to other people and groups. The sociomoral domain includes both social perspective taking and moral judgment, but social perspective taking can be done without moral judgment. There are many tests of social development. When we talk about assessment of moral development, we are talking about Kohlberg's assessment of moral judgment. Social development centers on capacity to take the point of view of others. Moral development basically refers to a sense of obligation to take the point of view of others in making value judgments and judgments of obligation in relation to others.

with some strengths and some shortcomings. Preplanned dilemmas like the one about Holly and the stranded kitten have the advantage of being balanced moral conflicts with the potential of inspiring the kind of conflict within and between children that leads to the development of better moral reasoning. Such dilemmas also have the virtue of being nonpersonal problems that may make it easier for children to listen openly to all sides of the argument. The strengths of the preplanned dilemmas, however, are also their weaknesses. Because they are hypothetical rather than real and immediate, they may be met with indifference on the part of children. An exclusive diet of hypothetical moral dilemmas, moreover, amounts to a moral education curriculum that is all talk and no action. Children are always debating somebody else's moral problem; they are never called upon to apply their moral logic to their own individual or group behavior.

Group games have the merit of going beyond merely talking about morality. They offer children the opportunity to experience what Piaget called the "moral necessity" of rules. Rules make the group activity—the game—possible: No rules, no game. The limitation of group games as social-moral education is that children must learn that taking the other guy's perspective and being fair are not just something you do when you play a game. They're what you should do all of the time.

Most teachers would readily agree that it is artificial and inadequate to have a few hours a week that is "moral and social development time." Just as the development of the child's logical reasoning must be continually fostered through a wide range of classroom activities, so, too, must the development of social-moral reasoning and behavior.

How then can a teacher conduct a program for social-moral development that is adequate to the needs of the child? The best way, we submit, is to build a just community in the classroom. In this approach, the social-moral curriculum is all-inclusive. It encompasses both the learning patterns that make up the academic curriculum and all the roles, rules, relationships, and interactions that make up the "human curriculum." The overarching goal is to create a classroom community in which the ideals of justice and co-operation become lived realities for children.

Background and Work with Older Children

The theoretical foundations of the "just community" approach to social and moral education through classroom democracy and co-operative projects were laid down by John Dewey (1916/1966) in *Democracy and Education* and other works. Dewey's ideas were repeated and supported by Piaget (1932/1965) in *The Moral Judgment of the Child*.

In the Dewey era, some experiments in classroom democracy and rule-making were conducted. Starting in 1920 Marion Turner, a student of Dewey, conducted an experiment in classroom democracy with children aged 4 to 6½ years. Her report, *The Child within the Group: An Experiment in Self-Government* (Turner, 1957), is still well worth reading.

In more recent history, efforts at school democracy began in the early 1970s. In 1973 Kohlberg started consulting with an alternative school in the Cambridge Public High School, the Cluster School, and in 1978 with the Scarsdale School. A colleague at Boston University with experience in moral discussion with high school students, Ralph Mosher, started about the same time consulting with the School Within a School, an alternative school in the Brookline High School. From this experience and its research evaluation has come a well-documented picture of the "just community" approach in secondary school practice (Mosher, 1980; Power, Higgins, Kohlberg, & Reimer, 1986). The research shows that school democracy, developmentally designed, stimulates stage advance both independently and in conjunction with classroom dilemma discussion. Parallel work at the early childhood level carried out by Tom Lickona consulting with preschool and elementary teachers, primarily in Cortland, New York, forms the experience base for the remainder of this chapter.

Involving Children in Making Rules for the Classroom

The research on moral reasoning in early childhood points consistently to this conclusion: Young children have a spontaneous tendency to view rules as the constraints that big people impose upon little people. Might makes right. Asked why children should obey their parents, for example, one 4-year-old replied, "Because children are the slaves of parents. We have to follow your orders."

As all parents and teachers know, however, the same 4-year-old who sincerely asserts the absolute right of adults to be the boss nevertheless fails to follow adults' rules much of the time. How do we make sense out of this inconsistency between judgment and action? One answer is that for the child who equates morality with obedience to the arbitrary decisions of adults, rules have no inner logic, no felt necessity, no perceived practical purpose in social relations—and hence no real grip on behavior. Morality is not yet "on the inside."

The way to get morality on the inside is not simply to try to put it there. Straightforward didactic moral instruction certainly has a place·in the education of the child, just as direct advocacy of justice has a place in the moral education of adolescents. But telling is not enough. Children must simultaneously *construct* or invent their moral understandings, much as they construct logical understandings like conservation, from the raw material of their firsthand experience. In the domain of social-moral development, that raw material consists of their day-to-day social interactions.

Challenging children to think about the rules that should govern the social life of the classroom is a basic way to stimulate their construction of moral knowledge. A teacher can pose questions such as:

1. What is a rule?
2. Why do we have rules?

3. Who should make the rules in a classroom? Why?
4. Should teachers have to follow the same rules as children? Why?
5. What rules do we need in our classroom? Why?
6. What should happen if a person breaks a rule?
7. Can rules be changed once you make them? How do you decide whether a rule should be changed?

Most teachers find that even before discussing rules for the classroom, however, they need to elicit rules needed for "good talking and good listening" in a discussion. Without such agreed-upon rules, attempts to discuss any topic are often frustrated by egocentric behaviors such as talking when someone else is speaking, being silly, getting up and walking around, and the like.

Some teachers prefer to let chaos reign temporarily in order to allow children to experience the need for rules of discussion. This is what Gloria Norton, a kindergarten teacher, did. She began her first class meeting with a discussion of the word "co-operation" introduced by reading the fable of the chicken and the wheat. She and the children then discussed the book, naming different situations in which people co-operate. "Many people listened with care," the teacher reports, "while others were disruptive or nonattentive. I waited a short time until I caught somebody listening. This is the scene that followed":

> *Teacher:* Mary, I saw that you were watching and listening to Susan as she shared with us. Susan, how did it feel to have Mary listen to you?
>
> *Susan (smiling at Mary):* It felt good when she listened to me.
>
> *Teacher:* When you listen to me, I feel good inside, too. I want to share with you, and when I look up and see your eyes, I know that you are listening to me.

"We continued our meeting in this way," the teacher says, "discussing co-operation and commenting on listening behavior. The next day we had a discussion about listening. I asked them how they knew when they were being listened to. I was very pleased with the results. They were able to identify good listening behavior. Together we began a list of rules for class meeting time:

1. Look at people when they are speaking.
2. Sit still and be silent when someone is speaking.
3. Everyone should get a chance to share.

These rules were then printed on a big sheet of paper and hung in the block corner where the class had its meeting."

Simply making rules, even with democratic participation, does not, of course, assure that all children will follow them. "The very next day," teacher Norton reports, "we had a lot of disruption, particularly by two boys, Kevin and Richard. They were talking, playing with blocks, and in general disturbing those people around them."

What should the teacher do at this point? If she disciplines the children herself (which may sometimes be necessary), she runs the risk of reinforcing the view of the classroom as a Stage 1 society where the teacher commands and children obey, or else. Teacher Norton handled this situation by asking the group to share the authority role: "Yesterday, the class agreed upon a list of rules. Today we have some people who are not following them. How can we, together, solve this problem?"

After discussing possible solutions, the class decided to add a fourth rule to its list:

4. A person will be asked to leave the group if, after one reminder, that person continues not to follow the rules.

Significantly, the "reminder" could be delivered by either the teacher or another child—another sharing of authority. Children asked to leave the meeting had to go to a quiet activity elsewhere. "After a couple of days of leaving the meeting, these children joined the group successfully," says the teacher. "Later we made an agreement that if any people were not able to follow the rules on a particular day, they would leave circle on their own." Authority sharing thus led to the development of children's own acceptance of and compliance with rules they had helped make.

Providing Support Structures for Children

Setting rules and consequences for breaking them does more than enable children to participate in building a social order in the classroom. It also provides a "support structure," an organizational feature of the social environment that helps children function at their best. Rules provide a structure, a form that shapes or "holds" individual and group behavior.

Frequently when children do not meet the responsibilities assigned them, teachers conclude that they are "not ready"; "not at the stage of development where they can handle that." This misleading half-truth is a distorted application of developmental theory. It is true that young children have a strong tendency to be egocentric. They may not be able to listen to each other in a class meeting, for example, without clear, posted rules, a system for taking turns, a short meeting time, a small group, defined personal space (a chair, a carpet square) around the circle, lots of teacher reinforcement for good listening, and so on. *With* these support structures, however, they can learn over time to listen to and interact with one another. For this reason, early childhood teachers, like any good educators, need to think of themselves as experimenters trying out different strategies to determine which enable children to operate at the cutting edge of their developmental capacity.

With this in mind, let us return to Gloria Norton and her class of kindergartners. Not fully satisfied with their behavior in circle meeting, she introduced further support structures. She proposed a Talk Ticket and a new rule, which was accepted by the children: Only the person with the Talk Ticket could speak. The Talk Ticket was handed from child to child around the circle, with a "pass" option. This new system, the teacher says, encouraged more participation and better listening.

To sharpen listening skills further, teacher Norton often invited someone to paraphrase what another had said. To help reticent children begin to participate, she frequently provided a sentence stem cue at the beginning of a meeting: "A time I helped someone...," "If I found some money in our class, I would...," "A project I would like to do in class..." In addition to "sharing meetings," the teacher says, the class had many "planning meetings, in which we planned two parties and six project days, the results of which we were all pleased with." Thus even 5-year-olds, properly guided, can take on the social responsibility of being consultants to the curriculum.

This teacher clearly gave her kindergarten children many real responsibilities of the kind that stimulate social and moral growth. By suggesting and eliciting new rules as needs arose, she helped them understand that rules are living, evolving instruments of human purpose. And at the same time that she challenged her children to engage in democratic decision making, she did a good deal of guiding, structuring, and supporting. Democratizing the early childhood classroom does not mean less leadership or authority on the part of the teacher, but a different kind.

Democracy with Preschoolers

Can this sort of participatory democracy be done with even younger children? Many teachers report that it can. Fern Cohen, for example, ran a nursery school for 4-year-olds in her home. She had 10 children in the morning, 10 in the afternoon. She asked each group to suggest the rules they should have for their classroom. To her surprise, the children took up this task with energy and enthusiasm. Here are the rules that the two groups came up with:

1. No punching
2. No fighting
3. No running (teacher's suggestion)
4. Don't stick your tongue out
5. Don't hurt the cat
6. You shouldn't grab things
7. You shouldn't break things
8. When you are finished playing with your toys, put them back on the shelf
9. Put covers on the markers
10. Don't throw a toy
11. Don't steal toys
12. Don't pull down your pants
13. Don't put paint on the toilet paper
14. Don't stand on the chairs
15. Eat over your plate

16. No spitting
17. Don't talk mean

We offer several observations about these rules. First, it is obvious that 4-year-olds see their world as full of opportunities to do evil. The teacher who wonders where to find topics for class discussion can rest assured that there is plenty of grist for the moral mill. Second, the "Don'ts" are far easier for 4-year-olds to formulate then the "Do's"; they need help with the latter. Third, although some rules ("Don't steal toys," "Don't talk mean") have a more salient moral dimension than others ("Eat over your plate," "Put covers on the markers"), all the suggested rules deal with behaviors that have some moral meaning. (If you drop the food on the table or floor, somebody has a mess to clean up; if you leave the covers off the markers, they'll dry out and be ruined for everyone else.) To draw out and develop children's understandings of the moral meanings of these different behaviors, each rule, or cluster of similar rules, warrants a probing discussion: Why shouldn't you grab or break things, or steal toys? Why shouldn't you hurt the cat or talk mean? Why should you put things back when you're finished with them? Is it ever right to punch or fight? What can you do instead that's fair?

A fourth observation is that we can hear in these 4-year-olds' rules the clear echoes of adult exhortations. Are these children parroting what they have been told by grown-ups time and again? In one sense, they are. But in another, more important sense, they are not. Though the content of their rules may be the old admonitions of adult authority, the process is new and exciting. Someone is asking them what *they* think the rules should be. They feel, therefore, a new sense of ownership of the rules. They experience them as *theirs*. And in the case of these children, that feeling showed up unmistakably in their social-moral behavior. "By the end of the week," the teacher reports, "the children were constantly reminding each other about their rules and creating new ones." She continues:

> Quite spontaneously, they would say things like, "Fern, sharing cookie cutters is a rule!" and, "I know a good rule—'No pinching, screaming, or yelling.'" They were very proud of their ability to come up with these new rules. We daily added the new ones to our list.
>
> During play, I could hear children talking about rules they had at home. For example: "When we don't treat our toys nice, Mom says to treat them nice—that's a rule!" and, "My Mom says, 'Don't smack your lips!' That's part of our rules."
>
> The children have become very much aware that rules exist inside and outside of the classroom. Parents even mention that their children are talking about rules at home, saying things like, "You have to have rules, you know."

Assessing the Developmental Meaning of Young Children's Rule Making

We do not have a report from this teacher about what happened in the weeks that followed. But we can safely predict that once the novelty of rule making wore off, the difficult task of getting children to follow their rules would remain. Support structures for that (e.g., visible reminders, follow-up discussions) would have to be found. And even with the most helpful of supports, the struggle to translate awareness into action—cognitive understanding into operative behaviors—would be an ongoing one.

Besides wondering about the enduring behavioral effects of the 4-year-olds' "adventure in rules," we might question its cognitive significance. Because children were able to make rules and treat them—at least for a while—as a serious part of their social environment, does this mean they have made a structural advance in their stage of moral reasoning? In the course of a week, could they possibly have moved from a Stage 1 view that rules are adults' orders to a Stage 2 view that rules are mutually beneficial agreements about how to behave? Without individually interviewing children and probing their reasoning, we cannot be sure. Since the research shows that stage advance is normally quite slow, it seems unlikely that change in the "deep structure" of the child's thinking would have occurred in so short a time.

And yet, something important happened. It may be that this teacher tapped into children's "practical moral judgment," which Piaget (1932/1965) believes runs ahead of the more "reflective judgment" that children use when asked to reason abstractly about hypothetical problems. In their concrete, familiar, real-life social interactions, these children may have had an understanding of the purpose of rules that is more mature than anything that would show up on a formal test of moral reasoning. Anecdotes about flashes of fairness or sensitive social understanding on the part of even very young children lend plausibility to the idea that children can do things in their natural social ecology that they would not do outside it. Or, less optimistically, it might well be if you scratched the surface of the rules these children made themselves, you would still find Stage 1 thinking underneath ("You shouldn't break a rule because the teacher will get mad"). Their respect for rules might still be heteronomous though democratically made.

Even if the last analysis were true—even if these children had not yet worked out higher-stage reasons for obeying rules—their experience still has value. They are engaged in a behavioral process of *acting on their social environment* in ways that open the door to the eventual development of more sophisticated social-moral reasoning. They are, in their group discussions, taking more initiative, doing more thinking, actively constructing rules instead of passively relating to them as external givens. In short, they are beginning to relate to their social world in ways that will make it easier to have equal-to-equal, reciprocal social interactions based on mutual respect that ultimately stimulate structural social-moral development. To take another example, a child who behaves in a friendly, helpful way toward others creates opportunities for friendships and other positive interactions, which then provide a context for developing his ability to take another's perspective and reason fairly. For this reason, teachers should encourage children to perform what we might loosely call "Stage 3 behaviors" of

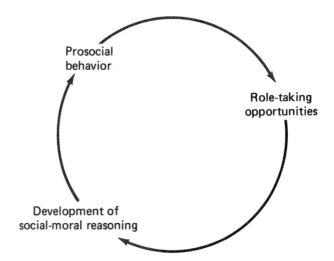

Figure 6.1

mutual caring and group responsibility long before they are capable of a full Stage 3 understanding of the Golden Rule. Viewed in this way, behavior and reasoning exist in a dynamic, interactive relationship (Figure 6.1). Prosocial behavior (rule making, group problem solving, co-operative work or play) leads to opportunities to take the role or perspective of others, which in turn leads to advances in social-moral reasoning, which in turn provides better reasons for engaging in prosocial behavior. This behavior-role-taking-reasoning loop is, we believe, an improvement over developmental psychology's earlier tendency to portray behavior as an outcome of reasoning without considering reasoning as a possible outcome of behavior.

The Developmental Benefits of Group Decision Making

We have urged teachers to involve even young children in group decision making about the life of the classroom. As teachers who have tried it will attest, this process takes time, patience, and persistence. What makes the commitment worth it? What are the benefits for the teacher and children? We submit that there are several:

1. Each child can come to feel a sense of participation in and responsibility for what goes on in the classroom. Such a sense of responsibility and participation has been found to be an important determinant of moral development.
2. The teacher's moral authority in the "democratic classroom" is based not simply on her status as an adult (though that certainly remains one source of her authority) or on her power to discipline, but more importantly on her ability to represent and promote within the classroom the legitimate interests of group members (e.g., their interest in fair treatment for all). Stated another way, the teacher is, through group decision making, returning a real

measure of authority to the children themselves. To be sure, the teacher always retains a special responsibility of holding the group accountable to a standard of fairness, insuring a reasonable conformity to the rules of the wider institutional environment, and the like. But to the extent that children are participating in formulating at least some of the rules that affect their lives, they are required to take the viewpoint of the "rule maker"—something that children in nondemocratic settings do not normally do.

When children experience the moral authority that comes from being part of a decision-making group, they are able to construct an understanding that lies at the heart of their continuing social and moral development: that rules have both a social origin and a social purpose. *People* make rules, and they make them so they can live together and get along.

3. Making rules a matter of collective decision sows the first seeds of moral community. Children can begin to feel a sense of belonging to a group in which each person has positive worth, has the right to speak and be heard, and where people try to be fair to one another without being forced to do so by adult authority.

4. When children feel responsibility for the rules of the classroom and part of the group that makes them, they are more likely to respect the rules in their behavior than when they have no hand in making or enforcing them. Morality begins to be internal rather than external. As a third-grade girl said to her teacher, "It feels weird to break your own rules.... It's like disobeying your own self!"

5. As children's felt responsibility, sense of membership in the community, and actual behavior changes, so, too, does the "moral atmosphere" of the classroom. Moral atmosphere can be defined as the stage of the norms or behavioral expectations in the group. This "group stage" in turn has real impact on the ongoing development of social-moral reasoning and behavior of individual children.

Using Conflict to Promote Social-Moral Development

Democratic decision making about classroom rules is one way to foster the social-moral development of individual children and the group's development into a just community. Group meetings, however, tend to tax the limits of young children's ability to sit still and pay attention. Experienced teachers know better than to overuse them. What other avenues are open for stimulating social-moral growth?

The spontaneous interpersonal conflicts of the classroom offer excellent opportunities to promote both social and moral reasoning and behavioral application. A moment's reflection tells us that every social conflict involves role-taking (social reasoning) and fairness (moral reasoning). When a conflict occurs between two children, there is almost always an issue of misunderstanding. Each child does not see the other's point of view. In discussing points of view, each child may begin to understand the thinking of the other. Beyond issues of understanding, however, social conflicts always involve the question, "Who is right?" If two children are in conflict, there is an issue of fairness. Can a way be found to meet the legitimate claims of both children?

When children have a conflict, then, the teacher has three tasks:

1. Helping them understand each other's point of view
2. Helping them work out a fair solution, one that takes into account both points of view (which will not always mean a 50-50 compromise, since one child's claim may be more legitimate than another's)
3. Helping them learn the behavioral skills needed to solve such problems without the intervention of an adult.

To illustrate this process in action, consider the following vignette supplied by Julie Morrow, a prekindergarten teacher in an inner-city program for low-income children. Scott and Brian, both about 4½, are working at the Play-doh table. Scott is cutting out heart shapes: Brian is making fishes. Scott puts down his cutter and grabs the fish cutter from Brian's hand, saying, "I want this!" Brian quickly grabs it back. Scott then grabs it again, and a tug-of-war ensues as Scott stamps his feet and whines, "I want the fish!"

At this point the teacher, who has been watching the conflict develop, intervenes.

Teacher: Okay, what's the trouble here?

Brian: I was using the fish, and Scott tried to grab it away!

Scott: I want the fish!

Teacher: Okay, let's cool down. Scott, *show* me what you did when you wanted the fish. (Scott takes hold of fish and unsuccessfully tries to pull it away.) What does Brian do when you try to grab the fish cutter?

Scott: Holds on tighter.

Teacher: That's right. And how does he feel when you try to grab it?

Scott: Mad.

Teacher: (*turning to Brian*) Brian, how does Scott feel when he wants to use the fish but can't have it?

Brian: Mad.

Teacher: What's a fair way of solving this problem?

Brian: Share.

Teacher: Okay. (*Turning again to Scott*) Scott, I'm going to show you what to do when you want somebody to share with you. Watch what happens when I ask Brian the *nice* way if I can use his fish cutter. (*Then to Brian, making a point of keeping her hands at her sides*) Brian, may I *please* use the fish cutter? (*Brian then gives her the fish as Scott looks on in surprise*) (*To Scott*) What did I do that you didn't do?

Scott: You said please, and you didn't grab neither.

> *Teacher:* I bet if you said please and didn't grab from Brian, he would give you the fish cutter.
>
> *Scott:* Brian, can I *please* have a turn with the fish?

To Scott's delight, Brian gives him the fish cutter. The teacher comments: "They played together co-operatively for the rest of the play time. Many other similar incidents have occurred in my class where I have used this approach with positive results."

What were the critical features of this teacher's role as conciliator and moral educator? In addition to promoting role-taking and moving the children toward a fair solution, she taught Scott a social skill that he apparently did not have: the simple act of saying "please." As a result, he now has at least one strategy for *inviting* co-operation from a peer. He has learned that words can be more powerful than force. And he is beginning to learn that he cannot impose his will on others but must instead consider their point of view and elicit their consent. These are obviously all important social and moral learnings for a child.

Note, too, that this teacher used a combination of asking and showing. She began by posing questions that got the children to think. This is a vital first step in a developmental approach. Once the cognitive wheels were turning, the teacher proceeded to her mini-demonstration of how to ask for something. Asking questions *first* gets the child ready to assimilate the lesson offered. This ask-then show sequence both respects children's capacity as problem solvers and allows the adult to teach children important social insights and skills that they might not develop on their own. To repeat an earlier theme: A developmental, constructivist approach to social-moral education does not mean that children have to discover everything on their own. Directly instructed in a new skill or insight, they are in fact better equipped to function independently as they make their way through their social world. Teachers need not feel embarrassed about the direct act of teaching.

Scott's use of the new skill he learned had a happy outcome; he got the fish cutter. Saying "please" does not, of course, always yield such satisfying results. Teachers can help children be better social problem solvers by teaching them many "words to say":

Making a request:	"Can I please have a *short* turn? I'll give it back in just a minute."
Inviting conflict resolution:	"Can we make a compromise?"
Challenging behavior:	"Is that fair?" (to a child who won't share or take turns)
Giving positive feedback:	"Thanks for sharing!"
Giving negative feedback:	"I don't like it when you grab! You should ask!"
Offering a compromise:	"I'll take a short turn, then you can take a turn!"

These social competencies not only can solve the immediate social conflict but can have long-range, general benefits as well. They contribute to a positive moral atmosphere in the classroom. They foster co-operative social interactions of the kind that give children access to each other's viewpoints and ideas. This ongoing interplay of perspectives, as we have pointed out, is an essential condition for social and moral growth.

Using the Group to Solve Conflicts

Dealing only with the children directly involved in a conflict is usually more efficient than involving the whole class. It is also developmentally sound, since it gives the children who are parties to the dispute maximum responsibility and opportunity to participate in its resolution.

Occasionally, however, a teacher may decide that a particular interpersonal conflict, especially one that persists despite individual negotiations, is best handled by bringing it up before the larger group. This should, of course, be done with care and only with the prior consent of the children whose conflict is to be discussed. To increase their feeling of control during the discussion and lower the risk level, they should be allowed to call upon persons to speak and to rule "out of order" anyone who violates an agreement prohibiting "put downs."

What makes group discussions of this nature developmentally worthwhile? They have several potential advantages. First, such discussions can help children learn to take the perspective of the group, something that is an important part of both social and moral development. As children listen to the views of their classmates, they get a sense of how their behavior affects the group and is regarded by it. Second, the embattled parties get to hear "objective" third-party views of their problem from people who do not have a self-interested stake in its outcome. Third, the group, for its part, can grow by taking the role not of fault-finding but of helping the individuals involved in the conflict to understand the causes of their problem and to think of ways of solving it that they might not think of on their own. Finally, when there are many interpersonal conflicts occurring in a classroom, it is more efficient to talk in group about the general problem than it is for the teacher to deal in a "fire-fighting" fashion with the separate crises as they keep cropping up.

A class of volatile 8-year-olds provides a good example of when it makes sense to take a group approach to discussing conflict. This class's typical day was filled with interpersonal collisions of one kind or another. "It's like popcorn in here," said the beleaguered teacher. "It seems as if someone is always poking, pulling, punching, kicking, or shouting 'That's not fair!' Even a *look* can trigger a fight!"

We helped this teacher conduct a class meeting to get at the problem of conflicts in the classroom: When and why did they occur? How could they be solved? After agreeing on rules for discussion (no small feat in this case), we said this to the children:

> We need your help in making a list of all the situations that cause conflict between people in this class. We don't want to name or blame any people. We just want to identify the problems. After we make a list, we'll all think about ways to solve these problems. Okay, who can describe a situation that causes conflict?

Hands waved. Children were eager to relate the many situations where interests clashed. We allowed them to "run" this part of the discussion: When one child finished speaking, he chose the next speaker from among those persons who were following the rules of discussion (a strategy we have found to be effective in motivating adherence to the rules). Here are some of the situations they described:

1. When you don't agree with what another person says, and it leads to a big argument
2. Two people are fighting about what to do, and somebody comes along and takes one side
3. Two people want to use the same thing at the same time
4. You're a new kid in the school, and kids say, "No, you can't play!"
5. When kids tease you, and you tell the teacher and that doesn't help, and then they do it more and more because they just want to make you mad
6. When somebody gets mad in a game and then tries to break it up
7. When you're in line, and somebody cuts in
8. When you're playing ball and there's an argument over whether somebody's safe or out.

After about a dozen contributions, we read back the situations that had been described (another technique that inspires good attending, since children like to hear their ideas repeated). Then we said, "Okay, let's start at the top of the list and have two volunteers to act out the situation."

Again, a flurry of hands. After each pair of children role-played how a given conflict developed, we said, "Now show a way to *solve* the conflict." Children demonstrated a variety of solutions to the different problems: talking it over; having a third person serve as a mediator (instead of taking sides); agreeing to take turns; finding a way to incorporate a newcomer to a game, and the like. One girl, in acting out a solution, used the words, "Let's work it out!" At our suggestion, the group adopted her approach as the class rule for solving conflicts of all kinds: as soon as an argument began, someone would say, "*Let's work it out!*" The parties to the conflict would then try to negotiate a solution, without the teacher if they could, with the teacher if help was needed.

When the class is used in this way, a group ethic is established that makes it easier to reach subsequent on-the-spot resolutions of problems between individuals. When those problems arise, the teacher and the children involved have something to fall back on, to appeal to: "What agreement did we make in class meeting?" The group discussion, moreover, has value as an enriched opportunity for perspective-taking, for finding out all the ways that other people see things. One of the things these third-graders liked best about their meeting, they said, was "hearing everybody's feelings about the problems and getting lots of ideas that can make this a better class."

What does the research show about the effects of group discussion of social conflict? At the prekindergarten and kindergarten level, several studies have used dolls or puppets to depict, concretely and dramatically, common interpersonal problems such as fighting over the same toy, name-calling, ostracism, and so on. Children are typically asked questions such as:

- What happened in this situation?
- How do the different characters feel?
- What are some other ways to solve this problem?
- What would happen if (*alternative approach described*)?
- Can you think of any problems that have occurred in our classroom that are like this problem?
- What should you do if you're having this problem?

Children who observe and discuss these little dramas, the studies report, offer fewer aggressive solutions as time goes on and become less aggressive and more co-operative in their own social play.

At the elementary level, three studies have done formal evaluation of the effects of group problem-solving discussions on children's social or moral development. These studies have reported significant stage advances in social or moral reasoning, and in all but one case, these gains surpassed those of controls. (Mosher, 1980)

Fostering Moral Community among Children

So far we have talked mostly about the "justice side" of the just community and only tangentially about the "community side." Making rules and solving conflicts can certainly be seen as a form of co-operation and a step toward the creation of a moral community. But they are not enough. People can make rules and negotiate conflicts and still not come to know or like or help each other. There is not much human support or warmth in merely being fair. As one teacher commented, "The development of a bond of caring within the class is more fundamental to me than the development of a fairness ethic. There is not enough real feeling in a fairness ethic for it to be the basis of a successful community."

If not from fairness alone, whence comes a sense of community? The source of community can be found within the word itself. A feeling of *unity*, of connectedness, of being part of a larger whole—this is its root meaning. To be a member of a human community in this sense is to identify, emotionally as well as intellectually, with something larger than oneself. Teachers refer to this kind of identification when they speak of trying to develop a "class spirit" or "group feeling."

The contribution of moral development theory is to try to move "a sense of community" beyond the status of a nebulous concept and give it clearer moral and psychological meaning. A community becomes a moral one when its sense of unity springs from a shared commitment to implicit or explicit moral values. The psychological impact of that shared commitment can be enormous. Individuals no longer stand alone in their moral convictions, but as members of a group that both supports them and holds them accountable to their common values. To think of the individual's social-moral functioning in these terms is to inform a theory of individual human development with the perspective of social psychology.

What does all of this mean for the classroom? How can a teacher of young children forge the bonds of community? One way, perhaps the most powerful, is to nurture the value of responsibility for each other's welfare. The teacher can encourage children to help each other in their individual interactions and support them when they do. But if helpfulness is to become a group value, a community norm, it must be developed and acted upon within the context of the group.

A teacher can foster group concern for the welfare of its members in at least two ways. The first is to raise a group issue that affects everyone in the group to one degree or another. This is what happened among the third-graders who formulated a group rule for solving social conflicts to "make this a better class." When a classroom is filled with strife, everyone suffers, and when it is characterized by harmony, everyone benefits. A second way to foster a sense of social responsibility is to make the group a source of help for any individual member. If some children in the class are new to the school, for example, a teacher can say, "How can we make our new members feel at home here? What can we do to make them feel part of the class?"

Even young children can respond to this kind of appeal. Nell Woodmancy, a kindergarten teacher, found in fact that her children, otherwise restless, paid closest attention and contributed the most in circle meetings when she posed the question, "Who has a problem they would like other people to help them solve?" All the discussion then focused on the one child's problem until a solution was reached.

How this sort of group responsibility works in a class discussion is illustrated by the following transcript of a meeting conducted by Kathy Kittle with her first graders. When six of them complained that class meetings on topics she proposed were "too boring," she wisely invited them to bring up problems they would like to discuss, and the whole class would help to work out a solution.

Mark: My problem is I don't have any place to park my bike because the bike rack is full.

Teacher: You feel bad because the bike rack is full when you get to school in the morning.

Mark: Yes, and if you leave your bike on the grass, Mr. Hurley [the principal] will get mad and take it away.

Teacher: Well, we certainly don't want to lose our bikes. How can we help solve
            Mark's problem?

Kevin: Let's build another bike rack.

Teacher: Could we build a bike rack?

Joe: No, it's made of metal. But maybe my Dad [the school custodian] could build
        one.

Erin: Yeah, or we could give each kid a name where his bike goes.

Jeff: Maybe we could talk to Mr. Hurley.

Robbie: All you got to do, Mark, is get to school earlier!

Troy: I know, Mark, you could move someone else's bike and put yours there!
        (*laughter*)

Teacher: What do you think about that? (*Note how the teacher uses Socratic
            questioning to get the children to examine Troy's statement.*)

Robbie & Joe: No.

Teacher: Why not?

Robbie: It wouldn't be fair.

Teacher: Why wouldn't it be fair?

Troy   (*the boy who made this suggestion*): 'Cause if everyone moved someone else's
        bike, no one would be able to find their own bike.

Teacher: So how do you think we should solve Mark's problem?

Jeff: I still think we should go and talk to Mr. Hurley (*followed by general
        agreement*).

The teacher went to Mr. Hurley on behalf of the children. Mr. Hurley found
out that the high school had an extra bike rack and had it moved to the
elementary school. Mark's problem was thereby solved.

Developing Caring Relations among Preschoolers

At what age can children begin to participate in this kind of caring community?
The conventional wisdom, supported by at least some of the research, would say
that prekindergarten is too early an age to expect children to be able to orient to
the needs of others. That view is called into question, however, by the
experience of teachers. Colleen Peterson, a Head Start teacher in a poor rural
area, recounts a meeting with her children that suggests what young children are
capable of when they are guided by a skilled teacher and acting on a real
problem that matters to them.

The problem in this case was a 4-year-old boy named Billy, soon to go into the
hospital for an operation. "As the day approached," the teacher says, "Billy
became noticeably more sullen and preoccupied. He seemed to avoid his best
friends and to shy away from even his favorite group projects." In a conversation
with the teacher, Billy revealed that he was afraid the operation would "hurt,"
but would say no more. The teacher comments: "I decided to talk about Billy's

surgery in a class meeting. I thought that most of the children were feeling hurt by Billy's deliberate avoidance of all of us and also that Billy was not happy with his relationship with the children."

Billy's feelings and behavior are obviously a sensitive subject for whole-group discussion, requiring the most sensitive handling by the teacher. In the meeting excerpt that follows, note her artful and many-faceted role: drawing out Billy; drawing out other children's feelings about his avoidance behavior; getting them to think about why he might be acting this way; carefully reflecting what children say; relating Billy's experience to that of other children; and guiding the discussion gently to its positive conclusion.

Teacher: Someone has told me that he doesn't like the room the way it is right now. He has told me it is not a happy place to be. Does anyone else feel this way?

Blake: Yeah, I do. Billy don't talk to me. He don't let me sit by him at snack.

Teacher: You feel bad that Billy doesn't want you to sit by him at snack?

Blake: Yeah.

Teacher: Billy, is there a reason you won't let Blake sit by you at snack?

Billy: I don't want him to. I don't want to sit by anyone.

Teacher: I think that Billy is feeling bad. Does anyone know why Billy is feeling this way?

Michelle: He doesn't like us.

Teacher: Is that true, Billy, that you don't like anyone here?

Billy: No.

Susan: Well, he doesn't play with us, and that's not nice.

Eric: I think he's sad because he got to go in the hospital.

Teacher: Billy, are you sad because you are going to go to the hospital?

Billy: It will hurt. Eric told me it does. And I want to go to school.

Teacher: You're afraid you will miss a lot of school if you go to the hospital?

Billy: Yes. (*Long silence*) And you will forget me.

Teacher: You think that we'll forget about you when you're in the hospital, away from school?

Billy: Yes.

Teacher: I don't think that will happen.

Eric: That won't happen because *I* will miss you.

Teacher: Will anyone else miss Billy when he's in the hospital?

Blake: Yeah, I will.

Susan: If he starts bein' nice again, I'll miss him.

Michelle: When I was in the hospital, everyone missed me a lot.

Teacher: I think Michelle knows what it is like to be in the hospital. You have been in the hospital many times, haven't you Michelle?

Michelle: Yes, I have.

Teacher: Michelle, when you were in the hospital, did many people visit you or send you cards?

Michelle: Just my Mommy and Daddy.

Teacher: Would you have liked it if all of us had known you then and had done something nice, like send you cards, when you were in the hospital?

Michelle: (*Emphatically*) YES!

Teacher: Do you think maybe we could do something like that for Billy when he is in the hospital?

Eric: Yes, we better do that, 'cause he's our friend, and we should be nice to him and try to make him feel better. (*Followed by unanimous agreement and a smile from Billy*)

The children did indeed all make Billy "get well" and "miss you" cards when he was in the hospital. The teacher remarks:

> I had very positive feelings about this class meeting and its outcome. I had never known the extent to which my children were able to sympathize with and feel compassion for others. Too often I attributed to the classic "egocentrism" of 3 and 4-year-olds what was, in reality, just an absence of situations in which they might demonstrate their feelings.

We take this teacher's experience as further testimony to the importance of providing environmental support structures, like a well-guided class meeting. Such structures enable children to use their available developmental capacities to the fullest and to engage in the kinds of interactions that will promote their further social and moral development.

Co-operative Learning

We have identified fair, democratic decision making and responsibility for the welfare of others as the critical components of the just community. An important means of developing both fair decision making and social responsibility is co-operative learning.

A half-century ago, Piaget roundly condemned schools for behaving as if their major goal were "the preparation of pupils for competitive examinations rather than for life" (1932/1965, p. 405). The school's determination to "shut the child up in work that is strictly individual," Piaget said, was "contrary to the most obvious requirements of intellectual and moral development" (p. 405). You do not learn co-operative morality, Piaget was saying, by working alone.

If we took Piaget's indictment seriously, we would look at the academic curriculum through different eyes. We would see that almost any learning task that is now assigned as individual work can readily be made a matter of collaborative effort. How does such collaboration help children develop socially and morally? It does so by giving them an opportunity and a reason to:

1. take the perspective of co-workers, whose ideas may differ from theirs

2. learn to communicate their own point of view in a way that will be listened to
3. make fair decisions about the division of labor
4. compromise when differences arise about what should be goals and how to achieve them
5. coordinate their actions with those of others
6. feel responsibility for the welfare (success) of their partner or group members
7. develop social-moral understandings and skills that they can transfer to a wide range of social interactions.

To illustrate the benefits of co-operative learning, we draw from the classroom of Judy Kur, a kindergarten teacher who first turned to co-operative learning as a way of dealing with discipline problems. Rather than following her initial impulse to use behavior modification with four especially aggressive and disruptive children, she decided to try a broader approach that might have positive effects on the general climate and interactions of the classroom.

She began by getting clear on the meaning of a "co-operative" project: Children would be not simply sharing and helping but *working together toward a common goal*. The first such goal she gave them was to build a group structure of their choice, working in teams of four and using only craft sticks, glue, and cardboard. To her surprise, she found that the co-operative mode had immediate salutary effects: "The children on the whole worked much better together this way than when they were at a table together but each working on their own thing. Only three arguments occurred."

Over the weeks that followed, the small co-operative groups seemed to pass through observable "stages." At the beginning, some groups floundered for lack of a leader. Then dominant children stepped into the leader's role and "ran the show" while less assertive children tended to hang back and contribute little. Eventually, however, more egalitarian relationships emerged: "Leaders became less important, shy children began to assert themselves, and decision making became a shared responsibility."

A communal "we" orientation also grew stronger in the groups. Says the teacher:

> I could hear children telling others to stop scribbling because "You are wrecking *our* picture!" The children were also becoming less dependent, calling on me only to see what they had done. There was very little idle chatter in the groups, most talk centering on the task at hand. I think this is because they were enjoying what they were doing. Every day now, my children ask if we can play those "group games."

Children were not only enjoying this new kind of activity; they were also developing important insights into the nature of co-operation. When the teacher asked at a class meeting, "What does it mean to co-operate?" these were some of the responses:

Robert: It means to help with the work, like, you know, don't goof off.

Matthew: You gotta talk nice, or no one will listen to you.

Anna: You can't be too bossy—everybody has to have a turn.

David: You help people do things. Like if they can't make a tree, you show them how.

In addition to fostering these social and moral understandings, the co-operative projects had a positive effect on the moral atmosphere of the class. This showed up in children's day-to-day behavior. "My children are kinder people now," the teacher said, "more attentive to each other's needs." A girl who had been hostile and aggressive before the projects, for example, took the lead in befriending a newcomer to the class. When a job needed to be done, all pitched in. "Clean-up time" (one of the best barometers of a co-operative spirit), the teacher reported, "has been cut in half since the projects began."

Co-operation and Conflict

Teacher Kur's experience is not an isolated one. Other teachers, working with older or younger children and in different circumstances (racially mixed classes, for example), have reported similar success with a co-operative approach, though they may encounter more bumps along the way. In any group, some interpersonal tensions or conflicts almost always occur at some point when social interaction, however co-operative, is intensified. More interactions mean more things to disagree about.

These "bumps," however, are part of a healthy social-moral curriculum. Having a co-operative classroom does not mean trying to eliminate conflict, just as it does not mean eliminating individual and competitive learning modes, which both have motivational value and a place in the educational process. Resolving conflict requires role-taking and moral judgment. The experience of conflict is therefore an important spur for social and moral development. The goal of co-operative learning is to help create a context, a community ethos, in which conflict is engaged and resolved in a spirit of fairness and mutual concern. DeVries provides an example of conflict from the University of Houston Human Development Laboratory School in which the teacher attempts to mediate conflict through appeal to fairness and democratic agreement.

The teacher (Ms. Rebecca Krejce) plays the game Concentration with two 5-year-old boys. The children's self-interests clash, and they struggle to resolve the problem of turns and other issues. The thought of the two boys, Yousef and Christopher, ranges from Stage 0 to Stage 2. The teacher invites the boys to find the matching pairs of animals and reads the rules from the lid of the box.

Teacher	*Boys*
Who should go first?	Y: Me.
	C: Me.
You both want to go first.	Y: Bubble gum, bubble gum...(begins rhyme, pointing to each player in turn).

C: I don't like to do "Bubble Gum, Bubble Gum."

Y: Let's take a vote.

C: No, there aren't enough people who want to vote.

The moral atmosphere of the classroom is reflected in Yousef's response to this conflict situation. Teachers in the Human Development Lab had worked hard to give children methods of settling disputes through the use of impartial procedures such as voting and rhymes (such as "eeney, meeney, miney, moe") that designate players successively and in which the last player designated wins. Yousef's practical reasoning is thus above a bald Level 0 insistence on what he wants. Christopher, too, focuses on the method for deciding rather than on what he wants.

O.K., so far we've talked about "Bubble Gum, Bubble Gum" or voting, and you don't like either of those. What do you think, Christoper?

C: I think that I'll just pick who goes first.

Yousef, do you like that idea? No?

Y: No.

C: I'll just pick.

Y: No, I said that first. And then you came and speaked when I was speaking. So, I'm just gonna do "Bubble Gum, Bubble Gum."

C: O.K., but that sure does disturb me.

Christopher's Level 0 insistence on what he wants brings another impasse, with each child repeating his solution. Christopher grudgingly agrees to go along with Yousef, but expresses his unhappiness. The problem for the teacher then is to respect Christopher's feeling, but try to get him to consider a Stage 1 view of fairness.

Do you think "Bubble Gum, Bubble Gum" would be all right with you, Christopher?

C: It's not all right with me, but if he wants to do it (shrugs).

Do you think your picking would be fair, Christopher?

Y: No, I don't think Christopher should pick.

With the impasse reasserted, the teacher continues to give the responsibility to the children for coming to agreement, but upholds the value of mutual agreement. By respecting the ideas of both children, she expresses the idea that conflict resolution should consider everyone's feelings.

Let's see if y'all can decide on
something that you both like.

C: I just wanta pick somebody. I
    don't like that "Bubble Gum,
    Bubble Gum."

Y: All right. Who says to do
    "Bubble Gum, Bubble Gum"?
    (He raises his hand.)

C: Nobody. I don't.

Y: (Turns to teacher) Do you wish
    to do "Bubble Gum"?

Well, if I vote, then whatever I say
will happen because you both
disagree.

C: It's O.K. with me if you do
    whatever you want because
    you're the adult.

Christopher's response is Stage 1 because it identifies fairness with whatever the
adult authority wants. The teacher upholds the idea of the importance of
agreement among players.

But y'all are playing the game, too, I
think y'all should decide, too.
Do you have any other ideas,
Yousef?

C: Well, I'd just like to pick.

Y: Well, you need to vote, too. So?

C: Well, Yousef, the only thing that
    doesn't disturb me is "Eeney,
    Meeney, Miney, Moe." You can
    say that, but not "Bubble Gum,
    Bubble Gum."

Y: O.K. Eeney, meeney, miney
    moe. Catch a tiger by the toe. If
    he hollers, let him go. Eeney,
    meeney, miney... (stops as he
    realizes that "moe" will land on
    Christopher). Wait a second.

C: No, no. You can't just stop.

Y: Wait. Let me pick somebody
    now.

Yousef's acceptance of a procedure agreeable to Christopher as well as himself
turns out to be rooted in the expectation that a rhyme procedure will get him
what he wants! When he miscalculates, it is Christopher's turn to defend the
rhyme procedure when it suits *his* self-interest! The teacher tries to uphold the
agreement made between the two boys on using a rhyme procedure to resolve
the conflict.

How did that work out? What happened with "Eeney, Meeney, Miney, Moe"?	Y: He was gonna get first.
	C: Wait, now let me do it (repeats the rhyme, and lands on teacher). You can go first.
That's what you want me to do?	C: Yeah.
	Y: Yeah.

Letting the teacher go first is an acceptable solution to both boys, so the teacher goes first.

Even though the eventual agreement is based on what Kohlberg would call a Stage 1 deference to the teacher's authority, it is a solution arrived at through a process of exchange of viewpoints and autonomous decision making of the two children. Sometimes educators think that if children are at Kohlberg's Stage 1, this requires the use of firm authority and discipline to match their stage. Even at Stage 1, however, children are open to exchange and agreement seeking, exchange that fosters movement to the next stage.

Opportunities for Co-operative Learning

The opportunities for co-operative learning are everywhere in the classroom. Teacher Kur, for example, went on to "incorporate co-operation into formal lessons—doing group terrariums for our plant unit and a class mural for our study of the circus." Teachers of young children have engaged them in co-operative blockbuilding, co-operative drawing, co-operative puzzles, and various other forms of co-operative problem solving. Teachers of elementary-age children have found many ways to foster co-operation and teach academic skills at the same time: partner learning (the smallest social unit and a good way to begin); small-group projects in subjects such as science and social studies; team research; and even team testing. Teachers of all levels have successfully involved their pupils in co-operative activities such as plays, a class newspaper, or a class project to help the wider school or community.

To reiterate: The moral curriculum and the academic curriculum can be two sides of the same coin. When students work together in a co-operative mode, their enthusiasm for learning and academic performance significantly increases. From a developmental perspective, of course, better grades or higher test scores are not the most important cognitive outcome of co-operative education. More significant in the long run is co-operative learning's potential for stimulating structural cognitive advance. As Piaget (1932/1965) has maintained, cognitive stage development is fueled by mind-to-mind interaction, through which children can compare their ideas with those of others, shed their intellectual egocentrism, and come to realize the necessity of logical argument and empirical verification in the common search for truth.

SUMMARY

Clearly, we regard a real-life just community as the most effective approach to social and moral education. At the same time, we believe that less comprehensive strategies such as group games and hypothetical moral dilemma debates make their own distinctive contributions. The richest social-moral curriculum is one that draws on all of the available strategies.

The Teacher's Role

How might we summarize the role of the teacher in the enterprise of developmental social-moral education? Without question, it is complex and demanding. It requires knowing how to use authority in different ways, ranging from unilateral action (as, for example, when a child is endangered) to democratic facilitation to letting children work something out entirely on their own. It requires all the skills involved in leading a good discussion: posing a question that children will be interested in discussing; asking stimulating follow-up questions; paraphrasing individual contributions; tying together related comments; putting challenging issues to the group; probing for social and moral reasoning; sharing with children the role of running the meeting and the responsibility for keeping its rules; helping them plan how to follow through on agreed-upon solutions to problems; and bringing the meeting to a close. It requires being able to teach directly as well as indirectly. It requires an imaginative ability to devise the support structures needed to optimize children's social-moral functioning. It requires a willingness to experiment, watch what happens, and revise and regroup as needed. It requires an ability to inject variety into the social-moral curriculum so that children do not satiate on any one form of class meetings, co-operative learning, moral dilemma discussion, or the like. It requires practicing what you preach, serving as a good model of understanding and fairness. It requires, finally, a sustaining commitment, despite the inevitable frustrations and failures, to doing what one believes to be necessary to foster the development of children.

The Goals

How might we summarize the goals of a developmental approach to social-moral education? From our discussion thus far, three major goals have been implicit:

1. *The individual child's vertical stage development*, defined as progress toward higher stages of social and moral reasoning
2. *The individual's horizontal development*, defined in three ways:
   a. Increasing use of one's highest available stage in *thinking about* social and moral problems
   b. Increasing *action* that is consistent with one's highest available stage

 c. *Acquisition of social skills* that mediate the widening use of social-moral reasoning

3. *The group's development as a just community*, which in turn serves as a support system for the development of the individual's reasoning and behavior.

There is, however, one great goal of social-moral education that is not addressed here. The ultimate end of just communities in classrooms and schools, like the ultimate end of individual human development, is the creation of a just community in the larger human society, as John Dewey clearly articulated in *Democracy and Education* (1916/1966). In Dewey's vision, which we take as our own, the society is obliged to support the full development of the individual, and the individual is obliged to contribute reciprocally to the shared life of the society.

We have argued in this chapter that there is much that teachers can do, even in the early childhood years, to make the spirit of participatory democracy "part of the bone and blood" of children's lives in the classroom. By building a just community, teachers are engaged in the most important task of education: helping children develop the intellectual, social, and moral competence, the "habits of thought and action," on which the survival of social democracy and individual human welfare so vitally depend.

PART III

Traditional School Objectives and Curricula from a Constructivist Perspective

Chapter 7

Number and Arithmetic

We turn now to the constructivist perspective on traditional arithmetic objectives. Piaget explicitly addressed the problem of children's widespread difficulty in mathematics. He stated:

> There is no field where the "full development of the human personality" and the mastery of tools of logic and reason...are more capable of realization, while in the practice of traditional education they are consistently being hampered." (Piaget, 1948/1973, p. 105)

Further, Piaget summarized the sad state of affairs:

> It is notorious that in classes that are normal in other respects only a fraction of pupils absorb mathematics, and this fraction does not necessarily encompass all of the more gifted in other branches. (Piaget, 1948/1973, p. 96)
>
> The teaching of mathematics has always presented a somewhat paradoxical problem. There exists, in fact, a certain category of students, otherwise quite intelligent and even capable of demonstrating above average intelligence in other fields, who always fail, more or less systematically in mathematics. (Piaget, 1969/1970, p. 44)

Piaget specifically decried the mathematical wastage in schools where children's education led them to fail and feel inferior about mathematical abilities. He felt this waste to be completely avoidable, saying:

> Every normal student is capable of good mathematical reasoning if attention is directed to activities of his interest, and if by this method the emotional inhibitions that too often give him a feeling of inferiority in lessons in this area are removed. (Piaget, 1948/1973, pp. 98–99)

The research and theory of Piaget and his collaborators on the child's construction of number is perhaps the best known of all the Genevan work. It is widely referenced in early education texts and books on mathematics education. Several authors of books on early math education acknowledge a primary reliance on Piaget's research and theory (for example, Dienes, 1960, 1963; Dienes & Golding, 1966, 1971; Lovell, 1961, 1971; Copeland, 1970; Biggs & MacLean, 1969; Ginsburg, 1977, 1983). A wide variety of different recommendations to teachers may be found in these books. Once again translations of Piaget's research and theory into educational practices may be understood in terms of the global, literal, and/or free translations discussed in Chapter 3. Before discussing specific recommendations for the teaching of number and arithmetic, let us review briefly some Genevan research and theory.

PIAGET'S THEORY OF NUMBER

It is significant that Piaget always refers to "number" in the singular, unlike many educators who refer to the child's learning of "numbers." For Piaget, knowledge of number implies a single system or synthesized network of logical classes and relations in which specific numbers can only be understood fully as part of this system. In its essence, the research of Piaget and his collaborators indicates that the child's "construction of number goes hand-in-hand with the development of logic" (Piaget & Szeminska, 1941/1952, p. viii). That is, to understand the sequence of whole numbers requires the construction of a coordinated set of relationships—conservation, seriated (and transitive) asymmetrical relations, and inclusion of classes. The construction of these aspects of operational knowledge of number is not an easy matter as demonstrated by the research that revealed children's many surprising difficulties.

Conservation of Number

Piaget's classic research on conservation of number is well known. Before about the age of 7 most children who establish the equivalence of two rows of eight objects by one-to-one correspondence nevertheless do not believe this equivalence is maintained (conserved) when the length of one row is made shorter than the other. That is, nonconservers say the two rows were equal before the transformation of one length, but that the longer row really has more than the other. A nonconserver bases judgment of quantity on global comparison. Since he has not acquired the notion of number, what he can think about is limited to perceptual wholes. For the nonconserver, the criterion of truth is *perception* not *conception* of number.

To put this phenomenon to a more stringent test, we (Kohlberg and DeVries) tried to heighten children's motivation by using M&M's candies and by having children compare unequal rather than equal quantities. In our modification of Piaget's task (see DeVries, 1971, for a complete description), children were shown a pizza board with a row of six M&M's longer than a row of five on another board. Children were easily able to point to the row of six when asked which had more to eat. Then the six candies were arranged in a row shorter than the five, and children were told they could take the row with more if they could correctly point to it. They were told, "If you don't pick the plate that has more to eat, you won't get any this time, but you'll get another chance later." Even in this situation where failure to conserve meant that a child took the *lesser* quantity of candy, 38% of the high-IQ 5-year-olds and about half of the average-IQ 6- and 7-year-olds (53% and 50%, respectively) failed to conserve.

What was amazing was to see so many children count the six M&M's, then the five, yet still maintain that the longer row of five had more to eat. One high-IQ nonconserving kindergartner (who was almost 6 years old) did not count but was encouraged at the end to do so. When she counted, she was a bit conflicted and commented, "This one [six] *should* have more because it's six and this has five, but this [five] has more because it's spreaded out." She seemed highly aware of the "moreness" of the *number* six, and it seemed possible that she might then change her mind and conserve. So she was given another chance and was asked, "So which has more candy to eat?" She said, "I would pick the plate with five." For her, six was more only when she counted, but what really "counted" in determining more to eat was the amount of space occupied!

Greco (1962) has distinguished this kind of reasoning as "quotity," a level preceding that of numerical "quantity." The child at the level of "quotity" feels no contradiction in saying there are six in each of two collections and that one has more than the other. It should be noted that nonconservation represents progress in the sense that it is an advance over the toddler who can make no comparison between two sets.

Correct counting may be misleading, since many children do a lot of counting as a method for getting adult approval, yet still without numerical comprehension. Reciting numbers each in correspondence with an object may thus signify no more than naming them "Jane, Susan, Bob, Sally ...," and the last number may mean simply the *last object* rather than the number in the whole set. Conscious attribution of numbers as "names" given to individual objects may not be observable in *all* children, as Gelman and Gallistel (1978) have argued. However, it is clear that it *is* observable in *some* children, and is thus something that teachers need to be on the lookout for. Consider, for example, the following incident reported by Biggs and MacLean (1969).

> A young boy was counting 5 pieces of candy. He picked each up in turn saying "1, 2, 3, 4, 5." Accidentally, the parent knocked 2 of the pieces onto the floor. Seeing this he asked the boy, "How many pieces of candy do you have now?" The boy replied, "1, 2, 5," again picking each piece up in turn. The helpful parent then told the child that he had three pieces of candy: "1, 2, 3." The boy, now quite upset with his parent, said, "3 is on the floor." (p. 111)

Correct ordering and counting are clearly necessary but not sufficient for an operational understanding of number, and the teaching of counting must be viewed in light of its changing significance for children.

Piaget (1953) emphasized that conservation of quantity is not in itself a numerical notion, but a logical concept—a logical deduction that goes beyond what is observable in the physical world. It is important, too, to be aware of the fact that operational reasoning about number implies not just conservation but also seriation and inclusion, discussed below.

Seriated (and Transitive) Asymmetrical Relations

The system of whole numbers is a series of asymmetrical transitive relations (Inhelder & Piaget, 1959/1964). It is asymmetrical because successive numbers are formed by adding 1. It is transitive because if A is less than B and B is less than C, A is less than C. Progress toward full apprehension of these aspects of the system involves qualitative seriation, the ordering of a set of elements varying in terms of observable differences such as length, then its arithmetization in the coordination of ordination and cardination. (Ordination refers to the position of an element in a set—eighth, for example. Cardination refers to the total number of objects in a set.) That is, a child may recite the number names serially in one-to-one correspondence without understanding that the last number refers not just to the ordinal position of the last object touched (eighth, for example), but to the cardinal number (eight) representing all the objects.

Piaget and his collaborators studied children's knowledge of seriation with a variety of "staircase" materials but those most closely resembling Montessori's rods (see Chapter 9) were 10 cards made so that the smallest (A) represented one square unit; the next-smallest (B) was the same width but twice as long (representing two units), and so on, to the last (K), which was 10 times as long as A. Children were asked to arrange the cards in a series and to count them. Then each child was asked, "How many cards like A could we make with (B) or (C)?" and so on, until he well understood that the second card could be cut into 2A, the third into 3A, and so on. When this was understood, and while the child still observed the array, a card was picked at random, and the child was asked how many units it represented. If a child had to measure each time to see how many times card A went into the others, it was assumed that he had not yet grasped the relation between ordinality and cardinality. Finally, the cards were disarranged, cards selected at random, and the child was asked to give the cardinal value.

This study revealed three stages in children's understanding of the relation between cardinal and ordinal value. At the first stage, seriation is global. That is, children make errors in placing the cards in staircase order. For example, one kind of error is to pay no attention to bottom alignments, and to make the tops form a staircase. At this level, the relation between order and cardination is understood only up to three or four, even when the correct seriation has been accomplished with help. For example one 5-year-old made a global seriation, was helped to correct it, and counted the 10 correctly. When asked, "How many cards like this one [A] could we make with that one [B]?" he answered correctly, "Two," and, "Three" for C. For card D, however, he said, "Five." Children at this level (those quoted were 4 1/2 and 5 years of age) can count the terms of the series correctly and even understand that the difference between adjacent cards is A or 1. Yet they are unable to find how many times A goes into longer cards simply by reference to the ordinal position. They do not understand the relation between position and cardinal value, even when the cards are taken in order. By direct perception, the relations up to three can be known, but after that, children at this level either count imagined divisions on a card (incorrectly) or judge by appearance. Piaget and Szeminska (1941/1952) comment that "they are in possession of all the empirical elements necessary for understanding the law, but they do not understand it" (p. 136).

The second stage is especially enlightening, in view of Montessori's use of staircase materials (see Chapter 9). At this level (children quoted are 5 years of age), children discover the law of the relation between position and cardinal value, but only when they consider the cards in order. They seem to understand a "rigid series" (Piaget & Szeminska, 1941/1952, p. 138), but only at an intuitive and not at an operational level. When cards are taken out of order or when the order is disarranged, they are baffled. Piaget and Szeminska relate the experience of one 5-year-old who arranged the cards in order, though with some trial and error. He answered correctly how many little cards make the big cards up to 10. However, when the experimenter started down the series, pointing to "Nine," he said, "Eleven," and he continued to count forward until he got to the second card, when he realized the absurdity of what he was saying. When cards were pointed to randomly, his answers were incorrect. Another more advanced child at this level, when the cards were disarranged, remade the entire staircase and counted to find the value of D. He then completed the series but began counting from one with the largest card, and said that D "makes 7, we can make 7 little ones" (p. 137).

It is clear that these materials represent "with the maximum of intuitive clarity the law governing the formation of the first ten finite numbers, each ordinal corresponding to each cardinal and vice versa" (Piaget & Szeminska, 1941/1952, p. 137). The behaviors described above showing systematic difficulties in grasping these relations reflect the same lack of understanding found in the conservation task. Successful one-to-one correspondence does not guarantee numerical (cardinal) correspondence. In counting the cards, children at the second stage appear to understand one-to-one correspondence, but this is not a system with conservation, and Piaget and Szeminska conclude that it is thus not true cardination. Correct answers are still intuitive, that is, dependent on perception of the staircase configuration and on the habit or "intuitive act of passing term by term from the beginning to the end" (p. 138). Thus, intuitive seriation, for Piaget and Szeminska, "becomes true seriation only when it becomes operational, and...it becomes operational precisely when there is co-ordination with cardination" (p. 138).

This coordination is found at the third stage (examples given are at ages 6 and 6 1/2 years), where children immediately find the value of a card, whether it is picked at random from the arranged or the disarranged series. Cardinal value and ordinal position thus have been organized into a stable system of relations. Piaget and Szeminska (1941/1952) point out that seriation prepares the way for number.

Inclusion of Classes

In seriation, each element must be understood as different from all the others. Classification, however, consists of putting together elements seen as equivalent in some respect, disregarding differences in other respects. Seriation consists of disregarding similarities (such as the woodenness of all the sticks) but may, of course, also be expressed as classes. For example, a series may be divided into "those bigger than or equal to" a given element, and "those smaller." Piaget thus points out that these two concepts are interdependent and develop simultaneously. That is, operational seriation implies understanding that "1" is included in "2," "2" is included in "3," and so on.

To better understand the development of this hierarchical inclusion of classes, Piaget and his collaborators did a series of studies. For example, a collection of flowers (B) containing 20 poppies (A) 2 or 3 bluebells (A') were shown to children who were asked, "Which will be the bigger bunch, one made with all the flowers, or one made with all the poppies?"

At the first stage, the child says the poppies will make the bigger bunch because she cannot think simultaneously of the whole and the parts. As soon as she thinks about the poppies, the whole no longer exists in consciousness, and the only thing left to compare with poppies is bluebells. In other words, she does not think of B as resulting from the addition of A and A'. She does not conserve the whole when focusing on the part. In the second stage, intuitive inclusion is possible when the child is encouraged to visualize which of two necklaces would be longer, that made with brown beads or that made with wooden beads (subordinate classes including more brown than white beads). At the third stage, the child grasps immediately that superordinate class B is larger than subclass A because she understands additive composition (for example, B − A = A'). In Kohlberg's (1966) study of 39 children, using the beads tasks, the percentages of 5-, 6-, and 7-year-olds not manifesting class inclusion were 94%, 67%, and 47%, respectively. With a sample of 96 children, DeVries (1971) used 4 brown M&M's and a mint and asked children whether they wanted to take all the chocolate or all the candy. At ages 5, 6, and 7 years, 88%, 69%, and 31% respectively of high-IQ children failed to assert that there was more candy than chocolate. Among average-IQ children the percentages failing were 100%, 94%, and 56% at the three age levels. It is clear from these results that a significant proportion of all 7-year-olds continue to be unable to reason from a grasp of the additive composition of classes.

The relation of inclusion to number may be illustrated with the following protocol from the research of Inhelder, Sinclair, and Bovet (1974).

CLA (6;3)

> The experimenter gives the boy doll LLLLOO[1] and asks for the girl doll to have less apples but as many *fruits* as the boy. The correct answer is given: LLOOOOO. "How did you work that out?"—"*There are six.*"—"Six what?"—"*Six apples . . . no, six fruits.*"—"Alright. How many has the boy got?"—"*Six.*"—"And the girl?"—"*Six.*"—"Six what?"—"*Six fruits.*"—"Yes, that's right. Tell me, does one of them have more *fruits*?"—"*Yes, the boy.*"—"You're quite sure? Because, remember that when you gave the fruit you made sure that they both had just as much, so that they'd both be happy! Show me the boy's *fruits*."— (She answers

---

1. "L" represents apples, and "O" represents nonapple fruit.

correctly.)—"Good. And now the girl's fruits."—(She answers correctly.)—
"Then, one of them has more fruits?"—*"Yes. the girl."*—"How many has she
got?"—*"Six."*—"And the boy?"—*"Six."*—"One of them has more?"—*"Yes, the
girl."*—"Six is more than six?"—*"Yes."*—"You're sure? One of them has more
things to eat?"—*"The boy got more, he's got a lot of apples."*— "Yes, but we're not
talking about apples, we're talking about things to eat. How many things has the
boy got to eat?"—*"Two."* (She points to the two "nonapples.")—"But he can also
eat those (apples)! In all, I mean."—*"Six. then."*—"And the girl?"—*"Six."*—
"Does one of them have more to eat?"—*"No."*—"What do they both have?"—
"They've got the same." (pp. 205–206)

Despite their efforts to foster progress in CLA's reasoning, Inhelder, Sinclair,
and Bovet note that she continued to have these kinds of difficulties and showed
little progress on the posttest after training.

The Interdependence of Conservation, Asymmetrical Relations, and Hierarchical Inclusion

Piaget found a close relation among conservation, asymmetrical relations, and
hierarchical inclusion. This led him to insist on the interdependence of the
development of logical and arithmetical relations, and their fusion in a single
operational system.

With educational concerns in mind, it is important to note, as pointed out by
Piaget and Inhelder (1966b/1969), that Greco "showed that numerical synthesis
of classes and serial order occurs only gradually for numbers higher than 7–8 or
14–15. Thus one can speak of a progressive arithmetization of the numerical
series" (p. 105).

All the aspects of number discussed above are logico-mathematical in nature,
as distinguished from physical and social-arbitrary (conventional) knowledge
(see Chapter 2). Genevan research has revealed that understanding number
involves logical deductions that go beyond what is directly observable in the
physical world and beyond mathematical truths given to children ready-made.
Let us turn now to educational issues.

A CONSTRUCTIVIST PERSPECTIVE ON SOME TRADITIONAL ASPECTS OF MATH EDUCATION AND EARLY EFFORTS TO ASSIMILATE PIAGET'S WORK

Beginning math education has traditionally approached this subject matter as if
its acquisition is a matter of social transmission of truths. This is reflected in
methods emphasizing practice through repetitive drill on "number facts" and
exercises on worksheets. Calculation has been taken as an important end in
itself, number has been assumed a "property of a set of objects," counting has
generally been regarded as the entry into number, and conventional notation has
been emphasized from the beginning. Most of what teachers do in this tradition

is to test children rather than encourage them to be active in constructing number. In addition, to deal with children's difficulties, figurative materials have been made as aids to beginners.

Genevan work on the child's construction of number, space, and representation of quantity indicates that many traditional assumptions and methods fail to take adequate account of the relation of mathematical knowledge to other aspects of cognitive development, and to cognitive stages. Even the efforts of educators explicitly attempting to develop curriculum based on Genevan work have often retained the stamp of traditional views contradicting Piaget's theory and research. These issues are discussed below.

Number as "Fact" and the "Property of Objects"

This aspect of math education reflects both old and new traditions. In the old tradition, children memorized and recited sums, differences, products, and dividends. Flash cards are still popular among teachers and parents taking the empiricist view that "number facts" constitute the essential raw material of mathematics. The new tradition of modern math reflects recognition that comprehension of the nature of these facts must be considered. Math educators became concerned because they recognized that recitation of the "number facts" often has little meaning for children. In an effort to expand the content and meaning of elementary math, number was defined as "a property of a set of objects in the same way that ideas like color, size, and shape refer to properties of objects" (Duncan, Capps, Dolciani, Quast, & Zweng, 1972, p. T30). Even educators explicitly basing curriculum recommendations on Piaget have sometimes taken up this definition despite its contradiction to Piaget's conception of the difference between physical knowledge and logico-mathematical knowledge (for example, Dienes & Golding, 1966, p. 9; Copeland, 1970, pp. 58, 265; Nuffield Foundation, 1970, p. 23). However, as noted in Chapter 2, Piaget even goes so far as postulating different kinds of mental action for knowing the properties of objects (simple or empirical abstraction) and knowing numerical relationships (reflective abstraction).

The notion of number as "properties of objects" led educators to design the well-known workbook exercises in which children are asked to draw circles around equivalent sets of pictured objects. Such an exercise may be diagnostically useful for finding out whether a child knows that four pencils are the same number as four dogs. However, it seems more like a *test* than an *activity* in which a child can learn something new. It is unlikely that the child who has not structured elementary number will learn from teacher's correction of such exercises. Moreover, these exercises generally focus on the numbers up to 10, and many of these can be grasped at a perceptual level, without operational structuring. It would be ridiculous to try to teach all numbers with the worksheet approach. As argued elsewhere:

> The distinction between the two kinds of abstraction may seem unimportant while the child is learning small numbers, say, up to 10. When he goes on to larger number such as 999 and 1000, however, it becomes clear that it is impossible to learn every number all the way to infinity by abstraction from sets of objects or pictures! Numbers are learned not by abstraction from sets that are already made but by abstraction as the child constructs relationships. Because these relationships are created by the mind, it is possible to think of numbers such as 1,000,002 even if we have never seen 1,000,002 objects as a set. (Kamii & DeVries, 1976, pp. 6–7)

The "progressive arithmetization of objects" noted above (referring to the fact that children first construct the network of numerical relations for numbers up to 7, then 8–15, and then 15–30) further emphasizes that number is not learned as "facts" or "properties of objects," but instead results from a gradual organization of relations.

Counting as the Entry into Number

Counting has classically been taken by teachers and parents as the entry into understanding of number. This view is consistent with the view of arithmetic as "number facts" to be learned by social transmission. However, most math educators, even those not attributing their views to Piaget, warn that rote counting does not signify understanding of number. Piaget's careful research makes it clear why this precaution is necessary.

Some aspects of Piaget's theory of number have become controversial with the research of Gelman and Gallistel (1978) who question the synchronous development of classes and relations with number. They attribute more importance to the role of counting in early number construction. That is, they point to what they call the "how to count principle" (present from about 3 years of age) as the basic procedure from which the child abstracts knowledge about number.

Sinclair (1979) notes that in a text in French (Beth & Piaget, 1961), Piaget's analysis is very close to Gelman's but that Piaget's theoretical objective leads him to a view emphasizing structural evolution rather than, as in Gelman's focus, "what the subject actually does when confronted with a problem" or "in what circumstances in real life the structures have been elaborated" (Sinclair, 1979, p. 1). The principal difference between the research of Piaget and that of Gelman is that Gelman's studies deal only with "specific numerosities, i.e., to collections the child has counted" (Sinclair, 1979, p. 4). Sinclair argues that Gelman "reduces the construction of number to a particular set of principles and procedures to do with specific numerosities" (p. 9). Sinclair raises the question as to whether the two views capture two different facets of development. She underlines the point that Piaget's conceptualization of number "does not mean that number concepts can be reduced to those of classes and relations—they can still be particular, even if they participate in the construction of logical concepts" (p. 8). She further emphasizes this:

> Number can neither be reduced to concepts of classes, nor to that of transitive relations, nor to that of one-to-one correspondences, but constitutes a new synthesis between all these in which the one-to-one principle and the iteration principle as a recursive procedure play an important part. (p. 9)

Sinclair's discussion suggests that it is important to understand the psychological difference between Gelman's hypothesis that numerosity (distinguished from number) is abstracted from procedures and Piaget's view, described by Sinclair as

> a broad description of basic characteristics of the organization of actions where ordering and classifying are considered to be amongst the most general, combined with some action patterns that are more specific such as establishing one-to-one correspondences and iterations. (p. 10)

Piaget and Szeminska (1941/1952) clarified their view of the role of counting aloud in experiments in which the child's ability to count without difficulty is first established in the absence of any objects. Then, choosing a number smaller than the highest number to which he can count, the child is given that many pennies and asked to give as many "sweets" as pennies to a doll. Then, after the child establishes an equivalent set and counts the pennies, the sweets are covered, and the child is asked how many sweets there are. Piaget and Szeminska found that accurate enumeration is often present in children who nevertheless do not assume the equivalence of two groups of objects having the same number. They discuss in the following way the role of counting in relation to the last stage in which the child knows the necessary equivalence of the two sets.

> It is therefore no exaggeration to say that the verbal factor plays little part in the development of correspondence and equivalence. At the point at which correspondence becomes quantifying, thereby giving rise to the beginnings of equivalence, *counting aloud may, no doubt, hasten the process* of evolution. Our only contention is that the process is not *begun* by numerals as such. (Piaget & Szeminska, 1941/1952, p. 64) (Italics added)

Counting is an acknowledged part of early quantitative thinking for both Piaget and Gelman. Although Gelman believes that reasoning on number goes on well before Piaget's fully elaborated concept, she, too, agrees that counting cannot account for the fully developed concept of number, even at the concrete operational level.

Figurative Materials as Aids to Learning

Many educators have proposed the use of physical materials based on mathematical relations as aids to children's learning. Montessori's effort to create "materialized abstractions" is discussed in Chapter 9. Her materials include, for example, staircase materials in which the smallest element is a unit of measurement for the rest. Cuisenaire rods are another example of efforts to use such materials to promote reasoning about number.

Cuisenaire's Rods

Georges Cuisenaire, a Belgian math teacher, developed materials in the 1930s to aid primary school children's arithemetic reasoning. These are colored lengths of wood with a cross section 1 centimeter square. The basic set comes in lengths ranging from 1 to 10 centimeters. Each different length is a different color, and the rods are generally referred to by their color names. The rods are not marked off in segments as were Montessori's red and blue rods, to avoid reliance on counting. Cuisenaire rods thus have more in common with Montessori's brown stair but are much smaller and, unlike the brown stair, are used for precise arithmetic computation. Cuisenaire's invention inspired Caleb Gattegno, and they wrote a book, *Numbers in Colour* (Cuisenaire & Gattegno, 1954), describing the use of the rods. Gattegno (1957, 1958, 1960) also wrote a set of arithmetic texts based on the use of the Cuisenaire rods. The rationale for the use of these rods is given in terms of perception and mental imagery. The rods are used first in free play. Then children are expected to associate a color with a length (but not with a number name at first). Then they are taught to put rods end to end, and find the rod that is the same length as those combined. For example, children are expected to verbalize addition ("The light green rod plus the red rod equals the black rod"), subtraction ("The blue rod minus a yellow rod equals a red rod"), and fractions ("The yellow rod is equal to half the orange rod"). This work with the rods is accompanied by exercises in which children associate numerals with groups of other objects and learn to write numerals. After a period of work with the rods without reference to numbers, children are taught to link a number with a length, and rods are used to work equations. Counting is specifically excluded from the educational rationale.

Constructivist Concerns

Several worries about these methods occur to educators informed by Piaget's theory. Piaget himself felt that the methods of Montessori, Cuisenaire, and Gattegno were based on an inadequate psychology. From a constructivist perspective, three characteristics of these methods at the beginning of young children's education in mathematics are problematic.

1. *The risk of substituting figurative for operative relationships.* The method of Cuisenaire and Gattegno emphasizes the exercise of reasoning based on perceptual judgment, in contrast with reasoning based on logico-mathematical relations.

    The constructivist skepticism and caution about the use of materials like those of Montessori and Cuisenaire in *beginning* math education is based on Piaget's theoretical distinction between two different but complementary aspects of thought—figurative and operative. The figurative aspect pertains to forms of cognition that are a kind of "copy" or imitation of qualitative aspects of reality. These include perceptions and mental images that correspond to figural aspects of reality—that is, to their configurations. The figurative aspect of cognition is a static apprehension of a state that offers only an approximate correspondence to objects or events. In contrast, the operative aspect of thought pertains to forms of cognition by which an object or event can be grasped in terms of transformations of static states. The operative aspect of cognition is a mobile apprehension that offers grasp of quantitative relations that go beyond what is directly observable. Seriated materials arranged in a staircase, for example, may be grasped figuratively without being understood operationally. The operative aspect of thought about seriation involves the whole network of exact relations discussed above by which an individual knows all the quantitative implications of a given configuration.

The use of physical properties of objects in figurative materials to represent logico-mathematical relations reflects to some extent a failure to distinguish physical knowledge from logico-mathematical knowledge, and empirical from reflective abstraction. Let us consider two of the prime examples of figurative materials used to teach operative (or logico-mathematical) aspects of knowledge—the methods of Montessori and Cuisenaire. Their view of number concepts as ideas to be discovered *in the materials* is in contrast with Piaget's emphasis on number as logico-mathematical relations that must be constructed in the mind of the knower. Figurative judgments based on simple abstraction of spatial configurations is very different from operative coordination of logical relations by means of reflective abstraction.

Piaget's research showing psychological difficulties in coordinating relations between cardinal value and ordinal position raises the question about whether the construction of this logical coordination can be aided by exercises dependent on figurative knowing. It is clear that children may be taught to arrange materials according to configurations. However, it is not clear whether or not such activities contribute to operative (logico-mathematical) aspects of reasoning. So long as the child relies on the perceptual aid of the configuration to get correct answers, reflective abstraction necessary for logico-mathematical knowledge is not exercised.

2. *Failure to take account of the psychological difference between reasoning about discrete and continuous quantities.* The use of figurative materials is based on the assumption of representation of discrete quantity (number) by continuous quantity (length). The child must be able to conserve length and impose on lengths a standard unit of measurement—to conceptualize segments as representing "countable" elements. This is problematic because Genevan research shows that the child's construction of continuous quantity develops independently of number and lags well behind it (about 6 months). In the quantification of discrete objects, the unit is given by the separation of objects. In the quantification of length, the unit is not given but is arbitrary and must be imposed by the knower.

For Piaget the danger is that young children are apt to see each rod as "one" rod rather than the cardinal number. Reasoning about continuous material calls for spatial operations that have some analogy to but are also distinct from logico-mathematical operations. Piaget (1953) remarked that "measurement develops later than the number concept, because it is more difficult to divide a continuous whole into interchangeable units than to enumerate elements which are already separate" (p. 78). He notes that beginning measurement with a rod used as a unit involves two operations of logic. One is the child's conception of the whole as composed of a number of parts added together (analogous to inclusion of classes). The second is the child's conception of displacement or substitution that is necessary to apply one length against another and build a system of units. Thus, to use Cuisenaire rods as representing numbers, the child must already be capable of logical relations akin to those of number. Moreover, it is possible that a child may learn that Red + Yellow = Blue without thinking that this means that $2 + 5 = 7$.

Montessori's segmentation of one set of rods into equal red and blue parts makes this material perhaps better for promoting reasoning about number (because there is some discreteness in units suggested) than her unsegmented brown stair (see Chapter 9) and Cuisenaire rods. Difficulties remain, however, with reference to the construction of the notion of equal units of measurement that requires conservation, and conceptualizing these units as representing discrete "countable" elements.

For children just beginning to construct numerical relations, the use of discrete "countable" objects seems preferable to single lengths representing cardinal values. We are thus very skeptical about the use of seriated materials with children at the beginning of their construction of number. What must be ascertained is how the child interprets the materials and what real meaning is reflected in his actions with them. This is, of course, an empirical question, and it would be interesting to study with Piaget's methods described above the reactions of young children with Montessori and Cuisenaire schooling.

Empirical data bearing on the issue of the relation between knowledge of elementary number and measurement comes from the experimental studies on learning of Inhelder, Sinclair, and Bovet (1974). They tested the hypothesis that "children who already possess an elementary conservation of number should have little trouble in reaching understanding of conservation of length problems if the lengths are broken down into clearly distinct units (matches) and lined up so that they touch each other (roads)" (p. 163). The research in which they tried to teach number conservation disproved this hypothesis. The findings "show that in the case of the conservation of length there is no direct developmental link between the concept of continuous quantity and that of number" (p. 163). Thus, Inhelder, Sinclair, and Bovet conclude that the conservation of "countables" precedes that of "measureables." The distrust of continuous materials as aids to promoting the child's early construction of number thus has some basis in empirical research.

The significance of Genevan research in relation to Montessori's method of teaching numeration and arithmetic is that it shows that understanding arithmetic relations cannot be reduced to association or sensory absorption. Montessori's method fails to take into account structural changes, that is, the qualitative changes in organization of thought about quantity.

3. *Emphasis on calculation as an end in itself.* The Gattegno program is highly structured in its emphasis on practice in calculation. Although experimentation is recommended, explicit teacher direction is necessary for more complex manipulations that would not be discovered in free play. A danger is thus that children's reasons for working with the rods may be heteronomous rather than autonomous. That is, children are not usually interested in calculation for the sake of calculation, except in a context of personal need to calculate—such as one finds in group games, to be discussed below. Whether this difference makes a difference in the development of children's knowledge of number is unknown.

Just as practice in calculation with equations may lead to right answers without understanding, so practice with Cuisenaire rods and other figurative materials may also be limited to skill with rods without broader understanding. A rather thorough set of studies indicates that Cuisenaire rods may not be as effective as Cuisenaire and Gattegno hoped. This work was done by the Canadian Council for Research in Education (1964), comparing classrooms in five provinces using Cuisenaire rods with classrooms using traditional methods. The main focus of the studies was on first and second graders. Although many of the findings were inconclusive, Cuisenaire students did better than traditional students on tests that emphasized computation. However, they did not do better on word problems, and it appeared questionable whether they maintained the advantage even in calculation beyond third grade.

Piaget's view of the value of Cuisenaire rods includes some of the above concerns. He expressed his view with important qualifications about the critical importance of the child's personal research:

> At the very first stages of initiation into arithmetic calculation, the Belgian teacher Cuisenaire introduced concrete teaching aids in the form of small sticks comprising groups of various units and known as "numbers in colors." Both the introduction of colors and the principle itself of the correspondence between spatial units and numbers can, however, give rise to extremely different interpretations and applications.... Though excellent when it gives rise to active manipulations and discoveries by the child itself, following the line of its spontaneous operational development, these aids may also tempt teachers to use them for demonstrations that are merely watched by the child, a process that does, of course, make comprehension easier than using more verbal or more static methods, but that runs the risk (and the risk is increased by the presence of the colors) of giving the configurations (and therefore the figurative aspects of thought: perception, imitation, and images) greater importance than the operations (and therefore than the operative aspects of thought: actions and operations). This risk becomes a

reality, with all its attendant dangers, when the emphasis is placed definitively on the relationships of the colors (which is why the Maison des Petits decided to do without this ambivalent aid), and when the teacher, while under the impression that he is being faithful to the lines laid down by the active school, is in fact employing merely intuitive methods of teaching. (Piaget, 1969/1970, pp. 48–49)

The rods or colored numbers of Cuisenaire-Gattegno may sometimes give the students scope for performing a constructive operation, but frequently they, too, fail, owing to substitution of a figurative for an operational activity. (Piaget, 1948/1973, p. 8)

Cuisenaire rods...are open to the most totally opposed methods of using them, some of them genuinely operative if the child is allowed to discover for himself the various operations made possible by spontaneous manipulations of the rods, but the others essentially intuitive or figurative when they are limited to external demonstrations and to explanations of the configurations laid out by the teacher. (Piaget, 1969/1970, p. 73)

Depending on how seriated materials are used, these may play a beneficial role at some point (though probably not in the beginning) in the child's construction of numerical relations. Piaget refers to some evidence on this point:

A series of research programs are at the moment being carried out, in Canada, in Great Britain, in Switzerland, and elsewhere, on the advantages and disadvantages of the various methods employed under the name Cuisenaire. One of the analytical processes being employed consists in using various operational tests of my own to compare the levels attained by comparable groups of children taught whether by the usual methods or by the numbers-in-colors method. It appears that in this respect a partial advance in development can be observed in cases where the numbers-in-colors method is used in an active and operational way, and where, needless to say, the teachers are sufficiently in command of the elements of modern mathematics and the psychology of intellectual operations. (Piaget, 1969/1970, p. 50)

Piaget did not specify what he means by using Cuisenaire rods "in an active and operational way," but we assume from his other remarks that he had in mind the child's own "invention" of relationships among the rods. Thus, the Cuisenaire-Gattegno method may be better than traditional methods at some point in a child's mathematical education. Piaget did not mention the ages of subjects in this study. More research is needed to establish the benefits and limitations to the use of Cuisenaire rods.

Calculation as an End in Itself

Traditional approaches to teaching arithmetic have emphasized calculation as an end in itself. The ability to compute has been viewed as the necessary foundation for mathematical competence, despite the well-known disparity between children's competence in calculation and intelligent use of calculation in "word problems."

Ginsburg (1977) and C. Kamii (1984) point out the less well-known learning difficulties that are *created* by teaching that emphasizes calculation. They make clear that incorrect calculation generally reflects intelligent effort to be systematic, and that errors arise when children view calculation apart from their reasoned knowledge about number. For example, Ginsburg quotes the following reactions of Patty, a 9-year-old.

I: I'm going to give you another problem. You seem to be doing pretty well adding. Suppose you have 29 again and 4.

Patty wrote:

$$\begin{array}{r} 29 \\ +4 \\ \hline 69 \end{array}$$

I: What does it say right here?

P: 29 and 4.

I: Are how much?

P: 69.

I: You're sure that 29 and 4 are 69?

P: Altogether?

I: Altogether.

P: No.

I: How much are 29 and 4?

Patty made a large number of tallies on the bottom of the page. She appeared to count them, at least sometimes using her fingers. Then she announced the result: 33.

I: 33. O.K. How come this says 69 (she pointed to the written work)?

P: Ooops! Because you're not doing it like that (she pointed to the tallies). Oh, this (the 69) is wrong.

I: How can you put a 3 here (referring to the second 3 in 33) if it says 9 here (referring to the 9 in 29)?

Patty looked at what was written
$$\begin{array}{r} 29 \\ +4 \\ \hline 33 \end{array}$$
and changed it back to
$$\begin{array}{r} 29 \\ +4 \\ \hline 69 \end{array}$$

P: That's 9 and that's gotta be 6. It's just that you're doing it differently than that.

I: So you get a different answer.

P: Yeah. 'Cause you're adding all of this up together (meaning the tallies). You're not adding it all up altogether this way (she pointed to the written work). You're putting the 9 by itself and that's 69.

I: So when you do it on paper you get 69 and if you do it with the little marks you get how many?

P: 33. Because you're adding all of it altogether. And you're not doing it over here.

For Patty, written work was a world apart from the addition of real objects. (pp. 137–139)

Ginsburg goes on to describe how Patty used her method systematically to add 100 + 1 to get 200, and 10 + 1 to get 20!

Kamii (1982b) calls attention to a case study by Erlwanger (1975) in which a bright fifth-grader expresses a clear distinction between two different methods of calculation. Unlike Patty, he feels no discomfort about the different answers he gets to the same problem. Kamii's description is quoted below.

> The interview concerned the addition of 3/4 and 1/4. Mat had two answers: 1) 3/4 + 1/4 = 4/8 = 1/2, and 2) "If you divide this (circle) into 4...and then add this (shading 3/4)...and this (shading 1/4)...it's a whole." He then wrote 3/4 + 1/4 = 1.
>
> *Erlwanger:* But when you did it the other way...you had 1/2...how come?
>
> *Mat:* I don't know! That's the way it is.
>
> *Erlwanger:* What method did you use when you got 4/8?
>
> *Mat:* I...uh...added the numerators and then the denominators...(and)...that's the one they taught me.... I think it was (level) E fractions.
>
> *Erlwanger:* How does this really work then...that...here you are doing it one way...
>
> *Mat:* (interrupting): Well...it's just like these (referring to examples on ordering fractions, in which he had obtained different answers).... You get a different answer every method you use.
>
> *Erlwanger:* And then how do you decide which answer is right?
>
> *Mat:* It depends on which method you are told to use.... And you use that method and you come out with the answer. And that's what answer is in the key.

These examples illustrate the dangers of teaching that emphasizes the importance of calculation for the sake of calculation.

Early Emphasis on Conventional Notation

A common practice in early education has been to introduce numerals at the beginning of mathematics education. This is often accompanied by drawings of sets of objects. The empiricist rationale is that children will associate the number of objects with the numeral. Movable counters are often used as well to give children practice in counting out the number indicated by a numeral. Practice in writing numerals is also a tradition in early math education.

From a constructivist perspective, the emphasis on numerals at the beginning of math education is problematic because it fails to take into account children's spontaneous ideas about how to represent quantity. Many of these ideas conflict with the convention of using numerals. That is, children's logic leads to certain feelings of necessity about what is an adequate representation of quantity, and our arbitrary conventions often do not make sense to children. While number is not arbitrary conventional knowledge, the shapes of numerals representing number are arbitrary and conventional.

Sinclair (personal communication; Sinclair, Siegrist, & Sinclair, 1982) reports studies in which children's logic leads to four different types of quantitative notation. In one study, children were asked to write down on paper what there was in a group of four round checkers, four square counters, or in a drawing of four birds. The four types of responses were as follows.

1. *The coordination of a number-word sequence with motor activity of making marks, but without any intention of counting.* Children may simply say numbers aloud while making marks, without one-to-one correspondence, or they may explain marks as "a lot."

2. *Use of the one-to-one principle.* Some children draw around each of the checkers, or draw objects in the same spatial arrangement as the objects represented. They thus represent qualitative as well as quantitative aspects of an array of objects. Soon after this type of correspondence, representation becomes more abstract when the child uses some kind of simple form to represent the number (circles, slashmarks, "balloons," and so on). These may sometimes resemble letter forms, but no longer resemble the forms of the objects. The same form is used, no matter what the objects represented. Soon after this kind of correspondence, children use conventional letters and number forms in an indiscriminate way. This is followed by use of the correct sequence of numerals. For example, children may write "1 2 3 4," with each numeral corresponding to an object. Or, they may write "4 4 4 4," with a feeling of necessity that there be a numeral for each object.

3. *Permutations.* Young children may feel that it is necessary to represent three balls differently from three houses. One way some do this is to use the same symbols in a different order. For example, three balls may be written "T I V" while three houses is written "I V T." Another way is to use different symbols for different objects. For example, three houses may be written "O O O" while three balls is written "T T T." In these ways, according to Sinclair, children can continue to represent the uniqueness of objects along with their "manyness." The use of permutations to represent differences in nonnumeric words was first observed by Ferreiro and will be discussed in Chapter 8. Sinclair notes that the reading and writing of numerals proceeds hand in hand with representation of language in general.

4. *Single numeral.* Conventional notation is the last to develop. Thus, its teaching in the beginning of young children's math education may be in conflict with spontaneous reasoning, and may constitute an obstacle to progress.

The Problem of Place Value

"Place value" refers to understanding the significance of numerals in tens, hundreds, thousands, and so forth, positions in Arabic representations of number. It is notoriously difficult for young children to understand "425," for example, as 4 hundreds, 2 tens, and 5 ones, whatever teaching methods are used.

From a constructivist perspective, place value is a problem for the child because it involves (1) intermediate to advanced construction of number itself, and (2) distinction between the representational significance of individual numerals and of combined numerals. On the first point, as we noted above, Greco found that number up to about eight was constructed first, then to about 15, and then to about 30. Can representation be expected to proceed in advance of knowledge of what is represented?

On the second point as C. Kamii (1984) has noted, place value requires knowledge of multiplication, which is beyond most first and second graders. Indeed, despite instruction, place value remains a problem for many 9-year-olds.

Children's comprehension of place value in the conventional notation system has been studied by M. Kamii (1980, 1981) as part of a larger study. In one task, 80 children 4 to 9 years of age were shown a Tinkertoy car, asked how many wheels it needed, and asked to figure out how many cars could be outfitted from a pile of 16 wheels. They were asked to make a drawing to show that that many cars could be made from all those wheels. Then the child was asked to write the numbers for "how many wheels you drew" and "how many cars we could make." Kamii drew a circle around each numeral the children wrote and explored their notion of the relation between this numeral and the cars and wheels. What she found was that many children who correctly wrote the numeral 16 did not know that it stood for all the wheels drawn. Of those who did know that the numeral represented all the objects, a number of different interpretations of the digits was found. One common interpretation was that the 6 represented 6 wheels and the 1 represented 1 wheel. Children making this interpretation drew one circle around 6 wheels and another around 1 wheel and were untroubled to see that they included only 7 wheels as showing what 16 meant. Three (of 5) 5-year-olds did this, 4 (of 13) 6-year-olds, 10 (of 17) 7-year-olds, 7 (of 12) 8-year-olds, and 4 (of 11) 9-year-olds. Clear understanding of place value—that quantities designated by the notational parts had to be exactly the same as the quantity represented by the whole numeral—was found in only 2 of the 7-year-olds, 2 of the 8-year-olds, and 5 of the 9-year-olds. These and other notions held by children indicate that understanding numerical quantity and understanding its representation are less closely related than adult intuition might suggest. M. Kamii (1980) makes the following observation on a contradiction in children's instruction on reading words and reading numbers.

> In reading, phonetics or sound-letter correspondences are important. But woe be to the child who tries to apply his phonics lessons to the reading and writing of numbers: in both "fourteen" and "forty-one," one hears or utters the "4" before anything else. In writing and spelling, the spatial arrangement of the marks and the order in which the letters occur are critical. In number, on the other hand, the spatial arrangement of the elements is irrelevant. Just as the child has grasped this important idea, he learns that the graphic representation of number demands that he pay attention to the spatial arrangement of the marks once again, and that digit order (positional notation) is critical. (p. 15)

Findings such as these suggest the need for more serious efforts to understand what it is children are learning from arithmetic instruction.

THE NEW MATH

The New Math has included some of the ideas discussed above. The work of its intellectual father, Zoltan Dienes, deserves special mention. Basing his work on that of Piaget, Dienes developed multibased blocks and described free play and directed activities aimed at "insightful mathematical-learning" that takes into account "the wholeness of the mathematical structure" (Dienes, 1960, p. 29). For each base (3, 4, 5, 6, and 10), a set of wooden materials includes units, longs, flats, and blocks. After a period of free play, children play a game with a die on which the numbers included in a given base are written. Taking turns throwing the die, children on their first throw take the designated number of blocks, on the second they take longs, and on the third, units. The player having the most wood wins. Children have the possibility for figuring out that the person who gets the largest number on the first number is highly likely to win because this determines the number of blocks a player has. This game could well be incorporated into the Kamii-DeVries approach described below, but with elementary school children. Dienes does not describe other games that fit the Kamii-DeVries definition of games. Other than this single game, Dienes's method is composed of exercises. It should be noted, however, that Dienes, like Kamii and DeVries, emphasizes the importance of a classroom atmosphere in which "the teacher is prepared to depart from his former position of unquestioned authority" (Dienes & Golding, 1971, p. 147).

Piaget comments on modern math and Dienes's work:

> As regards teaching of the new mathematics, . . . which constitutes such a notable advance over traditional methods, experience is often falsified by the fact that although the subject is "modern," the way in which it is presented is sometimes psychologically archaic insofar as it rests on the simple transmission of knowledge—even if an attempt is made (much too early as regards the student's manner of reasoning) to adopt an axiomatic form. . . . What makes this situation so surprising is that if mathematics teachers would only take the trouble to learn about the "natural" psychogenetic development of the logico-mathematical operations, they would see that there exists a much greater similarity than one would expect between the principal operations spontaneously employed by the child and the notions they attempt to instill into him abstractly.
>
> At the age of seven to eight, for instance, children discover by themselves assembling operations, the intersection of sets and Cartesian products, and at age eleven to twelve can discern sets of parts. The development of various forms or functions can be observed in very young children, and in many cases one can speak of "categories" in the sense of McLane and Eilenberg, which, although elementary or "trivial" in form, are no less significant as regards their educative value. But active intention and consequent practical application of certain operations are one

thing, and becoming conscious of them and thus obtaining reflexive and, above all, theoretical knowledge are another. Neither pupils nor teachers suspect that the instruction imparted could be supported by all manner of "natural" structures. Thus one can anticipate a great future for cooperation between psychologists and mathematicians in working out a truly modern method for teaching the new mathematics. This would consist in speaking to the child in his own language before imposing on him another ready-made and over-abstract one, and, above all, in inducing him to rediscover as much as he can rather than simply making him listen and repeat. The educator/mathematician Dienes has made praiseworthy efforts in this direction, but an inadequate psychological knowledge makes his interpretation of the success of certain "games" or exercises he has devised somewhat too optimistic. (1948/1973, pp. 17–19)

For older children, Dienes's exercises perhaps have promise, but we are skeptical about the real interest young children have in exercises out of the context of games and the needs of daily living. Nevertheless, such exercises carried out in the spirit of autonomy envisioned by Dienes may prove useful as a part of a constructivist program. Wadsworth (1978), however, is disparaging in his assessment of modern math (an assessment that no doubt refers to the work of others besides Dienes):

> The attempt to implement the "new math" in the United States during the late 1950s and '60s was an effort to get children to learn an important set of mathematical concepts that were neglected under the "old math." The failure of the "new math" to succeed in the United States on any large scale has probably been due to the fact that while the content of mathematics instruction changed somewhat, the teaching methods did not. In practice, instruction usually has been directed at teaching young children sophisticated concepts (and some that they were incapable of learning without formal operations, like induction and deduction) through the use of signs and symbols. Paper, pencils, and written and spoken words and numbers remained the media of instruction. From a Piagetian point of view, the "new math" did not succeed because its implementation in classrooms was no more in keeping with how children develop and learn mathematical concepts than was the old math! Without active methods that permit the child to construct mathematical concepts, a change in content can have little effect. This essential point was overlooked. (p. 171)

IMPLICATIONS OF GENEVAN WORK
FOR MATHEMATICS EDUCATION

The issue of the practical implications of Piaget's theory of number and mathematics education raises once again the knotty problem of the relation between theory and practice. At a general level, Piaget and his colleagues have demonstrated the link between logic and mathematics. They have shown that general cognitive structures such as the system of concrete operations account for fundamental competence in the establishment of specific concepts.

Principles Articulated by Piaget

Six specific principles related to math education can be gleaned from Piaget's remarks in various places. These include Recommendation No. 43 on the Teaching of Mathematics in Secondary Schools, adopted in 1956 at the International Conference on Public Education, sponsored by UNESCO and the International Bureau of Education (Piaget, 1969/1970, p. 48).

1. *Psychological structures must be developed before numerical questions are introduced.* Piaget (1948/1973) emphasized that in the psychogenetic evolution of children's thought, "all mathematical ideas begin by a qualitative construction before acquiring a metrical character" (p. 102). He argued that educators do not sufficiently dissociate questions of logic from numerical or metrical questions (p. 99). More specifically, he wrote:

> Yet mathematics constitutes a direct extension of logic itself, so much so that it is actually impossible to draw a firm line of demarcation between these two fields. . . . So that it is difficult to conceive how students who are well endowed when it comes to the elaboration and utilization of the spontaneous logico-mathematical structures of intelligence can find themselves handicapped in the comprehension of a branch of teaching that bears exclusively upon what is to be derived from such structures. Such students do exist, however, and with them the problem. (Piaget 1969/1970, p. 44)

The problem, according to Piaget (1948/1973), lies with methods of teaching. When numerical questions are posed before the child has certain logical structures, they have no meaning, and the child can only grope in an unintelligent way, with "the effect of blocking his reasoning powers" (p. 100). Piaget gives the example of the problem of velocities in which "the student must simultaneously manage reasoning concerning the distances covered and lengths utilized, and carry out a computation with the numbers that express these quantities" (p. 100). When the child does not solidly grasp the logical nature of the problem, numerical issues simply obscure the matter. Piaget recommends that:

> When, on the other hand, the two types of factors (logical and metrical) are dissociated, one can advance more surely, all in attaining the true goal of mathematical learning—the development of the deductive capabilities. It is easy, for example, to give children from ten to twelve years old even complicated problems of velocities (composition of the speeds of two moving objects where one changes place with another or in relation to another, acceleration on an inclined plane, etc.) without numerical data and by bringing the reasoning power to bear on the simply logical relationships (on the more and the less and not on the "how much"—that is to say, in the way Aristotle reasoned on the problem of speed!) Freed from the necessity of computation, the child enjoys building actively all the logical relationships in play and arrives thus at the elaboration of procedural operations that are flexible and precise, often even subtle. Once these mechanisms are accomplished, it becomes possible to introduce the numerical data which take

on a totally new significance from what they would have had if presented at the beginning. It seems that a lot of time is lost in this way, but in the end much is gained, and, above all, and enrichment of personal activity is achieved. (Piaget, 1948/1973, pp. 100–101)

Piaget refers to his research showing that young children represent spatial relations in nonmetric ways before eventually being able to reason in a precise mathematical way about them. The direct educational implication of this principle is that educators must focus on developing the child's general logical ability as the foundation for more specifically mathematical activity.

For young children this means, for example, encouraging children to think about quantity in qualitative but logico-mathematical terms such as "not enough," "too many," "more," and "less." The clear implication is that teachers should avoid pressuring children to acquire mathematical concepts too early. Duckworth (1964) quotes Piaget as follows.

> This is a...big danger of school—false accommodation which satisfies a child because it agrees with a verbal formula he has been given. This is a false equilibrium which satisfies a child by accommodating to words—to authority and not to objects as they present themselves to him.... A teacher would do better not to correct a child's schemas, but to provide situations so he will correct them himself. (p. 4)

2. *Psychological structures must be developed before formal symbolism is introduced.* Piaget (1948/1973) emphasized that "mathematics is nothing but logic," and since logic is not innate, that "failure in mathematics would signify a lack in the very mechanisms of the development of the intellect" (p. 96). Math as logic is distinguished from the technical language or symbolism of mathematics. Piaget (1969/1970, pp. 44–45) argues that the basic logical structures enable the child to reason about number before he can consciously reflect on the language of mathematics. He likens this to the ability to sing in tune without having a theory of singing or being able to read music. Wadsworth criticized methods based on early introduction of formal symbolism: "Children are introduced to *signs* (numbers) at the outset and encouraged to deal with abstractions *they have not abstracted*" (p. 163). Ginsburg (1977) also found that "children's understanding of written symbolism generally lags behind their informal arithmetic" (p. 90). Piaget (1969/1970) comments that children's problems in working with the written language of mathematics may not reflect a problem with the logic but, rather, a problem with its symbolic representation, or with the speed often required of children in written work. The work of Sinclair, Siegrist, and Sinclair (1982) described above further supports Piaget's caution that the logic in number and arithmetic and the representation of this logic are two aspects of intellectual development whose evolution are different. Even with regard to reading numerals, it is clear that reading numerals larger than 9 presents a different problem from reading writing. That is, the spatial order in writing is

relevant to reading words, but not so relevant to reading numbers. Therefore, educational methods must take account of this difference by refraining from introducing symbolism before the implicit logic is established. Ginsburg (1977) stresses that symbolism should be used to formalize what children already know (p. 75). The serious problems that can result when children's ideas clash with instruction are well illustrated by the foregoing discussion of children's difficulties with place value. Other difficulties will be discussed later in this chapter.

With regard to both these principles, Piaget's work makes clear that when instruction clashes with their own logic, children may begin to feel that math is incoherent and arbitrary. The negative effect of instruction out of synchrony with children's logic snowballs, and emotional difficulties can arise. Piaget (1969/1970) comments:

> Since everything is interconnected in an entirely deductive discipline, failure or lack of comprehension where any single link in the chain is concerned entails an increasing difficulty in following the succeeding links, so that the student who has failed to adapt at any point is unable to understand what follows and becomes increasingly doubtful of his ability: emotional complexes, often strengthened by those around him, then arise to complete the block that has been formed in an initiation that could have been quite different. (p. 45)

3. *Automatized knowledge should not be stressed before implicit logic is understood.* It is clear that children whose reasoning is operational have no difficulty making automatic their memory of sums, differences, and so on. C. Kamii (1984) notes that they thus are remembering their own past actions. Such automatic memory is acquired painlessly, in contrast to the agony often experienced by children having difficulty with worksheets and flashcards. It thus seems a waste of time, as well as damaging, to force young children to memorize arithmetic at a time when it makes no sense to them, when this can be so easily learned a little later.

4. *Children must have the opportunity to invent mathematical relations rather than simply confront ready-made adult thought.* Such opportunity occurs when children pose their own problems and struggle with numerical issues in the context of personal need and interest. Piaget (1948/1973) commented:

> In most mathematical lessons the whole difference lies in the fact that the student is asked to accept from outside an already entirely organized intellectual discipline which he may or may not understand, while in the context of autonomous activity he is called upon to discover the relationships and the ideas by himself, and to re-create them until the time when he will be happy to be guided and taught. (p. 99)

Personal research is fostered through concrete manipulations, though Piaget cautions that we should not confuse abstraction of knowledge from objects and abstraction of knowledge from actions. He notes that while "the most general structures of modern mathematics are at the same time the most abstract ... those same structures are never represented in the mind of the child except in the form of concrete manipulations, either physical or verbal" (Piaget, 1969/1970, p. 47). Piaget also cautions against confusion "with intuitive presentations (in the sense of figurative methods) since these operations are derived from actions, not from perceptual or visually recalled configurations" (p. 47). Teachers can aid children's personal research by providing materials and emphasizing children's efforts to think about approximations and to check and correct themselves. The emphasis is on reflection and reasoning more than on obtaining right answers.

5. *Teachers must understand the nature of children's mistakes.* Much of this chapter is devoted to exposing the meaning behind children's errors. To increase sensitivity to the psychological significance of errors, the reader can read further in Ginsburg (1977), C. Kamii (1985), and Labinowicz (1985). These authors discuss aspects of children's reasoning of which teachers are often unaware. Ginsburg (1977) comments, "Children solve problems in unusual ways of which teachers and tests are often unaware. And children—virtually all of them—possess important competencies which are sometimes ignored or suppressed in the process of teaching" (p. v). The challenge is for the teacher to permit children's honest (but often wrong) reasoning to flourish, in order to understand their competencies and difficulties in a way that goes beyond assessment of "skills" at getting right answers.

6. *An atmosphere for thinking must be established.* All the foregoing implications require a special atmosphere as the context in which they can be realized. This atmosphere invites children to pursue their personal goals, and supports their efforts with materials and interventions that reflect recognition that understanding number and arithmetic must be constructed by the child. In such an atmosphere, children's mistakes will abound, differences in opinion will be much in evidence, and nonstandard ways of calculating will flourish. In particular, children's conflicts and contradictions in reasoning will surface and even be fostered by the teacher. Inhelder, Sinclair, and Bovet (1974) argue against training isolated concepts or mechanics or reasoning and emphasize the importance of the child's growing discomfort over erroneous reasoning and efforts to recognize and resolve contradictions.

> Training procedures in which one type of reasoning is artificially isolated and exercised, as is often the case in certain programmed learning projects, are not, in our opinion, very useful since they eliminate the element we consider necessary for progress, i.e., the dynamics of the conflict between schemes. (p. 265)
> Questions and discussions at certain crucial points in the learning process can induce an awareness of contradictions, and provide the impetus for higher-level coordinations leading to new cognitive structures. (p. 166)

The challenge for educators who want to be informed by Piaget's work is to devise methods that take into consideration the nature of the child's reasoning and the kinds of difficulties children have in thinking about specific kinds of content. Keeping in mind the general principles of interest, experimentation, and autonomy discussed in Chapter 2, let us turn to the discussion of specific theoretical and practical efforts in mathematical education.

Constructivist Approaches to Beginning Number and Arithmetic

Diverse goals and methods in beginning number and arithmetic have been attributed to Piaget's inspiration. Goals have ranged from operational reasoning to success in traditional academic exercises. Methods can be categorized in terms of two types of translation discussed in Chapter 3—literal and free translations of theory into practice. These goals and methods are discussed below.

Goals

In contrast with traditional goals focused on accuracy in memory and computation, Piaget's work has inspired goals focused on process and understanding. However, Piaget-inspired goals in various programs differ in the way they relate to traditional product-oriented aims. For example, Labinowicz (1985) proclaims, "Nothing short of a moratorium on standardized achievement testing will free educators to listen to children and expand their perspective of teaching and learning" (p. 396). However, High/Scope's Hohmann, Banet, and Weikart (1979) hope to build "the links to traditional academic exercises in reading and mathematics" (p. xiv).

All Piaget-inspired objectives acknowledge the close relation between number and conservation, classification, seriation, and transitivity. These commonalities in objectives are manifested, however, in very different methods.

Methods

Literal translations of Piaget's theory of number into educational practices emphasize drill in exercises on one-to-one correspondence, conservation, and seriation. Lavatelli (1970b/1973), for example, directs children to put out one penny for each of eight small toys and asks "interview questions" such as "Do you have just as many toys as pennies? How do you know?" In one-to-one correspondence exercises, children are asked, for example, to put out pennies and toys "one for one" side by side and to put the pennies in a pile beside a row of toys. In addition, Lavatelli (19770b/1973) recommends the following "game," which we would term an "exercise."

> *T:* "You are the buyer and I am the storekeeper. You can take all the money for the shopping. Every time that you buy a toy, you must pay me a penny. Each toy costs one penny." (After the first exchange of 6 items, put the two remaining toys in the store.)
>
> *T:* "Do I have the same number of pennies as you have toys? Do I have more pennies than you have toys, or do you have more toys than I have pennies?"
>
> *T:* "How do you know?" "Why?"

(Next, the teacher is the buyer.) After six exchanges the child is left with two toys. Stop buying and ask:

T: "Can you tell me how many pennies I have left?"
"How did you know that I still have two pennies (one penny, three pennies)?"
Continue with the last two exchanges. "Now, with all the money that you have, can you buy all the toys I have?" "Could you buy more toys than are here, or could you buy only some of them? Why? How do you know?" (p. 41)

As noted in Chapter 3, Lavatelli recommends her exercises as short experiences that take place as part of a child-development program. However, her recommendations are almost exclusively for experiences outside the classroom. The closest she comes to integration of Piaget's work in classroom practice is her recommendation that children practice one-to-one correspondence by distributing crackers and napkins at snack time. Here, too, however, the activity is made into an exercise when it is recommended that the teacher increase the distance between the sets of objects or bunch together one set of objects and ask the child if there are still as many in one set as in the other. Finally the teacher is to have the child check his answer by reestablishing physical correspondence (Lavatelli, 1970b/1973, p. 42). Lavatelli thus believed that practicing the Genevan tasks would result in construction of the system of relations manifested by operational reasoning on these tasks. Piaget, however, was clear in expressing his opposition to such use of his experiments.

Lavatelli has not been alone in making a literal translation of Piaget's research experiments into exercises. Many examples of such reduction of the significance of Genevan work may be cited (Biggs & MacLean, 1969; Copeland, 1970; Thier, Karplus, Knott, Lawson, & Montgomery, 1979; Hess & Croft, 1972; and the first High/Scope program by Weikart, Rogers, Adcock, & McClelland, 1971).

Free translations of Piaget's work into methods to promote children's construction of number have two characteristics in common: (1) an effort to embed in activities opportunities for children to be interested in reasoning about relations of correspondence and inclusion, and to count and compare quantities, and (2) an avoidance of correcting children's errors in reasoning about quantitative relations. In recommending activities with these characteristics in mind, some authors succeed better than others, and some offer inconsistent recommendations. Our purpose is not an exhaustive review or critique, but an illustrative commentary on several approaches that may aid the reader in assessing other programs. We keep in mind Piaget's insistence on the importance of the child's psychological experience and the necessity for the child to be mentally active in constructing a logico-mathematical network of relations. We focus below on the approaches of High/Scope, Nuffield, Kamii and DeVries, and Labinowicz.

High/Scope

In their short chapter on number, Hohmann, Banet, and Weikart (1979) focus on one-to-one correspondence and conservation of number, the elements and precursors of operational reasoning about number. The activities they recommend are divided into "Key Experiences" in comparing amounts, arranging two sets of objects in one-to-one correspondence, and counting objects. High/Scope authors advocate meaningful contexts for counting, not mere drill. Contexts for these experiences include blockbuilding, pretend play, art, snack time, looking at pictures, and group games. Writing numerals is postponed. It is recommended that teachers ask questions about number and amount in the context of children's work with materials and then ask children to explain their answers. However, High/Scope authors caution teachers to accept children's wrong answers, stating, "It's pointless and frustrating to preoperational children to have their logic 'corrected' to conform to adult logic" (p. 231). Teacher-child interactions quoted to illustrate High/Scope principles of teaching show teacher's efforts to get children to compare, count, and think about one-to-one correspondence. The intention is that the teacher complement and extend rather than interfere with what children are doing.

In keeping with this intention, examples show teachers chatting with children about what they are doing. Teachers introduce number into situations in which children do not spontaneously think about it, and respond without correcting when children spontaneously express preoperational reasoning. This contrasts with Lavatelli's lessons. In their preoccupation with number, High/Scope teachers often seem to "parachute" questions and comments about number into activities in which children's preoccupations are elsewhere. For example, when a child pretends that pegs in spool holes are men repairing sewers, the teacher asks whether one man is put out for each hole. Such an intervention is a benign intrusion and may interest children in thinking about quantity. Nevertheless, many of High/Scope's classroom practices still seem to be thinly veiled attempts to teach selected "basic Piagetian skills," the objective stated in 1971. High/Scope practices are rather different from the Kamii-DeVries approach to be described below, in which situations derive from children's purposes in a more central way.

Like Kamii and DeVries, High/Scope authors advocate activities involving number in daily living—such as distributing cups or cookies at snack time, and card games and Musical Chairs. However, the recommendation of games is not elaborated, and the High/Scope rationale for these games is limited to one-to-one correspondence.

Nuffield Mathematic

The British Nuffield Mathematics publications acknowledge Piaget as the inspiration for a "revolt against [the] tyranny" of textbooks and mechanical practice that led to "the situation that a whole nation was viewing mathematics with disgust" (Nuffield Foundation, 1971, p. 72). Sponsored by the Nuffield Foundation, committees of authors produced a series of books on preschool and primary school education.

Nuffield Mathematics education occurs in a rich context of activities having multiple goals and rationales. It attempts to focus on children's interest, nourish curiosity, and promote group work. The title of one book, *Maths with Everything* (Nuffield Foundation, 1971), succinctly summarizes the orientation. Many of the same kinds of activities are recommended by Nuffield as by other Piaget-inspired approaches. For example, these encompass pretense and dramatic play, sewing, cooking, stories and nursery rhymes, puzzles, building with blocks and other construction materials, play with sand and water, painting, drawing, woodwork, and other art activities, music, and outdoor play with balls and jump rope, and reading. These are all linked with mathematics in some way in terms of global quantification (for example, "big" and "little," "a lot," "a few") or specific use of numbers (for example, in "buying" something at the pretend stores). The principle of encouraging global quantification prior to precise quantification with number and measurement is consistent with recommendations by Kamii and DeVries.

The Nuffield description of mathematics education includes many activities that do not specifically involve number. For example, preschool experiences include opportunities to find out that water in bowls and puddles behaves in the same way when struck. Noticing shape is considered related to math as well as properties of objects (as a ball can roll, but a block cannot). Other experiences considered of value to math but not involving number include comparing the difference between cleaning up spilled water and spilled puzzle pieces. The relations of these activities with math are not spelled out. While we would categorize these as physical-knowledge activities rather than as mathematics, the comparisons are logico-mathematical in nature, and we would agree that the physical experiences advocated do contribute in a general way to the development of reasoning that leads to number and arithmetic. However, failure to distinguish physical knowledge and logico-mathematical knowledge sometimes seems to lead the Nuffield teacher to interventions that may not be as productive as they could be. For example, experiences with continuous materials such as sand and water are recommended in terms of children's opportunities to "count, match, and sort" (Nuffield Foundation, 1970, p. 17).

We would not emphasize number objectives in such activities for two reasons. First, Piaget's work has shown that the quantification of continuous quantity is more difficult to structure and occurs later than the quantification of discontinuous quantity. Children's construction of notions of volume and units of measurement is not established before the age of 11 to 12 years (Piaget & Inhelder, 1966b/1969, p. 99). Thus, it seems a waste of time to worry about this kind of operational reasoning in the preschool and early primary years. Second, a focus on number may detract children's attention from physical-knowledge issues that are more compatible with their interest in action on the physical world. The teacher's decision about how to use materials and how to intervene in activities is thus a matter of priorities that are affected in important ways by the particular rationale and aspect of theory the teacher has in mind.

Throughout descriptions of Nuffield activities one finds a special emphasis on charting and graphing. Children are encouraged to make charts and graphs of everything—children's heights and weights, vehicles passing the school on a given morning, pets owned by class members, streets on which children live, birthdays by months, and those who go home for lunch and those who stay at school. These activities are linked to Piaget's theory of the relation between one-to-one correspondence, classification, and number. It emphasizes the representation of number without, however, considering the special difficulties related to the difference between constructing number and constructing its representation, as discussed above.

Nuffield Mathematics draws in a global way from Piaget's emphasis on the importance of play. In a more literal fashion, it draws from Piaget's tasks and derives activities from the aspects of reasoning studied by Piaget. Piagetian tasks are used to determine whether to provide certain activities. For example, conservation of area is ascertained before introducing activities involving comparison of surface areas (Nuffield Foundation, 1970, pp. 144–147). An abundance of sorting activities is provided, with the rationale that they are "a necessary stage towards understanding the meaning of number (Nuffield Foundation, 1970, p. 12). Activities designed to promote conservation are also in abundance. An activity recommended to promote conservation of length is described in the context of a project on buses. Children are to act out one of Piaget's tasks: "The 'teacher's bus' went along a straight road and the children were asked to move their bus *the same distance* along a winding road" (Nuffield Foundation, 1971, p. 6). To promote conservation of number, it is recommended that passengers in a queue waiting for a pretend bus be rearranged to show that the number does not change.

Although the Nuffield program is consonant in many ways with a free translation of Piaget's work, some of the practices advocated are more accurately categorized as literal translations. It seems that the reliance on tasks and structural stages leads to practices that are a literal translation, while the reliance on constructivism remains at the level of global translation.

Nuffield objectives focus on number as relations, but without Piaget's particular definition of relations constructed by the knower. In contrast with Piaget's view of operational relations, Nuffield authors state that "mathematics is the study of relationships between the facts of arithmetic" (1970, pp. 91–92), and take up the New Math view of number as a "property of sets" (see also Copeland, 1970, pp. 58, 265). This leads to an emphasis on sorting tasks and Venn diagrams that depart, in our view, from a free translation in which the child's purposes and interests are more organic to an activity.

For example, we would not show children a bulletin board on which same-colored circles and squares are connected by a string (Nuffield Foundation, 1970, p. 7). We would not bother with equipping the classroom with sorting boxes (Nuffield Foundation, 1970, p. 8), or with having children draw a circle around each group of different animals (1970, p. 9). These are tasks that do not "go anywhere" but are "dead ends" in terms of children's purposes. We would agree, however, with the value of activities involving grouping according to similarities and differences when these are in the context of physical-knowledge activities and group games and when they fit children's purposes. For example, sorting objects according to those that children predict will float or sink makes sense to children because they look forward and have the fun and satisfaction of testing their predictions.

Perhaps the most serious shortcoming of the Nuffield global emphasis on play and literal emphasis on Piagetian tasks and structures is its failure to take account of the importance of constructive error in children's progress in mathematical understanding. Nowhere in the Nuffield recommendations is there a focus on children's difficulties in reasoning in the course of activities. While Piaget's research findings about preoperational reasoning are well described, Nuffield authors do not attempt to take the Genevan discovery of constructive error into activities other than those directly reflecting Genevan tasks. Even these are recommended in terms of exercises as if repeated practice with the tasks will somehow lead to operational reasoning.

In comparison with the work of Kamii and DeVries and of Labinowicz, described below, the Nuffield approach focuses in a more concentrated way on the goal of correct reasoning than on the messy details of the incorrect aspects of the constructivist process. The Nuffield approach is an advance over the efforts of Montessori and High/Scope in some ways. Compared to Montessori, it provides a richer environment that appeals better to children's interests. In comparison with High/Scope, it provides a richer description of classroom life.

Kamii and DeVries

The Kamii-DeVries approach to the teaching of number in preschool was outlined in *Piaget, Children, and Number* (Kamii & DeVries, 1976), and revised by C. Kamii (1982c) in *Number in Preschool and Kindergarten*. The advantages of group games for promoting children's construction of number are discussed with many examples in *Group Games in Early Education* (Kamii & DeVries, 1980). Kamii's work on first-grade arithmetic substantially extends this approach in the book *Young Children Reinvent Arithmetic* (C. Kamii, 1985). We outline briefly the Kamii-DeVries approach to promoting the construction of number in daily living and group games.

DAILY LIVING.   Kamii and DeVries ask the teacher to be on the lookout for situations in the classroom when number is a natural issue, and to create situations in which children need to think about number in order to accomplish something they want. Such situations include:

1. *The distribution of materials.* For example, the teacher can ask a child at snack time to bring "just enough cups for everybody at your table." In a card game, five cards may be distributed to each player.
2. *The division of objects.* Faced with a quantity of raisins or apple slices to be

divided, a child must break the large set into many equal subsets. Similarly, in some card games, the whole deck of cards must be divided.

The other approaches discussed in this book also recommend experiences in daily living for promoting knowledge of number and arithmetic. Some of these are described above. In addition, it should be noted that Montessori (1909/1964) mentioned opportunities in daily life in which children have practice in counting. She gave as examples "when the mother says, for instance, 'There are two buttons missing from your apron,' or 'We need three more plates at table.' " Although Montessori mentioned children's opportunities for counting in the home, she did not build this kind of experience into her method for the classroom.

One of her first ways of introducing children to counting was to teach them to count to 10 and to make change with one-, two-, and four- centime pieces. Although such experiences are useful after children have well-consolidated counting ability, we would not use money to teach children to *begin* to count because of the confusion resulting from the fact that *one* piece must be understood as representing *five, ten,* and so on. Children's natural assumption that a penny is worth more than a dime because it is larger is well known. *After* children have learned to count and already understand that five pennies make a nickel, we would use a card game like Piggy Bank for practice in elementary addition. In this game, players attempt to collect cards (picturing from one to five pennies or a nickel) adding to five.

3. *The collection of things.* When parent permission slips must be collected, the children have the opportunity to think about the additive composition of number as they figure out the new total each day and how many more are needed. Milk-money collection can provide an opportunity to figure out how many cartons will be needed.

4. *Keeping records.* Some children can mark attendance, noting who and how many are present and absent. In games, discussed below, scorekeeping is a natural context for figuring out how to keep track of each person's accomplishment.

5. *Cleanup.* If boxes of activity materials (games, for example) are marked with a representation of the number of objects (pictures rather than numerals until children progress to reading), children will know how many objects to look for at cleanup time.

6. *Voting.* As discussed in Chapter 6, voting experiences are indispensable to the development of a sense of community and autonomy. These are also excellent opportunities for thinking about number as children count, record, and compare quantities.

GROUP GAMES.   Opportunities to construct number in the course of certain group games were mentioned in Chapter 5. Aiming games can provide an opportunity for counting and comparison of sets. The game of hiding and finding five objects makes set partitioning and addition and subtraction an integral part of children's purposes. C. Kamii (1984) notes that when 10 guesses are permitted in a game like Charades, children have to figure out how to keep track and usually need to make a record. The most fruitful games for reasoning about number are board games and card games. Board games in which a die is rolled to indicate how many spaces a player moves on a board are useful for children who are beginning to construct one-to-one correspondence and ordering in their counting. Use of two dice provides the possibility for addition and earlier strategies such as "counting all" and "counting on" to figure out how many spaces to move.

In many games with dice and spinners, chance plays a large role, and reasoning possibilities are thus often limited. These are nevertheless stimulating when counting is still a challenge in itself. Moreover, many games involving chance also include opportunities for constructing strategies as well. Individual games must thus be analyzed for their possibilities for reasoning. With regard to number, many card games are especially fruitful. For example, in War, all cards of a regular deck except face cards are dealt to two players and stacked face down. Players turn up their top cards simultaneously, and the player whose card represents the higher number takes both. The player who collects all the cards is the winner. In this game, children thus compare numbers in a context that mobilizes their interest and attention in a much more powerful way than, for example, drill or worksheets. C. Kamii (1984) found that when War becomes too easy, it can be modified into Double War, in which each player has two stacks and turns over two cards each time, to be added together and compared with the opponent's total.

In this constructivist approach to promoting construction of number, children's purposes and reasoning about number constitute an organic integration that seems qualitatively different from many of the situations described by other approaches. Kamii's books and Kohl (1974) are a rich source of practical suggestions with recommended activities and principles of teaching that are more detailed than those provided by other authors. In addition, Kamii discusses the disadvantages of traditional methods, such as the pervasive use of worksheets, and argues that addition does not have to be taught to children since it is inherent in the construction of number. She makes many practical recommendations based on her experience as a researcher in a first-grade classroom. For example, she presents rationales for sequencing work with addition in terms of the size of addends, rather than the size of sums that are customarily the basis of sequencing. She also recommends that written subtraction be postponed until second grade.

Labinowicz

The work of Labinowicz deserves special mention because it complements that of Kamii while differing from it in some respects. In *Learning from Children: New Beginnings for Teaching Numerical Thinking* (1985), Labinowicz describes his research with children in grades 1, 2, and 3. His account is made especially readable by the use of graphics panels to present vignettes from videotaped interviews. These accounts come from Labinowicz's study of children's reasoning in school-related tasks, which is much more extensive than Kamii's, both in scope and age range studied. It is impossible to read his report of experiences in probing how children really think about arithmetic procedures without becoming convinced that most mathematics teaching is doing a great deal more harm than good. Like Kamii, Labinowicz criticizes traditional methods and the use of achievement tests, and advocates teaching based on children's natural methods of reasoning about number.

Labinowicz's approach differs from Kamii's in that it does not aim for the same type of organic integration of number with children's interests in goals not related to mathematics. His goal is assisting the child in making a smooth transition to an understanding of paper-and-pencil algorithms. This approach may reflect Labinowicz's understanding of the dilemmas faced by teachers in most public schools. Therefore, he does not deal with number in problems in daily living and makes limited use of group games. Instead, Labinowicz takes a frank approach to teaching aimed at traditional goals, blending direct and indirect methods of teaching. While he clearly is aiming toward the child's construction of operational reasoning about number, he focuses specifically on children's work with traditional kinds of arithmetic problems.

The freshest aspect of Labinowicz's book is his description of how teachers can encourage "child-invented derived strategies" (what Kamii refers to as "intuitive methods"). One example quoted is a child confronted with the problem of $53 - 24$. She reasoned, "50 minus 20 is 30. 3, 4,...That's 1 more to take away. 30 minus 1 is 29" (p. 380). (Labinowicz points out the universal tendency of children to approach vertical sum and difference problems from left to right, rather than the right to left direction customarily taught.) He advocates encouraging children to think in their own ways and helping them extend these methods to higher levels of competence and efficiency. Children's own methods can therefore serve as a basis for teaching. In advocating that teachers encourage children to invent nonstandard algorithms, Labinowicz points out that those conventionally taught are not the only ones possible. He quotes Wheeler's (1977) example of a 9-year-old's procedures for adding $248 + 375 = 197$:

$$248 + 375 + 197$$
$$= 648 + 75 + 97$$
$$= 648 + 72 + 100$$
$$= 748 + 72$$
$$= 750 + 70$$
$$= 800 + 20$$
$$= 820$$

Labinowicz suggests classroom practices that emphasize exchange of views among children. The teacher's role is to circulate, observe children, and initiate interactions that encourage children to think. Recommended activities for pairs or small groups of children include various kinds of task cards with story problems, computations to check for errors, and "detective cards" with number obliterated by an "ink spill." While these differ little from workbook problems, the social context for their use results in a different experience for children. After children work with a set of problems, they return to a large group, and the teacher encourages children's presentation, clarification, comparison, and evaluation.

Presentation

- Would anyone like to show their methods (on the board)?
- Gloria, I noticed you were doing something different. Would you mind sharing it?
- Bill and Cindy, are you willing to share your methods? (Selected for contrast.)

Clarification

- Would you explain how your method works?
- Let me see if I understand you. (Teacher carefully verbalizes own understanding.)
- Does anyone want to ask any questions about Gloria's method?

Comparison

- How many different methods do we have on the board?
- Are any methods close enough to be called the same? (Different representation of the same procedure.)
- What's the same/different about these two methods?

Evaluation

- Is one method better than the other? What makes you think so?
- Suppose the problem was changed to ———. Would this method still be better?
- What kind of problem would this method be best for?
- Is there a method that's best for all problems we've tried so far?

Extension

- Have you got all the possible methods on the board?
- Would someone be willing to record these methods in a problem book for our class library? We'll leave some blank pages so that you can add other methods to the book as you think of them. (Each method is credited to its inventor.) (Labinowicz, 1985, pp. 387–388).

The central principle of teaching in this approach is for the teacher to understand children's thought processes.

In a Collect and Group (Trade) Game, children roll a pair of dice and put that number of cubes on a board called a "transition board" (having columns for tens and ones). With each new roll, they combine and regroup addends, trading for pregrouped unifix blocks when necessary. The goal is to collect the most objects in a specified time or to be first to reach a specified number.

Labinowicz's approach to primary-school arithmetic also differs from other methods in its recognition of the longer time needed by children to construct networks of number relations. He therefore advocates postponing written numbers and algorithms until children are comfortable with regrouping and renaming quantities of cubes. He also recommends that teachers practice lengthening the "wait time" after asking a question or making a suggestion.

Labinowicz concurs with Kamii and DeVries in specifying the importance of an environment in which the teacher's authority is reduced and children exercise autonomy. He recommends teaching by accepting children's answers, avoiding praise, encouraging self-evaluation, and redirecting adult authority back to children.

The approach described by Labinowicz for grades 1–3 differs from that of Kamii in its concentration on the transition to written algorithms through exercises or teacher-given tasks. It is also different in its assumption of children's interest in the mechanics of arithmetic as such. When children's interests can be harnessed, we would agree that the tasks in the social context described by Labinowicz may be constructive in the Piagetian sense. In addition to these tasks, we believe second- and third-grade children can also profit from playing group games and dealing with problems in daily living that require arithmetic calculation.

SUMMARY AND CONCLUSION

Much work remains to be done to formulate and demonstrate constructivist methods of teaching number and arithmetic. The beginnings described in this chapter derive from a central principle—to mesh instruction with the evolution of the child's reasoning. The teacher must be concerned with the ways in which mathematical ideas are established in the child's mind—that is, with the psychological construction. Similarities between the approach of Kamii and DeVries (and to some extent Labinowicz) and High/Scope, and that of Nuffield are summarized as follows.

1. Reasoning about number is embedded in a rich variety of activities that capitalize on children's interests in being active with countable objects. The specific nature of activities, however, differs in some respects, to be discussed below.
2. Logical quantification is encouraged. Like Nuffield and High/Scope, Kamii and DeVries stress the importance of children's opportunities to compare sets in logical terms such as "just enough," "as many," "too many," "more,"

"fewer," "the same," "less," "most," and so on. This characteristic differs from Montessori's emphasis on early calculation.
3. Wrong counting and calculation are not corrected. High/Scope is alone in its similarity to Kamii and DeVries on this point.
4. The writing of numerals is postponed. On this point, too, High/Scope is alone in its similarity to Kamii and DeVries.
5. Children's discussions about issues involving number are encouraged. This similarity is shared with Nuffield.

Characteristics of the Kamii-DeVries approach that differ from High/Scope and Nuffield are as follows.

1. The theoretical framework of Kamii and DeVries emphasizes the distinction among physical knowledge, logico-mathematical knowledge, and social-arbitrary knowledge, and between figurative and operative knowing. This especially contrasts with Nuffield's definition of number as a property of sets of objects. This theoretical uniqueness is at the heart of specific differences in practices. No earlier Piaget-inspired approach had made this distinction a foundation for deriving activities and principles of teaching.
2. Genevan tasks are not used as teaching contexts, either in the explicit way Lavatelli advocated or in the more veiled way advocated by High/Scope and Nuffield. Also, like Nuffield, Genevan number tasks are not used diagnostically as a basis for planning a sequence of activities.
3. Measurement activities are not included. Unlike Montessori, High/Scope, and Nuffield, activities involving continuous quantities are not considered to be important for mathematics, for reasons discussed above. Unlike High/Scope and Nuffield, play with fluid materials are included as physical-knowledge activities—elementary physics rather than number activities.
4. Group games are heavily emphasized, but are barely mentioned by High/Scope and are not mentioned at all by Nuffield. As described in Chapter 9, Montessori expressed abhorrence for the game of Hide and Seek, one of those recommended by Kamii and DeVries, and none of her number exercises uses a game format.
5. Children's specific interests in number are identified differently. Montessori assumed interest in her number materials and number itself out of the context of meaningful situations. Nuffield similarly assumed that interest in manipulating objects would arouse interest in teacher-designed tasks. High/Scope attempted more than Nuffield to integrate thinking about number into children's spontaneous interests in activities not defined as basically mathematical in nature. From our perspective, these are all less successful in harnessing the motive power of interest than problems in daily living and group games in which children have their own purposes for thinking about number. Kamii and DeVries have sought a still more organic integration of interest with children's activity.
6. Conflicts among children are capitalized upon. Although High/Scope and

Nuffield allude to children's interaction about number, the importance of confronting different views is not emphasized. However, in the Kamii-DeVries approach, children's confrontations with one another are a central part of the program. In activities involving number, the teacher capitalizes on situations in which children disagree by encouraging discussion to get consensus. In a board game when a child counts incorrectly, he is frequently corrected by other children, and the teacher encourages children to take account of others' ideas and come to an agreement. In Kamii's Double War, for example, one incident in a kindergarten involved the addition of 5 and 4, in comparison with 6 and 3. The child with 6 started to take all the cards, saying "Six is more." He was immediately contradicted by his partner. In the lively argument that followed, their concentration and attention to the question of equivalence was a powerful testimony to the effectiveness of games in promoting reasoning and construction of numerical relations.

A constructivist perspective is critical of New Math and Back to Basics methods because these approaches emphasize the production of right answers, ignore the nature of the child's reasoning, and thus can end up discouraging thinking. A constructivist approach involves understanding children's errors and confusions, and requires respect for the long time this process takes. As Inhelder, Sinclair, and Bovet (1974) noted, learning takes time, and children who progress furthest are often those who are most confused initially. The constructivist view of teaching number thus requires a fundamental reorientation of methods of evaluation as well as methods of teaching.

Chapter 8

Reading and Writing

In this chapter, consideration of reading and writing from a constructivist perspective—relying heavily on the work of Emilia Ferreiro and Ana Teberosky—has three objectives. The first is to present a summary of their research aimed at exposing the psychogenetic progression in children's knowledge and reasoning in the domain of written language. While other researchers have also revealed some of the phenomena described by Ferreiro and Teberosky (see, for example, Reid, 1966, Goodman & Goodman, 1977, Johns, 1977, and a review by Yaden, 1984), no one else has integrated them in a constructivist theory. A second minor objective is to discuss from a constructivist perspective two other approaches to conceptualizing developmental stages in reading—those of David Elkind and Jeanne Chall—in order to highlight the novelty of the Ferreiro-Teberosky approach. The third objective is to discuss implications of research in the constructivist tradition for teaching reading and writing, with illustrations from Teberosky's practical work in classrooms.

FERREIRO AND TEBEROSKY

After her training in genetic epistemology and psycholinguistics by Piaget and Hermina Sinclair at the University of Geneva, Ferreiro began psychogenetic research on reading and writing, to explore the question of whether a psychogenetic progression could be identified in the acquisition process. She observed that contemporary psycholinguistic theory had converged with Piaget's theory of intelligence in its understanding of the child as an active creator of spoken language. Research revealing children's constructive errors showed that the acquisition of spoken language could be reduced neither to a process of motor and sensory habit formation nor to associations between meaningless elements. However, there was no comparable theory of learning written language, and Ferreiro and Teberosky and other colleagues sought to fill this gap.

This constructivist theoretical orientation is in contrast to traditional assumptions about literacy that rest within the behavioristic tradition. Ferreiro's unique perspective leads to ground-breaking methods of studying children and to findings that move forward the frontier of our knowledge of the acquisition of literacy.

Ferreiro criticizes reading readiness tests because of their assumption that the capacity for reading and writing are based on "certain linguistic aspects (such as correct articulation) and non-linguistic aspects (such as visual perception and manual-motor coordination)" (Ferreiro & Teberosky, 1979/1982, p. 19). This collection of abilities or skills also typically includes left-right directionality and auditory discrimination. The behavioristic conception of the learner is as the passive recipient of knowledge given by the environment. In contrast, the research of Ferreiro and her colleagues supports the constructivist conception of an active learner who produces knowledge. That is, "an active learner compares, excludes, orders, categorizes, reformulates, confirms, forms hypotheses, and reorganizes through internalized action (thought) or through effective action (according to the level of development)" (Ferreiro & Teberosky, 1979/1982, p. 15). They tried to expose the positive aspects of what children know rather than what is lacking in terms of aptitudes and skills. The findings to be reviewed below show that preschool children try to understand written language, that they search for regularities, and test their predictions. As Sinclair notes in her foreword to *Literacy before Schooling* (Ferreiro & Teberosky, 1979/1982), "The authors show that children have ideas, and indeed, hypotheses and theories, which they continually test against the many examples of written text they encounter in their environment and against the information they receive from others" (p. v).

Concerned broadly with early school failure, especially in Latin America, Ferreiro began her work in 1974 in her home country, Argentina. Subsequently, she extended her studies to French-speaking children in Switzerland and to Spanish-speaking children in Mexico. This program of research and theory building is still in progress, but has already yielded important findings.

Methodology

Ferreiro's approach is to use Piaget's exploratory method to find out how children think about written language. Ferreiro and Teberosky sought to understand the child's psychological experience and changes in conceptions of print and writing from the viewpoint of the learner. Most research on reading and writing focuses on acquisition of what teachers try to teach—that is, on the degree to which children correctly interpret these culturally defined materials. In contrast, Ferreiro's method reveals how children transform these materials through an active process of assimilation. Her studies yield descriptions of many previously unsuspected "constructive errors" made by children. The picture of the child that emerges is of an active intelligence interacting with an object of knowledge—the print observable in the environment. What is "observable" to the child, however, is often surprising.

Ferreiro and Teberosky used a variety of ingenious techniques to study children's conceptions of written language. All their tasks involve an interaction between the child and the object of knowledge (written language) in the form of a problem to be solved. In each, the examiner introduces potentially conflictive elements, so that the solution requires reasoning and not just parroting of verbalisms given by adults. They studied children from the age of 4 years who could not read, 6-year-olds beginning to read, and compared lower- and middle-class children.

Hypotheses about Reading with Pictures

Young children who have had no systematic reading instruction interpret the relationship between picture and print in surprising ways. Ferreiro and Teberosky propose the following developmental progression in relation to pictures presented with a sentence written below (the same, but less elaborate progression was found for pictures with a word below).

1. *Picture and print are not differentiated.* At this level functions of picture and print are not yet differentiated. When asked to show where there is something to read, children go back and forth between the two symbol systems. While they *can* differentiate them, the term *to read* is understood to apply to both of them: Both picture and print are considered readable. It is clear that at this level writing is not considered to be a transcription of language.

2. *Print is differentiated from the picture.* Progress occurs when children begin to treat text as a somewhat independent unit. For example, children are shown a picture of a duck on the water with the sentence *"El pato nada"* (the duck swims). Children insist that it is "A duck," but that the print only says "duck." Thus a first distinction between picture and print is manifested when children systematically drop the article and accept only the name as represented by the text. Ferreiro and Teberosky call this the "name hypothesis." This differentiation constitutes progress, since the name is no longer confused with the picture. The text is a name, a unit of meaning distinct from the picture. Since writing does not yet represent language, the interpretation of what is actually written does not always correspond to their verbalizations. What is written is not necessarily the same as what can be read.

   Children categorized as 2A reject the possibility that a sentence is written. Category 2B is a response characterized by attributing a sentence to the text as a whole. An intermediate substage is characterized by fluctuation between name and sentence attribution. Text is still pointed to without precision, indicating that children at this level do not attend to graphic properties. They expect as many names in the text as there are objects in the picture.

3. *Initial consideration of some of the graphic properties of print.* At this level, children continue to assume that the text represents a label (answer type 3A) or a sentence (answer type 3B) close in meaning to the picture. What is new at this level is the establishment of a special relation between different segments of text and different aspects of the picture. The first graphic consideration is to distinguish between two lines of print. For example, a child might say that the first line says "Toad" and the second line says "Flowers" when the picture contains these two elements.

   For children at this level, graphic properties of the text pose a problem. The recognition of discontinuity in the print comes into conflict with the assumption of unitary meaning of print. This is reconciled by introducing sound transformations without changing the meaning (for example, attributing the first syllable of a name to the first line, and the second syllable to the second line) or introducing new meanings (attributing one sentence to the first line and a different sentence to the second line). Since writing is not connected to voiced aspects of language, it is often connected to quantifiable characteristics of objects. For example, large objects should be represented by graphics proportional to their size. Type 3C children often continue to believe that only names are written, but that a sentence can be read. What is written is therefore still different from what can be read from the name. Nevertheless, the effort at Level 3 to establish correspondence between parts of the text and parts of the picture paves the way for Level 4.

4. *Search for a one-to-one correspondence between graphic and sound segments.* Still considering print to be a label for the picture, children at Level 4 attempt to match a spoken segment with some written segment. For example, the sentence "*Raul rema en el río*" (Raul rows on the river) is read by one 5-year-old as "*Pescados*" (fishes). Pointing to "*Raul rema*," he says "*Pes*"; "*en el*" is read as "*ca*"; and "*río*" is read as "*dos.*"

While Ferreiro and Teberosky do not provide detailed numerical data on these levels, they note a concentration of Types 2 and 3 for children 4 to 6 years of age. The important point is that children's conceptualizations about written language possess an internal logic that is independent of schooling.

Ferreiro (in press) discusses the foregoing kinds of ideas of children as "typical examples of distorted assimilation, to use the classical Piagetian terminology" (p. 44). She goes on to say:

> The distance between the available information and children's ideas is too big: children are not able to understand because accommodation is impossible when assimilation is not possible either. The result is a distortion of the object (in this case, the written text) which is completely assimilated to the interpretive schemes of the subject, without taking into account its specific properties. (p. 44)

Coordination of Deciphering and Meaning through Conflict

Responses to the task discussed above led Ferreiro (1976, 1977; also reported in Ferreiro & Teberosky, 1979/1982) to hypothesize three aspects in the process that culminates in the coordination of decoding and meaning. Central to this process is the mechanism of cognitive conflict, observable in children's hesitations and vacillations. The classification of responses is described below.

1. *Separation of deciphering and meaning.*
   a. *Meaning without deciphering.* The child uses the picture in search of the meaning of the sentence. One or more names are suggested and sometimes a sentence. Some children try to consider properties of the text. For example, spaces between words may be assumed to indicate the end of one name and the beginning of another. "*El pato nada*" (the duck swims) may be read as "*pato, agua, flor*" (duck, water, flower).
   b. *Decoding without meaning.* The child focuses on isolated elements in the text without reference to the picture. For example, some letters may be iden-

tified, or meaningless syllables may be suggested. Ferreiro found no pre-school children responding in this way and concludes that this "pure deciphering totally devoid of meaning, an end in itself. . .is, without a doubt, a product of schooling" (Ferreiro & Teberosky, 1979/1982, p. 93).

c. *Attempt to relate deciphering and meaning.* The child tries to take account of the meaning of the picture, but also tries to find in the text something that will support the hypothesized meaning. For example, in the sentence "*La ranita solió de paseo*"), one child "reads" "*ra-na, porque está la a*," pointing to the last "*a*" in "*ranita.*" This effort eventually leads to conflict and category 2.

2. *Conflict between deciphering and meaning.*

a. *Primacy of deciphering.* The picture is used as a basis for predicting what the sentence says, but its unpredictability is appreciated. The child thus tries to decode, but in an effort to get an exact decoding, the meaning is lost. Ferreiro notes the extreme cases at this level in which children decode correctly (say all the sounds that are written) and thus appear to be reading, but they have no idea what the sounds mean. This effort is obviously unsatis-factory to the child, and leads to abandoning at least some of the meaningless sounds at 2B. This response type is also attributed to the unfortunate effects of schooling in which deciphering is emphasized.

b. *Primacy of meaning.* The effort toward coherence leads the child to eliminate or substitute parts that cannot be meaningfully integrated. What the text says is not distinguished from what it means. Ferreiro's example relates to the sentence "*La mano del mono tiene dedos*" (The monkey's hand has fingers).

> "La mano del mono tie-ne, ti-ne de-do, dedo; la mano del mo. . .ti-ne-dos. . . tinedos. . .tinedo. La mano del mono tinedo." When asked, "What does that mean?" the child answers: "Tinedo is the monkey's name," centering his response on the problematic element, having understood the rest of the sentence. (Ferreiro, 1977, p. 20)

c. *Oscillations between deciphering and meaning.* Efforts reflecting either a primacy of meaning or a primacy of decoding inevitably produce dissatis-faction in the child with his result. This conflict can lead to oscillation between decoding and meaning within the same sentence. The result is the correct decoding of some parts. Remaining parts may be decoded correctly but be incomprehensible to the child, or something meaningful may be added by looking at the picture. One child read "The monkey is peeling a banana" (pictured), then "The monkey is riding a scooter" (not pictured). In the latter case, "*mono*" (monkey) is read as "moto" and "*mano*" (hand) is read as "mono." Finally, this child focuses on "*dedos*" (fingers) as "de-do-s." This brings to mind the gesture of putting the finger to the mouth and saying "Shhh." He reads, "The monkey that tells the birds to be quiet."

3. *Coordination between deciphering and meaning.* Ferreiro includes cases in this category where success is achieved eventually, but not immediately. What distinguishes the child at this level is the effort to coordinate meaning and decipering, without compromising either. For example, "*ranita*" (the little frog) might be read at first "ra-ra-na" ("*rana*" is frog), in an effort to make the number of syllables correspond with the length of the word. In the case of grammatical errors resulting from incorrect decoding, children at this level know that what is said must correspond with what is written, and correct their reading by recourse to their grammatical knowledge.

Evidence for this sequence as a true psychogenetic progression comes from longitudinal study of 30 lower-class children in Buenos Aires during their first school year. While stating, "We are not saying that all children go through these phases," Ferreiro and Teberosky nevertheless are convinced that progress does follow this sequence in children whose instruction places principal emphasis on decipering. Ferreiro raises the issue, however, that the first separation of meaning and decoding may not be necessary—that is, may not be natural—but may be an artificial result of instruction that "from the beginning, leads toward such a separation" (Ferreiro, 1977, p. 25). This study shows that progress does require the child to go through a process of reconciliation between "linguistic knowledge...and the discovery of specific properties of the representation system of his language which is the alphabetic writing itself" (p. 26). Ferreiro concludes that conflict is necessary for the eventual coordination of meaning and decipering. She also notes that this conflict is independent of teaching methodology, since the oscillation between meaning and decoding cannot be attributed to the teaching of such oscillation. Conflict forces new analyses and inevitably leads to correct conclusions.

Conceptualizations about What Is Written in a Written Sentence

Ferreiro and Teberosky's procedure was to write a sentence (of the type noun + transitive verb + article + noun, or article + noun + transitive verb + article + noun) in front of a child and then to read it with normal intonation while pointing to the text in a sweeping, continuous gesture. The child was asked to indicate where each word is, and to say what is written in specific parts of the text. Subjects were lower- and middle-class children aged 4, 5, and 6 years. The psychogenetic progression is as follows.

1. *Separate parts of utterance are not matched with separate parts of text; whole sentence is attributed to one written segment; or only nouns are represented.* Three response types characterize the first level of conceptualization. The first includes children who find it impossible to separate the utterance into parts that can be matched to parts of the text. When asked where a certain word is, they point in a vague, erratic, and contradictory manner, referring as much to the whole sentence as to various parts, or to pieces of one part.

   The second response type includes children who attribute the whole sentence to one written segment. The leftover segments present a problem to which children respond by making up congruent sentences. Consider the following example.

> *Ximena* (4 yrs., MC) for PAPA PATEA LA PELOTA (DAD KICKS THE BALL): proposes the following for each of the segments from left to right:
> Papa patea la pelota.
> Papa grave (Dad sick).
> Papa escribe la fecha (Dad writes the date).
> Papa se va a dormir (Dad goes to sleep).
> (Ferreiro & Teberosky, 1979, p. 125)

Ferreiro and Teberosky conclude that the basic hypothesis of these children is that the sentence constitutes a whole that cannot be represented by several fragments of text.

The third response type in this first level is that only nouns are represented in the text. Children hypothesize compatible nouns for leftover text. For example, for the sentence "Dad kicks the ball," one 5-year-old says that one part is "Mama" because "Mama has to be there" (Ferreiro & Teberosky, 1979/1982, p. 127). Detailed analysis leads the authors to conclude that "written language is a particular way of representing objects, or, if one prefers, a particular way of drawing" (Ferreiro & Teberosky, 1979, p. 129). New objects are introduced as "background scenery or decorations of the action" (p. 129). Action cannot be drawn, and verbs are therefore not written but suggested by the whole picture.

Ferreiro and Teberosky report these Level 1 conceptualizations in 46% of the 4-year-olds they studied (45% of middle-class and 48% of lower-class), 30% of 5-year-olds (17% of middle-class and 60% of lower-class), and 41% of 6-year-olds (31% of middle-class and 43% of lower-class).

2. *Nouns appear independently in written form, but the verb is linked to the whole sentence or to the whole predicate.* At this level, children progress to stable placement of nouns but continue to have difficulty conceiving the verb as an independent written segment. They include it with a noun or insist that it is not written anywhere. Ferreiro and Teberosky (1979/1982) conclude that "written language consists of a series of cues regarding the essential elements of the oral message; on the basis of these elements one constructs the message" (p. 119). In Ferreiro and Teberosky's study, this type of response was found in 30% of 4-year-olds (24% of middle-class and 39% of lower-class), 27% of 5-year-olds (32% of middle-class and 21% of lower-class), and 16% of 6-year-olds (12% of middle-class and 24% of lower-class).

3. *Everything is written except articles.* This response type is characterized by correct location of nouns and verbs, but not articles. Children think the written article (consisting of two letters in Spanish singular) does not say anything and should be removed, or the article is another noun related to the general meaning of the sentence. The "leftover" problem is often resolved by making it part of the word it precedes or follows, assigning to it the first syllable of that noun. The latter belief stems from an assumption about

graphics—that in order to be read, a word must have more than two letters.

This technique also revealed that young children often believe that what one can read is not necessarily what is written. That is, they read the sentence including the article, but nevertheless believe the article is not written anywhere. Other research (Berthoud-Papandropolou, 1976) indicates that young children systematically reject articles as well as prepositions, pronouns, and conjunctions as "words" in orally presented sentences. Ferreiro points out that this is a key to understanding her findings. That is, if children assume that what is written is words, there is no reason for writing spoken elements that are not classified as "words." The problem of the article thus has its source in both graphic and metalinguistic aspects of children's thought. Ferreiro and Teberosky report this response type among 22% of 4-year-olds (29% of middle-class and 13% of lower-class), 35% of 5-year-olds (42% of middle-class and 29% of lower-class), and 30% of 6-year-olds (41% of middle-class and 8% of lower-class).

4. *Everything is written, including articles.* This response is not surprising among readers who have mastered deciphering. It occurs, however, among nonreaders as well, and even among those who can decipher, deduction rather than deciphering is often the basis for correct responses. That is, this correct response type rests on assumptions about what elements in spoken language are represented (nouns, verbs, and articles) and about the correspondence between temporal and spatial order. Ferreiro and Teberosky found this response type among only 1% of 4-year-olds (3% of middle-class and 0% of lower-class), 8% of 5-year-olds (10% of middle-class and 7% of lower-class), and 13% of 6-year-olds (16% of middle-class and 8% of lower-class). See also Ferreiro (1978) on children's ideas about what is written in a written sentence.

The Evolution of Writing

Five successive levels were hypothesized, based on initial research with children before schooling.

1. *Subjective intent and figural correspondence, hypotheses of minimum number, and variation of graphics.* At this level, the child's subjective intent counts more than objective differences in graphic forms. Nevertheless, Level 1 writing bears some global resemblance to what the child attempts to emulate. When this is print, children make separate characters of curved and/or straight lines. When this is cursive, children make closed or open curves linked by a wavy line. Thus writing is not viewed as a means of communicating, since children believe that one can interpret one's own but not others' writing. As one 4-year-old explained, "People know what they write and I knew what I was writing" (Ferreiro & Teberosky, 1979/1982, p. 180).

Level 1 is also characterized by some attempts to make a figural correspondence between writing and some quantifiable properties of the object referred to. Ferreiro and Teberosky describe one 4-year-old, for example, who felt a necessity to write "*oso*" (bear) bigger than "*pato*" (duck). A 5-year-old thought "*papa*" would have to be longer than "my brother goes to school," and another insisted that her name would have to be "longer because yesterday was my birthday" (Ferreiro & Teberosky, 1979/1982, pp. 183–184).

When print is what children try to emulate, two hypotheses are manifest at this level about what is needed to write something—that graphic characters are varied (the "variation" hypothesis), and their number is constant (the "minimum quantity" hypothesis). Generally, the minimum number is never less than 3 characters. Ferreiro and Teberosky emphasize that the assumption of a minimum number of characters is the child's construction, since no adult teaches that words with two letters cannot be read.

2. *Different graphics for different meaning.* At this level children feel that to read different things, objective differences in graphics are necessary. This is a higher level than that of children who use the same writing to represent different things. Intention is no longer sufficient. Characters tend to be better defined and more similar to conventional letter forms, although pseudo letters are also found. When the stock of graphic forms is limited, children indicate different meanings by varying the order of their graphics.

3. *Syllabic hypothesis.* Progress to this level is assignment of a sound value to each letter in a piece of writing. Ferreiro and Teberosky stress the significance at this level of children's hypothesis that each letter stands for a syllable. This represents "a qualitative leap forward in relation to the preceding levels" (Ferreiro & Teberosky, 1979/1982, p. 197). No longer is the correspondence between writing and oral expression global. Progress is manifested in a new "correspondence between parts of the text (individual letters) and parts of the utterance (syllables)" (p. 199). Still, letters may not all be conventional at this level, and sound values may not be stable. One 4-year-old wrote AO for "*sa-po*" (toad) and PA for "*o-so*" (bear). Ferreiro (in press) comments that the syllabic hypothesis is used first to justify and later to control the process of writing.

During the period of transition from global to one-to-one correspondence, fixed forms (whole word written from memory) and the syllabic hypothesis coexist. When children work with the syllabic hypothesis in mind, they need to write two-syllable words with two letters. This creates a cognitive disturbance that recurs continually because it conflicts with their minimum-quantity hypothesis that calls for three or more letters for something to read. One-syllable words create even more difficulty. Sinclair (personal communication) has hypothesized that the syllabic hypothesis may be much less evident in English-speaking children because so many of their words are one syllable.

What is especially interesting at this level is the conflict children experience with regard to the fixed forms, or stable strings, they have learned previously.

Using the syllabic hypothesis in trying to read fixed forms leads the child to confront the "leftover problem." This is especially evident with regard to children's names. During a visit to Houston, Ferreiro demonstrated this kind of conflict in an interview with a 4-year-old in the Human Development Laboratory School. Asked to write her name, the child wrote MAYA. When asked how it says that, Maya's efforts revealed a problem for her in relating the totality with the constituent parts. Covering first the YA, Ferreiro asked what the MA said. Maya responded "May," omitting the final "ah" sound. However, when MA was covered, Maya attributed both syllables to the final two letters. Pointing to Y, she pronounced "Mi," and pointing to A, she pronounced "yah." When the whole name was uncovered and Ferreiro asked, "And all of it?" she of course answered, "Maya." Ferreiro then asked, "So how does it go?" Maya then had difficulty because there were more letters than syllables, and attempted to reconcile this conflict in the following ways.

M   A (Y) A
Mah − ah − yah

She slid her finger over the Y without stopping, and Ferreiro repeated her attribution, then asked, "And this?" pointing to Y. Maya says, "No," and tried again, this time sliding over the first A.

M (A) Y   A
Mah − ah − yah

The next attempt omitted the final A.

M   A   Y (A)
Mah − ah − yah.

In frustration, Maya said, "I want to go now."

In another example of this conflict quoted by Ferreiro and Teberosky, a 5-year-old drew a car and was asked to write "car" (*carro*). Guided by his minimum-quantity hypothesis, he wrote four letters, AEIO. When asked to read what he wrote, he pointed to AE and said "*ca-rro.*" Hesitating when asked about the remaining letters, he said "*mo-tor,*" pointing to IO. This effort to account for the leftover part is consistent with Level 3 described above with regard to children's interpretations of written sentences. Left-overs in that context were interpreted as names of objects consistent with total meaning. Ferreiro and Teberosky again point out that these ideas are clearly children's original constructions, since they cannot be attributed to adult teaching.

4. *Syllabic-alphabetic hypothesis.* This level is a transitional period in which the alphabetic hypothesis begins to emerge. Conflicts beginning at Level 3 continue to occur as the child is confronted with known fixed forms whose reading according to the syllabic hypothesis is not in accord with reality provided by the environment. The child thus feels the necessity to revise this hypothesis and surpass it in order to resolve the conflict between internal constructions and external reality. Ferreiro and Teberosky describe the struggle of children who vacillate between syllabic and phonetic inter-pretations of words for which they have a stable visual image—such as their own names. For example, Maria, a 4-year-old, tries to make her name with movable letters. At one point MIA satisfied her feeling of necessity about syllabication, but she knows that an A comes after the M. When she places the A, she is not satisfied, either, because she now has one more letter than syllables. Her compromise is to start out reading phonetically and end up syllabically: "m/a/ri/a."

They emphasize that children do not abandon the syllabic hypothesis im-mediately upon beginning phonic analysis. Instead, they found that "children can go through long periods of fluctuation between syllabic and alphabetic writing, producing reading and writing which tend to begin syllabically and end alphabetically" (p. 270). Conflict with the minimum-quantity hypothesis and with written models given by the environment "can only be resolved by searching for an analysis that goes beyond the syllabic (dividing the syllable into smaller units of sound)" (Ferreiro & Teberosky, 1979/1982, pp. 269–270).

5. *Alphabetic hypothesis.* The end point of this evolution is reached when the child understands that each written character corresponds to a sound value smaller than a syllable. The syllabic hypothesis eventually is abandoned in favor of phonetic analysis because the syllabic hypothesis cannot reconcile the conflict between transmitted truths and the child's logic. Spelling and word separation difficulties remain, but Ferreiro and Teberosky do not view these as writing problems in the strict sense, since the code has been essentially broken.

What is most significant from an educational point of view is that in traditional schooling teachers begin teaching reading and writing on the assumption that children are at the last level of a lengthy evolution. Specific research findings regarding children's school failure in relation to their psychogenetic progress will be presented later.

Longitudinal Study of Hypotheses about Written Names

Ferreiro (in press) discusses the interplay between information provided by the environment and the child's process of assimilation. She describes the details of the psychogenetic progression in individual children with the main focus on the writing of proper names. Some of the hypotheses constructed by one of these children, Santiago (a middle-class child from an environment rich in literacy), and his related cognitive conflicts are described below.

One of Santiago's first hypotheses was that letters belong to persons. This hypothesis was inspired directly by the environment. At about 2½ years, Santiago wants to write and asks for some models. Someone in the family writes his name with capital letters, and the first letters of names of well-known persons. Santiago is told, "This is Santiago's, this is Ruben's," and so on. By 2 years 7 months, Santiago recognizes 14 different letters as belonging to known persons. This information leads him to certain problems and conflicts. While he knows that the first letter is not enough to "say" the entire name, he does not understand why someone's name includes other people's letters. Santiago recognizes in CARMELA "Carmela's, Anne's, Ruben's, mommy's, Ernesto's, Luis', Anne's," and asks, "Why did you put them all together?" Santiago experiences four conflicts. The first is that although Gabriel's letter is there in his name, it does not say Gabriel. . . and so on with the remaining letters.

The second conflict involves the reason for the particular number of letters in a name. One hypothesis is that there are as many letters as years of age. The conflict then is what the leftover letters say. Santiago resolves this at one point by adding "mommy and daddy," and at another by "Santiago washed his hands, he went to play, he ate a cracker." These are not satisfactory because of the absence of mommy and daddy's letters, and because Santiago believes that what is written are nouns. There is thus the problem of how the text can "say" what Santiago has done without repeating "his" letter. To this is added the difficulty that some people have two letters ("p" for "papa," and "R" for his name, "Ruben").

The third conflict is that some letters have no known owner. For example, W is "nobody's—mommy's upside down." The fourth conflict arises when "U" is presented by the family as "the one of fingernail" (*la de una*), and the figural similarity between U and the fingernail is pointed out. Now Santiago is conflicted when asked whether there are some letters that are not for people.

Ferreiro (in press) sums up Santiago's literacy development in terms of his reformulation of information given to him.

> He has quickly absorbed the information provided by the family, but he has reformulated it. The family has given information about the first letter of proper names, but Santiago has understood it as owners of letters. Each person may have his or her own letter, as a part of his/her own identity. This letter cannot be shared. For that reason, when the family gives the information that L—previously identified as "Luis," is also the letter of Leonardo, Santiago rejects this information, and is quite disturbed (obs. 8, 2 years 6 months old).
>
> The information provided by the environment has allowed Santiago to find a reason to discriminate among the arbitrary letter-forms, but this same rationality has its own limits: it is bothersome (but not more than that) to accept that there are letters that belong "to nobody"; it is a little bit disturbing to accept that someone

(but not anybody) has the right to have two letters, instead of only one; it is much more disturbing to accept that there is one letter "for fingernail," all the others being "for people"; it is extremely conflicting to accept that the letters of the others are a constitutive part of the proper name. With all the available information, but also with all these conflicts, Santiago will pursue his exploration into literacy. (pp. 12–13)

Santiago interprets texts using two different, coexisting procedures. One procedure is to take the first letter as a cue for a person. The other is to take the context as a starting point. Context predominates when Santiago says that a card with the text "*ELEFANTE*" says "elephant" when placed below a picture of an elephant, but that the same card says "lion," "donkey," "horse," "arm-chair," or "wall," depending on where it is placed.

At the age of 2 years 10 months, Santiago sometimes attempts a syllabic decomposition of a name in order to know how many letters are necessary. He decides there should be three to write "San-tia-go" and two for "Ru-ben." At this age, he begins to draw pseudo letters in addition to the conventional ones he has learned to draw. He invents absurd names for their owners and even writes his own name with three pseudo letters. Ferreiro (in press) interprets this apparent regression in the following way as an attempt to maintain the hypothesis that letters cannot be shared.

> Santiago does not succeed in reconciling the ownership rule with the fact that the same letters are used to constitute other names. As he cannot solve the problem, he tries to isolate both aspects: only the letter to each person, and the entire name in only one letter, working only at the qualitative level. On the other side, he tries to understand why adults use so many letters for a single name, and in this case he works only at the quantitative level, making his first syllabic analysis of words. . . . The pseudo-letters he is inventing allow him a momentaneous dissociation between quantitative and qualitative aspects of the written product (because the qualitative ones are so closely linked to the ownership rule). (pp. 18–19)

Ferreiro cites three incidents that make it clear how resistant Santiago is to the idea that letters can be shared. Disturbed at being told that P is not only "papa's," but also "Paula's," Santiago divides the letter into two parts, attributing the round part as "daddy's" and the straight part as "Paula's." He also refuses to accept the letter of Ana as also that of Anne, and says that Z can not be the letter of Zorro because "It's Nelson's." The surprising finding of this longitudinal study was that it took an entire calendar year for Santiago to accept that a given letter may belong to various names.

Hypotheses about the Results of Transforming Words and Sentences

Ferreiro and Teberosky explored children's interpretations of transformed words and sentences in order to understand what they consider essential in order for interpretation to remain the same. The procedure was to take words used in beginning instruction (such as "*mamá*," "*papá*," and "*oso*" [bear]) and first to ask children to write them. If they were unable to do this, the experimenter wrote them and children were asked to read them. Once the correct interpretation was agreed upon, the same letters were rearranged as the experimenter rewrote them. From *OSO*, for example, the experimenter wrote "OOS, OS, OSOS, SOS, and the child was asked if each was still the original word. If the child said it was not, he or she was asked what it said. The examiner was careful to refer to the original each time as the rearranged letters were written underneath ("I'll put this one here, this here, and this here"). In one study, Ferreiro and Teberosky also proposed transformations with the addition to one familiar word the initial letter of another familiar word (for example, going from "*oso*" to "*moso*" or "*poso*."

Two groups of low-socioeconomic-status children were studied with this procedure; those from 4 to 6 years had not received instruction in school, and 6- and 7-year-olds were receiving school instruction. Since the response types found were similar in the two groups, those presented below are from the schooled group who were interviewed at the middle of the school year. By this time, the teachers had presented at least six words, including those used in the transformation procedure. Responses were classifed according to the following categories.

1. Letters are viewed as graphic cues indicating the presence of a certain word. For example, the "p" in "*papá*" is not just one of the letters in the word. Rather, it is more important, being the cue that confers the meaning on the whole word. Estela thus identified the transformation of "*oso*" into "*poso*" as "*papá*," and into "*moso*" as "*mamá*." Griseldo said that the transformation of "*oso*" into "oos," "osos," and "soso" is still "oso, because it has the *s* and the *o*" (Ferreiro & Teberosky, 1979/1982, p. 231). Children thus use different graphic cues. In their examples, some use the initial letter, some two of the letters in the word, and some two identical letters with an accent mark.
2. The original number and type of letters are retained as essential, but the order is accepted as variable. Griseldo thus thinks that "*mamá*" transformed to "amam" is also "*mamá*" but with the accent mark missing.
3. Order is necessary, but only to produce symmetry. For example, "oso" and "sos" are considered variants of the same word.

These three response types are at the same cognitive level and may all appear in the same child. Ferreiro and Teberosky note that children giving these three responses all fail to conserve number.

4. A slight graphic change corresponds to a slight change in meaning. For example, Daniel thinks that when "*oso*" is transformed into "*osos*," it is "female bear," and when transformed into "soso," it is "little bear."
5. A slight graphic change corresponds to a slight change in sound, but the original meaning is conserved. For example, Miguel, who reads "*sol*"

correctly, nevertheless believes that "*solo*" is "*soool*" and still means "*sol*."

6. Mixtures of types 4 and 5 sometimes lead to compromise solutions in which a whole sentence may be used to interpret a transformation. For example, Omar, who recognizes the word "*nene*" (boy), reads the transformation into "pnene" as "nenepa," which means "boy who is grown up and is a father" (Ferreiro & Teberosky, 1979/1982, p. 232).

Most surprisingly, on this task preschool children and those who had already been systematically exposed to literacy instruction gave very similar responses. The authors comment:

> How many times must their teachers have written, broken down into letters and sounds, combined and recombined these beginning words? Nothing appears more simple: m-a, ma: ma-ma, mama. It is a question of analysis and synthesis, in the traditional conception of instruction. But this traditional conceptualization differs from reality: while teachers demonstrate the apparent simplicities of this analysis (of the word and its components) and present the synthesis of these components as obvious and natural, children are learning something else. (Ferreiro & Teberosky, p. 233)

Let us move now to the study of children's responses to transformation of a sentence. *EL PERRO CORRIÓ AL GATO* (THE DOG CHASED THE CAT) was changed to *EL GATO CORRIÓ AL PERRO* (THE CAT CHASED THE DOG). Children were asked to say what they thought it said. Ferreiro and Teberosky describe the developmental order of responses as follows:

1. It says the same thing. Although they take note of the transformation, children at this level see no reason to anticipate any change in meaning.
2. It says the same thing, but the reading order must be changed. That is, children say the meaning is the same, but it is necessary to read from right to left since what was at the right was moved to the left, and vice versa.
3. It says the same thing and it doesn't. Children feel that something has changed, but do not know what. They are indecisive about the significance of the similarities and differences of the transformed in comparison to the original sentence. Maximo (5 years), for example, says, "It's wrong. It's all turned around. It says the dog chased the cat but it's wrong" (Ferreiro & Teberosky, 1979/1982, p. 136).
4. It says something else. Children giving responses of this type say they don't know what the transformation says, but that it must say something else. They reject any suggestion of the correct reading. Jorge (4 years) thinks it says "the dog ran (*el perro corrió*)," and Leonardo (5 years) thinks it says "the dog is in the doghouse" (Ferreiro & Teberosky, 1979/1982, p. 136).
5. Discovery of the correct response after responding "I don't know" or "it says the same thing."
6. Immediate deduction. Deciphering is not attempted at this level because children arrive at the correct answer through deduction. As Alejandro (6

years) said, "it has to be the same but turned around" (Ferreiro & Teberosky, 1979/1982, p. 137).

Relation of Literacy Levels to Piaget's Stages

Piaget's stages pertain to adaptation to natural and universal content such as material aspects of reality, and to the development of logic. Levels in literacy pertain to adaptation to man-made written language. That is, written language is essentially arbitrary, conventional knowledge (though it has physical and logico-mathematical aspects). We might expect this difference in content to lead to differences in a description of structural stages and constructive processes. However, to the extent that stages are related across domains, it seems useful to consider the relation between levels in literacy and stages in operational development. Using the conservation of number task as an indication of a child's general cognitive development, Ferreiro and her colleagues provide some insights into the relation between this general development and literacy development. The establishment of this relation also serves to validate Ferreiro's hypothesis that her description of levels in literacy is a true psychogenetic sequence. She has reported the following findings.

Longitudinal Study

1. All except one of the five first-grade children who divorced deciphering from meaning (Type 1 response in sentence reading with pictures) throughout the year remained at the preoperational stage on number.
2. All except one of 15 children who coordinated deciphering and meaning (Type 3 response) by the middle of the school year, and all except one of 15 others by the end, were at the same time found to be intermediate or fully operational.

Word Transformation Study

1. All 6- and 7-year-old children in school who believed word transformations to be related to meaning (Response Types 1–3) rather than sound were pre-operational on the number task.
2. All children who believed that slight word transformations corresponded to a slight change in meaning or sound, or who offered compromise solutions, (Response Types 4–6) were at the transitional level on number.

Solid evidence is thus provided for Elkind's intuition (discussed below) that operational progress is related to phonetic word analysis. Ferreiro and Teberosky's analysis of the reason for the relationship between operational development and progress in literacy is very different from Elkind's discussion.

While they, too, believe that word analysis is related to the development of operations, they interpret this relation in the following way. The finding that it is the preoperational children (with regard to number) who focus on the number of characters to the exclusion of the order, or vice versa, leads Ferreiro and Teberosky (1979/1982) to comment:

> Our interpretation is that instruction forces cognitive activity which is beyond their competence. It is too much for them to work simultaneously with breaking down a whole (the word) into its constituents (syllables and letters), reconstructing the whole from its parts, understanding the composition of subclasses of similar elements, focusing on the number of elements of each subclass (two m's and two a's, two s's and one o), and finally, knowing the order of the elements as they form the whole. Preoperational children cannot do all these things at once. They can either take into account the order (in terms of alternations or symmetry), ignoring the number in each subclass of similar elements, or they can take into account the subclasses, disregarding the order of the elements within the whole....From a cognitive point of view, we have known for a long time that preoperational children are not able to work with wholes and parts simultaneously....The heart of the matter is that we must learn to mistrust what appears obvious to adults. (p. 234)

Ferreiro does not conclude that operational development is or should be viewed as necessary to reading. Clearer evidence is provided in untranslated later work (Ferreiro & Gomez Palacio y colaboradores, 1982), where it is stated that "the operational level 'facilitates the' access to the alphabetic writing system, but it is not a necessary condition" (personal communication, 1986). Ferreiro also suggests that children at preoperational and operational levels may learn to read through different processes. Ferreiro's views (see also Ferreiro, 1985a, 1985b) may be contrasted with those of Elkind and Chall, discussed below.

ELKIND

Elkind (1981) proposes five stages in the development of reading, based on Piaget's theory and his own theoretical elaboration. He criticizes information-processing and behavior-modification approaches because these lack a basis in the logic of the child. Elkind's stages are based on hypothesized theoretical correspondences between Piaget's tasks (especially seriation and classification) and reading tasks. The aim of this conceptualization, like that of Ferreiro, is definition of "hard structural stages" that share with Piaget's stages general cognitive characteristics. Elkind's Piagetian lens, unlike that of Ferreiro, is focused on the child's knowledge content in its approximation to that of adults, rather than on children's theories about written language. His five stages are as follows.

1. GLOBAL UNDIFFERENTIATION (3–4 YEARS). At this stage, children may learn the names of some letters, and a few in alphabetic order. This is said to be preconceptual and preseriational. By preconceptual, Elkind means

that the child cannot understand that all A's are alike in that they are all A's, but different in context, size, print, and script. By preserational, Elkind means that children do not scan from left to right or know that A comes before B, B before C, and so on. Children at the stage of global undifferentiation thus know an A in one context but not another, and recite letters in alphabetic order by rote and not as a result of "true seriation." For Elkind, the test of operational seriation is whether the alphabet can be recited backwards.

2. IDENTITY DECODING (4½–6½ YEARS).   At Stage 2, according to Elkind, children are capable of class inclusion (understanding that there are more children than boys or girls in their class). They are also able to seriate seven or eight size-graded elements, and to conserve number. Conservation of letters is indicated by recognition when they are upside down. Listening to stories is recommended for its value in "watching the adult transform printed marks into sounds" (Elkind, 1981, p. 273). Progress in classification and seriation finds its parallel in recognition that letters can be translated into sounds and that combinations of letters can be transformed into words. This is a transformation Elkind calls identity decoding. The child thus knows that a given letter remains the same as before when spoken. Elkind (1981) believes this decoding "can be acquired on the basis of experience and without the direct intervention of logic" (p. 275).

3. EQUIVALENCE DECODING (6½–9 YEARS).   This stage in reading coincides with the attainment of concrete operations. Whereas identity coding is restricted to single transformations of sounds or words, equivalence decoding is defined as understanding that the same letter can represent different sounds and that the same sounds can be represented by different letters. Elkind views this as analogous to logical addition and logical subtraction, and equates the position of a letter in the alphabet to the ordinal character of a number, and the letter's name to the cardinal value of a number (Elkind, 1975b). This analysis led Elkind to advocate that equivalence decoding be postponed until children attain concrete operations. He suggests practice in identity coding until that time.

4. AUTOMIZATION AND EXTERNALIZATION (9–12 YEARS).   During this stage, equivalence decoding is said to become automatic as children's attention is more and more given to interpretation rather than decoding tasks.

5. LEXICAL EGOCENTRISM AND RECEPTIVE DISCIPLINE (EARLY ADOLESCENCE).   This stage corresponds to Piaget's stage of formal operations. Children are able to "hold many ideas in mind at the same time, grasp metaphor and simile, think in terms of historical time and celestial space, grasp contrary to fact conditions, and much more" (Elkind, 1981, p. 278). Lexical egocentrism is defined as reading without the "receptive discipline" of listening carefully to what the writer is saying and putting it "into our own intellectual framework without at the same time changing the writer's message" (Elkind, 1981, p. 278).

Elkind (1975a, 1975b) asserts that average readers are superior in logical ability to "slow readers" of comparable overall intelligence, and that training in "logical skills" has a significant effect on some aspects of reading achievement.

In our view, Elkind's stages have a lot in common with "literal translations" of Piaget's theory into educational practice. That is, they include direct translations of parts of Piaget's theory into a conceptualization of literacy acquisition.

Along with Zimiles (1981), we view this description of stages as an over-extension of Piagetian constructs and cannot accept the idea that learning to read corresponds in the way Elkind describes to operational development. While some of the characteristics of Stage 5 may involve something akin to formal reasoning (for example, understanding historical time and celestial space), what Elkind calls equivalence coding does not require concrete operations. If concrete operations were required for successful beginning reading as Elkind (1975b) maintains, one would never find readers at age 3. Elkind fails to provide an account that explains the relation between learning the social-arbitrary aspects of written language and the logico-mathematical construction of classes and relations. For example, the order of letters in the alphabet has no logical necessity, and learning this order is in no way comparable to the logical necessity in numerical relations. In our view, it is unlikely that young children listening to stories "observe" that the adult is transforming printed marks into sounds. Elkind offers no evidence linking his stages in reading development to Piaget's stages. Nevertheless, his general intuition that reading and general cognitive development are related is validated by the research of Ferreiro and her colleagues, though in a way very different from what Elkind had in mind.

CHALL

Jeanne Chall (1983) describes macroscopic stages of reading development that she states "owe much to Piaget's work" (p. 10). She notes that although conceptions of reading imply developmental concerns and "although the work of teaching is essentially concerned with development, little of Piaget's scheme has been applied to education and reading" (pp. 166–167). Chall attempts to ameliorate this situation.

Chall's effort to describe broad stages in reading development stems from her observation that "the research on reading development, particularly since the 1950s, has been concerned primarily with the factors that influence reading development, not primarily with the development and growth in reading itself" (p. 261). These factors, according to Chall's historical analysis, were emotional and social factors (in the 1940s and 1950s), perceptual and neurophysiological factors (in the 1960s and 1970s), and linguistic and cognitive factors (in the late 1970s and early 1980s). The culmination was substitution of "scope-and-sequence" charts for stages. Chall criticizes the scope-and-sequence levels for omission of "broad characterizations and psychological explanations of the hierarchies and the transitions" (p. 262). She notes, "The concern for what should be taught, when, and how it should be taught, took over the developmental concerns of what is generally learned, when, how and why" (p. 140).

Chall suggests that "the detailed scope and sequence charts of specific reading skills thought to be essential at the different grade levels" have the danger of being used "prescriptively and rigidly to hold some children back and force others to move faster than they are able to" (p. 141). In her conclusions and recommendations, Chall criticizes the overuse of worksheets and asks, "Are we perhaps having students do too much of their reading by examination?" (pp. 172–173). She questions the emphasis on fun as an incentive in early stages and suggests that earlier introduction of adult literature might "give students a sense of the seriousness of reading" (p. 171).

We describe below the six stages Chall presents as "hypothetical" (p. 13) and "metaphorical" (p. 168). She offers these as an addition to current tests and textbooks, as "a useful guide for what to teach when, as well as for what and when to test" (p. 168).

STAGE 0. PREREADING: BIRTH TO AGE 6.　During this period, children develop "a fund of knowledge about letters, words, and books" and "some insights into the nature of words" (for example, rhyme and alliteration) (Chall, 1983, p. 13). Chall refers to research showing, for example, that preschool children can recognize and name most letters in the alphabet, distinguish writing from nonwriting, identify road signs and brand names of objects, and pretend to read by holding the book right side up, referring to words while telling a story, and turning pages one at a time.

STAGE 1. INITIAL READING, OR DECODING: GRADES 1–2, AGES 6–7.　In this stage, children associate letters with parts of spoken words. A qualitative change occurs at the end of this stage when children gain insight about the nature of the spelling system. An illustration of this transition is Sartre's memory of the moment when his hours of "grunting" and sounding syllables led to the insight that became reading. For Chall, this insight constitutes a structural change in the child's understanding of reading.

STAGE 2. CONFIRMATION, FLUENCY, UNGLUING FROM PRINT: GRADES 2–3, AGES 7–8.　The advance at Stage 2 represents a consolidation of Stage 1, and thus has no unique defining characteristic. Stage 2 readers are simply more fluent. They are better at decoding and also freer in use of context.

STAGE 3. READING FOR LEARNING THE NEW: A FIRST STEP. Chall's definition of progress past Stage 2 is in terms not of *how* children read, but *what* they read and *what they read for*. At Stage 3, beginning in grade 4, the task is no longer to master the "medium" of print, but to master the "message" of ideas (p. 61). Chall here subscribes to the traditional conception that primary schooling focuses on learning to read, while later schooling focuses on reading to learn (p. 20). At Stage 3 reading becomes a tool for knowing new information about the world. New words become more important, and children learn how to go about finding information efficiently.

Beginning at Stage 3, Chall's stages are heavily determined by existing school curricula. Two phases are described in Stage 3. Phase A (grades 4–6) involves reading conventional knowledge about the world, and ends with the ability to "read serious material of adult length but falling somewhat short of the reading difficulty of most adult popular literature" (p. 22). Chall does not specify the psychological nature of this difficulty that is beyond Stage 3 readers.

The end of Stage 3B (grades 7–9) is closer to the general adult level of *The Reader's Digest*, popular adult fiction, and local newspapers, for example. In comparison with 3A, readers become more analytic and critical in reacting to different viewpoints.

STAGE 4. MULTIPLE VIEWPOINTS: HIGH SCHOOL. The essential characteristic of Stage 4 is the reader's ability to deal with more than one point of view. The difference between 3B and 4 is unclear, except that critical reading is more consistent and "more developed" (p. 23) at Stage 4.

STAGE 5. CONSTRUCTION AND RECONSTRUCTION—A WORLD VIEW: COLLEGE, AGE 18 AND ABOVE. Chall takes W. Perry's (1970) definition of intellectual development in college as Stage 5. Truth is no longer viewed as absolute or simply relative, but depends on analysis, synthesis, and judgment, to "create one's own 'truth' from the 'truths' of others" (p. 24).

In intent, Chall shares our desire to define developmental stages observable to teachers in the classroom. However, Chall's stages, like those of Elkind, are not derived from research directly aimed at the study of stage development. Instead, they are drawn from the body of theories and research on reading and in part lean heavily on achievement-test data. They go beyond the limits of the achievement-test perspective, however, to the uses of reading by adults, including habits in reading behavior. Like Elkind, Chall focuses on progress from the perspective of approximation to adult comprehension. Her stages are not hard structural stages as are those of Piaget, but may be viewed as what Kohlberg calls "soft stages," since they emphasize the knowledge content and increasing competence as socio-culturally defined. Chall's stages in relation to Piaget's work are a "global translation" of his theory, since her stages reflect a loose matching of very general aspects of his theory with increasing reading achievement.

EDUCATIONAL IMPLICATIONS

Relation to Traditional Assumptions and Practices

Research in the Piagetian tradition summarized above indicates that children do not begin their understanding of written language by associating sound responses to graphic stimuli. Ferreiro and Teberosky's studies show that learning to read and write is not just a question of mechanics—of practice in phoneme-grapheme correspondence as in exercises like cat-fat-mat-rat-sat. Rather, it is one of progressive conceptualization, an active process of constructing and testing hypotheses. This view leads away from an emphasis on perceptual ability (with comprehension emphasized after mechanical practice) to an emphasis on broader cognitive competence (with comprehension emphasized from the beginning). Ferreiro et al. (1982) argue that literacy difficulties are not perceptual or motor, but more generally cognitive. While some literacy difficulties depend on instructional methods, some seem independent of instructional method. Ferreiro (1977) reports that great individual differences were found in children taught by the same teacher. Although they experienced the same method, they produced very different hypotheses that were "related to their operatory level more than to anything else" (p. 125). The fact is that all children face cognitive problems in literacy development.

General Pedagogical Principles

Teberosky (1982) cautions that this research on how children learn does not prescribe classroom practices or how children should learn. She emphasizes that the new knowledge "does not translate into formulas, recipes, or exercises." It does, however, suggest the possible fruitfulness of efforts to bring "what happens in the classroom" as close as possible to "what happens in the child's head' (Teberosky, 1982).

Ferreiro notes that teaching method can obstruct or favor the process of learning. She states that there is certainly not *one* method but a group of methodological options that derive from understanding the learning process.

Teberosky has especially taken up the issue of educational intervention in her work with teachers in Barcelona. While she emphasizes that it is not appropriate to create a new method or new pedagogy, she does explore with teachers how to take advantage of the insights resulting from constructivist research. Certain general pedagogical principles may be gleaned from the writings of Ferreiro and Teberosky. These are much like the principles of teaching discussed in previous chapters.

Begin with What the Child Knows

The principle of beginning with what children know requires the teacher to question naive ideas about the nature of a writing system and to consider instead what children think. It requires recognition that children are active knowers whose search for coherence is a long process that cannot be short-circuited without damaging it.

Perhaps the most basic finding of Ferreiro and her colleagues is that "children's criteria (for what can be written, read, etc.) only coincides with teachers' criteria at the final point in the process" (Ferreiro & Teberosky,

1979/1982, p. 280). They conclude that in their studies of children 4 to 6 years of age, "Only those at quite advanced levels of conceptualization can benefit from traditional instruction" (p. 280). They quote Vygotsky (1978), who said, "It is necessary to bring the child to an inner understanding of writing, and to arrange that writing will be organized development rather than learning" (p. 118). Ferreiro and Teberosky point out two dangers: of overestimating and underestimating what the child knows:

> The school's ignorance of these underlying processes implies the following presuppositions imposed on children: (a) they know nothing and so are underestimated; or (b) the writing system reflects language in an obvious and natural way, and so they are overestimated because they do not naturally share this assumption. (Ferreiro & Teberosky, 1979/1982, p. 281)

Respect Constructive Error, and Encourage Children's Predictions and Self-Corrections

As in other domains of learning, the constructivist view places great importance on the role of error. As Smith (1975) points out, traditional school practice abhors mistakes. However, Ferreiro (1977) argues that "all learning methods which proceed by discovery and active construction must necessarily undergo error" (p. 30). Ferreiro and Teberosky believe that "when teachers do not allow errors to occur, they do not allow children to think" (p. 218). They describe two kinds of errors: those that are a necessary part of the constructive process, and those that are unfortunately produced by instruction that focuses on phonetic analysis before children are able to accept the alphabetic hypothesis. Ferreiro (1977) points out that "blind mechanical skill dependent at every moment on the correction or on the synthesis given by someone else" (p. 122) is an artifact of such instruction, rather than error that is eventually productive. Constructive errors include the syllabic hypothesis which, though wrong, indicates an advancement in conceptualization. Many examples of constructive errors have been revealed by the research of Ferreiro and her colleagues, and by the practical work of Clay (1972, 1975, 1982), Schickedanz (1981), and other researchers. In particular, children's predictions should not be dismissed as "random guessing." Smith (1975) maintains that reading is not possible without prediction. Perhaps the greatest error in traditional methods of teaching reading is that teachers feel too responsible for correcting all errors. Ferreiro and Teberosky (1979/1982) recommend the importance of giving children sufficient time to recognize and attempt to pinpoint their errors.

Ferreiro and Teberosky found that children introduced to reading through the narrow use of deciphering ("make a noise with the mouth based on what they see with their eyes") are so centered on sounding out as the only access to a text that they are unable to use their syntactic knowledge. Continual interaction in the child's mind between prediction and verification are important for the conflicts that lead to more and more adequate hypotheses. Emphasis on deciphering can lead children into accepting flagrant incongruities and nonsense without any feeling that it cannot be correct.

In the excerpts from classroom interactions in the next section, Teberosky's teachers refrain from correcting children. Such restraint will only be comfortable after a teacher becomes convinced that children will eventually correct their own errors, and that spontaneous correction is what leads to solid understanding. It reflects recognition that correction beyond a child's possibility for assimilation may have the effect of destroying confidence and placing obstacles in the way of progress.

Support Children in Moments of Conceptual Conflict

Since cognitive conflict is an important mechanism in progress in literacy, the teacher is advised to look for moments in which it exists and when children may be susceptible to the introduction of conflicting information. Ferreiro and Teberosky emphasize that despite school practices that stress deciphering, "progress always occurs relative to the need to overcome a conflict" (p. 99). They point out that such conflict can occur between children's predictions and their efforts to decipher.

> The conflicting results that stem from deciphering, on one hand, and meaningful predictions and grammatical judgments, on the other, are a disturbance which can be overcome only by a process of coordination. Those who reach this point, in spite of school practice, are the ones who have not abandoned the search for meaning (linguistically transmittable) in the text. The others have remained in the initial divorce [between deciphering and meaning], without receiving the help that the school should provide. (p. 99)

Ferreiro and Teberosky suggest that some conflicts may present the child such a great problem for his conceptual level that blockage to progress can occur. For example, when a child is just beginning to construct the syllabic hypothesis, he cannot cope with the obstacle that constitutes one-syllable words (written in isolation), because he thinks that a written word needs more than one letter. But he will be willing to explore his new hypothesis when writing longer words or short sentences.

Expose Children to Written Language in all Its Variety

Ferreiro (1977) argues against presenting isolated letters and sounds to children by pointing out the different attitudes toward children's learning to speak and learning to read.

> No mother chooses to present some phonemes to her baby, to the exclusion of all others, in order to teach him to speak. She speaks to him, quite simply, and the child rediscovers around him all the sounds proper to his language, with their respective frequency of appearance, in "perfect disorder" with regard to a good

associationist program. This is not going to hinder him from making all of the pertinent distinctions. Why then, when we teach writing, do we think that the grouping of letters would be a factor of confusion, and not one of intelligent discrimination? In another connection, what happens with children who have learned by themselves, before entering school? [First results of research on children who begin to learn before entering school show that]...they seem to have made, by themselves, connections between letters which resemble each other, those very letters which the school presents as being as remote as possible from one another, in order to "avoid all confusion." (pp. 28–29)

In the Human Development Laboratory School, rather than following a packaged reading program, we surround children with written material of all sorts and call attention to it in the course of activities—rules for games, numerals and words on game cards or boards, cookbook directions, names of children (on grouptime mats, cubbies, attendance roster), lists for remembering (what to buy at the grocery store for cooking, which story to read after outdoor play, rules for grouptime), and so on.

Foster Social Interaction about How to Read and How to Write

Teberosky argues that although writing is an individual activity, it should not be reduced to a solitary activity. She emphasizes that even before learning to read and write in the conventional sense, preschool children can discuss and confront other children with their ideas about writing. Children are good sources of information for one another, even though their knowledge is incomplete. Awareness of many points of view can be a good source of constructive conflict. The examples of classroom interaction in a later section illustrate how teachers can support and promote collaboration and confrontation among children in the context of efforts to read and write.

Group Children Heterogeneously for Reading and Writing Activities

In contrast to the traditional practice of grouping children homogeneously in terms of their literacy, Teberosky recommends planning for fruitful collaboration and differences of opinion among children. Extreme differences should be avoided because this can result in dominance by the more knowledgeable and passivity in the less knowledgeable. The dynamic result of heterogeneous grouping is illustrated in the later section on classroom activities.

Provide Both Reading and Writing Experiences from the Beginning

Ferreiro and Teberosky observe that the order of acquisition of reading and writing varies from one child to another. Some formulate more advanced hypotheses about reading and others about writing.

Create Situations in Which Conventional
Writing, Spelling, and Punctuation Are Necessary

Teberosky does not elaborate this point. However, experience in the University of Houston Human Development Laboratory School suggests that situations focused on communication can include the writing of an invitation to parents for a Valentine brunch, a grocery list for the teacher who must shop for materials for a cooking project, or a message to the custodian to leave a block construction overnight. These kinds of activities are often found in traditional child-development programs such as Bank Street.

Encourage Children to Consider Quantitative Properties,
and Do Not Insist Exclusively on Qualitative Aspects

Consideration of qualitative properties (the names and precise forms of letters, and the sound correspondences) comes later than the child's consideration of quantitative properties (the number of letters, length of text, and correspondence of syllables to letters or words). This principle is especially relevant when text is accompanied by a picture. It is well known that children who cannot read often use the picture to predict the meaning of the text, without searching for any clues in the text itself. Such children do not associate the picture with a particular letter.

Do Not Restrict the Introduction of New Words to Those
That Are Monosyllabic with One, Two, or Three Letters

This principle is based on Ferreiro and Teberosky's finding that such words generally are below the young child's limit requirement for "readability." Depending on the child's active hypotheses, the imposition of short monosyllabic words may short-circuit the child's confidence in figuring out the writing system. This principle becomes especially important in light of Aukerman's (1971) report that 14 of the 15 words of highest frequency in children's readers are "a," "and," "go," "he," "I," "in," "is," "it," "not," "on," "the," "to," "we," and "you." Ferreiro (1977) believes the use of words with more varied letters better helps the child come to recognize a nonrandom order in writing.

Be Cautious about Using Dictation

Teberosky comments that writing what children say is not necessarily an activity that facilitates learning. She notes three ways in which teachers need to be sensitive to children's reasoning in the context of dictation activity. First, when children begin to make a distinction between what is drawn and what is written, they may respond differently to "What did you draw?" and "What can I write?" The latter question clarifies the child's understanding.

The second precaution results from the finding that at a certain conceptual level, children do not assume that what can be written is the same as what can be read. Acceptance of this idea occurs rather late. The teacher should therefore accept the child's "reading" of what is written, recognizing that reading and writing (as well as copying) require different processes, and do not translate automatically from one to the other.

The third precaution is that even after the child believes that all spoken elements are written, he does not necessarily assume that the order of writing corresponds to the order of enunciation.

Do Not Insist on Correct Pronunciation in Beginning Reading

Ferreiro and Teberosky discuss efforts to change nonstandard speech as a part of beginning reading instruction as "linguistic discrimination" (p. 282). They emphasize that the initial problem is not deciphering but more general conceptualizations about writing as a particular representation of language.

Allow Sufficient Time for the Constructive Process

Some indications from Ferreiro's research show that children, even highly advantaged children, need a lot of time for their work of hypothesis construction and revision. Study of the relation between passing to second grade and conceptual level revealed the shocking finding that passing is in many instances unrelated to conceptual progress in literacy. Of 1,000 children from schools selected randomly from school districts with high percentages of initial failure in Monterrey, Mérida, and Mexico City who were studied by Ferreiro et al. (1982), 75% of those who were strictly syllabic at the end of the year failed first grade. Of those who were still at the presyllabic level, 34% passed. Thus, progress reflected by the syllabic hypothesis was not recognized, and these children especially were punished. The unfairness to individuals is evident when teachers make opposite decisions about children at the same level according to Ferreiro's techniques. The Mexican data showed that decisions made in March determined whether children passed or failed. Ferreiro and Gomez Palacio urge that the time allotted for literacy development be prolonged.

Encourage Children to Write According to Their Conceptions

Ferreiro and Teberosky agree with Chomsky (1971) that children must be allowed to write according to "how it sounds." However, they go even further:

> We must let children write, even in a writing system different from the alphabetic one; we must let them write, not so they invent their own idiosyncratic system, but so they discover that their system is not the conventional one and in this way find valid reasons to substitute their own hypotheses with our conventional ones. (Ferreiro & Teberosky, 1979/1982, p. 277)

They also address the issue of copying as an instructional technique:

> Writing development as revealed in our work does not depend on children's
> graphic skill, on their ability to make letters which look conventional. It depends on
> what we refer to as their level of conceptualization about writing, that is, the set of
> hypotheses they have explored for the purpose of comprehending this object.
> When we keep children from writing (from testing their hypotheses as they produce
> written texts) and force them to copy (repeating someone's markings without
> understanding their structure), we keep them from learning; we keep them from
> discovering on their own. When we correct their copy-writing in terms of spatial
> relationships (stick to the left, two sticks instead of three, closed curve) or in terms
> of letters which don't belong or are left out, we ignore what is essential in the text:
> what it represents and how it represents it. (Ferreiro & Teberosky, 1979/1982, p.
> 278)

Teberosky describes how copying may be useful when integrated with children's
purposes in a larger context. This is discussed in the next section.

Examples of Activities

In one publication, Teberosky (1984) describes activities conducted by a teacher
in Barcelona with eight 5-year-olds. (See Willert & Kamii, 1985, Kamii &
Randazzo, 1985, and Long & Bulgarella, 1985, for other examples.)

Dictating a Story

In this situation, linguistic activity predominated as the children dictated a story
to the teacher who emphasized that they should tell her "only what has to be
written." In this way, she was careful to allow for children's distinction between
what is spoken to be written and what is spoken but does not have to be written.
However, children dictated the story at the same time they talked among
themselves, and what they told the teacher included both conversation and
narration. In one instance, the teacher wrote on the board, ". . . to the mountain
to look for weeds and the mother goat said to the seven little goats not to open
the door Olga what are you putting? the fierce wolf?" When the teacher then
read what she wrote, all the children protested, and the teacher then asked what
and where to erase. Children were then motivated to look in the text to find
precisely what should be erased. The effort to read was thus in the purposeful
context of correcting the text. Since they did not know what was written in each
fragment of text, the teacher told them when they asked. For the children in this
group (though not for all children in the class), the teacher confirmed that they
made a correspondence between what is said and what is written, that they
distinguished the utterances that should be written from those that did not
belong to the narrator, and that they tried to locate the parts not belonging the
the story.

Copying

In the same session, it was proposed that children copy a piece of the story from the board. In this activity, the technical aspect of writing prevailed as children focused on the qualitative properties of each letter. Their challenge was to figure out how to transform visual information to graphic action. This was not easy, and children were often very conscious that what they wrote differed from the model. Conversation included "letter recitation" as one child called out letters and others wrote, and some asked one another questions such as "Which one is this?" The teacher was able to confirm that most of these children knew the names of the letters and could match them with their forms. It was clear one child's preoccupation centered on making good copies of individual letters rather than on the interpretation of their meaning. Since this child's copying activity involved naming letters, it was more than just a motor activity, but it had lost the connection with the language of the story.

Reading What is Written

After copying, the teacher always asked children to read what they copied. She found that what they "read" was more related to memory of the story than to what they actually wrote. When she asked more precisely what was written in a particular segment, seven of the eight children responded in terms of a syllabic hypothesis, usually including two letters for each syllable. On another occasion, each syllable was made to correspond with a whole word. Only one child was able to read his copy correctly in the conventional manner. When pressed to say what was written in a given segment, the other children retreated to letter recitation and refused to interpret the segment.

Writing

The teacher proposed that children write a noun fragment from the text. Children were free to use the model on the board or their own copy, or they could write without a model. The results reflected children's conceptual levels. Some wrote it correctly with correct left-right sequencing. Others were nearly correct, and some relied on a syllabic guide or a mixture of alphabetic and syllabic hypotheses.

Teberosky also mentions the following writing activities:

1. The children all write the same thing on paper or on the blackboard, and compare their results;
2. Only one child writes, on paper or on the blackboard, while the others watch and/or collaborate;
3. Each child writes something different.

She believes the first is the most fruitful in promoting collaboration. The second is also productive because children are able to participate in the production, even if they are not the one designated as the scribe. The last was the least productive from the point of view of promoting constructive collaboration.

Group Interaction

In another paper focused on the longitudinal study of 20 children over a period of 7 months, Teberosky (1982) identified forms of group discussion that correspond to conceptual development for individuals.

1. *Independent Writing and the Primacy of Intent.*
   When children are inexperienced in working in a group, they tend to concentrate more on their own work than on that of others. Children do exchange some information. However, the general tendency is to make individual productions, and Teberosky notes that the information given by others has only a momentary and local influence on the child's writing. Since everyone writes in her own way, and what matters is the writer's intention, writing cannot be understood by others or serve as a vehicle for transmission of information. Group work with children at this level can be important in providing stimuli for imitation. Consider the following protocol of interaction in a situation in which everyone is trying to write the word "*vaca*" (cow) on her own paper. (Some bilingual children interact sometimes in Castilian and sometimes in Catalan.)

OS: An "a"

HE: Va, va

OS to HE: "A"

RO to OS: This is an "a" (making a gesture of an "a")

Teacher: How many letters are in the word "vaca"?

HE to teacher: (Shrugs his shoulders indicating he doesn't know) An "a," ca, a ca, another "a," no, it can't be, ca, ca.

HE: (Writes ARO)

DA: (Writes AEO)

HE: (Writes AROU) A "u"

RO to HE: It ends with the same letter, "a."

HE to RO: I'm not finished.

HE: (Writes AROURA)

RO: (Writes AROA)

OS: (Writes ANAOURA) Va-ca (pointing to the first five letters she wrote).

Teacher to OS: What about these (the ones she didn't point to)?

OS to Teacher: Oh, they don't count. Here I finish with the "a", and I put too many letters so these are extra.

OS: (Writes AIAUA)

Teacher to everyone: Which one should we choose?

RO: (Points to his own)

HE: (Points to his own)

DA: (Adds an "A", making AEOA)

Teberosky comments that in this example, the interactions refer to:

    a. The graphic form of a letter (how to make an "a");
    b. The necessity of including a letter with an assigned value ("a");
    c. Control over the quantity of letters required for the word (between four and six);
    d. Beginning and ending letters having a fixed value.

Teberosky also points out that in this example the objective differences in children's productions do not bother them, and they show no conflict about the claims of two children who select their own when the teacher suggests picking one of the products.

2. *Collaboration and the Search for Coherence.*
Children more advanced in group work confer with one another about how something is supposed to be written. They thus focus not on communication, but on representation. While children are able to be resources for one another, they are not always conscious of convergences and divergences in their products. Challenging one another thus occurs only occasionally. The intention, however, no longer rests entirely with the individual's arbitrary purpose but has shifted slightly to the goal of a certain consistency. Children thus discuss the external aspects of written forms but do not arrive at a final consensus. In the Barcelona classroom where both Catalan and Castilian are spoken, children sometimes attribute differences in writing to the language differences. The greater exchange of information provides latent possibility for conflicts that become manifest at more advanced levels of group work. Consider the following interchange in which children give one another information on the form of letters, their names, and their phonetic values.

IV: (Tries to write "elefante") An "e"

AL: Does it end in "e"?

IV: (Writes "E") El, el, e-le, "l"

ME to IV: And an "e"

IV: How do you make an "l"?

JO and ME to IV: Like this (they make an "L" in the air).

JO to IV: Like an "e," but without a little line.

IV: (Writes EL)

ME to IV: Now another "e," another "e."

IV: Fan-fan-le-fan

ME to IV: Another "e," because if you wouldn't say le, you have to put another "e."

IV: E-le-fa, an "e" and an "f."

ME to IV: If that is an "l," you have to put an "e."

IV to ME: Another "e"?

ME to IV: Yes.

IV: (Adds E, ELE) Don't fool me!

ME to IV: No!

AL: (Reads ELE) E-le

IV: E-le-fa ... fante. "F" and "a." "F," how do you make it?

Teacher to IV: Like an "e," but without the little line on the bottom.

IV: (Writes ELEF)

JO: "F" like in Felix.

AL: Felix, my grandfather's name is Felix.

Teacher to IV: What else do you need to put?

IV to Teacher: Fan-te

AL to IV: An "n" and an "a."

IV: Fan-te, a "t," a "t."

AL to IV: Fa, an "a," you need.

IV: (Writes ELEFA) E-le-fa-te, a "t"

ME to IV: Well, a "t."

AL to IV: A "t," should I make it for you?

IG: Which is the "t"?

ME to IG: Look, it's easy (points to a T in pato that is written on another child's
paper)

IV: (Writes ELEFAT)

AL to IV: "T," an "e." Put it! I already told you!

IV: (Adds E, ELEFATE)

AL: Now, elefante.

The alphabetic hypothesis is in evidence in this interchange, and children are
trying to assign a value to each sign in their writing. Since the coherence that
is achieved is individual, it is often difficult for a product to be read by anyone
else. Teberosky notes that this kind of exchange does not emerge in a dictation activity. She also comments that although the final result approximated
the conventional form, this is not a condition for interaction.

3. *Confrontation and the Movement toward Interindividual Agreement.*
Children later become more open to social influence, and to considering the
parts of words by themselves. Teberosky notes that confrontation is not only
a possibility, but that children seem to seek it actively. Because they feel a
necessity for agreement about their products (when they attempt to write the
same thing), arguments occur "in which each person tries to defend his work
and criticize the work of others" (Teberosky, 1982, p. 172).

Teberosky emphasizes that the interpersonal dynamic is more than an
exchange of individual opinion. What happens is more than progress in
individual construction. Rather, what happens is "a reflective integration and

not a passive acceptance of opinions of others" (Teberosky, 1982, p. 172). Teberosky comments as follows.

> The convictions that the children have about their work are not just the result of their individual labor, but also the concordance of their work with that of others. This serves to confirm or rectify their convictions.... The conviction is reaffirmed as a result of the shared and accepted convention. The paradox of this situation is that a certain conviction is required in order to argue with others, but when the arguments lead to agreements they reinforce the convictions. (1982, p. 172)

Consider the following interaction.

> All were writing the same thing on the blackboard with each child writing in his own language "elefant" (Catalan) or "elefante" (Castilian).

IG: "A"

AR: (Writes A) "L"

GE to AR: An "l" is like this (makes an "L")

GE: (Adds L, AL)

GE: An "f"

AR to GE: If you don't know how to make an "f," I'll do it.

AR: (Writes F, ALF)

IG: Like an "e"

GE: (Writes A, ALFA) An "a." (Reads over each one of the letters ALFA) A-la-fan-te. I start in Catalan and end in Castilian.

IS: How do you make an "n"?

AR to IS: An "a" and an "s" in order to elefante, a "t," elefante.

IG: (Reads above each of the letters of ALFA) Yes, "a," a-la-fan-te. How do you make a "t"?

GE: (Writes ALFT and reads above each of the letters) A-la-fan-te (beginning in Catalan and ending in Castilian)

IS: (Writes ALNFAN and reads showing two letters for each syllable) (While writing, he says: a, la, a-la-fan)

AR: (Writes ELFT) Elefant

Teacher to everyone: This is how Ar wrote it (points). IG, GE, and IS wrote it this way. Where could it be (pointing to all the writing)?

IS to Teacher: Here, elefant (showing A-NFAN)

AR to Teacher: Me, elefante

IS: Here it is al-fan, al-fet (pointing to ALFT), he el-fe-e, el-fe-te (pointing to ELFT) and here is elefant (pointing to her own writing, ALNFAN).

Teacher: Do we need this "E"?

IS to Teacher: If it is in Castilian we do, because with an "e" it is elefante, with an "a" it is elefant, here it is el-fe-te (points to ELFT)

AR to IS: There, nothing (referring to IS's writing)! "A," "l," "n," "f," "a," "n" (points to ALNFAN).

IS to AR: No! From three on three al-la-fan. From two on two (above ALNFAN, two letters for each syllable)!

Teacher: How many ways can it be written?

GE to Teacher: Many.

IS to GE: Only one way. If not, it says another animal.

AR to IS: Two ways, Castilian and Catalan.

IG to AR: Two, like these (points to cursive writing) and these (points to print).

IS to IG: Yes, in capitals and in small letters. (Teberosky, 1982, pp. 173–174)

In this interchange the final results are not exactly the same, but collaboration flowers in consultation and argumentation. It is important to note that conclusions about conventions include recognition that there can be many ways to write the same word (in different languages, cursive or print, capitals or small letters), and that there has to be one way (in any one language).

Teberosky proposes the notion of "socialization of knowledge" to reflect the nature of the constructive interaction among children and with the teacher, in contrast to the traditional view of individualization of knowledge. She also suggests that in a bilingual setting, languages should not be separated.

In other accounts of classroom interaction, Teberosky gives examples of collaborations in which a child asks another for information, and gives critical opinions and corrections.

Assessment of Individual Children

The following behaviors of children seem significant for teachers to notice:

1. Consciousness of the differences among children's products;
2. Uneasiness over observed differences;
3. Challenging the "correctness" of other products;
4. Effort to make copy exactly like the model;
5. Asking for information and giving it to others;
6. Conviction about own ideas, and openness to opinions of others;
7. Arguing about graphic products, using interpretation of others' writing as a tool for comparison;
8. Making conclusions about conventions, coordinating own ideas with those of others.

The Teacher's Role

The research of Ferreiro and Teberosky leads to a view of the teacher as *not* "giving, initially, all the secret keys of the alphabetic system, but of creating the conditions in which the child will discover them for himself" (1981, p. 15).

Much like our description of the constructivist teacher's role in other chapters, Teberosky describes the teacher's role as a helper behind the scenes, facilitating children's interactions, responding to questions when no child can, and providing concrete reading and writing examples. The teacher does not correct errors, but accepts all ideas as valid. When differences of opinion are expressed, the teacher's idea is presented as one of the possible alternatives, and resolution comes from children. Answers are given in terms of clarification of what children are thinking or doing. It may be useful to reiterate what the teacher did in the examples above.

1. How many letters are in the word "*vaca*"?
   What about these (leftovers)?
   Which one (of the products) should we choose?
2. This is how AR wrote it. IG, GE, and IS wrote it this way. Where could it be (pointing to all writing)?
   Do we need this "E"?
   How many ways can it be written?

In these descriptions, Teberosky demonstrates in part how the teacher can influence children at various conceptual levels. She emphasizes that the teaching method depends on the child. That is, it depends on the child's interpretation of what the teacher does.

Much research remains to be done on the teacher's role and classroom activities that foster progress in reading and writing. Teberosky provides us with a beginning in what is still frontier territory for research.

CONCLUSIONS

In this chapter, efforts to understand the acquisition of literacy in light of Piaget's constructivist perspective are reviewed. The most useful description is provided by Ferreiro and Teberosky. Their account of the psychogenetic progression reflects children's hypotheses about the meaning of written language. Constructive error plays an important role in this picture of children's construction of knowledge about this aspect of their environment.

Chall's stages in reading development are defined by competence in academically successful adults. This is a "global translation" of Piaget's theory, since these stages reflect a loose matching of very general aspects of his theory with increasing reading achievement.

Elkind defines the acquisition of reading in terms of some of Piaget's characteristics of operational reasoning. Elkind's stages are viewed as a "literal translation" of Piaget's theory, since they reflect a direct application of parts to some aspects of reading achievement.

The levels of conceptualization presented by Ferreiro and her colleagues end at the point other stage descriptions begin. That is, Ferreiro studies children in Chall's Stages 0 and 1 and in Elkind's Stages 1 and 2. While the Chall and Elkind stages are defined in terms of child knowledge that agrees with adult knowledge, Ferreiro's method makes possible a description of levels that includes constructions that do not agree with adult knowledge.

The educational implications of Ferreiro's work are discussed in contrast with traditional assumptions about how children learn. Fourteen principles of teaching are presented:

1. Begin with what the child knows.
2. Respect constructive error, and encourage children's predictions and self-corrections.
3. Support children in moments of conceptual conflict.
4. Expose children to written language in all its variety.
5. Foster social interaction about how to read and how to write.
6. Group children heterogeneously for reading and writing activities.
7. Provide both reading and writing experiences from the beginning.
8. Create situations in which conventional writing, spelling, and punctuation are necessary.
9. Encourage children to consider quantitative properties, and do not insist exclusively on qualitative aspects.
10. Do not restrict the introduction of new words to those that are monosyllabic with one, two, or three letters.
11. Be cautious about using dictation.
12. Do not insist on correct pronunciation in beginning reading.
13. Allow sufficient time for the constructive process.
14. Encourage children to write according to their conceptions.

Examples of constructivist classroom interactions are given. These principles and the role of the teacher described by Teberosky are consistent with our presentation in other chapters. (See Holdaway, 1979, for additional useful techniques harmonious with a constructivist perspective.)

The full significance of the constructivist perspective on the teaching of reading and writing is only beginning to be articulated. Further psycho-educational research is needed to generate new problems and new insights.

PART IV

*Early Education Program
Comparison and Evaluation
from a Constructivist Perspective*

Chapter 9

Montessori
Theory and Practice

There are many reasons for including a chapter on Montessori here. First, Maria Montessori was one of the few creative modern early education theorists. Piaget (1939b) commented that Montessorian pedagogy constitutes a particularly important stage in the history of progressive education. Second, Montessori's theory fits broadly within the cognitive-developmental stream. After John Dewey, Montessori may be considered a founder of cognitive-developmental early education, the first to carry the romanticism of Jean-Jacques Rousseau, Johann Pestalozzi, and Friedrich Froebel to the next level of development. And third, Montessori created a practice, or "program," that has experienced a revival since the late 1950s and is currently widely available in private and some public schools. Started in the first decades of the twentieth century, it will almost certainly be with us in the first decades of the twenty-first, something that cannot be said with assurance of all the other programs discussed in this volume.

This chapter looks back on Montessori from the perspective of subsequent Piagetian psychology. One current of opinion over a number of years is that Piaget's theory is compatible with and provides justification for the Montessori method (Rambusch, 1962; R. Gardner, 1966/1968; Murray, 1979). Piaget's theory is even being taught in some Montessori teacher-training centers as harmonious with Montessori's ideas (for example, see C. Perry, 1980). Although several developmental psychologists have pointed out some common strands of theory connecting Montessori and Piaget (Hunt, 1964/1968; Elkind, 1967, 1983), there is also a certain tension between the cognitive-developmental tradition and Montessori which led Kilpatrick (1914) to write a polemical criticism of Montessori from the Dewey framework. The contrasts between Dewey or Piaget on the one side and Montessori on the other may be considered, however, as contrasts within a general cognitive-developmental approach, which together contrast with both the cultural transmission and romantic approaches discussed in Chapter 1.

Divergencies between Montessori and Piaget or Dewey arise because Montessori as an educational genius was relatively unconcerned with scientific theory or with systematic logical consistency in her psychological theorizing. In particular, Montessori's ideas concerning cognitive stimulation were a somewhat syncretic synthesis of two separate and contradictory streams of thought in psychology. The first stream of thought was developmentalism, a stream commencing with Rousseau (and continuing through Dewey and Piaget). The second stream of ideas contributing to Montessori's thought was that of the associationistic psychology of the eighteenth and nineteenth centuries, in which ideas were viewed as arising from associations between simple sensations. This assumption was inherent in the educational methods of Jean-Marc-Gaspard Itard and Edouard Seguin from which Montessori started. The tension between these two streams of thought is the major focus of this chapter. What follows is an exercise in integrating similarities and differences. After a brief overview of common threads and divergencies in theory and educational practices advocated by Montessori and Piaget comes an examination of their ideas in more detail, calling upon research findings when these help in discussing the relative merits of theories and practices. Only Montessori's own published works are considered, in order to avoid controversies that exist among her advocates.

COMMON STRANDS IN MONTESSORI AND PIAGET

Both Montessori and Piaget were essentially concerned with, as Montessori (1916/1965) put it, "the progression from the known to the unknown" (p. 162). Piaget (1980) summed up his basic concern as the essential question of genetic epistemology: "How to explain the construction of new relations" (p. 10). Although Montessori's aim was to find ways to foster progression in the child's knowledge and Piaget's aim was to understand the nature of this progression, the commonality of their concern with novelty in conscious individual thought led them to some similar theoretical ideas.

Briefly, we point out three similarities. First, in common with the general developmentalist line of thought, Montessori stressed that organism and mind form a structured whole, that the child is not a little adult but is a qualitatively different organism, and that there is an invariant succession in the structural development of the child's mind. These assumptions are most specifically set forth in the Piagetian doctrine of stages, where stages refer to qualitative or structural changes in reasoning proceeding through an invariant sequence.

A second common thread is the notion that transformation of mental structure occurs through active experience. Both Montessori and Piaget emphasize that experience is not passive response to external stimulation. Like Piaget and Dewey, Montessori stressed that competence and epistemic motivation exist from the beginning of life. Montessori's view is expressed in a way reminiscent of Piaget's constructivism: "The known establishes itself in the child as a *complex system* of ideas...actively constructed by the child himself during a series of psychical processes representing an internal formation, a psychical growth" (Montessori, 1916/1965, pp. 162–163). Both criticized educational methods that made children mentally passive. At the heart of Montessori's theory about how experience transforms mental structure is her emphasis on attention as fundamental in her dialectic between liberty and discipline in the child's development. Piaget (1948/1973) similarly remarked upon the educational value of exercising the powers of observation and emphasized that interest is the fuel that makes the motor of the intelligence go.

The third commonality between Montessori and the cognitive-developmental view is the major focus on general cognitive development, in contrast with a narrow focus on linguistic development and academic skills. While the Montessori approach includes a strong concern with academics, its emphasis is upon the acquisition of logical and orderly thought, consisting especially of classification and seriation. In a very broad sense, this emphasis is consistent with Piaget's theory of the formation of concrete operations that are necessary for classification and seriation (and also other manifestations of operations). Both view logical classificiation and seriation to be hallmarks of general intellectual development, not just the result of specific verbal learning of category labels. Both agree that the development of logical thought depends upon the child's activities of grouping, ordering, comparing, and so on. In all these views the Montessori approach differs markedly from approaches such as that of Bereiter and Engelmann (1966), which treat the development of classification and number knowledge as problems in the teaching of a language system. In contrast with empiricist or cultural-transmission views of learning and development, both Montessori and Piaget view action as the means by which the child acquires knowledge.

The similarities between Montessori and Piaget, emphasized by Hunt (1964/1968, 1969) and other writers, seem supported by certain similarities in statements made about education by Montessori and Piaget themselves. Piaget advocated education that is active, and Montessori's method *is* active. Piaget emphasized the importance of experiences with concrete objects, and Montessori's materials *are* concrete. Piaget stressed the importance of autonomy, and Montessori advocated independence of action and choice. Both emphasized the importance of moral development. Furthermore, in viewing general cognitive development as occurring in stages, both agree that this development cannot be taught, and that education must be guided by the way the child thinks and by natural laws of development.

These broad similarities do, indeed, make it tempting to conclude that we have in Montessori's method the educational expression of Piaget's theory. The temptation is, moreover, abetted by the fact that Montessori's theoretical ideas about children's development were not always rigorously expressed, and by the fact that Piaget's practical ideas about education were never developed very far. It is thus easy to read Montessori's often vague theoretical ideas as consistent with Piaget's theory, and to read Piaget's often vague ideas about practice as consistent with Montessori's method. However, as we shall see, when one takes the writings in which each is clearly specific, one finds many differences in meaning behind similar words, and that many apparent consistencies weaken or disappear. Divergencies between Montessori and Piaget are discussed below in terms of their different views of the nature of knowing and mental organization.

A certain awkwardness in comparing Montessori and Piaget should be noted; it derives from their different professional concerns. Montessori's emphasis was practical, and her theoretical ideas were largely intuitive. It may not seem fair to place Montessori's theory alongside Piaget's well-elaborated and research-based theory resulting from a lifetime of work, especially since some of this work was done after Montessori's death. However, given the insistence of some present-day Montessori advocates that Piaget's theory is consistent with the theory and method of Montessori, it is necessary to examine the degree to which this is the case.

It is also somewhat awkward to compare Piaget's educational ideas with Montessori's well-elaborated method, since Piaget disclaimed being an educator. His theoretical emphasis led him to make only broad, skeletal educational recommendations, and he left to others the task of specifying practices informed by his work. In discussing the Montessori method from the Piagetian perspective, we will thus rely on our own elaborations and derivations from Piaget's work, as well as on his writing about education.

THEORETICAL DIVERGENCIES BETWEEN THE MONTESSORI METHOD AND CONSTRUCTIVIST EDUCATION: SENSORY ABSORPTION VERSUS INTELLIGENT CONSTRUCTION

While Montessori and Piaget were both concerned with the issue of the development of knowledge, they differed in fundamental ways in their conceptualization of the nature of knowing and the acquisition of knowledge (that is, the *functioning* of human mentality), and the organization of knowledge (that is, the *structure* of mentality).

Montessori: Discontinuity in Mental Functioning

Sensory Absorption

Montessori viewed the knowing process of the child as a basically different kind of function from that of the adult. She characterized the child's knowing in the years from birth to age 6 as a function of sensory absorption, in contrast with adult reasoning. She stated in her last book (significantly titled *The Absorbent Mind*) that during the first 3 years of a child's life, knowledge comes totally by absorption through the senses, without even any effort on the part of the child. She believed that abstractions are directly based on the pure perception of simple sensory attributes. For example, she believed that if the child would only become clearly aware of the pure sensation "red," he would then have an abstract concept or basic classificatory category. (This view is shared by many kindergarten teachers who believe that "knowing colors" promotes logical thought.)

We indicated in the discussion of commonalities between Piaget and Montessori that Montessori believed that experience is not passive. We find contradictions in Montessori's writing on this point, as discussed below.

The external nature of the origin of knowledge which is reflected in the idea of passive sensory absorption is also seen in Montessori's explanation of the sensory process. Like stimulus-response psychologists in the behavioristic tradition, she said that external stimuli act directly upon sense organs, and that the external stimulus activates a motor impulse in a nerve center. The child's internal reaction is an automatic biological or psychochemical change. By this process, Montessori argued that the child's mind copies the external environment. However, Montessori also emphasized the child's internal reaction as the most important factor and denied that intelligence is built up in mechanistic fashion.

Montessori's theory about the sensory absorption of knowledge as images led her to view the ordinary result of naturally disordered experience of reality as chaos in the organization of knowledge. She criticized the typical "over-stimulating" experience of the young child who must exert great effort to continually correct errors given by the senses. Thus, for Montessori, the educational challenge was to aid the child in organizing sensations and images. Her goal was to develop an ordered mind through regulating the orderliness of experience.

Action Combined with Sensory Absorption

While Montessori viewed the nature of mental functioning as basically the same throughout the years from birth to age 6 (that is, knowing as characterized by absorption), she distinguished a subphase during the years 3 to 6 in which action begins to combine with sensory absorption. The importance for intellectual development of spontaneous activity was also stressed as the key to internal regulation and discipline. For Montessori, spontaneous action was defined as contrasted with disordered movements. She saw a necessity for the child to move from disordered movements to spontaneous and ordered movements. As we shall see in the later discussion of the educational expression of this idea, Montessori saw the importance of spontaneity within the constraints of the development of correct ideas, in contrast with the Piagetian idea of spontaneous activity as filled with errors that have constructive value.

Shift to Memory, Understanding, and Thinking

Montessori pointed out a shift in the child's mentality at the age of 6, when the capacity for memory, understanding, and thinking appears. This constitutes the discontinuity in the nature of the child's knowing that contrasts with Piaget's notion of continuity, described later.

Attention in the Knowing Process

At the heart of Montessori's sensory psychology is her fundamental emphasis on attention as a crucial component of the "hidden labor," the means by which sensations become conscious. Montessori's concern with attention represented the principal component in her dialectic polarity between liberty and discipline in the child's development. She claimed her method was a method of liberty, which promoted spontaneous, self-regulated discipline as opposed to the imposition of discipline upon the child from the outside. Inner discipline, she claimed, grew out of free attention and hence out of liberty. While Montessori agreed with William James as to the crucial nature of attention as a foundation of will and discipline in the classroom, she disagreed with his inference that young children are by nature distractible and that their attention must be maintained by the teacher. In contrast, she argued that even young children can cling long and ardently to objects or tasks of their choice. The reason for a low opinion of the attention of the young child, Montessori claimed, is that it is studied under the wrong conditions—when adults are trying unsuccessfully to direct a child's attention.

In Montessori's day, the debated issue was whether attention was a function of spontaneous interest or of imposed discipline or will resulting from adult authority. Montessori's observations led her to the conviction that attention is the most intense with no intrusion of authority when the child is relating spontaneously to objects. She compared the attention of the absorbed child to our impressions of the absorbed genuis—the Sir Isaac Newton or the Archimedes—whose attention is certainly not a product of will in the sense of internalization of authority.

For Montessori, attention is not only the key to sensory absorption of knowledge, but also to the development of will and discipline necessary to more advanced intellectual work. In her view, attention becomes will when an element of habit enters the persistence and directedness of attention. To illustrate the development of attention in individual children and in classrooms, Montessori (1916/1965, pp. 98–108) drew a series of impressionistic graphs representing advance from a period of disorder to a "superior stage" of habitual orderly behavior characterized by serene, self-disciplined interest in work. The beginning of order is illustrated by an attention graph showing a period of easy work, a period of restlessness, a phase of serious work, and a final period of rest, recreation, or social activity. Surprisingly, the development of attention for Montessori (1916/1965, p. 107) culminates in obedience. She considered it progress when the child can control his actions in accordance with the demands of someone else.

Modern educational psychology has not yet pursued with systematic observational methods Montessori's impressionistic graphs of attention. In principle, such a pursuit would seem to be a feasible and worthwhile endeavor. We can, however, report a modest pilot study coming out of a Montessori project that did focus upon some of the issues we have raised.

Like Montessori, one of us (Lawrence Kohlberg) was struck by some outstanding examples of attention in both middle-class and disadvantaged children in the Ancona Montessori preschool program in Chicago. Although not conclusive, some evidence indicates a facilitating effect of this Montessori program on attentional disposition. Children in a Head Start program were rated by both the Binet testers and the teachers on a distractibility scale ranging from 1 (complete and persistent task-absorption) to 9 (difficult to get and hold attention).[1] In the first two years of the program there was a significant decrease in distractibility among the disadvantaged children. This decrease correlated 0.65 with Binet IQ increases during the year among this group of children (Kohlberg, 1968b). (In later years of this program this gain in attention related to IQ increase was not found in other groups of Head Start children, probably because Head Start children in later years were on the whole more attentive or less distractible on entry than the initial group had been. Indeed, the overall ratings of attention for the Head Start children in the later years were no different than those of the middle-class children [Karlson, 1970]). To the extent, then, that the Montessori program did lead to increases in rated attention, the effects were "compensatory." By "compensatory" increases we mean that meaningful change was found only among the initially highly distractible children, and this occurred only among "disadvantaged" distractible children, that is, only where the Head Start children as a group tended to be low in attention.

This research does provide some support for the rationale of Montessori's focus on individual tasks, particularly for disadvantaged children. Other research on classroom behavior (Jackson, 1967) suggests the importance of attention, as does experimental psychological study. Grim, Kohlberg, and White (1968) were struck intuitively by the meaningfulness of William James's classical analysis of attention as a foundation of moral will. Accordingly, they engaged in a series of studies of older children which related both experimental and teacher rating measures of attention with measures of children's moral behavior— willingness to cheat in a series of experimental situations, as well as honesty rated by teachers. The factor analysis of the experimental and rating measures indicated a general attention-will factor that cut across both experimental and teacher rating methods, and cut across both pure cognitive attentional tasks and tasks that involved moral behavior. This factor was found both in young children—for instance, second graders—and in junior high school-aged children. The younger children rated lower in both attention and honesty than the older children, showing that in large part the attention-moral will factor is age-developmental.

Piaget: Continuity in Mental Functioning

Like Montessori, Piaget tried to understand the development of scientific thinking. He, too, observed that child thought was incoherent or "chaotic,"

---

1. Low to moderate correlations were found between tester's and teacher's ratings and between ratings and experimental measures of attention used by Grim, Kohlberg, and White (1969).

although he did not view this as random chaos, but as having internal coherence. Piaget (Piaget & Inhelder, 1964) shared with Montessori a concern with the development of logical coherence and classification ability as significant in the general development of intellectual competence. However, in contrast with Montessori, Piaget (1961/1969; Piaget & Inhelder, 1966a/1971) rejected the notion that everything in intelligence has passed through the senses or comes from perception in the form of mental images. As discussed in Chapter 2, Piaget believed that the sensorimotor roots of thought lie in action, not in sensation. This view is based on extensive research on intelligence, perception, and mental imagery. Consistently, Piaget found that children have ideas about objects and events in reality which could not possibly have come from perception. Moreover, after studying perceptual mechanisms, Piaget concluded that these are inadequate in themselves to bring objective knowledge. Rather, he found that their organization and direction depends on a more general form of action which goes beyond perception.

Piaget called this form of action "equilibration." It is equilibration that for Piaget constitutes the basic *functional continuity* of knowing throughout life, in contrast with Montessori's discontinuity view. As for mental imagery, Genevan studies showed that it, too, depends on this general form of action rather than resulting directly from perception. Thus, for Piaget, knowledge is not a copy of reality, and knowing cannot be explained in terms of sensory, or even perceptual or imagery, processes. Piaget himself expressed the difference between his view of the role of perception and that of Montessori:

> What appears first in the evolution of infant perceptions is not the sensation; it is not even perception isolated from action. It is total activity, that is, sensory-motor or practical intelligence, intelligence itself which, from the first months of existence, organizes perceptions as a function of action. Madame Montessori certainly caught a glimpse of this great truth; she made use of admirable observations in this regard...but she was not sufficiently aware that perceptions like that of form or depth presuppose, from the point of view of development, not only isolated and static sensorial analyses, but a construction of a group where the combinations of the intelligence play a much more important role, in their dynamism, than the sensations which are the product of it. (1939b, p. 3)

Piaget admired Montessori's effort to enrich laboratory psychology with anthropological analysis of behavior in nature. However, he felt that with respect to her belief in sensory exercise she herself was the victim of what she feared: projecting onto reality a laboratory doctrine that became obsolete.

As for classification, Piaget went further than Montessori in his effort to understand the dynamic structure underlying or making possible not only classification but scientific reasoning in general. While Montessori glimpsed the general significance of classification for intelligence as a whole, her sensory psychology led her to an emphasis on avoiding errors in logical classification. For Piaget the child's "illogical" reasoning is a normal and necessary stage in development toward logical consistency. In contrast with Montessori, Piaget did not view children's "wrong" ideas as something to be squelched or prevented, but as something to be understood as valid intellectual activity.

Piaget (1961/1969) concludes that "it is impossible simply to divide cognitive functions into perceptions ('the senses') and reason, because action as a whole is both the point of departure for reason and a continuous source of organization and of reorganization for perception" (p. 361). His view is counter to that of Montessori because he finds that perceptual processes do not function autonomously but depend on crucial contributions in terms of the activities and decisions of the knower.

In contrast to Montessori's view of the mind as absorbent, formed by sensory impressions, Piaget's research led him to a view of the mind as self-regulating, formed by its own action. He (Piaget, 1975/1985) described the dynamic self-regulatory process of "equilibration" in part in terms of "constructive errors." It is not possible in this context to explore this topic thoroughly, but Genevan research has shown that young children's cognitive progress often involves errors and contradictions. For Inhelder and Piaget (for example, Inhelder & Piaget, 1955/1958, Chapter 2), error is not random chaos, and coherence is not the result of sensory absorption of adult logic. Rather, it appears that the construction of an internally consistent logical system depends on an emerging awareness of contradictions arising in part from these incorrect ideas.

In summary, with regard to their theories, Montessori and Piaget are in basic opposition in their views on the way in which intelligence functions. Montessori's theory of sensory absorption of external order cannot account for the active but wrong or incomplete and contradictory hypotheses children construct. For Piaget (1972b) the child's ability to assimilate any given information or to organize ideas logically depends on the structure of his intellectual instrument. Intellectual competence improves through a process of equilibration or self-regulation that includes as important aspects the construction of inadequate ideas, the awareness of contradictions, and the feeling of necessity to create more adequate ideas that eliminate contradictions.

THE MONTESSORI METHOD: A CONSTRUCTIVIST CRITIQUE

Montessori's writings are peppered with criticisms of the traditional education of her day, which she saw as enslaving children in unhealthy immobility. She especially criticized stationary desks and chairs and lecture programs designed to keep children still, the use of prizes and punishments to control and motivate children, and an emphasis on teacher correction of children's mistakes. Traditional education of today continues these same practices Montessori criticized so long ago, and those of us today who advocate more active methods of education carry on the countertradition articulated by Montessori, Dewey, and many others.

Montessori's great respect for the child and her belief that the child's mind absorbs the environment like a sponge led her to recommend a special "prepared environment." Montessori (1914/1965) believed that the environment must be adapted for children (p. 38). One of her great contributions to early education is the idea that furniture should be child-sized. She designed furniture and implements to suit the child's proportions and strength because she thought it desirable for children to carry out as many adult activities as possible. The ideal was to have all the equipment necessary for the management of a family of children. Montessori described this as a house including a garden, bathroom, dining room, parlor, room for manual work, gymnasium, rest room, and a place to keep live animals. In great detail, Montessori described the ways in which these rooms should be furnished. For example, little armchairs and sofas should be in the parlor, and the dining room should contain low cupboards where children could take and put away real china and glass and real knives. A dressing room should contain a small cupboard or shelf for each child, small sink, basins, and soap. In the "Children's House" children themselves would do everything— sweeping, dusting and washing furniture, polishing brass, laying and clearing away the dining table, rolling up the rugs, washing clothes, and cooking eggs (Montessori, 1914/1965, p. 44). Montessori contrasted this environment with toys like doll houses and activities such as dressing dolls, pretending to cook, and playing with toy animals. She said that her method gives all this to the child in reality (Montessori, 1914/1965, pp. 46–47).

Most Montessori schools today do not realize fully this idea of the prepared environment. That is, they do not provide houses with rooms corresponding to family dwellings, and children do not perform much real housekeeping work or manual labor. In considering our critique below focused on Montessori's didactic materials, the reader should not forget the context of her general ideal with which we agree to a great extent. That is, although we do not see the necessity for the particular house Montessori described, we do agree that to the extent practical it is useful for children to care for and clean materials in the classroom, and especially that this work should fit children's purposes and the interests of the group.

Montessori's belief in the necessity to capitalize on the child's spontaneous activity also led her to design materials that would make it easy for children to know what to do with little instruction. These materials were to be "self-correcting." That is, children should be able to judge their own success and see the need to correct errors without teacher intervention.

In the Montessori Method (1909/1964) the curriculum is conceptualized in terms of eight categories of activities.

Practical Life Exercises

Montessori's (1909/1964, Chapter 7) Practical Life exercises are concerned with the care of the child's own person, with the care of the environment, and with lessons in social courtesy. They were designed to promote cleanliness, order, poise, and conversation. These constituted the first hour's activities in the Children's House, beginning with an inspection of each child's body and appearance of hair and clothes. Children were taught how to take a partial bath with small pitchers and basins, and how to brush their teeth. Following the inspection of persons was an inspection of room and materials, and cleaning by the children. Poise and equilibrium were the aim in the next activity in which children sat with hands on table, feet on floor, and head erect. They sang a hymn, and stood and sat without being noisy. Exercises gave children practice in moving gracefully, greeting each other, lifting objects carefully, and receiving objects from each other politely (Montessori, 1909/1964, p. 123). Montessori described the encouragement of conversations about children's experiences outside school for language development. She recommended teaching children not to introduce certain topics because they do not make pleasant conversation (Montessori, 1909/1964, p. 124).

Practical Life exercises include polishing shoes, peeling carrots, pouring water and juice, and washing hands and tables. For these exercises, Montessori specified a sequence of steps to be followed (for example, 17 steps in the ritual of hand washing). Over time, children are encouraged to perfect their movements (for example, to wash hands without spilling a drop of water, and to put a cup on a saucer or a chair down on the floor without making a noise). Standing (1957) points out Montessori's emphasis on means rather than ends in Practical Life exercises—on the importance of performing an action in a logical sequence in order to avoid confusion and an unnecessary expenditure of energy. He gives the example of the subsidiary actions in the logical sequence of opening and closing a door: "(1) approach the door, (2) raise the arm and (3) turn the handle, (4) pull the door a *little* way out, (5) let the handle go back, (6) pull the door well out" (Standing, 1957, p. 222). This is what Montessori referred to as the "analysis of movement," designed to bring better coordination between mind and muscle.

The Constructivist Perspective

The parallel with Practical Life in the Kamii-DeVries approach is the use of daily living situations as contexts in which to promote development and as a source of curriculum content. Like Montessori, many of the same sorts of practical life activities are valued for their potential in developing children's self-sufficiency— one aspect (though a minor one) of the emphasis on autonomy. Also advocated in the constructivist approach are polishing shoes, washing things, pouring juice, cutting carrots, and tying shoelaces (Kamii & DeVries, 1973, pp. 395–396; 1978, pp. 304–309). Personal care is not mentioned as a part of constructivist education, but we have no objection to this priority.

Although some constructivist activities bear a general similarity to Montessori's Practical Life exercises, Kamii and DeVries do not subscribe to the analysis of movements or sequential steps in performing activities such as handwashing. Instead of teaching children a method for washing hands and tables, they try to capitalize on children's desires and personal needs to do these things by encouraging their efforts to figure out how to accomplish them in whatever way they can. In the constructivist approach, there is no right way to wash a table.

Social courtesies are not taught as correct forms of behavior, but consideration for others is expected to emerge over time and in part out of conflict as children are encouraged to decenter and take others' perspectives into account, as described in Chapters 5 and 6.

Montessori's emphasis on poise through sitting and walking a line in certain ways seems to place children in a situation in which what they do is done simply because the teacher demands it. It is difficult to see how such rules and values could seem anything except arbitrary from the point of view of the child's feelings of necessity.

We would agree with the encouragement of conversations, but would not make some subjects taboo. Rather than emphasizing that children should learn to talk only about what is socially desirable, we think that respect for children leads to acceptance of their expressed feelings and ideas.

The reader may note from our presentation of constructivist education that the constructivist rationale for activities similar to Montessori's Practical Life exercises is very different (for example, physical knowledge, spatial reasoning, logico-mathematical structuring, autonomy, and moral development). This leads to differences in the child's actual experiences in the two programs.

Muscular Education—Gymnastics

Montessori (1909/1964) criticized the coerciveness of gymnastics in which children follow movements given by commands (p. 137). She felt that exercises of this sort repress spontaneous movements. In this aspect of her method, Montessori was concerned with development of physiological movements such as walking, breathing, and speech. Her aim was to encourage movements that are useful in ordinary life such as dressing, undressing, carrying objects such as balls, cubes, and so on (p. 138).

Montessori's (1909/1964) observations of children led her to design and have manufactured special apparatuses, including a little fence made of "parallel bars supported by upright poles firmly fixed on to the heavy base" (p. 141), a special swing in which children could push themselves away from a wall, a pendulum for children to push to one another while sitting in chairs, a small spiral stair with a balustrade and a low wooden platform painted with lines to gauge the distance of broad jumps. She also adopted Seguin's trampoline and rope laddar.

Free Gymnastics advocated by Montessori (1909/1964) included use of balls, hoops, bean bags, and kites, and the games of Pussy Wants a Corner and Tag (p. 144). Free gymnastics also incuded marching, aimed at developing poise. These exercises involve walking slowly around a circular line painted on the floor, by carefully putting one foot in front of the other, heel to toe. This is made more difficult as children are challenged to perfect the control of their motions by carrying water in a glass without spilling it, carrying a bell without making it ring, or balancing a basket on their heads.

Educational Gymnastics include exercises to prepare children for the Practical Life exercises by developing coordinated movements of the fingers. In these, children use 10 wooden frames mounted with two pieces of cloth or leather to practice fastening and unfastening buttons and buttonholes, hooks and eyes, eyelets and lacings, and so on.

Respiratory Gymnastics aim to regulate the respiratory movements by learning the art of breathing (Montessori, 1909/1964, p. 147), and develop correct speech habits. In these exercises, the directress has children breathe deeply, expel slowly, and repeat certain words in order to learn correct movements of lips and tongue necessary for proper pronunciation.

The Constructivist Perspective

Some constructivist experiences are essentially the same as those in this part of the Montessori Method. Although the rationales are different, children in both types of programs are encouraged to play a few of the same group games. (However, we have never observed these in the Montessori schools we have visited.) Nevertheless, Montessori did not see intellectual value in these games and specifically disapproved some games we advocate, as indicated later in this chapter. We tend to agree with Montessori's rejection of group gymnastics by command, but see little difference between this and her Marching exercises in which children are also regulated by the directress' orders that may be felt arbitrary by children. We do not object to the Dressing Frames if children are interested in fastening. While in constructivist programs, like other child-centered programs, children also have available a variety of equipment on which to exercise their muscles, close attention is not given to physical movement. The more casual attitude reflects an assumption (which may or may not be warranted) that muscular development is adequately fostered in a variety of ways without the specific exercises that Montessori advocated.

Nature in Education—Agricultural Labor: Culture of Plants and Animals

This part of Montessori's method was designed for spiritual purposes, observation of phenomena of life, foresight, patience and confident expectation, and trust and confidence in living creatures. In the course of gardening and caring for animals, the child feels a purpose when he sees that living things depend on him. Montessori was impressed with children's spontaneous interest in earthworms, insect larva, and growing flowers and fruit.

The Constructivist Perspective

No serious differences are found between our constructivist approach and this aspect of the Montessori Method.

Manual Labor—The Potter's Art and Building

Inspired by an artist's school and cultural universals in human history, Montessori's (1909/1964) goal in having children do clay work was to complete a socially useful object (p. 162). Although we have not observed it in Montessori schools, Montessori described how children are to make clay vases and tiles, with which they construct miniature walls and houses. In this work, children are supposed to use the same processes as masons, using mortar and trowel (p. 165). Montessori also described how children can dig foundations for their walls and houses, sometimes made for their chickens.

Montessori (1909/1964) made it clear that in these exercises children are free to create according to individual aesthetic taste. She did not like copying, but also felt that no educational result occurred when children were allowed to use clay in their own way (p. 162).

The Constructivist Perspective

Activities such as these are harmonious with the constructivist approach, except that children's spontaneous actions are encouraged with materials such as clay. It seems that Montessori may have overlooked the physical-knowledge advantages (discussed in Chapter 4) of exploring the properties of materials. She also did not discuss the contribution of such activities to the development of symbolic thought (when, for example, a child experimenting with the properties of clay suddenly "sees" an object represented by the clay and begins to fashion representational objects).

Education of the Senses

Montessori's convictions about the role of the senses in knowing led her to develop a set of didactic materials whose purpose was to educate the senses (Montessori, 1909/1964, p. 167; 1914/1965, p. 50). To promote general cognitive development, Montessori attempted to provide order to the child's mind through materials organized according to systematic variations in physical qualities or dimensions such as brightness in color (light-dark), pitch and intensity of sound (low to high musical tones and soft to loud), and size (short to long, narrow to wide, small to big, and so on). Montessori referred to these as "materialized abstractions"— as the means by which the mind can become capable of ordering and classifying sensory impressions. She took from Itard the idea of isolating the sense as much as possible in order to limit the consciousness to the object of the lesson (Montessori, 1909/1964, p. 224). The method aimed to isolate the child's inner attention and focus it upon the perceptions.

For example, Montessori described the process of teaching "hot" and "cold" by blindfolding the child in a quiet place and drawing his hand first over a dry rubber bag filled with water at 60° C and then over one filled with water at 10° C. The teacher simply says, "It is hot. It is cold," and the lesson is finished. Montessori explains that this accomplishes a projection on consciousness of two images, and helps the child distinguish differences.

Sensory education was designed to proceed from a few strongly contrasting stimuli to many finely differentiated stimuli. Montessori saw sensorial education as preceding intellectual education per se.

Materials and exercises were designed to permit the child to recognize and correct errors without teacher correction. In relation to intellectual activity, sensory exercises were believed "to lead the child from sensations to ideas— from the concrete to the abstract, and to the association of ideas" (Montessori, 1909/1964, p. 224). Montessori listed 13 didactic materials (1914/1965, pp. 50–51) for the education of the senses.

Solid Insets (The "Cylinder Blocks")

Four solid oblong pieces of wood have 10 round holes into which the wooden knobbed cylinders fit. In one block the 10 cylinders are the same height and decrease in diameter only. In the second they decrease in diameter and height, and in the third in height only. In the fourth, they decrease in diameter and increase in height. In order to train the eye (Montessori, 1909/1964, p. 169), children are to take out the cylinders, mix them, and put them back in their proper places. Montessori observed that this material was preferred by 2½- to 3-year-old children, and it thus became the first material presented to children of this age. Montessori described how children who make errors see their mistakes in concrete form when they end up with one that will not fit the last hole. Thus she said that the control of error is in the material itself (Montessori, 1914/1965, p. 71), and that it is not the teacher's role to correct the child.

Pink Cubes (The "Pink Tower")

Ten wooden cubes painted pink decrease in size from 10 centimeters to 1 centimeter. This material is to be used to build a tower with the largest cube on the bottom and the others in order of decreasing size to the smallest on top. Montessori (1909/1964) pointed out that this material is more difficult than the cylinder blocks because error is not controlled by the material but by the child's perception (p. 26).

Wooden Prisms (The "Broad Stair")

Ten brown prisms, each 20 centimeters in length, decrease from 10 centimeters to the side to the smallest having 1 centimeter to the side. The child scatters these over a light-colored carpet and then carries them to a table in order of gradation, sometimes beginning with the smallest and sometimes with the longest.

Rods (The "Long Stair")

Ten rods painted green all have the same square section of 3 or 4 centimeters but differ in length by 1 decimeter. Montessori also had this material painted in decimeter sections, alternating red and blue. Children are to scatter and mix these rods on a carpet and then arrage them in order of length.

Rectangular Tablets with Rough and Smooth Surfaces

A small rectangular board has its surface divided into two parts—rough and smooth. Montessori (1914/1965, p. 14) described how the child is to wash her hands and then pass the fingertips as lightly as possible over the two surfaces. Through noticing their differences, the child develops "tactile sense," to which Montessori gave an important place in her method.

A Collection of Various Stuffs

Two pieces each of many different fabrics in bright colors are matched by the child according to the degree of fineness or coarseness from coarse cotton to fine silk. "Touching" thus graduates to "feeling," and this exercise is repeated with the child blindfolded.

Wooden Tablets

Various types of wood are used so that the small rectangular tablets differ in weight and color, though they are the same size. The child is supposed to rest a tablet delicately on the inner surfaces of outspread fingers, and move hands imperceptibly up and down as though to weigh them. Later, this baric sense is further exercised when the blindfolded child holds the tablets two at a time and puts the heavier on the right and the lighter on the left (Montessori, 1914/1965, p. 80).

Two Boxes, Each Containing 64 Colored Tablets

These tablets are covered with eight tints of silk, each of which has eight shades. Today, the tablets are simply painted. The child begins with this material by matching colors from a small collection, then arranges shades of a given color in order, beginning with the darkest. These exercises of the chromatic sense are described as leading to "color memory." That is, a child can look carefully at a color and then, without looking further at it, find its match in a mixed group of tablets (Montessori, 1914/1965, p. 86).

Geometric Solids

A sphere, prism, pyramid, cone, and cylinder are made from pale blue wood. The child is taught to touch them with eyes closed (exercising the stereognostic sense), and to guess their names. He is also encouraged to observe the differences in how they move when pushed.

Plane Inset

This material consists of a cabinet with six shallow drawers, each of which contains six wooden knobbed insets that fit into a frame. Each drawer specializes in a particular geometrical form (circles, triangles, etc.) in different dimensions. Like the cylinder block, the child takes out the insets, mixes them, and replaces them. Tracing the outline of the inset and aperture with the index and middle fingers is encouraged, and the teacher must show the child how to touch, to make sure she touches all the angles and sides. Montessori believed this exercise especially helpful in preparing the child for later writing (Montessori, 1914/1965, pp. 95–96).

Cards with Geometric Forms

Three series of cards repeat the same geometric shapes as in the plane insets. In the first series, the shapes are filled in (that is, they are blue paper cut-outs pasted on the card). In the second series, the shapes are outlines about half a centimeter in width (cut out from the blue paper). In the third series, the shapes are outlines in black ink. Exercises with these cards include arranging according to shape, putting the wooden forms and solids on the cards, and tracing the outlines of the forms. Montessori believed that the ability to see the similarities among these series of solid and outlined shapes represented progress from concrete reality to an abstraction.

Sound Cylinders

Six closed hollow cylinders are filled with objects to produce sounds varying in intensity from loud to almost imperceptible sounds. A double set is used by the child who arranges them in matching pairs and in a series from loudest to softest.

Musical Bells

A series of bells identical in appearance sound the tones and half-tones of an octave when struck with a hammer. A mixed double series is used by the child to match tones. With a single mixed series the child arranges the bells in order of an ascending scale.

Exercise in Silence

To further refine children's perception of sounds, Montessori devised a "lesson of silence" (Montessori, 1914/1965, p. 118). Children are taught to sit absolutely still, breathe without sound, and to listen to slight sounds, unnoticed before—such as the ticking of a clock, chirp of a sparrow, flight of a butterfly. The lesson of silence ends with whispered calling of children from behind the group or from the next room.

Montessori believed that through all these sensory exercises children classify sensory impressions and acquire an "alphabet" for their experience.

The Constructivist Perspective

Montessori's method of educating the senses is not generally consistent with the constructivist focus on the exercise of reasoning. From our perspective, sensorial exercises do not lead to thought that is the precursor to operatory or even preoperatory reasoning. The general constructivist reservation about Montessori's sensorial exercises is that logico-mathematical knowledge cannot be fostered directly through the senses but depends on experimentation in physical-knowledge activities. Kohlberg (1968b) found that after kindergarten children's experience in a Montessori program, they were not operatory in reasoning on Piagetian tasks.

Nevertheless, a number of Montessori's ideas are consistent with the approach of physical-knowledge activities, for example, appealing to children's spontaneous attention and activity, and promoting the observation of similarities and differences. However, the notion of what is the most desirable form of spontaneous activity differs, as the reader will recognize from descriptions in Chapter 4. Kamii and DeVries also agree with the desirability of communication of error through children's observations of the results of their actions rather than through teacher correction. However, the child's possibilities for spontaneous activity are very limited with Montessori's didactic materials. Montessori did recommend free action on the geometric solids, but this kind of experimentation is emphasized to a much greater extent in constructivist physical-knowledge activities.

Materials having mathematical size relationships are also found in constructivist programs, and their free use is advocated, as has long been the practice in the child-centered tradition. Blind activities may also be found in constructivist programs but are not restricted to matching or simply identifying objects by feeling them. For example, in a group game, blindfolded children exercise spatial reasoning and construct mental images as they try to add missing parts to a pig mounted on a wall (Kamii & DeVries, 1980, Chapter 8). While we agree that some children *may* be spontaneously interested in the goal of matching fabrics, we would give it a low priority because we think it has low general appeal in terms of purposes children feel a necessity to pursue for their own interest. Moreover, this activity has a dead end, and we prefer activities that are likely to lead to new problems that children will be intrigued by.

We will discuss further the theoretical basis for our criticism of Montessori's education of the senses in the later summary of general contrasts with the constructivist approach. Suffice it to say at this point that the essential difference between our approach and that of Montessori with respect to her sensorial materials is that we do not try to give the child ready-made, already-organized materials. In our view, by trying to isolate children's attention to perceptions, Montessori seriously limited the possibilities for exercising and developing reasoning.

Language, Writing, and Reading

Montessori's emphasis on sensory methods of education may also be found in her approach to language, writing, and reading. Viewing language as learned by absorption through the sense of hearing, she taught teachers to pronounce clearly and completely when speaking to a child (Montessori, 1914/1965, p. 123). Learning correct pronunciation was viewed as necessary for providing the basis for correct writing through phonetic analysis of spoken language. The Montessori child first learns the sounds (not the names) of alphabetic signs and spells words as he sounds them out before he can read. Reading thus emerges out of writing in the Montessori Method. It should be noted that Italian is a phonetic language and that the relation between sounds and written symbols is much more regular than in English. However, English-speaking Montessori teachers use the same approach. For nonphonetic languages, Montessori recommends that the teacher make words with movable letters, pronounce them, and have the child repeat the exercise of arranging and rereading them (Montessori, 1914/1965, p. 154).

Language teaching involves reading to children about real people and things of nature—omitting fantasy, myth, and fairy tales (Montessori, 1917/1973, p. 202). Vocabulary enrichment is provided through use of precise names and correct terminology. For example, the child may be asked to "Bring me Australia" (from the world puzzle map) or "Bring me the solid triangle."

Montessori viewed writing as based on the ability to manage the writing instrument, as well as on knowledge of alphabet forms. She justified many practical life and sensory exercises in terms of "preparing the hand for writing" (Montessori, 1914/1965, p. 139). For example, muscle control necessary for writing is developed first through large muscle exercise—such as requiring children using the graduated rods to carry each one separately from the shelf to a rug, holding it by the ends. Small muscles are developed through exercise in pouring rice and water from one small pitcher to another, lacing and buttoning, polishing silver, cutting vegetables, and in using the pincer movement of thumb and index finger in picking up sensorial materials with tiny knobs. Montessori also devised specific exercises to develop muscular ability directly to manage the writing instrument. For these, she had sets of metal insets made similar to the wooden Plane Insets, and had children follow their outlines and color in the resulting shapes.

Exercises designed for writing letters begin with sandpaper letters (cursive) and movable cut-outs of the alphabet. These (light-colored vowels and dark-colored consonents) are to be traced with the finger, using the same movements the child would use if he were writing. The teacher pronounces the sound of a letter and the child repeats it. The next part of the lesson with each letter is for the teacher to ask "Give me i. Give me o," and so on. Finally, the child is asked, "What is this?" (Montessori, 1914/1965, p. 152).

Montessori saw her method of teaching writing as preparing the child for reading. Her beginning reading materials are well-known objects and cards with the objects' names written on them. Later, pictures are substituted for objects. The child sounds out the letters in the word, and the teacher encourages him to say them faster until "finally the word bursts upon his consciousness" (Montessori, 1909/1964, p. 298). Then children read and perform actions written separately on cards, for example, "She gazed slowly around the room" and "The boy ran away as fast as he could" (Montessori, 1917/1973, p. 183). The first series of cards contains one action, followed by six other series that require interpretation of more and more complex sentences.

Montessori's method of teaching reading includes early grammatical analysis for children between ages 5 and 7. Each part of speech is coded by a different color, and boxes with word cards have compartments labeled "noun," "article," and so on. Children combine article and noun cards, putting them side by side on a table. Montessori (1917/1973) prepared many such materials and exercises. For example, to teach descriptive adjectives, the child reads phrases such as "the green color," "the rough cloth," and "the blue rectangular prism," and places the designated objects from the sensorial materials beside the descriptive phrases.

In all Montessori's writing about her experiments and the method she eventually recommended for teaching language, writing, and reading, she emphasized the joy and intense spontaneous interest with which children responded. The anecdotes she recounts are indeed impressive (see, for example, Montessori, 1909/1964, p. 287). The beginning of writing is described as occurring in an explosive and joyous way. Although Montessori stressed the development of writing before reading, she was not rigid about this and expected individual differences in whether children would find one or the other easier.

The Constructivist Perspective

While we are heartily in agreement with Montessori's emphasis on the importance of children's spontaneous interest in writing and reading, we have reservations about the preparation she saw as necessary. The principal reservation is that so much of the preparation for controlling the writing instrument must seem arbitrary from the child's point of view. Our emphasis on the importance of children's felt purposes leads us to question the desirability of many of Montessori's exercises that may not, in fact, appeal to the spontaneous activity she viewed as ideal. For example, we have seen children dutifully filling in shapes made with the metal insets without any joy or personal interest. This is but one example of how, in many cases, Montessori's materials led to exercises that are tasks and not activities. That is, children do them out of respect for the teacher's purposes, not out of their own intrinsic interest or sense of purpose.

It is somewhat difficult to compare Montessori's and constructivist approaches to language, reading, and writing because a constructivist alternative does not exist in fully develped form. Some principles of teaching are described in Chapter 8, which the reader may compare with Montessori's method. Characteristics in common include the emphasis on reading stories to children and providing children with phonics information (though the constructivist approach is not didactic). Children in constructivist classrooms have the opportunity to construct the rules of phonetic analysis for themselves. For example, they might notice that a word beginning with the same letter as their name also begins with the same sound. (Willert & Kamii, 1983, have described how children in one classroom taught themselves to read.) When children in constructivist classrooms copy a word, it is a word they have special motivation to write, not a word selected by the teacher. Movable alphabet letters are available, and, as in Montessori's approach, children are encouraged to try to form words on the basis of sound. Ferreiro and Teberosky have indicated new considerations about the teaching of writing and reading from a constructivist perspective. These are discussed in Chapter 9.

Arithmetic

Montessori (1909/1964) noted the many opportunities in daily life in which children have practice in counting—as when the mother comments that a child has two buttons missing or that three more plates are needed on the dinner table. One of her first ways of introducing children to counting was to teach them to count to 10 and make change with one-, two-, and four-centime pieces. Beyond this, she devised exercises using the sensory materials to begin direct teaching of arithmetic.

The cubes, prisms, and rods were designed so that the smallest is a unit of measurement for all the rest. Montessori (1909/1964, 1914/1965, 1917/1973) began arithmetic instruction with a set of 10 long rods divided into alternating blue and red sections 10 centimeters in length. She described how the child should be taught to say "One" for the smallest piece, then "One, two" for the segments of the next one, and so on. Each rod is also "named" with its number. Following this, the directress mixes the rods, selects one, and asks the child to give her the one next in length. He is supposed to select it "by his eye" and then to verify it by putting the two together and counting the sections. These exercises are repeated many times (Montessori, 1909/1964, pp. 327–328).

Montessori thought it important that children get an idea of a collective number as a unity, represented by a single object, yet composed of equal parts. She criticized the practice in schools of using beans or marbles because she thought their use gave the impression of $1 + 1 + 1 + 1$, and so on, and not the idea of adding united wholes.

To learn addition and subtraction up to 10, children put the shorter rods together to form 10s. They are shown how to put the last rod (1) systematically next to the 9, the 2 rod next to the 8, and so on to the 5, which is turned on end to show that $2 \times 5 = 10$. Putting the rods back in their places is supposed to provide exercise in subtraction from 10. As these exercises are repeated over time, the child is taught the technical language. When the child can write, she is taught the signs "+," "=," and "x." Many other similar exercises are devised, and the child fills many pages with written equations.

Graphic signs for numbers are taught with sandpaper numerals in a manner like that of teaching the alphabet. After the child has learned to trace and name the numerals, he is taught to place numeral cards on corresponding rods. The next exercise aims at further practice in associating the numeral with the quantity, using two trays (or spindle boxes) divided into five compartments. Each compartment is labeled with a numeral, from 0 to 9. Children put the designated number of wooden spindles into each compartment. Lessons on zero are greatly emphasized, and involve asking children to "Come to me zero times," "Throw me zero kisses," putting nothing in the compartment labeled 0, and so on. Memory of numbers is taught by giving children slips of paper on which numbers are written and having them leave the paper and go to collect the number of objects (such as discs) written on the paper. The teacher verifies whether the number of objects is correct.

Children are taught to arrange discs under numerals in rows of two, with odd pieces placed under and between the last two (this arrangement taken from Seguin). Montessori (1914/1965) also described an exercise in which children lay the numerals 1 through 10 on a table and put below them the corresponding number of cubes or counters in this same arrangement. They are taught to begin with 1 and to add 1 for each subsequent numeral after copying the preceding arrangement. Putting out 4 objects, for example, is achieved by copying the row and a half of 3 and adding one to make the symmetrical arrangement of two rows of 2.

To teach numerals larger than 10, Montessori adopted Seguin's boards. One has the numeral 10 printed nine times in a column. The child changes the first to 11 by placing a card with the numeral 1 over the 0. The numeral 2 is placed over the second 0, and so on. The 10 rod is combined with the smaller rods to represent these numbers. The directress may give a numeral and ask the child to combine the 10 rod with another, and the sums may be recorded in the conventional way (for example, $10 + 6 = 16$). Another Seguin card is used to teach children to count by 10s, by covering the 1s in the column of nine 10s with consecutive numbers from 2 to 9, thus making 10, 20,...90. Subtraction exercises are similar, and multiplication and division exercises are also done with the rods. For example, the child is challenged to make 2 rods equal to the number 4 by noting that $3 + 1 = 4$ and $4 - 3 = 1$ and $4 - 1 = 3$ (Montessori, 1909/1964, p. 334). Then rod 2 is turned over to show its relation to 4, 3 to 6, 4 to 8. The Seguin arrangement in rows of 2 used in the memory activity is also used in relation to the rods, and arrangements of discs are made to correspond to the rods. Montessori used this to teach the idea of odd and even numbers, and felt that division by 2 was made easy because children can get the right answer simply by counting the 2 lines of 2s under a numeral (Montessori, 1909/1964, p. 335).

Montessori designed bead materials to further illustrate the base 10 system and to enable children to work concretely with larger numbers. Beads strung on wires represent different numbers. The 10-bead bar is orange, 9 is dark blue, 8 is lavender, and so on; 1 is gold. With this material, Montessori emphasized again the conception of a collective number represented by a single object, to save mental effort and clarify the idea (Montessori, 1917/1973, p. 205). Like Cuisenaire (see Chapter 7), Montessori described recognizing and counting numbers by color, to facilitate performing arithmetic calculations.

Bead work also includes cubes and chains of 100 and 1,000. The chains are composed by attaching the rigid 10 bars with flexible links. Children thus gain an idea of quantity by examining the lengths of the chains when stretched out, and the surface when folded by 10s or 100s. Through counting these chains, it is expected that children will at some point become conscious that the 100 chain has ten 10 bars, and the 1,000 chain has ten 100 chains.

The next material Montessori introduced was an abacus-type counting frame. It has four wires, each strung with 10 beads. The top wire is marked with the numeral "1," the next, "10," then, "100," and the bottom one, "1,000." A second frame with seven wires is used to represent numbers up to the millions. Special lined paper provides a green line on the far right for units, a blue line to its left for tens, red line for hundreds, and a line on the far left for thousands. Children thus learn to write units, tens, and so on in their conventional positions. Children make up their own numbers on the frames and write them down. Later, the frames are used for addition, subtraction, and multiplication exercises. Here we begin to go beyond the preschool curriculum and therefore discontinue our presentation of Montessori's method of teaching arithmetic.

The Constructivist Perspective

Montessori's method of teaching numeration and arithmetic clearly aims at genuine understanding of number and calculation, and not just rote memory of arithmetic facts. It has in common with a constructivist approach (articulated in Kamii & DeVries, 1976, and revised in Kamii, 1982c) an emphasis on the use of discrete, "countable" objects. However, important differences must be noted that reflect a different conceptualization of the nature of knowledge about number and the development of this knowledge. The Piagetian view of number is presented in Chapter 8, along with a summary of the constructivist approach to teaching number.

Principal differences between Montessori's method of teaching numeration and arithmetic and a constructivist approach may be summarized as follows. In Montessori's method, first, counting and calculation are presented as tasks and ends in themselves, rather than as part of activities in which they are means to ends reflecting children's purposes. Second, figurative materials are used to avoid and to correct errors in operative knowing (see Chapter 7 for a definition of this distinction), and measurement is confounded with number. For children who are incapable of logical classification and conservation, Montessori's exercises may make sense only in terms of creating configurations such as a staircase (without numerical significance), or making some arrangement of material that seems arbitrary. It is clear that children may be taught to arrange staircase materials correctly and to count them. However, it is not clear that the construction of coordinated relations between cardinal value and ordinal position is aided by the use of such materials. It may be, in fact, that these materials retard this coordination by prolonging dependence on perceptual or figurative aspects. So long as the child relies on the aid of the configuration to get correct answers to exercises, she is not exercising the operative aspect of knowing (through reflective abstraction described in Chapter 2). It remains an open question whether Montessori's exercises in intuitive reasoning can contribute to operative development.

A third feature of the Montessori approach to numeration and arithmetic is that exercises in calculation with large numbers are given very early, rather than giving children a lot of time to consolidate relationships (such as inclusion) for smaller numbers. And finally, children are preoccupied very early with conventional notation and written exercises, rather than with activities in which writing is unnecessary or in which children invent their own systems of notation.

The constructivist perspective on teaching number and arithmetic is discussed further in Chapter 7.

GENERAL CONTRASTS BETWEEN THE
MONTESSORI METHOD AND CONSTRUCTIVIST EDUCATION

Piaget (1939a) praised Montessori's recognition of the importance of the child's liberty and activity, and noted that her intention was to prolong adaptive behavior and promote discovery. However, he felt that it was necessary to distinguish between intention and realization of intention, and said that "Madame Montessori did not go far enough with her own ideas; she was not faithful to her initial intuition" (Piaget, 1939b, p. 3). In the course of presenting the Montessori Method, we have commented on some similarities and differences with the constructivist approach we advocate. Now we comment on six general contrasts we see as critical differences between these two approaches. We highlight those already mentioned and elaborate several others. Each contrast may be traced back to underlying theoretical differences in views of the nature of knowledge and its acquisition.

Exercise of Senses versus Exercise of Reasoning

As discussed above, Montessori's view of knowledge as acquired by absorption through the senses led her to plan activities to exercise the senses separately and to sharpen sensory awareness as the instrument of knowing how to classify. Montessori viewed her "materialized abstractions" as providing the child with "analyzed attributes of things," "order for content," and to lead from "concrete to abstract" and from "simple to complex."

By "analyzed attributes of things," Montessori referred to her variations in dimensions, forms, colors, textures, weights, temperatures, flavors, and sounds. The intention was not to teach forms, colors, and so on as information content, but to foster an ordered way of receiving sensory impressions. Montessori assumed that the organization would be absorbed first and the content or meaning later.

Piaget's view of knowledge as acquired by active, intelligent construction led to activities (described in Chapters 3–8) to inspire the child's exercise of reasoning. While Piaget also regarded classification an important result of mental development, he gave it a less exclusive role and emphasized the operative rather than the sensory nature of its evolution. According to Piaget (see Chapter 7), the operation of classification represents more than the ability to discriminate perceptual sameness or differences among pairs of objects. Rather, it implies forming a network of groupings or relations that are consistent, inclusive of all members, exhaustive of all objects, and organized in terms of hierarchical inclusion of one class in another.

While birds or animals may be trained to *discriminate* objects as same or different, they do not *classify*. In a similar sense, while infants and animals may be readily trained to *discriminate* the biggest of a number of stimuli, or the heaviest, or the brightest, they do not possess *relational operations*. Relational operations are indicated by understanding, for example, that an ordered series is transitive (i.e., that if A is greater than B and B is greater than C, then A is greater than C).

Studies reviewed by Piaget (1936/1952, 1937/1954) and by Werner (1948/1961) suggest that children's first classification systems focus on meaningful objects ("things of action"), not upon sensory attributes. The child's first categories (for example, boy, girl, dog, cat, mother, father, bicycle, car) are not based on a single sensory cue given by perception. The first classes are groupings of characteristics (for example, hair, clothes, behavior in the concept of "boy") to indicate an underlying similarity among objects with a common function, rather than a common sensory meaning. According to Piaget, even the first concepts are thus organizations of relations rather than of sensations. Furthermore, the development of these concepts into logical classifications is not a process of induction from perceptual instances, but is rather the deductive organization of a reversible group of logical operations consisting of various conceptual relations. By "reversible" we refer to Piaget's finding that well-consolidated reasoning about number implies conserving number and knowing its transitivity (implying seriation) and hierarchical inclusiveness. Operational reasoning about number is flexible and mobile.

At first glance, it may be tempting to conclude that Montessori's idea of progression from concrete to abstract ideas is similar to Piaget's notion of the development of concrete operations. However, Montessori's conception of abstractions as perceptual discriminations is in striking contrast to Piaget's distinction between simple abstraction from actions on objects and reflective abstraction from coordinating mental actions themselves (see Chapter 2). Contrasting with Montessori's intuitive notion that thought arises from perception, Piaget (1970d/1972) found coordinating actions practically from the beginning of life and concluded, therefore, that "perception never acts alone" but always "implies a logico-mathematical schematization of perceptions as well as actions" (pp. 72–73). Distortions and corrections of perceptual activity imply that even perceptual knowledge is not by sensation alone, but also involves the intelligence. Thus, Montessori and Piaget resolved the problem of the relationship between action and thought in very different ways. The conception underlying Montessori's materials lacks the mechanism transforming "sensing" and "doing" to "knowing." As Piaget (1974d/1978) pointed out, "know-how" at the level of practical action may lead to success, but "understanding" involves "a true conceptualization, that is, a transformation of action schemata into concepts and operations" (p. vi).

In contrast with Montessori's assumption that order may be absorbed without content or meaning, for Piaget order or organization does not exist apart from the content known. Operations are not formed and then "applied" to content, but characterize the structure of knowledge in a specific content domain. Operations as characteristic of reasoning come into being and can be exercised only in the course of thinking about particular content. Montessori was under no illusion that children understand the number, classification, and so on in early work with her materials. In constructivist education, children would not be asked to go through exercises with content that is meaningless to them.

Since Montessori did not study the natural evolution of knowledge in children, her efforts to sequence ideas from simple to complex were necessarily based on her adult analysis of what was simplest and what was most complex. Piaget's work has shown that what is simplest for the adult is almost never simplest for the child. His research shows that children first know something in a global way that is wrong in certain respects. Gradually, they modify their "wrong" ideas and differentiate their global notion. Simple elements and their relation to the complex whole actually tend to be known last rather than first. Further, the effort to sequence small details from simple to complex is complicated not only by individual differences in order of correct acquisitions, but also by individual differences among children in the sequence of "wrong" ideas.

The differences in viewpoint between Montessori and Piaget have crucial implications for interpreting the meaning and effectiveness of Montessori's sensorial approach to cognitive education. To summarize this central point of divergence between the Montessori Method and our constructivist approach, we quote from Piaget (1939b):

> Does...development really proceed from sensation to idea? Is the exercise of sensations or perceptions, isolated from their context and usual meaning, the best way for the education of intelligence? This question of relationships between the senses and ideas, or between sensory education and education in general, seems to us to be the central problem of Montessorian pedagogy.... She did not realize sufficiently that perceptions such as that of form or depth imply...not just isolated and static sensory analyses but a construction of a group where intellectual combinations play a much more important role...than sensations. (pp. 2–3)

Self-Correcting versus Open-Ended Materials

Montessori's concern with insuring the absorption of orderly knowledge led her to design self-correcting materials for the prevention and control of error. She believed that by correcting mistakes in material arrangements, the child would correct his sensory knowledge.

In both Montessori and constructivist approaches children are encouraged to find out from acting on materials whether their ideas are right or wrong. The practical difference is that constructivist materials are more open-ended. Montessori's self-correcting materials present a single problem with one right answer. In contrast, constructivist materials may be used in a wide variety of ways, and problems are more often introduced by children than by the teacher. These problems do not necessarily have one right answer, and as discussed in the following section, constructivist teachers do not try to prevent "wrong" answers.

Error-Free Repetition versus Error-Filled Experimentation

For most effective absorption, Montessori believed in indefinite error-free repetition of her exercises. Exercises should be done for a long time without mistakes. Teachers were cautioned, however, not to correct the child when he carries out some actions incorrectly. The material should be presented on another day, emphasizing the aspect the child missed.

In contrast with the notion of error-free repetition, Piaget advocated experimentation and saw "constructive error" as a necessary part of mental development. As discussed in Chapter 2, Piaget (1948/1973) pointed out that "the child must pass through a certain number of stages characterized by ideas which will later be judged erroneous but which appear necessary in order to reach the final correct solution" (p. 21). Piaget's definition of spontaneous activity recognized the important role of error.

> Only this [spontaneous activity], oriented and constantly stimulated by the teacher, but remaining free in its attempts, its gropings, and even its errors, can lead to intellectual autonomy....It is in learning to master the truth by oneself at the risk of losing a lot of time and of going through all the round-about ways that are inherent in real activity. (Piaget, 1948/1973, pp. 105–106)

Piaget's notion of knowledge as actively constructed by the knower himself leads to educational methods that encourage children to think their own preoperational thoughts, which are often "wrong" from the adult's point of view. From the Piagetian perspective, the child's "wrong" answers contribute to the development of his reasoning because they reflect an active intelligence with its own logic in the process of development. In an experimental context, error and repetition are of a different character than in Montessori's exercises. Take, for example, the child in a Rubber Band Activity[2] who persists for a long time in trying to attach loose playdough to a paper clip hanging on a rubber band. She does not realize that this is an impossible task and is surprised when it falls off every time. Her spontaneous repetition testifies to her continued belief in the possibility that it will work, and it is only after many such repetitions that she may finally conclude on her own that it will not. We think a teacher should be pleased to see a child trying out her own ideas, even when these are wrong. From the constructivist perspective, intelligence develops by being used, and preventing children's errors prevents children's development.

To sum up this commentary on the difference between error-free repetition and error-filled experimentation, we quote Piaget's comment on Montessori's self-correcting materials.

> The best made material must serve real experimentation; otherwise it becomes an obstacle after having been a support. Mrs. Montessori, who wanted to protect the free development of the child against clumsy adult intervention, ended up precisely limiting this natural evolution too often with a material inspired partially by adult psychology and, worse yet, by an artificial psychology....In spite of everything, the pupil remains half passive, and his action is continuously restrained by rigid frameworks. (Piaget, 1939b, p. 3)

Work versus Play

The constructivist and Montessori views diverge sharply on the role and value of work and play in child development. Montessori (1936a/1956) felt that "in the life of the child play is perhaps something of little importance which he

---

2. In the Rubber Band Activity, children play with rubber bands, a cardboard box with a skinny dowel rod stuck through opposite sides, string, paper clips, pipe cleaners, and miscellaneous objects. They impose many problems on these materials, including predicting whether rubber bands strung on the rod will break when particular objects are hung on them.

undertakes for the lack of something better to do" (p. 122). Piaget viewed children's play as "thought's most spontaneous manifestation" (Piaget, 1928b/ 1964, p. 202) and a means whereby "they shall come to assimilate intellectual realities which would otherwise remain outside the infantile intelligence" (Piaget, 1969/1970, p. 157).

While Montessori made it very clear that children following her method work and do not play, she made an important distinction between "work" as intrinsically motivated and "labor" as extrinsically motivated. Intrinsic interest is characteristic of most definitions of play. Whether or not an intrinsically motivated activity is called "work" or "play" is not so important as understanding the contrasting views of certain kinds of activities referred to as "play." Montessori rejected fantasy and pretense, painting and drawing that do not reproduce reality, puzzles, and games such as Hide and Seek. All are considered valuable educational activities in constructivist education.

In terms of basic psychology and epistemology, Montessori's opposition to play stems directly from the same roots as her emphasis on sensory absorption. A view of "reality" or conceptual truth as directly provided in sensation implies that the symbolic and the playful are opposed to "truth" or "reality." Montessori valued imagination only when rooted in sensation and when reflecting reality (Montessori, 1916/1965, pp. 245, 248, 254).

Pretense

Montessori saw fantasy and pretense as disorderly and undesirable, as indicating unsatisfied desires, a weak will, lack of concentration, and mental instability (Montessori, 1916/1965, pp. 256–265; 1936a/1956, pp. 154–156; 1949/1967, p. 267). For Montessori, the decline of play was evidence of progress to a state of "normalization" in a child.

Free Drawing and Painting

Montessori viewed children's free drawing and painting as "horrible daubs" that are "monstrous expressions of intellectual lawlessness," and said these were not found among her children (Montessori, 1917/1973, p. 308).

Picture Puzzles

In the course of discussing the advantages of geometric insets, Montessori dismissed play with puzzles as having no educational value. She argued that work with insets resulted in clear concepts, but that play with puzzles resulted merely in vague notions about geometry (Montessori, 1917/1973, p. 260).

Group Games

Despite her aversion to play, Montessori did suggest some games for muscular education, including Tag and games involving balls, hoops, bean bags, and kites

(Montessori, 1909/1964, p. 144). However, her rationale for these activities was to prevent atrophy of the muscular system (Montessori, 1949/1967, p. 145).

It is revealing to note that the game of Hide and Seek did not receive her approval. She described observing the following behaviors among children of 2 and 3 years of age:

- the hider would take his place before the seeker left the room;
- the seeker would nevertheless leave the room and return to "find" the hider;
- players took turns "hiding" in the same place, and seekers continued to "find" them repeatedly, with no loss of joy in this success;
- when an older child pretended not to see the younger one, the younger called out, "Here I am";
- when Montessori herself hid in a place different from the ritual place the children were using, they were disappointed not to find her in the expected place and asked why she didn't play with them (Montessori, 1936a/1956, pp. 54–55).

Montessori concluded from these observations that the child is endowed with a sensitiveness to order. Piaget (1932/1965) described similar behaviors in Hide and Seek, but interpreted them in terms of egocentric assimilation or simple imitation of the form of the game, in the absence of understanding of the reasons for rules, and lack of competitiveness due to inability co-operate (see Chapter 5 for discussion of the significance of the incorrect ways in which young children play games).

In summary, Montessori believed that many playful activities of the type that we advocate were trivial and a waste of time, if not damaging to children. Montessori believed children should spend their time working to absorb factual, reality-oriented knowledge, in contrast with play.

In contrast with these views, Piaget saw play as a natural precursor to "work" and as a legitimate form of thought indispensable to both intellectual, social, and affective development. The four categories of play that he distinguished are described in Chapter 2. In contrast with Montessori's insistence on children's work, we advocate children's play in activities that include the very ones Montessori excluded. Our rationale for these activities concerns their general role in contributing to the child's cognitive development, representational thought (in pretense, drawing, and painting), spatial reasoning (in puzzles), physical knowledge (in painting and construction), and both cognitive and sociomoral reasoning (in group games).

The opportunity to engage openly in make-believe is a facilitating condition for the differentiation of reality and appearance rather than a force leading to fixation in the realm of fantasy. The role of symbolic play in cognitive advance is matched by an even more distinctive role in social advance. Many aspects of social role-taking are only available through the channel of pretend play. Furthermore, when symbolic play is understood as one of the symptoms of the general symbolic (or semiotic) function, its significance for communication becomes clear. Along with verbal and gestural language, symbolic play involving others permits evocative thought and also communication with others. These open the way for decentering to recognize separate and multiple perspectives that are eventually differentiated and coordinated. Through play, the child makes progress toward operational reasoning about physical and social worlds.[3]

If the Montessori restrictions on play and on the verbal conceptual (as opposed to the sensory) seem overrestrictive, the Montessori emphasis on the sensory-cognitive provides interesting forays into aesthetic early education. A number of Montessori activities involve sensory discrimination and ordering of an aesthetic variety, for example with musical scales. The spontaneous interest of many children in such activities does suggest that these could form a beginning of a developmental aesthetic education.

Individual versus Collective Activity

Montessori's method emphasizes individual activity because she saw development as a task for individual sensory absorption. She did not elaborate an early education developmental approach to the social in the same sense as she did for the cognitive. Nevertheless, she had in mind social objectives as well, and believed her method offered possibilities for social training that was superior to the education of her day. She criticized schools where the only social life was during recess or on field trips, and where children's life was for the most part regimented, with everyone doing the same thing at the same time (Montessori, 1949/1967, pp. 11, 225). For Montessori, "social sentiment" is better developed in a community of work where children attend to their individual business, but where mutual aid and courtesy are expressed. Montessori (1909/1964) saw her method as "preparing the child for the forms of social life" (p. 121).

Montessori's (1949/1967) social objectives were based on the belief that the child absorbs the social patterns of his group (p. 189). She aimed for children to develop internal inhibitions of impulses and discussed these in terms of an internal "construction" of will (Montessori, 1916/1965, p. 173). While she took conformity to societal norms of politeness as an aim, she made it clear that she had in mind the establishment of volitional following of the "code of manners" (Montessori, 1916/1965, pp. 172–173). While Montessori tended to see desirable social behaviors as stemming from an individual rather than an interactive process, she described the results in terms of interactions. The effects of liberty include pleasant relations among children, courtesy, respect for others' work, and patience to wait for something in order not to infringe the rights of others (Montessori, 1916/1965, pp. 174, 324). Montessori (1916/1965) aimed to create attitudes and habits of orderly movement that could not happen by

---

3. The interested reader may refer to Chapter 9 in Kohlberg and Colleagues (1987) for a more in-depth discussion of issues concerning the role of play in development.

keeping children motionless (p. 174). Orderly movement is described in terms of walking without knocking against or stepping on others, without overturning tables, and without grabbing from others.

Many people observe Montessori classrooms and object to the limited social interaction. Montessori (1949/1967) defended her approach by pointing out that children in classrooms oriented to her method live in an active community, and by comparing her method with that where children sit and listen to a teacher talk (p. 225).

Montessori pointed out the social advantages of mixed-age grouping where older children help and protect the younger. She described a spirit of cooperation, affection, and community (Montessori, 1949/1967, p. 231). Montessori noted that when teachers in her classrooms succeed in engaging children in productive work, clashes between them do not occur.

It would be false to characterize the differences between Montessori and constructivist approaches as a strong contrast between individual versus collective activity. Montessori's view is compatible with the kind of group feeling, real respect for others, and co-operative interaction we also hold as an aim. Although the specification of so much individual work operates against this aim in Montessori classrooms, individual play and work are also found in our classrooms. We would therefore caution against unnecessarily dichotomous thinking on this point.

While the Montessori approach stresses individual cognitive performance, some research suggests that it does not lead to less classroom affiliation and co-operation. In one of our studies (Stodolsky & Jensen, 1969), episodes of peer interaction were coded for two mornings in each of the three classrooms (permissive, school readiness, and Montessori[4]). Average number of social acts per minute were about the same in each classroom. Frequency of affiliative and co-operative acts was higher (but not significantly) in the Montessori class than in either of the other classrooms. In a study by Mayer (1973) two Montessori second-grade follow-through classes were compared with Bank Street, Engelmann-Becker, and Weikart cognitive classrooms. After the Bank Street classroom, the Montessori classrooms were highest in peer interaction. The differences between the Bank Street classes and the Montessori classes were not significant.

Montessori's emphasis on cognitive development was meant to be compatible with social development in a classroom where co-operative social interaction occurs. Nevertheless, it must be admitted that Montessori did not provide a well-elaborated developmental approach to the social as she did to the cognitive in early education. On balance, our constructivist approach emphasizes to a greater extent the role of social interaction (collaborative and oppositional) in cognitive, sociomoral, and affective development. Montessori did not have a

---

4. It should be noted, however, that this Montessori school was considered by more orthodox Montessori advocates to be too loose in its implementation of the Montessori Method.

conception of the psychologically interdependent and interactive relations among these aspects. Perhaps for this reason her method does not seem to realize fully her vision of social experience for children.

The constructivist view leads us to identify educational methods emphasizing peer interaction that differ from Montessori's in important ways. For example, as described in Chapters 2, 5 and 6, we advocate self-government through group discussion and voting, debates about social and moral issues, and the use of group games. In our view, conflicts are inevitable, normal, and educationally useful situations in which children can decenter to appreciate the feelings and ideas of others, and develop feelings of moral necessity about their relations with others.

Perhaps the feature of social development that child-development or child-centered preschool approaches in early education focus on most has been the child's participation and co-operation in the peer group. Our view of the importance of social interaction is closer to this view than to Montessori's ideas (though other differences with one realization of the child-centered tradition are discussed in Chapter 10).

The importance of peer interaction has been commonly understood as a function of the child's deep needs and their satisfaction. However, research studies suggest that it is closely related to intellectual maturity. Parten and Newhall (1943) found maturity or co-operativeness of social peer play was correlated .61 with age and .38 with IQ, so that mental age or cognitive maturity appears to be an important determinant of peer co-operation. Accordingly, it may well be that the experiences leading to increased intellectual maturity and functioning may also lead to increased social participation and co-operation. In Chapter 2, we elaborated a view of social and cognitive development as structurally parallel which is harmonious with these findings. In Chapters 5 and 6, we also elaborate a view of educational objectives in terms of moral and ego development which crosscuts the cognitive/social dichotomy.

In summary, the theoretical assumptions and classroom methods related to individual and collective activity are significantly different in Montessori and constructivist approaches. In our view, the constructivist approach is based on a more integrated theory of cognitive, sociomoral, and affective development, and offers a broader range of opportunities for social experience.

Obedience versus Autonomy

Both Montessori and Piaget deplored the coercive and verbal methods of traditional public schools where discipline and moral training were based on the cultural-transmission model. They pointed out the shortcomings of such methods in terms of failure to produce autonomous personalities. Montessori summarized three unfortunate precepts governing most education: (1) The child is expected to acquire virtue by imitation instead of through development; (2) Virtue rests on domination of the child's will; and (3) It is the teacher who forms the child's mind. Both Piaget and Montessori emphasized the importance of the child's construction of will for the development of self-regulated morality, in contrast with blind obedience to authority. However, we find some contradictions in Montessori's statements and recommendations, and, once again, we find significant theoretical and practical differences between the Montessori Method and constructivist education.

While Montessori aimed at will as an interior guide, she clearly believed that self-disciplined will meant willing obedience to adults. While believing that character and morality develop through self-discipline rooted in liberty, she outlined methods that seem at least equally rooted in authority.

Just as she saw intellectual education from the perspective of a sensory psychology, Montessori conceptualized social and moral education in terms of sensory attention and the absorption of order. She believed that customs, morals, religion, and aesthetics are absorbed (Montessori, 1949/1967, p. 189; 1909/1964, p. 221). Further, she emphasized the importance of directly communicating what is right and what is wrong, as another way of providing the child with order (Montessori, 1916/1965, pp. 335–336). Montessori did not make a distinction between knowledge as arbitrary or conventional "truths" and sociomoral knowledge requiring cognitive and affective decentering to consider multiple perspectives and construct relations of reciprocity. In contrast with the constructivist view of sociomoral development forged through the fire of interpersonal exchanges in play, Montessori saw sociomoral development in terms of a parallel development of will and obedience in work.

For Montessori (1909/1964, 1916/1965, 1936a/1956, 1936b/1956, 1949/1967), willpower is the basis for obedience of moral rules; self-discipline is reflected in an ability to obey. In connection with her studies of attention and development of ability to work, Montessori described stages in the evolution of obedience. In the first level of obedience the child sometimes obeys, but not always. At the second level the child always obeys—absorbing the other's wishes and expressing them through his own behavior. At the third level the child can control actions in accordance with the other person's desires with a joyful sense of submission to a superior personality. Montessori likens this advanced level to the dog who loves his master and wags his tail while joyfully obeying (Montessori, 1916/1965, p. 104; 1909/1964, p. 116; 1936b/1956, pp. 138–139; 1949/1967, pp. 260–261). Montessori emphasizes that will and obedience go hand in hand, and obedience may even be a sublimation of the child's will (1949/1967, pp. 256–257). She describes the obedient group as recognizing the superiority of the directress, looking to her, intent and ready to follow her sign (Montessori, 1916/1965, p. 116).

Montessori writes about the futility of trying to get children to obey through praise, begging, orders, or violence. She viewed obedience as arising spontaneously later than ages 4 or 5, as the result of the self-discipline derived from repetition of her didactic exercises (Montessori, 1909/1964, p. 364). Thus, as the child patiently repeats lessons, inhibits impulses, and exercises self-control (for example, in lessons of silence, walking slowly and quietly, and refraining from any action when told to do something zero times), he is training positive willpower and habits of moral behavior.

Basically, we view as false the ideological polarity often involved in discussions of Montessori, namely, the polarity between the "structured" and the "permissive." Montessori was a believer in permissiveness only if that is opposed to discipline viewed as severe regulation of the child through imposition of a large number of adult rules for behavior. Montessori clearly stated that her method had its basis in the liberty of the child, and from this perspective was therefore not structured. Nevertheless, Montessori did believe in ordering the environment to the end of stimulating the development of cognitive and moral order in the child's mind, and in this sense was not permissive.

In practice, it is evident that Montessori's ordered environment involves a fair number of classroom management rules. A central short-term function of most ordinary classroom management rules is that of preventing distraction from tasks in a crowded setting (Jackson, 1967). Rules of order do not necessarily imply "discipline," however, in the sense in which discipline means the cultivation of obedience and the elimination of misconduct through punishment and reward.

Two research findings may be cited indicating the value of Montessori's notion of order through self-directed activity, as opposed to discipline, in classroom functioning. The first is a finding by Kounin (unpublished) that teachers' methods of discipline (type, style, and amount of punishment and reward) are unrelated to amount of classroom misconduct, while effectiveness in structuring instructional activities is related to low classroom misconduct. The second more tentative finding comes from one of our own studies (Stodolsky & Jensen, 1969). Observation of three summer classrooms indicated about equal frequency of statements of rules in the Montessori and the school-readiness classrooms, with far fewer statements of rules in the permissive classroom. Observers agreed that the direct rule enforcement techniques of the school-readiness teacher were the most effective of those used by the three teachers. Episodes of what might be considered misconduct were least frequent in the Montessori classroom. In both the permissive and the school-readiness classes, 16% of the episodes of social interaction were episodes of physical aggression, while only 2% of the Montessori classroom episodes involved physical aggression. This suggests that the greater cognitive structure of the Montessori classroom may reduce misconduct without use of strongly coercive discipline by teachers. After 6 weeks in public school, however, when the children in the three preschool programs were rated by their teachers, no clear or significant differences were found.

However, another of our studies (DeVries & Goncu, in press), reported in Chapter 11, suggests that the Montessori Method may not result in the internal discipline Montessori hoped to achieve. The order in children's behavior in Montessori classrooms may depend on the presence of adult authority. In a comparison of children playing a board game by themselves, significantly more conflict and significantly less conflict resolution were observed in the Montessori children than in children from a constructivist program. This study suggests that suppression of classroom conflict may be counterproductive in children's construction of the internal guide for conduct toward which Montessori aimed.

Teacher as Directress versus Companion/Guide

A number of similarities may be noted between Montessori's description of the role of the directress and our description of the teacher as companion/guide. In both cases, the role of the teacher includes engaging children's interest in activities, allowing free pursuit of these, and making it possible for children to become aware of and correct their mistakes. We agree with Montessori's (1909/1964) statement that "the teacher. . . must be more of a psychologist than a teacher" (p. 173), and with her insistence that the child's activity is more important than the teacher's. We especially agree with her view that "one must limit the action of the adult upon the child so as to give him the possibility to develop without having always on top an oppressive will which is stronger than his own" (Montessori, undated/1973, p. 3). However, in comparison with our ideal teacher, Montessori's teacher seems more heteronomous and impersonal in relations with children. She is more active in providing didactic instruction but less active in engaging in activities with children and in stimulating social interaction and experimentation.

It is significant that Montessori changed the name "teacher" to "directress." She explained that the function of the teacher is "to direct the psychic activity of the children" (Montessori, 1909/1964, p. 173). This direction, however, occurs principally through the materials that take the place of the teacher. Montessori's method calls for the teacher to "teach little and observe much" (Montessori, 1909/1964, p. 173). The aim is for the teacher to become more of a passive than an active influence (Montessori, 1909/1964, p. 87). Montessori cautions against interrupting or interfering with children's work, and describes the ideal in terms of the teacher's noninvolvement. Individual lessons should be concise, simple, and objective to facilitate absorption. Her idea was that the truth to be absorbed should be highlighted through brevity, elimination of unnecessary verbiage, and presentation "in such a way that the personality of the teacher shall disappear" (Montessori, 1909/1964, p. 108). The purpose of lessons is to fix an idea by calling attention to the sensory impression (Montessori, 1909/1964, p. 115). An example of a good lesson was given earlier with regard to teaching "hot" and "cold." Similar lessons focused on colors (Montessori, 1909/1964, p. 109). The brief instruction is followed by testing (asking the child for the correct answers), but errors are not corrected. We have already discussed Montessori's views on obedience and correction of error, pointing out certain internal contradictions in her statements on these issues.

In contrast with Montessori's conception of the teacher's role, ours is that of an adult who cultivates a more personal and egalitarian relationship with children. Rather than striving to be a "passive influence," the constructivist teacher is often an active participant as well as observer of children. Rather than striving to provide isolated truths in simple didactic lessons, the constructivist teacher tries to foster reasoning and the child's invention of knowledge especially when physical, logico-mathematical, or moral in nature. Telling children truths is generally limited to knowledge that is social-arbitrary (conventional). Unlike Montessori's directress, we would not hesitate, for example, to correct a child's mistake in naming colors since this is an arbitrary, man-made item of knowledge that can only be known through social transmission.

SUMMARY

Montessori criticized the education of her day in which children sat at desks in unhealthy immobility. Those of us today who advocate more active methods of education carry on the countertradition, articulated by Montessori, Dewey, and others.

The Montessori Method belongs within a broad conception of cognitive-developmental programs of early education because it is based on recognition that the child's mind is qualitatively different from that of the adult, that mental transformation occurs in stages through active experience, and that logical thought results from general intellectual development, and is not just verbal learning. Montessori emphasized attention as fundamental in her dialectic between liberty and discipline. Piaget similarly remarked upon the educational value of exercising powers of observation and emphasized interest. Like Piaget, Montessori advocated education that is active, uses concrete materials, and emphasizes moral development.

Despite these commonalities, theoretical divergences between Montessori and Piaget outweigh the similarities. In contrast to Montessori's view of the mind as absorbent and formed by sensory impressions, Piaget viewed the mind as self-regulating, formed by its own action through equilibration involving constructive errors.

Montessori's educational ideas were dominated by her conviction that the environment must be organized and tasks planned so the child absorbs logical order. She saw the ordinary result of absorption as chaos in the child's mind. Her goal was to develop in the child an ordered mind through an orderly experience, avoiding error. Spontaneous activity, for Montessori, occurred within the constraints of orderliness and correct ideas. These are in contrast to Piaget's ideas. He too recognized incoherence or chaos in the child's thought, but saw not random chaos but internal coherence. He saw spontaneous activity as filled with errors having constructive value, as valid intellectual activity.

In this chapter, Montessori's method is described, and similarities and differences with constructivist education are discussed. Similarities in activities include practical life activities (such as washing things, pouring juice, and cutting carrots), care of plants and animals, molding with clay, using blocks with mathematical size relationships, use of balls, hoops, bean bags, and kites. In contrast with constructivist education, Montessori excludes from her method children's pretend play, free painting and drawing, modeling with clay according to children's ideas, and stories involving fantasy. Montessori also criticized some of the group games we find most educationally useful, and in general excludes group games, mentioning only two for the purpose of muscular development.

The Montessori Method is especially different from constructivist education with regard to Montessori's 13 didactic materials for the education of the senses. Though some of these materials resemble those used by Piaget to study seriation, the Montessori exercises are more like tasks than activities, and fail, from the constructivist perspective, to arouse the kind of spontaneous activity we seek to inspire.

Montessori's emphasis on sensory methods of education are also found in her approach to language, writing, reading, and arithmetic. Many of her exercises in controlling the writing instrument seem arbitrary and purposeless from the child's point of view. Montessori's emphasis on phonics in beginning reading contrasts with the constructivist approach described in Chapter 8, while her emphasis on counting, use of figurative materials, and emphasis on conventional notation in beginning arithmetic contrasts with the constructivist approach described in Chapter 8.

Divergences between the Montessori Method and constructivist education are summarized as: exercise of senses versus exercise of reasoning, self-correcting versus open-ended materials, error-free repetition versus error-filled experimentation (and, as Don Holdaway has suggested, also error-informed experimentation), work versus play, individual versus collective activity, and obedience versus autonomy.

Chapter 10

Bank Street
Theory and Practice

Bank Street theory and practice deserve consideration in this volume because among the articulated, identifiable programs in early education, Bank Street is the closest relative to the constructivist, cognitive-developmental approach. Bank Street writers (Franklin & Biber, 1977) also acknowledge that a large area of common ground is found in these approaches. They observe that the Piagetian notion of the child as a constructor of knowledge leads to an objective very close to that of Bank Street—helping children be as active as possible.

Bank Street is the most vital contemporary representative of the "child-centered" or "child-development" tradition in early education from which the more recent Piagetian programs have drawn heavily for designs of classrooms, types of activities, and methods of teaching. This tradition was developed in the United States by preschool and kindergarten educators, especially those connected with universities, child-development institutes, and colleges devoted to teacher education.[1] The thinking behind child-centered practices as currently expressed in Bank Street rationale derives from what we called in Chapter 1 the romantic and progressive streams in educational thought. Bank Street's most significant original and continuing roots lie in John Dewey's progressivism, articulated by Harriet Johnson (1928/1972), Lucy Sprague Mitchell (1950), and Caroline Pratt (1948/1970).

The Dewey influence gave the Bank Street tradition a basic commitment to the stimulation of thinking, beginning as early as 1919 when Harriet Johnson, inspired by Dewey, established the school later named for her, which is now the Bank Street School for Children.

The influence of psychodynamic theory is also acknowledged as having directly influenced practice, as recounted by Biber (1979).

> On our part, there was increasing sensitivity to young children's problems in managing the feelings of ambivalence, conflict, and guilt about the anger they felt toward the very people they loved; the pull between following impulse mixed with the fear of where it might lead, and the ignominy of accepting restraint; between the lingering comfort of dependence on the strength of adults and the deep wish to be brave enough to test the world in one's own right. As adults, as teachers, we became increasingly more aware of early childhood as a period of emotional weathering, involving pain alongside the opening vistas of the growing mind and its

---

1. See E. Weber (1969), *The Kindergarten: Its Encounter with Educational Thought in America*, and (1984) *Ideas Influencing Early Childhood Education: A Theoretical Analysis*, for excellent accounts of this history.

pleasures, all part of a far more complex growth process than had once been envisaged. (p. 7)

Biber recalls the struggle of early progressive educators with how to develop educational practices that took these insights into account. She cites Susan Isaacs (1930) as especially influential.

Long after the development of techniques to foster self-initiated play in activities permitting the child's release of unconscious feelings and working out conflicts, the mental health movement in the 1950s and 1960s led further to emphasis on the importance of the educator's concern with emotions and their role in learning and development (Biber, Gilkeson, & Winsor, 1959). By the late 1950s Bank Street's emphasis on emotional development seems to have been dominant and better elaborated than the emphasis on intellectual development. Although Bank Street thought clearly distinguished between the role of therapist and the role of the teacher, the teacher role included some characteristics of interaction often stressed by therapeutic models. The most fundamental concern was to facilitate the play and social interaction of the child in a way that would promote ego strength or positive mental health. Curriculum stressed self-selected, self-directed activities in "centers of interest" (such as housekeeping, blocks, sand, water, art, books and puzzles, science, and woodworking).

Piagetian program developers have often acknowledged that they stand on the shoulders of those who developed many child-centered practices that are borrowed because they are justified by cognitive-developmental and constructivist theory. Bank Street and Piagetian approaches stand together in contrast to behaviorist emphases on habit training arising out of the cultural transmission tradition (Franklin & Biber, 1977).

Bank Street and Piagetian program development were influenced by the fact that programs for the disadvantaged to enhance intellectual development were sought during the 1960s and 1970s (Biber, 1967a, b, d, 1970).[2] The compensatory education focus did lead Bank Street to a new stress on the cognitive and linguistic competencies of the child and to new conceptualizations of how to promote ego strength. Despite the special consciousness about intellectual development in both approaches in recent years, both take development as their aim in a comprehensive sense and strive to identify practices that promote at the same time specific aspects of intellectual, ego, and socioemotional development.

The term *developmental-interaction* first emerged in Bank Street writing in 1971 (Biber, Shapiro, & Wickens, 1971; Shapiro & Biber, 1972), although the concept had developed gradually over several decades. This more explicit conceptualization served as a reaction against the emphasis of both behaviorists and cognitive-developmental psychologists on the cognitive with

---

2. However, in contrast with Montessori and early Piagetian programs, which were developed for poor children and later adopted for the advantaged, Bank Street began as a private school for children from liberal professional homes and was extended to programs for the disadvantaged.

little or attention to emotional aspects of development. "Developmental-interactional" indicates the premise that a concern for development as an aim of education rests on recognition both that development is an interaction between cognition and emotion and that it arises through active interaction between the child and the environment. A basic tenet is that cognitive functions (such as acquiring information, reasoning, and using symbols) cannot be separated from personal and interpersonal processes (such as self-esteem, internalization of impulse control, and relatedness to others) (Biber, 1972).

Both Bank Street and Piagetian approaches represent a commitment to articulate a comprehensive and coherent theoretical rationale for early education, including an integration of Piagetian, Deweyan, and psychoanalytic theories. However, Bank Street draws from a greater variety of theories, and aims at a comprehensive "super theory" that integrates shared assumptions from a "family of theories," including Tolman, Wertheimer, Lewin, Piaget, Werner, Freud, Erikson, Sullivan, and Hartmann (Biber, 1977, 1984; Franklin, 1981).

What are the differences in theoretical underpinning among Bank Street and Piagetian programs? Bank Street theory is strongly rooted in John Dewey's progressivism which has influenced Piagetian programs only indirectly. In Bank Street thought, Werner's conception of intellectual development is more emphasized than that of Piaget (Biber, personal communication), and psycho-dynamic theories of ego development are more self-consciously combined with cognitive theory. While teachers in the Piagetian programs described in Chapters 4–9 are expected to be sensitive to implications of neopsychoanalytic theories of development,[3] the programs are built with Piagetian theory primarily in mind, and the integration is not made explicit.

Bank Street theorists agree with our general view of the High/Scope and Lavatelli programs as being in some respects inconsistent with the implications of cognitive-developmental theory (Franklin & Biber, 1977). They acknowledge that some Piagetians have not limited programs to a narrow focus on cognitive development and have emphasized development as a whole. From the Bank Street perspective, however, the cognitive-developmental and constructivist perspective seems too cognitive to provide the basis for a comprehensive educational program. Franklin and Biber (1977) express doubt about the adequacy of the Piagetian approaches.

> The program descriptions reflect—to varying degrees, to be sure—a rather preponderant emphasis on cognitive functioning as such, and insufficient attention

---

3. This expectation has been manifested by efforts to hire teachers with training from Bank Street and the Erikson Institute for constructivist demonstration programs and university teacher-training programs. In developing the constructivist approach informed by Piaget's work, Kamii and DeVries took for granted much of the established necessity to consider continually the child's feelings and internal conflicts. This did not imply, however, a blanket acceptance of all psychodynamic tenets. Many of these are in contradiction with cognitive-developmental and constructivist assumptions. See DeVries (1974a) for a discussion of some of these.

in our view to feelings and fantasy as they reflect and feed into the child's aesthetic as well as his inter- and intrapersonal development. (p. 16)

Bank Street proponents also worry that the individual may be lost in a focus on developmental stages (Shapiro & Wallace, 1981; Biber, 1984).

We agree with the view that Piagetian theory does not offer a fully elaborated description or explanation of "affective-social" development. However, we feel that it does provide a more comprehensive framework than that assumed by Bank Street writers, and as we argued in earlier chapters, that it is an excellent integrative framework for taking into account all aspects of development. While Piagetian programs need a more elaborated conception of socioemotional development, the Bank Street program might profit from a more elaborated conception of cognitive development.

This chapter, written from the constructivist perspective, represents an effort to gain a better understanding of similarities and differences between these programs whose aims and practices share so much. Our intention is to provide a comparative examination that will more sharply define current issues and problems in the effort to articulate a theory of educational practice congruent with child development research and theory. With this in mind, a dialogue was sought with those at Bank Street who have been in the forefront in developing this approach.[4] Their responses to drafts of this chapter left us with a clearer picture of some similarities and differences, but also with somewhat more confusion about Bank Street theory and practice. Through its 60 years of evolution, Bank Street has incorporated emerging theory from related fields in its rationale (Biber, 1981, 1984), but it is often unclear whether these influenced changes in basic practices, or to what extent they were simply cited as new justifications for established practices.

We concluded that it may be impossible for anyone outside the Bank Street circle to present this approach entirely accurately, based on published descriptions. However, the analysis undertaken here may serve to identify those areas in which clarification is needed. Most of all, we hope that the critical look at Bank Street work from the constructivist perspective will lead to a clearer view of what is yet needed for progress in both Bank Street and constructivist programs. We focus in depth upon what we see as both achievements and limitations and contradictions that have resulted from the Bank Street effort to integrate a wide range of theories.

4. We would like to express our deep appreciation to Dr. Barbara Biber and Dr. Edna Shapiro for the time and effort they spent in reading and responding in writing and in person to earlier drafts of this chapter, and for permission to quote some of these personal communications. Responsibility for the perspective on Bank Street presented here, however, is the authors', and, in fact, as we indicate where appropriate, our view is not entirely shared by those identified with Bank Street.

OBJECTIVES

Bank Street aims are derived from a developmental-interactional theory as this interacts with what Biber calls a "humanistic value position, both as to what constitutes optimal development of the individual and as to priorities of social organization" (Biber, 1977, p. 429). Biber (1964) notes that individual fulfillment alone does not comprise the Bank Street system of values. It is embedded in a universal concern for eveyone else's individuality. What Biber calls a "humanistic value position" we referred to as the "ethical principles of the liberal tradition" in Chapter 1.

From this position, four broad objectives are listed in terms of four "major processes of the developmental sequence" (Biber, 1977, p. 429). These reflect an effort to capture the functional dimensions of cognitive and social-cognitive structural stage development, as stage development is modified or qualified by an adapting ego.

Broad Objectives

The first of the four aims is "enhancing competence." In the Bank Street view, competence involves not only "objective" standards of ego strength (such as adaptive use of knowledge and skills), but subjective standards of ego strength (such as self-esteem, self-confidence, resourcefulness, resiliance, and a feeling of competence). The goal of competence is also discussed in terms of specific skills, excellence of performance, and language proficiency for communication and as a conceptual tool for acquiring knowledge.

The second aim, of "individuality or identity," is oriented to objectivity in identifying "self qualities," the variety of roles occupied ("worker, learner, member of a group, and so forth"), and "realistic expectations and aspirations" (Biber, 1977, p. 430). This goal overlaps with the competence goal in its inclusion of a sense of self-worth. Autonomous functioning is emphasized as "the ability to make choices, develop preferences, take initiative, risk failure, set an independent course for problem-solving, and accept help without sacrificing independence" (Biber, 1977, p. 430).

The third virtue posited as a Bank Street aim is "socialization." This includes the child's rechanneling highly charged impulses in order to participate in the social order of the classroom. "This involves yielding individual drive to group purposes, adapting behavior to a rational system of controls and sanctions, and, finally, internalizing the regulating codes" (Biber, 1977, p. 430). According to Biber, two ingredients are central to this goal. First is the ability to be sensitive to others' points of view and to engage in co-operative or mutual (as opposed to predatory) relations in play, work, talk, and argument. Second is having available "a variety of modes of communication necessary as a means for understanding commonness of human feelings and conflicts as well as for extending knowledge and finding emotional refreshment" (Biber, 1977, p. 430).

The fourth general objective is "integration of functions," as opposed to their compartmentalization, and involves a synthesis of inner and outer worlds, and of thought and feeling. It is unclear what Biber means by the compartmentalization she wishes to avoid. However, she specifies the stimulation of "openness" or "sensitivity and responsiveness...to a wide range of phenomena, including freedom of affect to move across a wide span of emotional experience" (Biber, 1977, p. 430). This goal includes "having a sense of ease with multiple modes of expression and interaction—logical and alogical, reasoned and intuitive" (Biber, 1977, pp. 430–431). Perhaps this goal is intended as a synthesis of the three prior virtues of competence, individuality, and socialization.

In general, the constructivist perspective is comfortable with these broad Bank Street objectives, though the reader will note that some are not mentioned specifically as constructivist aims while others are elaborated with a different rationale.

Specific Objectives

More specific Bank Street aims consistent with these broad objectives are elaborated as eight "Educational Goals for the Preschool Years" for children aged 3 to 5 years. These are intended to show how cognitive and affective aspects "interpenetrate one another" (Biber, Shapiro, & Wickens, 1971, p. 17).

1. *To serve the child's need to make an impact on the environment through direct physical contact and maneuver.*
   - Exploring the physical world: e.g., equipment, space, physical protection.
   - Constructive, manipulative activities with things (presymbolic): e.g., variety of materials—blocks, clay, sand, wood.
2. *To promote the potential for ordering experience through cognitive strategies.*
   - Extending receptiveness and responsiveness: e.g., variety of sensory-motor-perceptual experiences, focus on observation and discrimination.
   - Extending modes of symbolizing: e.g., gestural representation; two dimensional representation with pencil, crayons, paints; three-dimensional representation with clay, blocks, wood.
   - Developing facility with language: e.g., word meanings and usage, scope of vocabulary, mastery of syntax; playful and communicative verbal expression.
   - Stimulating verbal-conceptual organization of experience and information: e.g., verbal formulation; integration of present and nonpresent; accent on classification, ordering, relationship and transformation concepts in varied experiential contexts.
3. *To advance the child's functioning knowledge of his environment.*
   - Observation of functions within school: e.g., heating, water pipes, kitchen, elevator.

- Story-reading: e.g., stories about nature, work processes, people's roles and functions.
- Observation of functioning environment outside of school: e.g., to observe work processes, natural processes, building construction, traffic regulation; to visit police, firemen, farm and dairy.
- Discussion of contemporary events which children hear about: e.g., war, demonstrations, strikes, space activities, street violence, explorations, earthquakes.

4. *To support the play mode of incorporating experience.*
- Nourishing and setting the stage for dramatic play activity: e.g., experiences, materials, props.
- Freedom to go beyond restraints of reality in rehearsing and representing experience.

5. *To help the child internalize impulse control.*
- Communicating a clear set of nonthreatening controls: e.g., limits, rules, regulations.
- Creating a functional adult authority role: e.g., understandable restraints, alternative behavior patterns, nonpunitive sanctions.

6. *To meet the child's need to cope with conflicts intrinsic to this stage of development.*
- Dealing with the conflict over possession displaced from the family scene: e.g., fostering special relation of child to single adult, guidance in learning to share things as well as people.
- Alleviating conflict over separation related to loss of familiar context of place and people: e.g., visits from home people to school, interchange of home and school objects; school trips to home neighborhoods.
- Accepting ambivalence about dependence and independence: e.g., selection of areas of curriculum most suited to independent exploration, acceptance of regressive dependent behavior under stress.

7. *To facilitate the development of an image of self as a unique and competent person.*
- Increasing knowledge of self: e.g., identity, family and ethnic membership; awareness of skills.
- Clarifying sense of self: e.g., as initiator, learner, autonomous individual.
- Advancing integration of self: e.g., self-realization through re-expression in symbolic play, latitude for individual mix of fantasy with knowledge of objective reality.

8. *To help the child establish mutually supporting patterns of interaction.*
- Building informal communication channels, verbal and nonverbal: e.g., adult-child, child-child.
- Cooperative and collective child-group relations: e.g., discussion periods, joint work projects.
- Creating supportive adult role: e.g., source of comfort, trouble-shooter, solver of unknowns, invested in child's learning.
- Establishing models of human interchange which value individuality; e.g., teacher-teacher and supervisor-teacher relationships. (Biber, Shapiro, & Wickens, 1971, pp. 10–11)

The Bank Street position certainly succeeds in presenting goals in terms of a concern with the "whole child." However, from the cognitive-developmental perspective, the effort falls short of theoretical coherence in a number of important ways discussed in the following section.

Limitations in Conceptualization of Bank Street Goals

From the cognitive-developmental perspective, the foregoing conceptualization seems to work against the Bank Street intention of presenting a unitary framework. Two limitations may be identified.

Fractionation of Socioemotional and Cognitive Goals without Theoretical Unification

The intention of theoretical unity seems contradicted by Bank Street's conceptualization of cognitive and affective or ego-developmental goals as separate and juxtaposed. This position offers unity in its "whole child" conception, but such a solution to the problem of integration still leaves the question of how the eight goals are functionally linked. The cutting up of cognitive development in the first three goals departs from the standpoint of a more unitary conception. It makes knowledge one thing, cognitive functioning another thing, and competence motivation a third thing.

Aspects of social and moral development throughout the last four goals differ from the cognitive-developmental perspective. For example, "limits, rules, and regulations" are emphasized in the service of impulse control, "learning to share things as well as people" is presented in terms of coping with conflicts, "identity" is listed in terms of self-image, and "cooperative and collective child-group relations: e.g., discussion periods, joint work projects" are given as examples of mutually supportive patterns of interpersonal interaction.

From a cognitive-developmental perspective, "limits, rules, and regulations" are emphasized in terms of the child's construction of a self-regulating system which, as a by-product, results in impulse control. This is part of the development of moral and social judgment, which also involves affective and cognitive decentering essential to sharing and reciprocity in interpersonal interaction as well as all other aspects of adaptation. "Identity" and self-image develop in this same broad context that includes cognitive constancy and decentering to become conscious of others and to situate (construct) the self in a network of moral and other social relationships.

From our point of view, the Bank Street approach is more eclectic than the constructivist perspective. Biber and Franklin (personal communication) emphasize that Bank Street's base in not arbitrary, but is a careful assemblage of compatible theories (excluding behaviorist theory).[5]

5. Theoretical roots are discussed by Bank Street writers in Biber (1959a), Biber and Franklin (1967), Biber (1967c), Biber, Shapiro, & Wickens (1971), Shapiro and Biber (1972), Biber (1977), and Franklin (1981).

Inconsistencies with Cognitive-Developmental Theory

Bank Street goals also differ from a cognitive-developmental point of view because they are in some ways inconsistent with cognitive-developmental theory. Let us consider the Bank Street conceptions of "levels of experience," representation, and moral development.

LEVELS OF EXPERIENCE. Bank Street goals reflect a recurrent theme emphasizing three levels of experience—sensory, motor, and symbolic. Bank Street writers do not intend to present a sensory theory and do intend to stress the importance of action. However, the description of this theme contrasts with the cognitive-developmental view to the extent that the role of action is presented in terms of muscular exercise and manipulation, physical experience in terms of sensory experience, knowledge in terms of information, and representation in terms of cognitive strategy. Bank Street stresses activities for sensory, motor, and symbolic experience. Consider the following elaboration of this Bank Street theme.

> The program as a whole is designed to initiate the children into many different kinds of experiences; experiences that, on the sensory level, sensitize them to seeing, feeling, tasting, hearing and discriminating elements of the environment; experiences that, on the motor level, widen their knowledge of the physical world through their own activity in it—strenuous activity such as climbing, stacking, riding and steering, and also manipulative activity such as filling pails with pebbles or cutting with scissors; and experiences that, on a symbolic level, develop their representational functioning through drawing, painting, building with blocks, dressing up, playing at making supper or pretending it is moving day. (Biber, Shapiro, & Wickens, 1971, p. 17)

> The variety of materials in the schoolroom offers opportunity for a wealth of sensory experience—rough sand in box.... Through these constructive-manipulative activities (experiences in transforming objects—changing bulk, form, consistency and pattern) the "things" in the environment become better known. At the same time, the children develop facility with the kind of action responses that are the basis for later symbolic reorganization of experience. (Biber, 1977, pp. 435–436)

From a cognitive-developmental perspective, the three levels of Bank Street experience differ from the constructivist perspective because they are not functionally linked, do not correspond to developmental stages, and remain largely an intuitive conceptualization.

In a personal communication, Biber and Shapiro have stated that the Bank Street method acknowledges the constructivist emphasis on action and thought. They say, "Throughout our writing it is plain that our method is not based on a sensory psychology but is centered on action; knowledge serves thinking beyond 'information,' and representation involves multiple functions in addition to 'cognitive strategy'."

While Bank Street theorists acknowledge the importance of action and play, they do not elaborate physical-knowledge activities. While certain elements suggest something like the Piagetian construction of physical knowledge, these are not conceived in terms of Piaget's theory, which gives a distinct role to physical (and not merely sensory or manipulative) experience in the child's construction of knowledge and intelligence. The Bank Street goal of "direct experience" clearly does not mean the same thing Piaget means by physical experience, and Bank Street "sensory-motor-perceptual experiences" are not the same as the physical-knowledge activities of Kamii and DeVries (although general similarities in materials are found in some activities).

REPRESENTATION. The significance for Bank Street of creating representational objects from clay, blocks, and wood is "to promote the potential for ordering experience through cognitive strategies." Pretense is "to support the play mode of incorporating experience." From the constructivist perspective, we see the value of these activities as exercise of the symbolic function, which in this form has a particular role in the sweep of development toward operational thought.

LANGUAGE. The Bank Street view of the role of language in cognitive development also seems to differ from the cognitive-developmental view as that is elaborated in Kohlberg and Colleagues (1987). For Bank Street, language proficiency is seen as necessary to working with concepts as "the tools for organizing experience and acquiring knowledge and cognitive power to judge, to reason, and to infer." In Piagetian theory, concepts are not words, and especially for the young child, it is not by language that experience is organized, knowledge is acquired, or powers are increased to judge, reason, and infer, though language is an important auxiliary instrument of thought. Bank Street seems to give language a role closer to conceptualization than to representation as in the constructivist view.

MORAL DEVELOPMENT. The fifth Bank Street goal seems to reduce moral development to impulse control and to substitute the notion of internalization for construction. While this reduction is not intended, nevertheless certain language suggests it. For example, it is stated that "to help the child internalize impulse control," the teacher should function as an adult authority by "communicating a clear set of nonthreatening controls" in the form of "limits, rules, regulations" and by providing understandable restraints, alternative behavior patterns, nonpunitive sanctions."

From the cognitive-developmental perspective, the role of rules and regulations in the development of impulse control is not "an important aspect of establishing a rational authority system to which the children are invited" (Biber, 1977, pp. 442–443). Rather, as noted above, adaptation to external rules and the construction of internal "rules" is a process not limited to impulse control, but involves the whole of moral, cognitive, and affective development (see Chapters 2 and 6). Furthermore, the psychoanalytic notion of internalization is inconsistent with the Piagetian notion of constructivism because "internalization" seems to imply that something external becomes internal without any change in form or content.

In contrast to the notion of acceptance as the way external regulations are internalized, the constructivist perspective is that the child actively constructs self-regulating principles and that this process is characterized by qualitatively changing understanding of the content of external rules, and by qualitatively changing forms of internal regulation. Biber and Shapiro (personal communication) agree that there is a real difference between the concept of internalization of impulse control and the concept of constructivism. Contrast between the two approaches on this point is softened by Biber's (1984) recent statement that in her view, "psychodynamic theory calls for reeducation of impulses, parallel to the reeducation of thought processes in cognitive psychology" (p. 320).

In summary, despite the common broad developmental aim of Bank Street and cognitive-developmental programs, a close examination reveals certain important differences in goals and rationales. In our view, these differences appear at least partly due to Bank Street's theory, a theory that is more eclectic and less unified than cognitive-developmental or constructivist theory. Biber, however, calls attention to the distinction by Reese and Overton (1970) between "good eclecticism," where ideas from different theoretical structures are drawn into a whole structure, and "random eclecticism," where strands from different theories are combined without sufficient attention to questions of compatability (p. 324). Franklin (1981) also emphasizes the theoretical cohesiveness of developmental-interactionism.

In the Bank Street view, psychological theories in curriculum building serve as "channels through which to navigate toward the selected educational goals" (Biber, 1977, p. 428). This is in contrast with the effort of constructivists to derive aims and methods from Genevan theory and to use this theory as the framework within which practices (including those inspired by other theories) must be reconciled and shown to be coherent.

But do these sometimes fine theoretical distinctions in aims and rationales make a difference in practice? From both Bank Street and Piagetian points of view, their theoretical differences have important practical effects. As Franklin and Biber (1977) comment, the difference "is crucial to the planning of learning experiences, the teaching strategies, and the nature of the teacher-child relationship" (p. 17). We address this question in the following section.

CLASSROOM PRACTICE

The Bank Street approach, like the constructivist or cognitive-developmental approach, is neither a curriculum nor a method. Descriptions of its practice tend to be general principles and types of activities with summary accounts of what life in a Bank Street classroom is like. Some excellent exceptions are found in the book designed to elaborate the cognitive aspects of children's experience in

Bank Street classrooms (Biber, Shapiro, & Wickens, 1971) and the recent overview chapter on the Bank Street program in action (Biber, 1977). In this section, we focus both on the Bank Street articulation of general principles of practice and on the specific protocols of classroom interaction. We wish more of the latter were available because the gap between a principle and its living expression leaves room for misinterpretation. The constructivist approach provides more illustrative protocol material and since we also know it first-hand, the comparison of practice is better-informed on this side. If we err in our comparison, we hope our effort will stimulate the production of literature that will correct our perceptions.

We begin with a focus on the teacher's role because so many aspects of Bank Street practice flow from this central conception. Next, we consider the outline of kinds of experiences emphasized in a Bank Street program, highlighting detailed teacher-child interactions presented as models of Bank Street practice.

The Teacher's Role

In the Bank Street approach, principles of teaching related to socioemotional aspects of objectives are distinct from those related to cognitive goals. We therefore consider these separately.

Socioemotional Development

Two major themes can be identified, derived from neopsychoanalytic theory, particularly Erikson and Sullivan. The first theme is the role of the teacher and school as a mediator between the world of the family and the world of the peer group and the larger society. The job of the school is to facilitate this transition in such a way as to preserve the positive values of the child's life in the family while "stretching" these values and notions to accommodate the requirements of a larger, less indulgent and less intense world than the one of the family. The second theme is the role of the teacher and school in fostering the child's ego development and mental health. A third theme that Biber and Shapiro call to our attention is the teacher's role in stimulating "extensor" processes related to interaction with the world around.

These themes unite to create a certain image of the teacher's role (Biber & Snyder, 1948; Gilkeson, 1962). It includes a quasi-maternal nurturant aspect emphasizing mutuality between teacher and child. At least within the preschool era, the teacher's first central concern in the Bank Street schema is to be a figure of trust so that the child feels that the world is more safe than threatening, more giving than denying, more accepting than rejecting. If this is established, the teacher can help the child overcome separation anxieties and other conflicts whose resolution is necessary to increasing initiative and confidence in an expanding world outside the family. The teacher's role is to encourage and support children's ventures beyond the familiar, thereby promoting increments in the ego strength of initiative, the key polarity for the preschool child in the Eriksonian scheme.

In addition to trust and initiative, another Eriksonian stage concern represented in Bank Street thinking is that of autonomous self-control. The importance of autonomy is conceptualized differently by Bank Street writers than by constructivist writers. For Bank Street, autonomy is related to concerns about holding on to possessions versus voluntarily letting go or sharing. The Eriksonian issue of autonomy involves feelings of possessiveness and jealousy toward favored persons such as the teacher, as well as feelings toward objects. The teacher's role in facilitating the resolution of this conflict is to give particular attention to the child who, for example, must always sit next to the teacher at grouptime. Gradually, the child sees the teacher giving similar attention to others, and becomes less possessive though still dependent. The child's possessiveness in relation to things is also expected to change gradually. The teacher aids this process by "diminishing the emotional charge, by putting possession on a functional basis ('When he is through using it, you will have it') or by bringing to the surface for the children the paradigm that the other side of giving is getting" (Biber, 1977, p. 443).

The Bank Street teacher's role therefore combines many characteristics of the good mother and the good therapist. Yet, the teacher is not quite a mother and not quite a therapist because she must introduce the child to the wider world of peers and life outside the family context.

To a considerable extent, Piagetian programs also include these aspects of the teacher's role (although as noted in Chapter 3, the High/Scope program emphasizes socioemotional aspects least). While Kamii, DeVries, and Kohlberg are in basic agreement with Bank Street in considering it essential for the teacher's role to include the characteristics discussed above, an important difference should be noted with regard to the authority aspect of the teacher's role.

The Bank Street conception of the authority aspect of the teacher's role is related to the goal of developing the child's trust. Trust is viewed as necessary to the child's acceptance of the teacher's authority as representative of the larger society's knowledge and social/moral rules. Trust is also necessary for acceptance of the teacher's authority in controlling the child's impulses. The various aspects of the Bank Street teacher's role thus converge to place her necessarily in a clear authority relation to children, but this is conceived as positive motivation rather than submission to power. "For the children, experiencing control and support from the same authority figure should reinforce internalization of a rational, nonpunitive authority mode as part of the growing conscience" (Biber, 1961b, p. 340). The Bank Street conception of the teacher's authority role clearly contrasts with the authoritarian attitude in rigid school systems which requires children to submit their will to that of the adult. The Bank Street teacher defines and communicates rules and motivates children's desire to follow them out of recognition of their rational necessity.

Considerable overlap exists between the Bank Street and constructivist visions of the teacher's appropriate use of authority. Both emphasize the importance of children's view of it as nonarbitrary. Teachers try to help children see the reasons for rules—for example, that they safeguard individual interests and make group life more satisfying.

We agree that the teacher must protect children from their own and other's destructive or intrusive impulses, aim at the development of children's self-control, and employ nonpunitive sanctions. Especially at the beginning of the year with a group of young children, the constructivist teacher may have to exercise adult authority by insisting that certain safety or schedule rules be followed. As in the Bank Street approach, this heteronomy is softened as much as possible by a relation of affection, sympathy, and trust, and by appealing to children's ability to understand at some level the reason for the teacher's exercise of control.

The basic difference between Bank Street and constructivist practices in relation to the authority issue is that the constructivist teacher aims in a more concerted way to minimize the exercise of constraint. The constructivist goal of establishing trust is not to create the condition for the child's acceptance of the teacher as authority but of the teacher as companion/guide.

As discussed in Chapters 2 and 6, in our view adult control or regulation of the child can interfere with the construction of a system of social and moral values by which he can regulate his own behavior. Accordingly, the constructivist teacher's goal includes giving authority to children for making and enforcing rules. Biber and Shapiro (personal communication) question how realistic this is, and Shapiro comments, "We may have a real difference of opinion here because I do think it is unlikely that 3, 4, and 5 year olds can truly be given authority for making and enforcing rules." Further, they state, "We disagree with your image of the Piagetian authority role, positioning the teacher as an egalitarian member of the group with the children." They disagree partly because they feel that the constructivist definition of the teacher role does not take account of the child's ambivalence about being his own authority. We would certainly agree that children sometimes need the teacher to take control for them and that it is not always possible to reduce authority.

The difference that remains in conceptions of the teacher's authority role seems to stem from different emphases in views of the way in which social and moral judgment develops. The Bank Street teacher role emphasizes the psychoanalytic belief that conscience or internal regulation results from internalizing the experience of control and support from a consistent, trusted, nonpunitive adult authority. The constructivist teacher role emphasizes the Piagetian notion that inner regulation based on a feeling of necessity results from the individual's active construction. In this view, therefore, to the extent that a child simply accepts and follows the teacher's rules, the child is failing to construct autonomous self-regulating values and rules of her own. Rather than perpetuating an authority role, the constructivist teacher makes a self-conscious effort to facilitate the establishment of a children's society based on co-operation and dialogue, and a shared sense of community, a community in which the teacher functions as much as possible as an egalitarian member. From the constructivist perspective, this kind of interpersonal dynamic is crucial because it permits the kind of psychological autonomy necessary for development in all domains to occur. Biber and Shapiro (personal communication) insist that the Bank Street teacher also establishes a child society based on co-operation, dialogue, and a shared sense of community, and that this is not diminished by the teacher's "modulated authority role." We again leave the reader to decide the significance of this conceptual difference, discussed again later with respect to specific classroom practices.

Cognitive Development

The role of the Bank Street teacher as outlined above already includes a concern for intellectual aspects of development as these are involved in social adaptation, ego development, mental health, and creativity (Biber, 1955, 1959b, 1961a; Biber, Gilkeson, & Winsor, 1959). Accommodation to the world outside the family requires knowledge of social and physical worlds. Such knowledge contributes in a positive way to ego development and mental health insofar as it is accompanied by a sense of efficacy and competence regarding one's place in this broader world. More specifically, however, Bank Street writers address the issue of cognitive development in the book *Promoting Cognitive Growth* (Biber, Shapiro, & Wickens, 1971). They state that the purpose of this publication is "to define and illustrate how the teacher of preschool children can strength cognitive development, which is seen as one of several goals in the developmental-interaction program of education" (p. 4). Four principles of teaching may be extracted from the chapter on "Guidelines for the Development of Cognitive Proficiency":

1. Assess a child's thinking as to how particularized to a given act or how generalized and transferable, and lead the child to new levels of conceptual mastery, or broaden the scope of content under control;
2. Verbally respond, amplify, rephrase, and correct children's comments, confusions, actions;
3. Foster intuitive and associative thinking;
4. Pose problems to promote inductive thinking.

Let us examine each of these teaching guidelines briefly in light of the constructivist, cognitive-developmental view.

Assess a Child's Thinking as to How Particularized to a Given Act or How Generalized and Transferable

By this guideline, Bank Street writers mean, in part, what Kamii and DeVries mean by saying that the teacher should "figure out what the child is thinking."

However, the Bank Street guideline differs from the constructivist guideline in its focus on the child's conceptual mastery. The Bank Street orientation may be illustrated by the following example.

> While reading a story about firemen, the teacher recalls the children's confusion about the different roles people carry. She asked, "Is the fireman a daddy?" The children answer, "No." The teacher does not correct them, but waits for the girl whose father she knows is a fireman to enlighten the children, which the child does. Here there is another gain: another child, not the teacher or the book, is the source of knowledge—a way of gaining knowledge the teacher wishes to encourage. (Biber, 1977, p. 440)

Piagetians stress the difficulty young children have with multiple classification, but the constructivist teacher would not think of this as "confusion" to be ameliorated by verbal enlightenment, and would not ask a question so far beyond children's ability. From the constructivist perspective, the Bank Street model reflects a lack of distinction between logico-mathematical and arbitrary-social sources of knowledge. The "enlightenment" of the children requires more than information from the child whose father is a fireman. Bank Street writers (personal communication), however, do not intend to suggest that the interchange about the fireman will somehow make children able to classify.

Verbally Respond, Amplify, Rephrase, and Correct Children's Comments, Confusions, Actions

The Bank Street teacher reinforces concepts through verbalizing in the context of children's play and life experience. To further cognitive development, Bank Street authors (Biber, Shapiro, & Wickens, 1971) state, "in her effort to help the child clarify an idea, see a connection, express his thought, notice a similarity, the teacher responds to, amplifies, corrects the child's comments, confusion, action, whenever and wherever it occurs, not only at a designated lesson time" (p. 17). Verbal methods include "translating the children's activities into verbal statements, accenting words with tone and gesture" and "rephrasing the child's thought or action so as to lead toward a next step in generalization" (p. 19).

These teaching principles suggest to us an empiricist view of the relationship between language and thought. That is, the teacher seems guided by an implicit belief that by providing a verbal label, she provides a concept, and that by repeatedly accompanying a child's actions with verbal conceptual descriptions, she reinforces conceptual learning. However, Bank Street writers do not mean to express the role of verbal methods as empiricist. They comment:

> You are treating what we say as excessively mechanistic. I thought that the implication here was that the children knew these concepts, to some extent at least, and that the teacher was trying to help them consolidate their ideas by introducing the terms in different contexts, making their concepts and knowledge more explicit. (Shapiro, personal communication)

We would agree that the introduction of new vocabulary in the context of a child's activity provides aliment the child may assimilate in a way that enriches knowledge of word meanings. However, even in instances where the child does learn a verbal label, this does not reflect a higher level of generality from the point of view of development of cognitive structure. Our worry is that the type of language emphasis proposed by Bank Street will operate against the encouragement of thinking.

The Bank Street emphasis on modifying and extending a child's language does not intend to suggest a belief in straightforward correction. Bank Street writers have been long-standing critics of the teacher-child relation in which the child's thought and logic are corrected. Nevertheless, in specific examples of teaching it is difficult to avoid the impression of a commitment to the power of the teacher's words in modifying, extending, and even correcting thought and logic. The Bank Street (personal communication) assumption underlying these verbal methods, however, is that when a teacher says something, it highlights, makes explicit, or "draws a circle around" it for the child who is enabled to "discover what he knows but doesn't know he knows."

After reading our manuscript, Biber and Shapiro commented, "Our statement using the term 'correct' is unfortunate. We should have made it clear that the teacher keeps the child's confusion in mind and finds opportunities to clarify in the course of ongoing experience in the stream of events in school." This comment underscores the Bank Street aim to change children's thinking in terms of correct content. Constructivist teachers have a more casual attitude to conceptual errors. They note when preoperational reasoning occurs but generally do not direct teaching efforts toward its verbal content. Constructivist teachers expect children eventually to correct their own logico-mathematical "confusions," and believe it more fruitful to focus teaching efforts on what children can do rather than on what they cannot do. The constructivist teacher is not oriented toward reinforcement or presenting concepts. Rather, he is oriented toward stimulating reflection in terms of the kind of knowledge involved in a particular content.

Foster Intuitive and Associative Thinking

The Bank Street definition of "intuitive" thinking is thought that is not characterized by logical precision and accuracy. "Associative thinking" is described as "the association of ideas." In some ways, these views are similar to intuitive thought in Piaget's theory. Like the Bank Street teacher, the constructivist teacher also encourages thought at the level of practical intelligence—for example, in mixing paint, building with blocks, and anticipating temporal sequence on the basis of classroom routine. It is unclear whether intuitive thought in the Bank Street framework refers only to correct apprehension or whether it also includes regulations that may be incorrect from the point of view of adult logic.

Unlike the Piagetian view, Bank Street rejects the view that intuitive thought is a stage of cognitive development that is a precursor to logical or operational thought. In addition to defining intuitive thought in terms similar to the Piagetian definition, Bank Street theory also refers to intuitive thought as a form of fanciful or idiosyncratic thought found in adults as well as children. The fostering of intuitive thought in Bank Street practice is presented in terms of its long-range contribution to adult creativity. Piagetian theory has little to offer on aesthetic development and adult creativity.

The lack of more specific examples of Bank Street practice to illustrate this guideline makes it difficult to ascertain whether these theoretical differences lead to practical differences between Bank Street and constructivist approaches. A general difference, however, seems to lie in attention to the role of intuitive regulations in the development of logical or operational thought. We find nothing in descriptions of Bank Street practice akin to the constructivist teacher's analysis and encouragement of children's construction of specific intuitive regulations or coordinations.[6]

With regard to "associative thinking," the difference may be more theoretical than practical. Again, practical differences cannot be assessed due to lack of more specific classroom illustrations. Certainly, constructivist teachers, as well as Bank Street teachers, are tolerant and supportive of children's "digressions" in a discussion when they want to recount something personal of which they are reminded. The Bank Street view of the value of such "associative" thinking is presented in terms of the child's construction of links between personal and socialized meanings, which help the child understand "formal symbol systems."

In some ways, the cognitive-developmental interpretation is opposite to the foregoing. The tendency of young children to participate in group discussion by "associating" in a personal way to what someone else says is viewed as egocentric assimilation rather than as the association of ideas. The behaviorist notion of association fails to take into account the role of the individual's cognitive structure in giving personal meaning to the stimulus of the association. The cognitive-developmental view is that the association occurs because it is the only way the child can give meaning to what the teacher views as a general topic. The process of coming to see oneself as a participant in a discussion where

6. For example, in the game Don't Spill the Beans (Kamii & DeVries, 1976), in which players take turns placing a bean on the top of a delicately balanced pot, trying not to tip it over, one 5-year-old began by dividing the 200 beans in a way that showed intuitive regulations having to do with equal quantities. She alternately gave one to both players, then two to each, sometimes giving to one twice in a row. When the division was finished, the teacher asked, "Are you sure I have just as many beans as you do?" The child replied, "No." "How can you be sure?" the teacher asked, and the child suggested, "If we count them." She decided after counting that the teacher had five more than she did. When asked, "What can we do so we have the same?" the solution proposed by the child was, "Put these five in the pot [and not use them]." Reasoning here is clearly not characterized by reversible operations, but intuitive regulations are present in the qualitative recognition that equality may be realized by alternately distributing one or two to each player. The final solution, too, shows qualitative coordination of the relation between the two equal quantities and the amount left over.

everyone tries to "stick to the topic" involves decentering to take account of other's ideas as well as differentiated conceptualization of a topic to which one's personal experience is relevant only insofar as what is general is abstracted from it. From the constructivist perspective, it is difficult to see how association of personal experience to a general theme could result in a better understanding of socialized or conventional meanings, since "digression" occurs as the result of the young child's inability to comprehend the socialized meaning.

Pose Problems to Promote Inductive Thinking

The Bank Street teacher emulates hypothesis making by using "if-then" questions. For example, the teacher may ask, "If you hit Johnny, then what do you think he will do?" or, "If you mix blue and red, then what color will you have?" (Biber, Shapiro, & Wickens, 1971, p. 18). This kind of questioning is consistent with the constructivist perspective. It is also recommended by Kamii and DeVries, especially in physical-knowledge activities, but their emphasis on prediction is justified for somewhat different reasons, has somewhat different aims, and looks different in practice. They put the emphasis on the child's active anticipation about the results of actions, and putting actions and reactions into relationships—which occur more often *without* than with a verbal hypothesis. Bank Street examples often seem oriented to getting the child to give an answer to a question of fact, or to prevent actions such as hitting. Biber and Shapiro (personal communication) disagree with this interpretation, stating that Bank Street literature is also full of examples of how to get a child to think about what he does not yet know and find out by acting on objects.

As we noted above, in addition to these four principles of teaching oriented to cognitive development, Bank Street specification of the teacher's role is as an authority who communicates a set of controls in the form of limits, rules, and regulations, and who provides restraints, alternative behavior patterns, and nonpunitive sanctions. This view of the authority role has ramifications for cognitive development and is in contrast to the constructivist teacher's focus on reducing the exercise of authority and giving authority to children for making and enforcing rules.

The Program

Bank Street program content has long been known for the kinds of activities described as the child-centered curriculum: singing, playing instruments, listening to stories, pretend play, sand and water play, clay, painting, and other art activities, field trips, block building, puzzles, caring for and observing animals and plants, and outdoor play with swings, tricycles, wagons, see-saws, and slides.

Many convergences in program content are found in Bank Street and constructivist programs. However, important differences should be noted. First, we consider differences between Bank Street and constructivist approaches to activities involving the physical world of objects and space. Next, we compare approaches to social and moral development. Finally, we present in detail a Bank Street applesauce-making activity in comparison with an applesauce activity conducted by a constructivist teacher.

The Physical World

Bank Street and constructivist approaches both place great emphasis on the importance of children's experience with objects in the physical world. Although the fractionation of Bank Street goals makes comparison difficult, parts of the first three specific objectives can be seen as having something in common with constructivist emphasis on physical knowledge and on autonomy, insofar as this implies, in part, confidence as an agent in the physical world. Let us examine the degree of commonality.

First, it should be noted that the Bank Street program includes activities viewed by Kamii and DeVries as good physical-knowledge activities—for example, sand and water play, and mixing paints and playdough.

> The variety of materials in the schoolroom offers opportunity for a wealth of sensory experience— rough sand in the box; smooth soft covers for the doll bed; hard wooden blocks; soft playdough; effervescent soap suds; contrasting colors on the paint easel and in the crayon box; multishaped pieces in the form boards; and musical instruments with a range of sounds. The possibilities for manipulative kinds of play with these materials are endless—pounding away the roundness of a ball of clay, making mud out of sand and water, making purple with blue and red paint, covering an empty paper with green circles, and filling up the emptiness of a pail with pebbles and listening to the sound as they are dumped out.
>
> Through these constructive-manipulative activities (experiences in transforming objects—changing bulk, form, consistency, and pattern) the "things" of the environment become better known. (Biber, 1977, pp. 435–436)

These examples reflecting the Bank Street emphasis on sensory experience illustrate how this theoretical orientation leads to special value being placed on activities in which actions are oriented to observation of properties of objects such as texture, color, shape, and sound, and to transformations of these properties. This contrasts with the broader Piaget-derived orientation to physical experience (including sensory experience) and its relationship to logico-mathematical experience. From the constructivist perspective, the Bank Street notion of sensory experience seems to relegate the role of action to that of service to the senses and makes knowledge more the result of observation than of action more broadly conceived.

In relation to the three types of physical-knowledge activities included by Kamii and DeVries (see Chapter 4), we find examples of these also in Bank Street descriptions. Examples of activities involving the movement of objects, however, are rare in Bank Street description while these are the most emphasized by Kamii and DeVries. Bank Street activities involving physical objects tend to fall mainly in the categories of activities in which the child structures his observations of interactions among objects.

Bank Street activities involving the movement of objects are oriented to increasing the child's information. For example, by balancing boards, swinging on a swing, and sliding down a slide, children are said to "develop rudimentary knowlege of the world and how it works, gaining experience with space and direction" (Biber, 1977, p. 435). No elaboration of this kind of activity is given to suggest the emphasis found in Kamii and DeVries on encouraging children's sustained experimentation with, for example, simple mechanical phenomena in the interest of general intellectual development.

Similarly, in Bank Street examples of activities involving changes in objects, the emphasis is limited to observation of properties and does not extend to experimentation to observe variations in properties resulting from variation in the factor causing a transformation. The difference between the two approaches may be illustrated with the following Bank Street description: "To advance the child's functioning knowledge of his environment. . .[children] go to see how the building works—. . .where the heat comes from. . . . The world becomes known, spatially and functionally, through direct observation and contact" (Biber, 1977, p. 439).

The constructivist objection to this particular activity is that what the child can observe and contact directly is very limited, and possibilities for structuring are therefore limited. The young child can know "where the heat comes from" only at the level of arbitrary social information. Because of the young child's difficulty in reasoning about the unobservable and his relatively far more sustained attention to phenomena he can control (and not just observe), Kamii and DeVries derive criteria for physical-knowledge activities that exclude many Bank Street activities (see Chapter 4). The Bank Street emphasis on sensory experience, observation, and object properties seems to provide less extensive possibilities for structuring physical experience than the broader constructivist emphasis on action to produce object phenomena.

Social World

Bank Street and constructivist approaches share an emphasis on the importance of social interaction. The eighth Bank Street objective is "To help the child establish mutually supportive patterns of interaction." Constructivist approaches such as that of Kamii and DeVries include the same kinds of efforts described by Bank Street writers to encourage children to take others' perspectives, to co-operate in mutual endeavors, and to develop a community of interests.

While the direction of overall aims and practical efforts are very similar with regard to the social world, some differences may be noted. Constructivist approaches have made more explicit efforts to develop activities and principles of teaching that directly stimulate particular kinds of social interchanges. For example, the approaches to democratic group decision making described in Chapter 6 have no parallel in Bank Street program descriptions. Nor is there in Bank Street anything like the direct stimulation of moral dilemma conflicts and resolution through discussion. Group games, whose advantages are discussed in Chapter 5, are also absent from the Bank Street program. In addition, in constructivist programs there is more self-conscious effort to create and take advantage of opportunities to get children to take responsibility, without, of course, directiveness on the part of the teacher. It is unclear whether these curriculum elaborations would be viewed by Bank Street theorists as appropriate expressions of their eighth goal or compatible additions to their approach. In the absence of more detail about the more specific ways in which Bank Street teachers realize goals related to the social world, a closer comparison is not possible.

BANK STREET AND CONSTRUCTIVIST PROGRAMS IN ACTION: COMPARATIVE ANALYSIS OF APPROACHES TO MAKING APPLESAUCE

Similarities and differences at the level of articulated/formal theory are not always accompanied by the same similarities and differences at the level of practice. Similarities in general rationale often mask differences in specific practices, and apparent differences in rationale may not be reflected in practice. It seems useful, therefore, to present a detailed description of one Bank Street activity and to compare it with an account of a constructivist approach to the same activity. No single activity can ever represent an entire program, of course, and the following comparative analysis is not intended to be a comprehensive analysis of the programs as wholes. Nevertheless, the examination of similarities and differences seems useful to developing an approach to the problem of a theory of educational practice.

The most detailed available protocol of Bank Street practice involves making applesauce. Therefore, in a first step toward clarifying the operational differences between the Bank Street and constructivist approaches, preschool teachers in their first year of exploring constructivist teaching at the Merrill-Palmer Child Care Center[7] were asked their reactions to the Bank Street applesauce account. Many of these reactions were highly positive. For example, teachers liked the Bank Street ideas of labeling a tray with each child's name, labeling jars with names of family members, and figuring out how many jars each child needed. Reading and number are integral with a child's purposes in such a situation. The use of the recipe chart seemed similar to their use of recipe books. The desirability of "strengthening the connection between home and school" by making something to give family members was also appreciated. Going to the

7. This was the first and only year of a demonstration project begun by DeVries at the Merrill-Palmer Institute during its last year of existence as a private institution.

store together was viewed as an especially desirable way to encourage a feeling of purpose in common in the group. Letting children core the apples was recognized as a valuable opportunity to observe the properties of apples when these are unfamiliar. The use of two kinds of apples provided an excellent context for logico-mathematical comparison and the exercise of classificatory schemes. Cooking in a Pyrex pot was viewed as excellent because children could easily observe the apples' reaction to being heated. Fostering a sense of responsibility with cleanup, introducing new vocabulary in the activity context, and learning to use cooking tools were viewed as desirable. Along with these favorable reactions, however, were comments concerning important differences between the Bank Street account and the teachers' own experiences with cooking activities.

As a result of this conversation, Ms. Jane Wienner, a Merrill-Palmer kindergarten teacher, volunteered to make applesauce in her classroom, to see how differences would be manifested. Discussions followed regarding which features of the Bank Street activity should be retained, which should be modified, and which were optional. Instead of cooking with four children as the Bank Street teacher did, Ms. Wienner decided that her regular practice of having two cooks work from a recipe book should be followed. Given the constructivist objective that children become able to carry out cooking activities on their own, the teacher felt that she wanted to avoid the possibility of being forced into too directive a role with four children.

Although the value of the Bank Street trip to buy ingredients was recognized, a conscious decision was made to eliminate this, for several practical reasons. The market was some distance away, and transportation was not easily arranged. Bad weather was also a factor. Further, the children had made such a trip the week before, and the teacher felt that another would add minimal benefit to the activity. Biber and Shapiro (personal communication) criticize this decision: "Your eliminating the trip to the market stripped the cooking experience of a vital connective in the children's thinking: experience focused by thinking ahead and the psychological value of integrating thinking and acting."

Another deliberate change in the Bank Street activity was to continue the Merrill-Palmer teacher's emphasis on making something to give classmates, rather than family members. While the teacher in a variety of ways included children's home experiences at school and tried to extend school experiences into the home, she had another primary objective of creating a feeling of community and common interest in her group. Cooking had come to be an important ingredient in this group dynamic, and the teacher felt that cooking for the group would be a better demonstration of her emphasis than cooking for family members.[8]

The two applesauce accounts are presented side by side in Table 10.1 to

---

8. Cooking for family members had, however, been done earlier in the year when the class made a Valentine's Day lunch for their parents, and each parent brought a cooking utensil as gift.

permit better comparison. In the interest of conserving space, the first part of the Bank Street account is edited and partially summarized, since there are no Merrill-Palmer segments comparable to the preparation and trip to buy apples. The focus of comparison is primarily on the accounts of cooking, which are given in their entirety. The Merrill-Palmer activity is organized according to three categories in which major differences between the two accounts may be noted. These categories are related to children's interactions, the general nature of the teacher-child interaction, and teacher interventions to promote cognitive goals.

In both activities, the emphasis is on informal interaction in an atmosphere of mutual pleasure in a mutual endeavor. Both are characterized by co-operation and communication. However, the Merrill-Palmer account contains more frequent, sustained, and reciprocal interchanges between children that can be termed truly co-operative in the Piagetian sense of decentered and mutually adaptive activity. In the Bank Street account, in contrast, most of the children's verbalizations are directed to the teacher or to no one in particular. No child asked another a question or gave another a direction. Instead, verbalizations, as well as actions, tend to be parallel rather than efforts at reciprocal communication and adaptation.

The two accounts also differ in the general nature of teacher-child interaction. While warmth and pleasure in the company of children characterize both, the Merrill-Palmer teacher relates to children more as a companion and less as a leader. While the Bank Street teacher's role is central in terms of regulating the activity and bringing it to a successful conclusion, the Merrill-Palmer teacher relinquishes the lead to the children. The conversational style of the Merrill-Palmer teacher is oriented to the preoccupations of children, to eliciting their honest preoperational ideas, trying to understand more fully what they are thinking, and consulting children about what to do. The Bank Street teacher's conversation is more oriented to encouraging what is correct in children's thought, although she refrains from correcting preoperational ideas.

More preoperational thought is expressed by Merrill-Palmer children, and the Merrill-Palmer teacher pursues these kinds of ideas in an effort both to understand them more fully and to encourage children's further reflection. Her specific interventions to promote cognitive development are self-consciously aimed at getting children to think, experiment, and figure things out. In contrast, the Bank Street teacher's interventions are more focused on communicating and eliciting correct information. Comments on the Bank Street account from a constructivist perspective appear to the right of the account; comments on the Merrill-Palmer account from a constructivist perspective are to the left of the account.

Discussion

While considering the differences between the two approaches to applesauce, it should be remembered that these differences rest within a context of similarities that include emphasis on encouraging children's action when they have personal reasons for engaging in an activity, promoting feelings of competence and mastery, fostering communication by creating a situation in which children need and desire to communicate, teaching reading and new vocabulary in a casual way as it is naturally integrated with what children are doing, and creating an interpersonal milieu that fosters individual expression as well as group solidarity. Let us now look more closely at the differences that emerge from the two accounts.

Children's Interaction

In the Bank Street account, several interactions are described between children. Rosina responds to Joey's question (although he does not seem to be asking anyone in particular) regarding which bucket will be used for red apples; she later suggests there are maybe a hundred when he says "So many apples." Fernando offers to go with Janice to borrow a hot plate and pot. Co-operation is explicit in the efforts to pour applesauce through funnels into jars. Mutuality is certainly clear in Joey's humorous imitation of Fernando and their sharing of the "mushy-gushy" joke. Janice responds to Rosina's observation that her applesauce is pinker. The children are involved together in the task, and there is some sense of group involvement. From the constructivist perspective, however, little co-operation is described. The incidents of children's interaction are not only few in number, in comparison with the Merrill-Palmer account, but tend to be limited to a single exchange rather than being part of the kind of reciprocal dialogue between children that frequently occurs in the Merrill-Palmer activity. The Bank Street protocol gives a feeling that most of the conversation and communication flows between teacher and child or is directed to the group in general. In relation to one another, children's actions and verbalizations tend to be parallel rather than interactive.

Part of the reason for the limited co-operation apparent in the Bank Street account may lie in the nature of the activity itself. In the course of doing this activity at Merrill-Palmer, it became clear why applesauce had never before been selected as a recipe in our constructivist programs. Applesauce is not the best recipe to select when the criteria for selecting activities are possibilities for autonomy and co-operation. Preparation of the raw apples is too difficult and dangerous for children to do without close supervision and considerable help. The hot mixture is dangerous, its cooking must be monitored, and its transfer to bowls and strainers also cannot be entrusted to children alone. The project is too long for many children (an hour and a half for Merrill-Palmer kindergartners) unless the teacher does most of the work, and in that case the value would be largely lost. Furthermore, and most important, the nature of the work to be done presents little necessity for co-operation. Cutting apples, stirring, checking on cooking progress, straining, and serving are all essentially individual activities that require little negotiation or discussion. While many teachers see

TABLE 10.1

Applesauce at Bank Street[1]	Comments on the Bank Street Account from a Constructivist Perspective	Comments on the Merrill-Palmer Account from a Constructivist Perspective	Applesauce at Merrill-Palmer[2]
A MULTIPLE GOAL ACTIVITY The fresh *pears* at lunch evoked the excited comment "Apples" from Spanish-speaking Fernando. "Well, this is a fruit," said Miss Gordon, encouragingly, "but it has another name. Do you remember the apples we had last week?" "They were hard to bite," said Joey. "And we made applesauce," said Rosina. "This fruit is called a pear, Fernando; let's taste this pear now. We'll have apples again." *The teacher responds to what is correct in the child's response, valuing his category association. First, she wants to support communication and willingness to experiment with language; later she gives the correct name. The children*	The teacher here respects the principle of capitalizing on children's spontaneous	In a constructivist program, too, cooking activities might arise from children's suggestions, and such initiative is viewed as highly desirable from the point of view of goals of autonomy. Goals of autonomy and co-operation led constructivist teachers to feel that it is indispensable to have available homemade recipe books that children can follow. The objective is for children to rely on themselves and consult the recipe rather than depend on the teacher to be told what to do and how to do it. By setting up the situation so children can figure out what to do and how to do it, the teacher gives the possibility for the exercise of reasoning (including reading) and reciprocity.	The teacher asked whether the prospective cooks would like to make applesauce. When they responded with enthusiasm, she promised to make a recipe book and bring it the next day. *Note:* The cover and final page show the end product, and the first page pictures all the necessary ingredients and utensils. Each page thereafter contains a single direction, with a clear picture of what to do. The usual routine is for the cook to be selected by rotation from a list on the wall. Everyone knows that the person whose name is at the top is the next cook, and anyone can figure out how many days it will be before their turn. The cook picks an assistant cook, and they must agree on which recipe to select for the next day. (This procedure was modified in the present case because of the researcher's particular interest in

strengthen the experience by relating it to previous experience in which they were active.

"Mine's soft," said Joey.

"Can we make applesauce again?" begged Rosina.

The teacher replied, "Perhaps we could do what Janice wanted to do. Remember? To take some home to her family?"

"To my mommy, and my grandma, and Danny."

"Not to my baby," said Rosina. "He's too little. Him only drink milk."

"Tomorrow we'll buy lots of apples," said Miss Gordon.

The teacher is building a sense of continuity by recalling earlier intentions that had been expressed by the children.

She rarely corrects use of pronouns for four-year-olds. She knows the child will learn through greater social maturity and hearing language. (Biber, 1977, p. 446; Biber, Shapiro, & Wickens, 1971, p. 47)

The teacher later capitalizes on the situation by asking interests and Janice's express request. However, it is the teacher who decides and announces that they will buy apples the next day. This seems to be a missed opportunity to exercise reasoning and autonomy. From a constructivist point of view, it would have been better to ask children if they would like to make applesauce and what they would need to do. Such an opening would have given children the chance to exchange ideas and take a more active role in co-operating with one another, as well as with the teacher, in planning what to do.

Co-operation may begin with disagreement over what recipe to select—a discussion highly valuable for intellectual and moral development because children are confronted with the need to decenter and feel the necessity to figure out how to resolve conflicting viewpoints. In the beginning, the teacher helps children become conscious of the need to co-operate and anticipate events by asking questions such as: How can you agree on what to cook? Did you ask your assistant if that's O.K. with him? How can you decide who gets to stir first? Maybe you'd better talk it over and come to an agreement. Can you figure out a fair way?

This decision was made out of consideration for time, safety, children's frustration tolerance, and to clear the way for children to do the rest of applesauce. Had the cooks been uninterested, their wishes would have been respected.) They check to see if they have everything they will need, and the teacher makes a list of any items that are missing. On the following day, the teacher showed the recipe book to the two cooks, and went through each page with them. They were beginning to read, and the children read for themselves what they could. The teacher used the opportunity to show them new words. She emphasized that they would be able to do the cooking by themselves the next day, and called their attention to the need for care in using sharp knives.

To make the teacher's role less arbitrary, a page was included that said, "Have a teacher cut 10 apples in half and core them."

For practical, but not theoretical, reasons, the teacher decided to use only one kind of apple in this first attempt.

CHILDREN'S INTERACTIONS

(While the teacher is away, Lee and Lana huddle over the recipe book.)

TABLE 10.1 (continued)

Applesauce at Bank Street	Comments on the Bank Street Account from a Constructivist Perspective	Comments on the Merrill-Palmer Account from a Constructivist Perspective	Applesauce at Merrill-Palmer
children how they can take the applesauce home. "What can we put it in?" Rosina reminds the teacher of all the baby food jars she had brought previously. "A good idea! And your mommy said she would keep more for us. Let's write a note to tell her we need them tomorrow." The teacher writes a note dictated by Rosina, telling her mother she needed to bring "bunches of jars to school" (Biber, 1977, p. 446; Biber, Shapiro, & Wickens, 1971, p. 48). The next day, each child washes jars and puts out one for each family member on a tray labeled with his or her name. One child figures out with the teacher that he needs six while another child needs nine. The teacher had made a recipe chart with magazine pictures next to the names of	The question of how the applesauce will be taken home is an excellent example of how the teacher can use such a motivating context to inspire reasoning about a problem and to encourage and support autonomy in figuring out and achieving a solution.	the cooking on their own. Specifying the teacher's role with a page in the book protects children's autonomy by shifting the directive from the teacher to the book. It is thus clear to the cooks that the teacher's role is to be a limited one, and that the project really is theirs. The physical experience of exploring the properties of raw apples is de-emphasized because it would not add much to what children already know about apples. Co-operation without the teacher, asking questions of another child, giving information, correcting misreading, reasoning about meaning of written symbols.	Lana: (Reading) Here . . . . Lee: (Joins to read in unison) Here is what you need. Lana: One-ten apples. Ten apples. Lee: That's sugar, cinnamon, water, one teaspoon. . . . Lana: (Correcting) One over four is a quarter. Lee: What 'bout this (picture of knives)? Lana: Those are knifes. Lee: But what about this (picture of cutting board)? Lana: Oh, this is the cutting board. Lee: *This* (picture of skillet) is the cutting board. She wrote "cutting board" here different. Oh no, there it is. (It is unclear whether Lee changes his view that "cutting board" is written with two different sets of letters.) Lana: Two spoons.

Lee: Two bowls. Two everything!

Lana: (Turning to next page and reading laboriously) Cut the ... Cut apples into ...

Lee: ... little tiny pieces.

Lana: *No!* Cut apples into real

Lee: ... eensy, eensy, teensy

(The teacher returns with a cutting board she brought from home. Following a conversation about procedures and being careful with knives, Lana turns to the next page in the recipe book.)

Lee: ("Reading") Let a teacher cut the apples into real teeny pieces. (He reads the idea, but not the words which say, "Have a teacher cut 10 apples in half and core them.")

Lana: No, just a half. (Imperiously to child who stops in passing) And don't you eat none, Allen. I cut faster than him.

Child correcting child.

Child correcting child.

items needed, and had taped a stick of cinnamon to the chart. "Let's look at the recipe chart. I have a list so we can remember to buy everything." The children call off the items and the teacher checks her list. When children cannot name the stick of cinnamon, the teacher suggests, "Smell it. Have we had it before?" One child remembers, "Toast! What we put on toast!" and the teacher gives the word "cinnamon" (Biber, 1977, p. 447; Biber, Shapiro, & Wickens, 1971, pp. 48–49.)

The teacher and four children then walk to the fruit stand to buy apples. On the way, the teacher asks if they remember the way, and children point out familiar places. At the fruit stand, the teacher lets the children feel and look at a yellow apple from the array of varieties, and they decide to buy some red MacIntoshes and some Golden Delicious. The teacher

TABLE 10.1 (continued)

Applesauce at Bank Street	Comments on the Bank Street Account from a Constructivist Perspective	Comments on the Merrill-Palmer Account from a Constructivist Perspective	Applesauce at Merrill-Palmer
comments, "Then we can taste two different kinds of applesauce." (Biber, 1977, p. 448; Biber, Shapiro, & Wickens, 1976, p. 50) Children help the teacher count the three dollars needed. At another store, they smell spices and buy cinnamon. In addition to notes quoted above, the following indicate Bank Street's multiple goals involved in preparation and going to the store. COGNITIVE COMPETENCE GOALS The lumber yard is a known landmark, and serves as a point of departure and return. Young children are reassured by having small understandable pieces in a confusing city environment, and the teacher helps them by encouraging them to begin to	Again, the teacher makes the decision. She might have taken advantage of the opportunity to ask children whether the different kinds of apples would make different kinds of applesauce—whether they expect it to look and taste different and whether they want to find out. Discussion of predictions could then have led children to suggest cooking the apples separately. Or, the teacher could have suggested it in this context, and children could then decide.	Thinking ahead to anticipate a possible problem. Child regulation of eating privileges. (Had this not been accepted by other children, the teacher could have taken advantage of the opportunity for a discussion of what is fair. Such an extended discussion at grouptime might lead to the establishment of a rule by children to avoid future conflicts.) Child consults child. The teacher does not correct Lana, but asks her a question that stimulates her to think about the written symbols. Both children take	Lee: I cut 'em faster. … What if we need some more sugar? T: We can get that if we need it. Lana: … I get to eat another one. (As passing child reaches into the bowl) No—only the cooks! When you be a cook and you cook something, nobody else except (unintelligible). Only me and Lee can eat 'em. … (The cooks huddle over the frying pan.) Lee: Where do you put it at (temperature)? Lana: On the hot part—on that red. T: What's it supposed to be on? Lana: Thirty hundred—three hundred. Lee: (As it cooks) It smells like applesauce. It smells like cider!

perceive familiar objects as guideposts.

The colorful array of fruit is a visual display of classification. The children use color as the criterion for selection. The teacher exploits this incidental experience with classification and uses it in connection with the plan to make applesauce.

These children have more than the usual experience in handling money in store situations.

The teacher welcomes the children's blending their intimate personal recalls with the knowledge-focused trip.

The children's knowledge of their functioning environment—buying and selling, money exchange, locating one's self in a neighborhood—is being accented by this experience. (Biber, 1977, pp. 447–448; Biber, Shapiro, & Wickens, 1971, pp. 49–51)

Advantages described by Bank Street writers related to cognitive aims include

responsibility for deciding what to do and whether the apples are done. They cooperate in using the colander, and Lana suggests a division of labor.

(Discussion about whether it's too hot or cooking too fast and how long it will take)

Lana: It's not done, Lee. (They fan steam) It has to get warm. It can't be hot.

. . .

(Both children begin to work with colander over the bowl)

Lana: Mushing it through. I'll pat it. You mush it.

(During this activity, the teacher comes and goes, attending to other children in the room, inviting one child to paint, pinning her paintsmock, responding to children at snack and in other activities, getting a helper to clear snack and do other chores.)

While Lana takes leadership here, she is clearly oriented to the mutuality of the endeavor, as indicated by her repeated use of the word "Let's."

Lana: Lee, let me see. Put some more in (the colander). Let's take it out and put some more in.

Lee: Oh, you're putting in the mushy part already. . . .

Cooks continuously relate to one another in their common concern.

Lana: Let's put a little more (she spoons). Let's put a lot more. Let's put all of it in.

Lee: Oh, we'll have to hold it forever (laughs)

TABLE 10.1 (*continued*)

Applesauce at Bank Street	Comments on the Bank Street Account from a Constructivist Perspective	Comments on the Merrill-Palmer Account from a Constructivist Perspective	Applesauce at Merrill-Palmer
nonpresent experience, learning symbol systems, object and person names, classification, past time orientation, quantifying general amount and money, and geographic orientation. SELF-IMAGE GOALS: The sense of identity with family members is enhanced by providing jars for each member. The children are given opportunity to be the problem solvers in response to the questions raised. INTERACTION GOALS: This experience contributes to mutually supporting patterns of interaction by the meaningful communication with the fruit vendor, the teacher's extension of family-school connections, her accepting response to a child's individual experience. The teacher is strengthening her	The extended dialogue and cooperation in this interchange involve deciding what to do, giving advice, joking, asking for information, and deciding when to move to the next step.		Lana: (Reprovingly) Lee, you should help me get it. (As he starts to spoon) Get a lot in your fork and it'll be faster.
			Lee: I'll get a lot. Ow! (Laughs) You burned me! I'm going to lick it (licks the fork).
			Lana: Now is it sugar time?
			Lee: Not yet (looks at recipe). We're on this. We're doing this page. (They pat the applesauce a little more) We're done. We're on the sugar page.
			. . .
		Teacher's guidance takes the form of consultation, leaving room for children to decide not to follow her suggestion. . . . and the cooks feel free to say no!	T: Do you want to put this little bit in there too (some left on colander)?
			Lana: No—Yeah.
			Lee: No, we don't want to put it in there. We want to eat it.
			T: Are you going to have enough, though, for everybody if you eat all that?
			Lee: Yeah.

role as the one who guides the steps when learning is complex and elicits the children's knowledge as she does so. The children's sense of group is being reinforced by participation and recall of joint experiences that have been important to them.

Back at school, the teacher picked up two buckets in the play house area; one was green and one was yellow. "We can put my Golden Delicious yellow ones in the yellow bucket," said Rosina. "But which bucket will we use for the red apples?" asked Janice.

"Oh, the green one, silly," said Rosina.

"Mine rolled right in."

"My gold apples go bump, bump. Gold apples."

The teacher suggested that they cook each type separately.

The teacher is reinforcing differentiation—separation into two buckets, and cooking separately.

The children begin to think actively about the apple classification, but, again, the teacher's suggestion of cooking the apples separately seems to close off a possibility for children's further reasoning.

When children cannot regulate the amount they eat out of consideration for the amount to be cooked and eaten later, they can only experience a teacher's regulation as arbitrary and external to their reasoning. Later spontaneous comment by the children that they had enough suggests that the question did take root in their thought and that they took up the concern as their own.

Lana does take up the teacher's concern as her own, and decides she wants to add the applesauce to the bowl. The difference between the two cooks is resolved by a sort of good-natured compromise. Had an impasse occurred, the teacher would have refrained from intervening unless children could not settle the issue themselves. Teacher intervention, when necessary on occasion of such clashes, takes the form of supporting children's efforts to negotiate their own settlement. She

Note: The teacher is somewhat concerned that the cooks will have little left to cook. She does not want to tell them not to eat so much, but she wants to give them a chance to reflect on the consequences. Here, and later in the activity, her attitude is that if children cannot anticipate the possibility of not having enough applesauce when she calls it to their attention, then they should be permitted to experience what happens. She feels that the risk of disappointment is a lesser danger than the imposition of her idea that they should eat less. If disappointment later occurs because there is not enough applesauce, she plans to comfort and sympathize, and capitalize on the opportunity to get children to reflect on the need to plan ahead. In this case, the children did have enough to cook and serve.

Lana: *No!* I want it in here (bowl). (She protests Lee's desire to eat the applesauce on the colander)

TABLE 10.1 (*continued*)

Applesauce at Bank Street	Comments on the Bank Street Account from a Constructivist Perspective	Comments on the Merrill-Palmer Account from a Constructivist Perspective	Applesauce at Merrill-Palmer
"I think we'll need another hot plate and another pot." "Me go with Janice," offered Fernando, "to Mrs. Palmer's room." "If she doesn't have another hot plate you'll have to ask in other classrooms." "I know, up the stairs to Mrs. Kerr's—my brother's teacher, Danny's teacher," Janice said. *The teacher is previewing a problem and decides that the children need preliminary help in solving it.* The teacher said, "Golden Delicious apples here. And the red ones are called MacIntosh apples." "So many apples," exclaimed Joey. "Maybe a hundred," Rosina said. Joey lifted one bucket. "I am very strong."	The teacher identifies and solves the next problem. Instead, she might have presented it to the children by simply asking if they have enough things, or commenting that there is only one hot plate and pot and asking what they can do to cook the apples separately. The constructivist teacher would agree that an affective	might, for example, ask something like, "If you both want to do something different, how can you figure it out? Did you explain what you wanted to each other?" This "plotting" together reflects a solidarity that results from the general establishment of a feeling of community among children. Consciously manipulating the teacher to dry the dishes reflects both a recognition of her as a helpful resource and an egalitarian attitude toward her as approachable in a peer-like way. The children call the teacher by her first name. This is one of the ways the teacher tries to reduce her authority role and practice equality. The teacher lets herself be manipulated, asks a child for	(Lee gets spatula and eats some, puts some in bowl) . . . (They gather utensils, put them in sink, and Lee begins to wash.) Lana: One part is we're all done cleaning it. Lee: How we goin' dry stuff? Lana: (Looks calculatingly over her shoulder toward the teacher who is with other children, then grins in a conspiratorial way at Lee) Let's get Jane. . . . Jane, we need your help. T: What do you need? T: Oh, am I the dryer? Lana: Yeah. T: Where are the towels? Lana: In the kitchen. (Teacher goes to get towel.) . . . Lana: (Takes colander to garbage can and scrapes) T: Will it come out, Lana? Lana: No

element certainly enters into Rosina's statement. However, it is also viewed as a preoperational gross quantification. The teacher might have extended the opportunity to think further about the number of apples by wondering aloud about how they could find out how many, asking children if they want to try to count them.

direction, and follows it, thereby strengthening the egalitarian relationship she endeavors to maintain.

Again, the cooks have a slight difference of opinion about what to do. This is again resolved good-naturedly, apparently because Lee's initial objection is overcome by seeing that Lana's idea will work.

Lee's lack of anticipation that water would flow through the colander indicated an unexpected advantage of the activity for his construction of physical knowledge.

Lee's desire to share his amusement with Lana reflects his decentered feeling of shared interest.

The foregoing section of the protocol illustrates the kind of decentered social interaction the constructivist teacher tries to promote. Earlier in the year, the teacher had worked especially to get children to take account of and operate in

The value of the recipe chart for the Bank Street teacher is the symbolic representation of the sequence in the activity. While this is also important to the constructivist teacher, she also thinks of the value of the recipe book in terms of its role in reducing the necessity to exercise authority, by enabling children to do the cooking on their own. The constructivist approach is to encourage children to figure out what to

---

Lee: Is it comin' out, Lana?

Lana: Only a little. (She finally returns) Can you take that big bowl out of the sink, please?

Lee: We need to wash. . . . (the bowl first)

Lana: (Plops colander in the sink) Take the big bowl off the sink (to make room for the colander). (She turns the water on.)

Lee: Put some bubbles in it.

Lana: Yeah, get some soap.

Lee: (Screeches) Oh! It's coming from that one! (He notices that water goes through the colander into the bowl) It's coming from that one to this one, Lana. (Giggles) Isn't that funny?

Note: The teacher is surprised at Lee's surprise that water drains through the holes in the colander. She thought this would be easily anticipated, and makes a mental note to plan follow-up activities involving draining. This illustrates how the constructivist teacher's focus on the nature of children's reasoning leads to curriculum elaboration.

By keeping the kinds of apples separate and reminding the children of their distinctive names, she is once more teaching the concept of difference within commonality.

The teacher does not stop for an accurate count of the apples. She accepts the exaggerated guess as an affective rather than strictly numerical statement.

The teacher had prepared a second chart with pictures showing children washing apples, peeling and cutting

It showed that they would need a bowl, a board, and cutting utensils.

The teacher and the children reviewed the recipe chart.

The children knew where to get the boards and bowls. Miss Gordon distributed the knives and corers.

The teacher uses pictures to depict the sequence of actions the children will perform and the materials they will use. She cross-references the experience and the symbols of the experience.

TABLE 10.1 (*continued*)

Applesauce at Bank Street	Comments on the Bank Street Account from a Constructivist Perspective	Comments on the Merrill-Palmer Account from a Constructivist Perspective	Applesauce at Merrill-Palmer
"Now we're ready—what first?" said Miss Gordon. "I want red." "I want yellow." The children chose a color and with full bowls went to wash the apples. "Just with water," the teacher added, remembering past incidents of soapy diligence. As the children returned with their bowls of wet apples, the teacher helped them core the apples. "Here's the picture. It shows where we take out the seeds on the very inside—the whole core." Joey dug at his apple. "I got a pit." "Joey, now see if you can twist the corer around for the rest." They sliced the apples, with the teacher watching their careful use of the knives. "Chew, chew," commented Joey, eating as he worked.	do by consulting the book. One negative Bank Street reaction to this was the view that displacing the authority from the teacher to the book made it too impersonal and failed to promote the teacher-child relationship.	terms of one another. As a result, they did not need support in relating to one another by this time of the year.	

"Dee-licious, Golden Delicious." "They isn't gold inside," commented Rosina. "Dat isn't real gold, is it?" asked Janice. "It's just a word," she decided, looking for confirmation to the teacher, who agreed.

The children are being trusted to use knives under the teacher's watchful eyes, and through their own action to investigate inside-outside differences.

"Now, into the pot. We'll need a little water."

Rosina carefully put in two drops, added more at the teacher's suggestion.

Rosina's comment suggests that she expected the Golden Delicious apples to be gold inside, and Janice seems to wonder whether real gold may be involved. These expressions of intuitive thought could have been extended by the teacher. She might have asked other children whether they think it's real gold, or she might have wondered aloud or asked children why they think the apples are called Golden Delicious. Janice seems to conclude that the name is arbitrary when with a little encouragement she might have made the correspondence of the name with the color of the apple.

Here the teacher misses another opportunity to encourage children's initiative. She decides for them that the next step is to put the apples into the pot and add water. She might have asked children to figure out what they need to do next. When Rosina's idea is to put only two drops of water

TEACHER AS COMPANION/GUIDE TO PROMOTE AUTONOMY

Foregoing passages illustrate some of the ways the Merrill-Palmer teacher seeks to establish a context of companionship within which to foster children's initiative and pride in accomplishment. In setting up the activity and interac-

335

TABLE 10.1 (continued)

Applesauce at Bank Street	Comments on the Bank Street Account from a Constructivist Perspective	Comments on the Merrill-Palmer Account from a Constructivist Perspective	Applesauce at Merrill-Palmer
"Were those apples sweet enough?" asked the teacher. "We'll only need a little sugar, then. Just up to here on the measuring cup." She showed them the line with her finger. "Later, we can add more sugar if we think it needs any." *The teacher points up the relation between an amount and an effect.*	in, she simply tells her to add more when she could have stimulated children's thinking and co-operation by asking others what they think. The question "Were those apples sweet enough?" was an excellent one to open the possibility for children to experiment and compare. Unfortunately, the teacher then goes on to decide that only a little would be needed and even tells the children how much to put in the measuring cup. When the teacher makes all the decisions, children's opportunities to think are restricted.		ting with children, she emphasizes that the applesauce-making is for the two cooks to do on their own. Having introduced the recipe book the previous day (as a reading and planning activity), on the day of the project she casually says to the cooks, "Why don't you guys read over the recipe? If you have any questions you want to ask me, you can ask when I get back (from getting a cutting board from her car)." Upon her return she asks if they are ready to start and if they have everything they need. Then she says, "Then I'll help you with my page, and then you can do it all by yourselves." They wash the apples, and she cuts and cores them, emphasizing "That's my part." During this time, the teacher follows the children's conversational leads.
They watched as the teacher took photos of them putting the pots of apple slices on the hot plates.			Lee: Turn the next page. Lana: I love apples. T: You do? Lana: They're so juicy.

The teacher highlights the experience by taking pictures of the children which will go into their books about what they do in school.

"While the applesauce is cooking, we'll paste the labels on our jars." The trays of jars and the gummed labels were given to each child.

"Perhaps we should ask someone to help you, Fernando. You'll have a lot to make." Janice volunteered.

Crayons and felt markers were placed in the center of the work tables. The teacher wrote some names, but everyone took a hand in writing a name or putting a mark on at least one label, or decorating the label for a family member's jar.

The children are initiated into the "writing" experience before they can actually use letters. The teacher encourages the children to be helpful to each other in a situation where the need for help is real and apparent.

Again, the teacher announces what children are to do next. They follow her direction rather than directing themselves.

The teacher takes excellent advantage of the opportunity to integrate writing into the activity when children can recognize the need for written symbols and are motivated to think about their significance.

The idea that apples grow on the ground as well as in trees is an intelligent construction, based on observation of apples in reality. This could also involve

---

T: They're good, aren't they? What kind of apples do you like best?

Lana: Red apples, real red ones.

T: I like the green ones.

Lee: I like green ones, too.

Lana: I like green ones.

Lee: I like green *and* red ones.

Lee: I'm glad I'm a cook.

Lana: I love apples.

T: Do you know what kind these are?

Lana: No—They come offa trees, these kind do.

T: What kind don't come off trees?

Lana: The kind that are in the ground.

T: Oh, are there apples that are in the ground?

Lana: Uh huh. My Mama growed some apples in the ground and they turned out just right.

T: Were they apples?

Lee: (Looks at recipe book to see what's next)

T: Lana, I want to hear about these apples that were on the ground. Were they just on the ground from the tree, or

TABLE 10.1 (continued)

Applesauce at Bank Street	Comments on the Bank Street Account from a Constructivist Perspective	Comments on the Merrill-Palmer Account from a Constructivist Perspective	Applesauce at Merrill-Palmer
From time to time they stopped to look at the cooking apples through the Pyrex pots. "There's bubbles." "They wiggle." "Hot stuff!" The teacher asked a bit later, "Are they almost cooked?" "Look, Miss Gordon. They are mush." "Mushy gushy," said Fernando. "Mushy gushy," echoed his friend Joey, provoking gales of laughter. "We're making mushy gushy." *The teacher encourages the children to observe the transformation by using transparent pots. The children have a chance to be discriminating observers and find their own verbal forms. Their invented language, with exciting overtones, is not censored by the teacher as she proceeds with the goal-directed activity.*	The Pyrex pots are excellent materials to enable children to observe the reaction of apples to heat. The children call the teacher "Miss." This is presumably one of the ways the Bank Street teacher stresses her authority.	assimilation of observations of tomatoes growing. When a child genuinely holds such an idea, verbal correction is a very delicate matter. The danger is that acceptance of the correction may result in damaged confidence in what can be known by actively thinking. Lana's case is ambiguous. She may have given the teacher what she thought she wanted to hear. Or, she may have possessed enough differentiated knowledge about how things grow to enable her to use the teacher's thinly veiled suggestion to correct her own idea.	did you think they were growing on the ground? Lana: They fell off the tree. *Note:* In retrospect, the teacher felt her last questions might have had the unfortunate heteronomous effect of making Lana feel her idea was being corrected. What the teacher intended, however, was to clarify what Lana meant. She decided she might have pushed this a bit too far, but hoped Lana's conclusion was a result of genuine reconsideration and not just submissiveness. Lee: Jane, I have apples in my backyard. The apples fall off and I pick 'em up. (Conversation about trees in Lee's grandmother's yard.) Lana: Jane, they're getting brown. T: What's getting brown? Oh, the apples *are* already! Why do you think that's happening?

338

The teacher took a pot from the burner and stirred the contents, letting them drop from the spoon. ''Do you think it's cooked?'' They said yes, and the teacher removed the other pot.

While the sauce cooled, the labeling process was finished, knives were washed, cinnamon grated, sniffed, tasted, and discussed.

The strainers and funnels were brought out, placed over the bowls and jars. Each child had a bowl, a small paper cup and spoon ''for tasting'' and a large stirring spoon.

They held bowls steadily for each other as the sauce was strained, and helped each other pour the applesauce through wide-mouthed funnels into the jars.

''Mine's sour,'' declared Fernando.

''What does it need?'' Miss Gordon asked.

''More sugar.''

''That will take the tartness away,'' said the teacher. ''It

Had children done the stirring, they might have had more knowledge on which to base their judgment as to whether the apples were cooked. The teacher might have asked children how they would know when the apples were done.

The task of straining and pouring the applesauce creates a good context in which children see a need to co-operate.

The teacher asks Fernando to figure out what his sour applesauce needs. Instead of pronouncing the effect sugar will have, she might have asked him how he thinks it will change it.

Since the task of cutting the apples is not problematic, it provides a natural setting for conversation, revealing children's preoccupations. The teacher's respect for the child's thought is evidenced by her interested response and questioning.

Lee: They're sour.

Lana: Because you should eat 'em *now*.

T: But why do you think they're getting brown?

Lana: So it tastes good.

T: You think the brown part tastes good?

Lana: Yeah, I love brown parts—*and* the white part.

Lee: Ooo! The brown part is *sour*.

T: Have you tried eating the brown part before?

Lee: Yeah, it tastes sour.

Lana: I tried eating it before and I said, ''Mmm, I love a little sour thing. It tastes good.''

T: I like the sour apples like Granny Smith apples. You know those are the kind I was bringing?

Lana: Yeah, those are the kind that turn brown.

T: They do?

Lana: Yeah, I like those, too. Those are the only ones that I eat because it has brown in it, but the other

TABLE 10.1 (continued)

Applesauce at Bank Street	Comments on the Bank Street Account from a Constructivist Perspective	Comments on the Merrill-Palmer Account from a Constructivist Perspective	Applesauce at Merrill-Palmer
will be sweeter." They added more. "Mine's pinker," declared Rosina. "Your apples was red," Janice reminded her. "Mine was yeller. Golden . . . Golden Delicious." "Yum, yum." They tasted each other's. *The teacher asks the children to make judgments. Again she points up the relation between amount and effect.* *She uses the children's replies to introduce a new word. The children spontaneously review the experience, noting the consistent difference between apples when raw and when cooked.* Janice pushed her head under the teacher's face. "Rosina has more jars than me."			kinds I only eat the white kind. There's no seeds in that one. T: There are a few. See? They're all on one side. There. I'm almost done with my part, and you guys can do the rest. . . . The teacher feels she cannot leave the activity while children are using sharp knives, so she remains at the table while children cut. Conversation continues as follows: Lana: My cousin is a vegetarian. T: What is a vegetarian? Lana: It's a person that only eats vegetables, not meat. And I'm not a vegetarian, so I don't believe him. He says meat is not good for you. T: Why does he say meat is not good for you?

The teacher said, "Let's see whom they are all for." She turned the jars around, reading off the labels: "One for her Mommy, one for her Grandma, one for Aunt Rosa-Maria, one for Billy."

Fernando added, "And Daddy."

"No," said the teacher, "no Daddy, and one for her sister Ellen, one for Rosina, and one for her baby."

"Fernando also has a lot of people in his family. Let's count his jars."

After the counting, Janice announced that she had four. "They are all very full up."

When they looked at all the jars, they were impressed by the large production. "We made hundreds."

As a matter of course they washed their bowls and spoons and, with teacher's help, the glass saucepans.

It is not easy for the young child to accept the logical basis for one child having more jars, which the teacher has

The teacher seems to assume that Janice will see the reason Rosina has more jars if she reviews the labels. From the teacher's point of view, the inequality has a rational basis, but Janice appears to view it as unjust. Since she already knows about the labeling, this review in itself seems unlikely to convince her. Moreover, it fails to acknowledge her real concern. A recognition of the limitation of her ability to judge the justness of the inequality might have led the teacher to address the feeling and take advantage of the opportunity to get children to think about the moral issue of whether it was fair for Rosina to have more jars.

When Lee asks for help, the teacher turns the question back because she thinks he can figure out his own solution if she refrains from solving the problem for him.

Lana: Because he's a vegetarian. I'm not.

T: But what does he think is wrong with meat? Did he tell you?

Lana: He doesn't like it. He just told me it.

T: But he didn't tell you why he didn't like meat? Just that it wasn't good for you?

Lee: Who?

Lana: My cousin. When we took us some Burger King McDonald's I saw him.

T: Oh, you did? Was he eating hamburgers?

Lana: No, it was when we were looking at the play.

T: Oh, now I remember, Lana.

Lee: Where do we put 'em (the cut apples)

T: Where do you think would be a good place to put them?

Lee: In there—no, in this bowl. (He sets bowl between Lana and himself and dumps his apples in.) I like cutting apples so I can taste 'em. (He does.)

TABLE 10.1 (continued)

Applesauce at Bank Street	Comments on the Bank Street Account from a Constructivist Perspective	Comments on the Merrill-Palmer Account from a Constructivist Perspective	Applesauce at Merrill-Palmer
established. The teacher repeats the formulation in a step-by-step explanation. Counting has a clear personal charge, associated, as it is, with family members; also a review of family membership per se. The exaggerated idea of the number of jars expresses the sense of great accomplishment. The reality of "no daddy" is not skirted over by the teacher—a reality to be accepted. (Biber, 1977, pp. 448–451; Biber, Shapiro, & Wickens, 1971, pp. 51–56.) Aspects of the experience as they relate to the eight goals are summarized: *Goal 1. Impact on Environment.* ... The children are involved in a series of activities that alter the condition of things; taking		Observation of the juicy property of the apples is an important empirical abstraction, but does not lead to real experimentation such as occurs in activities involving the movement of objects.	Lee: Jane! I made apple cider come out! (He notices the juice from the apple as he cuts.) T: You did? Lee: When I stabbed it through, it made apple cider. Oh! More apple cider! More apple cider! (He is very excited.) Jane, I see apple cider coming out! T: You do: Like at the cider mill. .... (As the cutting is completed) Lana: It's going to be enough. T: Think so? That was a lot of work. Lee: Then we go on to the next page. The next page is the frying pan. ... Lana has two more. I got one more. ... We didn't cut ourself. ... Jane, we told you we wouldn't cut ourself. Lana: Apples! Yum, yum, yum.

the insides out of apples, reducing them to mush by cooking, changing taste qualities and, in the end, producing a known food. Some of the manipulative activities—slicing with a knife, coring—require new mastery.

Goal 2. Cognition. ... The intrinsic cognitive elements are similar to those noted in Part 1 of this Episode: identity, classification, differentiation, quantifying, and orientation in time and space.

Goal 3. Knowledge. ...
The cooking experience acquaints the children directly with an important work process—the preparation of food. They are learning a sequence of steps and a selection of tools that are essential in changing the fruit from the raw to the cooked condition.

Goal 6. Conflicts. ...
Through the cooking experience the children are connecting school life with home realities. Taking home a

The recipe pictures enable children to "read" the idea when they cannot read the words exactly. Such experience seems important in creating an attitude of expecting writing in books to communicate something one wants to know.

It is not clear whether Lee believes he is making more detergent by adding water, but his initiative is intelligent and of value for the exercise of causal reasoning.

By expressing her own wish as a member of the group to hurry and go out, she leaves open the possibility for children to decide if they want to hurry or not.

I get the last one to eat.

T: (As Lee consults the recipe book) Do you remember what it says on that page?

Lee and Lana: No.

T: (Points to picture of frying pan) What's that?

Lana: A pot. Put the apples in there and wait and see if they cooked enough to take 'em out.

(Flurry of activity in taking apples to the pan, plugging it in)

...

(At cleanup, while starting to wash dishes)

Lana: (Adds soap)

Lee: (As teacher returns) Know what makes more bubbles?

T: What?

Lee: Water. (He adds water to the liquid soap container, which was almost empty.)

T: I'm anxious to get outside. Let's hurry and wash these dishes.

Note: The teacher does not wish to cut short the cooks' meaningful involvement with clean-up if this is more important to them than going outside.

...

TABLE 10.1 (continued)

Applesauce at Bank Street	Comments on the Bank Street Account from a Constructivist Perspective	Comments on the Merrill-Palmer Account from a Constructivist Perspective	Applesauce at Merrill-Palmer
gift for each member of the family helps the child bridge the separation between home and school.			Lee: (Squeals as he picks up the colander) I picked it up and it's coming out. It turned brown. I wonder why.
Carrying through a complete activity and using the tools for cooking contribute to the child's sense of independence.			Lee: Oh, I have one of those (colander) at home, but it's a different color. It's grey.
Goal 7. Self-Image .... The experience helps the child review his family constellation and position himself in relation to smaller and bigger siblings; it builds toward an image of being someone who can both make and give. This sense of themselves and what they do as important is enhanced by the teacher taking pictures of them in their school activities. This also emphasizes the teacher's interest in them as learners.			T: It's like mesh? Or is it plastic?
			Lee: No, it's those kind of holes (like the colander, not like the sieves).
			T: Oh, it's metal.
			Lee: This isn't metal, Lana. This is silver (skillet).
			Lana: Silver's metal.
			Lee: Metal is silver!
Goal 8. Interaction .... The children observe, enjoy and	Despite the failure to see the hierarchical, inclusive		*Note:* The teacher's effort to understand Lee's description of his colander at home led her to conclude that he meant it was metal. The conversation between Lee and Lana reveals that Lee has not yet constructed the class

344

help each other spontaneously, as part of the work activity. They talk to each other about what they are doing. The question-answer pattern moves both ways between children and teacher; and, when puzzled, the children turn to the teacher. (Biber, Shapiro, & Wickens, 1971, p. 57; Biber, 1977, p. 451)

classificatory relationships, the discussion probably has value in the exercise of classificatory schemes.

The teacher consciously uses a logical quantifier rather than a numerical quantifier. She expects this to inspire counting but refrains from telling children to count because she wants them to reason that counting is necessary to find out whether there are enough.

inclusion relation between metal and silver. Lee fails to grasp Lana's correction and the teacher realizes further discussion would not help him construct this logico-mathematical relationship.

(Lana finds a burned peel that won't come off the skillet. She gets a strong cleanser and squirts it on.)

TEACHER INTERVENTION TO PROMOTE REASONING

The constructivist teacher's interventions oriented toward activating and extending children's reasoning are illustrated in some of the above excerpts. She asks why the apples are getting brown (after a child calls attention to this) and whether they will have enough applesauce for everyone. Other examples (including sometimes refraining from answering children's questions) are found in the following excerpts.

T: (As children check ingredients and utensils) Do we have enough apples?

Lee and Lana: (Count the ten apples)

TABLE 10.1 (*continued*)

Applesauce at Bank Street	Comments on the Bank Street Account from a Constructivist Perspective	Comments on the Merrill-Palmer Account from a Constructivist Perspective	Applesauce at Merrill-Palmer
		When a child has to figure out how to make two equal subsets from a larger set, she does not know ahead of time how many each will get. The problem of dividing things among children is a common one in a constructivist classroom. (See Kamii & DeVries, 1976)	Lana: (Pushing four to Lee and keeping four for herself) Now you have four and I have four. Lee: We all have *five!* *Note:* The teacher specified the number of apples in the recipe because she expected it to inspire children to think about number. She was prepared to ask them how many each cook should cut, but the idea of division occurs spontaneously. Lana: How do we cut 'em in pieces?
		Again, the teacher does not solve a problem for children which they can figure out themselves.	T: However you think is the best way. Lee: I'm going to eat some. T: (Teasingly) Make sure you leave enough for the applesauce. Lee: Me and Lana do this page. (Conversation about being careful with knives) Lana: (Starts to cut) I'm going

to cut 'em into little bitty pieces.

Lee: (Stabs an apple half) Look. Me and Lana didn't cut our hands.

Lana: The skin keeps on comin' off when I cut it.

Lee: Wow-eee!

. . .

(Both are eating fairly continuously.)

T: Do you think there's going to be enough applesauce for everybody to have some?

Lee: Yeah. (He continues eating)

T: O.K. Better make sure you have enough for everyone, Lee (in a teasing tone).

Lee: Yes, Jane (with mock compliance).

Lana: That's twelve.

Lee: That's a hundred—a million!

T: Do you think there's a million pieces in there?

Lee: Yeah—more than a million.

Note: The teacher realizes that Lee's idea about the number of pieces is not just due to playfulness. She has observed in

Again, the teacher light-heartedly gives children a chance to anticipate the possible problem of not having enough, but she refrains from regulating how much they eat.

TABLE 10.1 (continued)

Applesauce at Bank Street	Comments on the Bank Street Account from a Constructivist Perspective	Comments on the Merrill-Palmer Account from a Constructivist Perspective	Applesauce at Merrill-Palmer
			many other situations that he still tends to reason globally rather than in a precisely quantitative way. His number vocabulary outdistances his conceptions about number, and he uses "hundred" and "million" to express the judgment of "a lot." Qualitative comparison is evident in his use of "more than." In this instance, the teacher supports his effort to think about the number without expecting it to contribute specifically to an advance in numerical reasoning. Lana: What makes six and seven and one? (Various guesses from children at the next table) Lana: Fourteen! . . . (Discussion about whether it's too hot or cooking too fast) T: I don't know. What do you think? How long do you

Child corrects teacher who accepts correction.

think it's going to take to get soft?

Lee: Mushy, you mean!

T: Mushy. How long do you think it will take?

Lana: Five minutes.

Bystander: I'll get the timer out.

Lee: (Sets timer for five minutes, then after a moment says the time is not up, that four minutes are left, then makes it ring early)

T: Bing. Time's up. Boy, time went fast.

Note: The teacher wonders if Lee thinks that he makes time actually go faster by advancing the timer. However, she feels the best response is simply to express surprise, with the idea that this might result in reflection. If this is not what he thinks, and he is simply being humorous, she hopes to express recognition of this idea.

Lee: (Takes lid off and checks apples) Not ready. (Resets timer) We've got one more minute. (Makes it ring) Jane, time's up. Almost

TABLE 10.1 (*continued*)

Applesauce at Bank Street	Comments on the Bank Street Account from a Constructivist Perspective	Comments on the Merrill-Palmer Account from a Constructivist Perspective	Applesauce at Merrill-Palmer
			done. (Checks with fork) It's done! (Checks recipe book) Sieves. Push apples through some sieves.
			T: There are several different ones. You can decide which one the apples go through best.
			(Discussion of problem that apples are very hot. Children decide the teacher should pour them into the bowl.)
		Child directs problem concern to child.	Lana: (Tries sieve) It won't mush through. It won't go through these tiny holes, Lee.
			Lee: (Forks mixture into colander) I'll push mine through. Jane, it's comin' through this one! (He uses the colander as it sits on the table, not anticipating where the applesauce will fall.)
		The teacher, after inspiring children's efforts to figure out	T: (To Lana) Is it working in that one?

Lana: No, because none of it goes *through*. (She scrapes the apples out of the sieve.)

Lee: I'll push mine through. It's comin' through this one.

T: Is it?

Lee: See? Applesauce!

Lana: You said we needed sugar. (Accusingly, as if it has been forgotten)

T: Uh huh, when we get to that page.

Lee: Then why is the applesauce ready already? (Notices apple puree dripped on the table and moves colander over bowl)

Lana: That one (sieve) doesn't work.

T: It doesn't work? Maybe another one will work better.

Lee: This one works better.

Lana: (Takes a strainer with larger mesh) Mush it through, pick it up, and put it back in the bowl!?

T: The idea is to get the applesauce mushy. That's what the recipe calls for. But you can get it mushy

which sieve is best, supports them with her interest and companionship as she shares their experimentation experience.

When a cook addresses the teacher with the question of sugar, she refers her back to the authority of the recipe book, thus continuing to reduce heteronomous dependence while still maintaining a companionable relationship.

The cooks have taken up the teacher's idea of comparing sieves as their own purpose. She continues to encourage comparison.

Lana seems to be asking if her method is correct. The teacher refrains from explicitly sanctioning, restates the recipe goal, and supports autonomous effort in figuring out how to accomplish the goal.

TABLE 10.1 (continued)

Applesauce at Bank Street	Comments on the Bank Street Account from a Constructivist Perspective	Comments on the Merrill-Palmer Account from a Constructivist Perspective	Applesauce at Merrill-Palmer
			however you want.
			Lana: It's not coming through this one, either.
			Lee: It's coming through this one (sets it on the table again).
			T: (To Lana, as some of the apple mixture goes through the strainer) A little bit.
			Lee: It's coming through this one.
			T: Is it going through that one, Lee?
		The teacher's question is aimed at focusing Lee on where he wants the applesauce to go, to encourage him to think of the means for accomplishing this, without telling him what to do.	Lee: (Picks up colander and looks at the bottom, looks at the table a little sheepishly)
			T: Where do you want it to go? Do you want it to land on the table?
			Note: The teacher is surprised at Lee's lack of anticipation that the applesauce will drip onto the table. She hopes that the unforeseen result of his action makes him feel a need to take

into account more aspects of the situation and thus to coordinate new relationships.

Lee: (Shifts colander to bowl)

Lana: Pushes apples through colander, sees how the puree clings to the underside) It won't come out. It's coming out, but it won't fall off of it.

T: O.K. So it doesn't work so well, huh?

Lee: This works well.

T: I wonder why that works better than Lana's. Lee.

This question aims at stimulating construction of logico-mathematical relationships by getting children to notice differences and make comparisons.

Lee: Because it's the good—It's the better . . . .

Lana: It has bigger holes.

Lee: . . . than everyone.

T: Why does that work better?

Lee: Because all these three (strainers) have the same holes.

Lana: Turn it. Jane, we're on the sugar page!

. . .

TABLE 10.1 (*continued*)

Applesauce at Bank Street	Comments on the Bank Street Account from a Constructivist Perspective	Comments on the Merrill-Palmer Account from a Constructivist Perspective	Applesauce at Merrill-Palmer
			T: Oh, it does look nice and mushy. Do you think that looks mushy enough? Do you think that looks like applesauce?
			Both: Yes.
			T: I think it does, too.
			Lana: How do we pour it out?
		The child's question about what to do is turned back to the child with a challenge to figure it out.	T: However you want. How do you think you can get it in there (from colander to bowl)?
			Lana: Oh, look-it, Jane (surprise at applesauce on bottom side of collander)!
			T: (Laughs)
			Lee: (Holds up colander and looks at the mashed apple on the bottom)
			Lana: It slobbered (laughs). Pour it out, Lee.
		Child directs child.	T: What's it doing?
			Lee: Comin' out there (turns upside down over bowl)
			T: Yeah, it goes through the

holes on this, doesn't it?

Lee: We told you. . . . Oops (a little spills on the table). Have to lick it. Mmm, it tastes like applesauce.

Lana: Put the sugar in now and stir it up?

Lee: No, we have to put this in (more from colander).

T: Let me read you what it says again. O.K.?

Lana: O.K.

T: It says, "Add sugar until it tastes sweet."

Lee: Wow! We'll have to keep on tasting it!

Lana: Jane, taste this. It tastes sugary even though it doesn't have sugar in it.

T: Mmm, it does taste sweet.

Lana: O.K., now put sugar in it?

T: Do you think it needs more?

Lee: Jane, what does it say after this?

Lana: It needs sugar. I didn't even put none in it.

T: I know, but it tastes sweet. Do you think it needs some?

Lana: Yeah.

T: O.K., but do you think it needs a lot . . .

Child takes initiative in deciding what to do.

Teacher again responds to child's question about what to do by referring to the recipe book.

The teachers refrains from telling what to do, but asks what the child thinks.

355

TABLE 10.1 (continued)

Applesauce at Bank Street	Comments on the Bank Street Account from a Constructivist Perspective	Comments on the Merrill-Palmer Account from a Constructivist Perspective	Applesauce at Merrill-Palmer
		The teacher wants the cooks to have the opportunity to compare the results of adding sugar more than once and perhaps to construct the serial correspondence involved (the more sugar, the sweeter the applesauce). She therefore tries to get them to reflect on how much sweeter it needs to be. Lana seems ready to do this, and when Lee starts to dump all the sugar in, the teacher intervenes a bit more strongly, partly to protect Lana's effort. It might have been better if the teacher had suggested that Lee and Lana consult one another about what to do.	Lee: Yeah, put all of it. T: . . . or do you think it needs a little? Lana: (starts to pour) T: Lee, do you think it tasted sweet already? Lee: Yeah. T: So does it need a lot or a little bit? Lee: A *lot* (emphatically). T: Did it already taste sweet? Lana: (Carefully sprinkles in a little, sets rest aside) Now, after you put su . . . Lee: (Takes cup and starts to put the rest in) T: Lee, do you think it needs that much? Lee: Yeah. T: Maybe you should taste it now and see what it tastes like now. It might be sweet enough now.

356

Lana: (Pushes cup in Lee's hand away)

(Both taste)

T: What do you think?

Lee: A little more sugar.

T: A little more?

Lee: Yeah (he dumps in the rest in the cup).

T: Was that a little more?

Lee: Yeah (grins).

T: (Laughs) How do you think it's going to taste now?

Lee: Applesaucy. Oh, it looks like applesauce! We put the skin in, Jane.

Lana: (Tastes) Mmm (grins and rubs stomach with look of satisfaction).

T: Do you like it that way?

Lana: (Nods)

Lee: (Tastes)

T: How does it taste?

Lee: *Good!*

T: (Laughs) Let me taste it. (She does) You're right. It does taste good. Do you think there's enough sugar in it now?

Lana: Yeah. (Offers taste to Foster Grandparent)

TABLE 10.1 (continued)

Applesauce at Bank Street	Comments on the Bank Street Account from a Constructivist Perspective	Comments on the Merrill-Palmer Account from a Constructivist Perspective	Applesauce at Merrill-Palmer
			FG: Have you finished putting everything in it?
			Lana: No, we're not finished putting everything in it.
			Lana: It has sugar in it. Taste a little.
			FG: (Does) That's very good.
			Lana: (Laughs) We cook good.
			FG: You haven't put no spice in it yet, huh?
			Lee: (Looks in recipe book) Jane, what about the spice?
		The teacher again refrains from giving an answer the cooks can find out for themselves.	T: Well, what does it say?
			Lee: Add spice.
			T: Remember how much?
			Lee: A little pinch (He gets can of cinnamon and adds some)
			Lana: (Stirs) I know it's going to taste good after we get through stirring it.
			(Both stir and taste)

Lee: MMMm (laughs). I'm
        going to taste it again.
        (Both taste, look at each other
        and laugh)
T: Did you add the cinnamon?
Both: Yeah.
T: Well, what do you think?
Lana: All done.
T: What does it say next?
Lee: Serve it to the children for
        lunch.

The teacher consults the
cooks about what to do.

T: Where do you think we
        should keep this until snack
        time?

Lana: In the refrigerator.

        . . .

T: Are you almost ready for me
        to dry?
Lee: Yeah, we need you to dry.
T: So which of these things do
        you think worked best?
Lee: The big-holed one.
T: Do you know what this is
        called?
Lee: No. What?
T: Lana, do you know?
Lana: No.
T: Did you ever see one like it
        before?
Lee: No, but they sure are big.

TABLE 10.1 (*continued*)

Applesauce at Bank Street	Comments on the Bank Street Account from a Constructivist Perspective	Comments on the Merrill-Palmer Account from a Constructivist Perspective	Applesauce at Merrill-Palmer
		The teacher provides new vocabulary (arbitrary social knowledge).	T: They sure are. It's a colander.
		The teacher promotes a feeling of community among children through interest in giving and receiving the highly valued snack. Goals also involve promoting feelings of competence and mutual respect.	*Note:* At grouptime, Lana and Lee showed the other children the applesauce and told how they made it. They "read" the recipe book to the group, and told which worked best to make the apples mushy, and how they knew when it had cooked enough. They counted the number of people, and served it with great pride at afternoon snack.

[1] This activity was first published in 1971 by Biber, Shapiro, and Wickens; it was later reprinted as part of Biber, 1977.
[2] Conducted in May 1980.

360

this as an advantage, since possibilities for conflict are minimized, constructivist teachers seek recipes offering more possibilities for co-operation (including conflict).

Despite the potential individual nature of the applesauce activity, the account of interaction between the Merrill-Palmer cooks contains many instances of reciprocity and co-operation. They ask one another for information (identification of recipe pictures, where to set the skillet temperature, whether it's time to add sugar, and how to get the dishes dried). They correct one another (the teacher is to cut apples in half, not in little pieces) and even the teacher (the apples are to be "mushy" as the recipe said and not "soft"). They disagree moderately (as to when the apples are done, what to do with what's left on the colander), advise (how to work at the same time with the colander, on adding soap to the dishwater, and how to make room for the colander in the sink), and communicate amused reaction (to water going unexpectedly through the colander). They also regulate who gets to eat apples during their preparation.

Bank Street writers point out that their protocol was written to show that such a routine activity involved many actions, thoughts, and much talk that could be seen as promoting cognitive development. With this purpose in mind, perhaps Bank Street writers simply chose not to emphasize co-operation and peer interaction; perhaps more occurred than was reported. However, if the difference in peer interaction lies less in what occured than in what is reported, this difference still remains at least theoretically significant. From the constructivist perspective, the reciprocity in dialogue and co-operative activity is of central importance for cognitive as well as all other aspects of development. Its de-emphasis in a description oriented to cognitive aspects therefore represents a major difference in conceptualization about what in an activity *is* promoting cognitive development. It also further illustrates the difference in conceptual integration of cognitive and socioemotional aspects.

General Nature of the Teacher-Child Relationship

The differences in children's interactions in Merrill-Palmer and Bank Street accounts are partly due to the general difference in the teacher-child relationship in the two approaches. Differences in conception of the teacher's appropriate use of authority are reflected in the two applesauce accounts. The Bank Street teacher is "Miss Gordon," the leader whose role is central in regulating the cooking and bringing it to a successful conclusion. The constructivist teacher is "Jane," a companion/guide who makes a self-conscious effort to remove herself as the center of the activity and give the cooks the responsibility. In light of this difference, it is not surprising that Bank Street cooks relate more to the teacher and Merrill-Palmer cooks relate more to each other.

In the context of relatively greater teacher direction, Bank Street children seem to take much less initiative and, instead, to follow the teacher's lead for the most part. The Merrill-Palmer teacher, by relating to children as a companion/ guide, deliberately delimiting her role and helping only when necessary, opens the way for children's initiative. She asks for children's honest ideas and pursues their leads by trying to understand more fully what they think and know, and she consults children about what should be done. Her companionable style creates an interpersonal dynamic that frees children to say and do what they really think and feel. In the Merrill-Palmer project are many instances of preoperational thought. Children freely discuss the idea of apples growing in the ground, why apples turn brown, and the relationship between silver and metal. They "read" the recipe in terms of how it makes sense to them, exclaim over "cider" coming out of apples, express surprise over (and reveal lack of anticipation of) water draining from a colander, add water to a bottle of liquid detergent to make "more," and use the colander on the table, only then becoming aware that applesauce drips on the table. They struggle with reading combinations of numerals.

In comparison with the Merrill-Palmer account, the Bank Street activity contains much less frequent and extended preoperational thought. Content of Bank Street children's thought is presented for the most part as correct and "reality-oriented." This difference seems to reflect the difference in attitude toward teacher authority. It is consistent with the observation that when children exercise more autonomy in regulating their activities, they exercise their reasoning more and express it more openly. It seems that when children orient their energies to following the adult's lead, they necessarily direct less energy to spontaneous reflection (or feel less free to express it).

Teacher Interventions to Promote Cognitive Development

Different conceptions of the teacher's role are also reflected in different specific interventions having cognitive aims. The account of applesauce is consistent with the Bank Street conception of the teacher as an authority representing the larger society. As noted, "The teacher is strengthening her role as the one who guides the steps when learning is complex." The Bank Street teacher tries to make children conscious of the various aspects of the cooking process by verbally directing next steps, previewing problems, and explaining. Interventions seem focused on insuring children's success in producing the applesauce.

From the constructivist perspective, the Bank Street activity involves too much teacher direction while at the same time too little intervention fostering children's reasoning. Interventions are not self-consciously aimed at getting children to think, experiment, and figure things out. The intention is for children to be problem solvers (to enhance self-image), and children are involved in carrying out many solutions. However, as noted in our commentary, it is the teacher for the most part who identifies problems and their solutions and makes the decisions. Full advantage is thus not taken of opportunities to encourage children to reason. For example, the use of two kinds of apples offers possibilities that are missed for getting children to anticipate and compare differences. The idea of cooking them separately was given to the children when it might well have come from the children themselves if the teacher had asked whether they think the two would taste the same, look the same, and so on, and whether they can think of what to do to find out. An ideal opportunity for a moral discussion of what is fair is missed in the situation of Janice's concern with the injustice of having fewer jars than Rosina. The teacher also misses opportunities to appeal to children's judgment or get them to refer to the authority of the recipe when she decides they need another hot plate, that more water is needed, and that they should paste labels on the jars. In the instance of showing children how much sugar to add, it is noted, "The teacher points up the relation between an amount and an effect." From a constructivist perspective, this is precisely the problem. Because the teacher does it, children are robbed of the opportunity to construct these correspondences. In the instance of the richest preoperational expression (the exchange concerning "gold" in Golden Delicious apples), the teacher failed to use this opportunity to encourage children's honest thought and exchange of ideas. Rather, she seemed oriented toward reinforcing the child's somewhat uncertain conclusion that "gold" is just a word. In light of the Bank Street teacher's dominant role in this activity, it is perhaps not surprising to find it noted that "when puzzled, the children turn to the teacher." Children in the constructivist activity, too, view the adult as a resource, but rely to a greater extent on themselves and turn to the teacher less frequently.

In contrast with the Bank Street account, the Merrill-Palmer teacher's interventions are designed to foster reflection, experimentation, and co-operation among children. The constructivist conception of the teacher as mentor who facilitates autonomy leads the teacher to refain from directing, making decisions, and solving problems for children. While she remains available to guide when children are unable to take the lead, the teacher capitalizes on opportunities to encourage children to figure out what to do and how to do it. Her questions inspire children to count and divide the apples, think about what size the pieces should be, which strainer is best, how much sugar to put in, and whether they might not have enough applesauce if they eat too many slices. When children ask questions whose answers the teacher thinks they can figure out for themselves, she encourages them to do so (how to cut the apples in pieces, how to get applesauce from the colander into the bowl, how to find out about the spice). As children experiment with the strainers, the teacher intervenes sparingly, supporting their efforts with her interest, and casually focusing on comparisons. When Lee realizes his appleasauce has gone through the colander and onto the table, the teacher simply asks indirect questions to get him to think about how to avoid this.

Bank Street Response to the Constructivist Critique

Biber (personal communication) responds to our analysis with a good deal of disagreement.

In the Bank Street record I see interaction in many forms, not the parallelism you describe. I see children's verbalizations representing communication, cooperation, help and sharing among the four Bank Street children, intermingled with communication with the teacher. They communicate about what they are doing, ask each other questions, check their obervations about what they are doing, ask each other questions, check their observations of kinds of apples, communicate enjoyment, etc. Everyone partakes in labeling the jars.

I see many repeated instances in which the Bank Street teacher, sometimes with content, sometimes with questions, extends the potential that each experience has for cognitive advance in a continuous process of active interchange with the children. I repeat that the teacher role in the Merrill-Palmer image is focused and restricted to the cognitive dimension. In negative criticism you say of Bank Street procedure "when puzzled, the children turn to the teacher." In our view this places the teacher as a resource, not a "dominant" force. The teacher shares her thinking, questions and answers with children; this represents a deeper kind of friendliness. She is not an investigator of cognitive processes, a role which, when dominant, neglects, even denies, the complexity of adult-child interaction.

I consider that the Merrill-Palmer role of the teacher—reducing communication to asking questions, removing the teacher's presence as a way of giving children more autonomous functioning—expresses a lack of recognition of the teacher's complex responsibility in relation to noncognitive processes and her awareness of their interaction with ongoing cognitive processes.

To sum my response to the Merrill-Palmer teacher role: I see the displacement of the teacher role as a knowledgeable, adapting guide of a complex activity to the fixed authority of directions read out of a book (which the teacher as well as the children reads assiduously); I see the repeated use of the question form by the teacher that has directive, at times corrective more than inquiry intent; I see a one-sided, predominantly interrogatory climate in the communication from teacher to children; a false equality in which the teacher tries to position herself as a member of the child group. This does not, as I read it, create an atmosphere of "natural conversations" which is your description of the Merrill-Palmer situation.

To put it mildly, I am surprised at your choice of a book for the children to use as a source for procedures and understanding. How is a depersonalized authority to be taken to signify less authority? Does it make sense to substitute the formalized book instructions for a teacher as the source for enacting procedures—a teacher who will, presumably, take into account and respond to the variability with which individual children undertake unfamiliar operations?

Response to the Bank Street Critique

Our commentary on this Bank Street critique focuses on the teacher's use of questions, the use of the cookbook, and the teacher's egalitarian attitude.

The Teacher's Use of Questions

Questions did dominate the Merrill-Palmer teacher's interaction with the cooks. These were oriented to four aims: (1) to foster children's reasoning about the process of making applesauce, (2) to provide support and share concerns, (3) to respond to children's initiatives, and (4) to gain information she herself could not know.

To foster children's reasoning, the teacher raised issues children seemed not yet to consider, and tried to stimulate thinking about what they were doing. For example, when she noticed that the cooks were eating a lot of the apples, she asked, "Are you going to have enough, though, for everybody if you eat all that?" Later, she reminded them of this consideration in a teasing way. When one of the cooks asked the other where to set the temperature on the frying pan, and the child gave an inadequate answer, the teacher hinted by asking "What's it supposed to be on?" Not telling the answer provided the opportunity for the child then to focus on the number. Many of these questions were consultative in tone. For example, she asked, "How long do you think it's going to take?" and "Do you think it needs more (sugar)?" Particularly important questions stimulated logico-mathematical comparison of the results of using different collanders.

Bank Street critics see these kinds of questions as directive or corrective. While the teacher does aim at getting children to think about particular issues, the children's reactions are not controlled. For example, even though the teacher hoped the children would experiment with adding sugar a little at a time, she did not prevent Lee from dumping in all that was in the cup.

The teacher provided support and shared children's concerns with affirmative rhetorical questions when, for example, cooks exclaimed that cider came out of the colander, and commented that there would be enough applesauce.

Children's initiatives that prompted questions included asking for help with washing dishes ("What do you need?" "Oh, am I the dryer?" "Are you ready for me to dry?"), stating a love for apples ("You do? What kind do you like best?"), and asking "Know what makes more bubbles?" ("What?")

Finally, the teacher asked many questions to elaborate topics introduced by children—about apples that don't come off trees, change in color of apples, an incident with a vegetarian uncle, a different kind of colander at home, and the taste of the applesauce.

In the context of much talk by children, we do not see the teacher's talk as "one-sided" or as creating a "predominantly interrogatory climate." It seems to us that the teacher did "take into account and respond to the variability with which individual children undertake unfamiliar operations."

Directions from the Cookbook

We certainly agree that the cookbook is a source of authority in the Merrill-Palmer activity, as the teacher intended it to be. The cooking context seems to us an excellent opportunity for children to develop good attitudes toward reading, as well as an opportunity for autonomous self-regulation. However, the teacher did not give up all authority, as seen by the instances in which she gave information—reiterating that the idea is to get the apples mushy, rereading the recipe when children forgot what it said, and providing vocabulary ("colander" and "metal"). Further, she took responsibility for coring the apples and pouring the hot applesauce from the frying pan into the bowl.

The Teacher's Egalitarian Attitude

The teacher reduced authority by respecting children's autonomy in a variety of ways. As discussed in Chapter 2, complete equality is not possible, and it is not the constructivist goal. We do not see a "false equality" in the constructivist teacher's interaction with the cooks. Since this Bank Street criticism was not elaborated, we do not know where a false equality seemed to be manifest.

CONCLUDING REFLECTIONS

In this chapter, we have looked at similarities and differences between the developmental-interaction theory and practice of Bank Street and constructivist theory and practice. Differences between these approaches in themselves underline the need in early education for more explicit analyses of all approaches to educational practice in relation to child-development research and theory. Bank Street was selected for analysis because it has for many years represented the best in educational efforts to draw upon theories about child development. However, we argue that further progress is necessary, and that integration with cognitive-developmental theory and practice would address two problems in the Bank Street approach: weakly unified theoretical perspective, and gap between theory and practice.

Weakly Unified Theoretical Perspective

In an effort to provide a comprehensive theory of the "whole child" that integrates socioemotional and cognitive development, Bank Street writers draw upon many sources. These, however, are sometimes contradictory, and it is not specified how they select from and combine theories to constitute a coherent, internally consistent system. Developmental-interactional "theory" seems to be less a unified theory than a collection of points of view supported by unsynthesized bits and pieces from many theories. Our criticism is not based on an objection to eclectic integration as such in educational theory. In Chapter 1 we acknowledge that educational programs cannot be spun directly out of psychological theory but must emerge from a dialectic collaboration between practitioner and formal theory. We do object, however, to eclectic combination of theories that sets the serious practitioner simultaneously down conflicting paths of instructional approaches. The Bank Street eclecticism contains such a troublesome conflict in its orientation to socioemotional and cognitive development.

We noted how Bank Street goals are fractionated, having no common theoretical construct to unify cognitive and socioemotional aspects. While Bank Street writers strongly assert the interdependence of these aspects, the way they are integrated is never adequately articulated, at either the theoretical or practical level. Moreover, while the developmental-interaction approach uses both cognitive and ego stage formulations, the primary emphasis on neopsychoanalytic stages in socioemotional development is not matched at the level of practice with a similar emphasis on stages in cognitive development. This leads to a certain contradiction between principles of teaching related to socioemotional aspects and those related to cognitive aspects. When the teacher's goal in realizing the cognitive aspects of Bank Street goals is specified, the emphasis on constructive error in stagewise development from within frequently disappears.

While Bank Street theory shares many strands with the constructivist view (commonly acknowledged, too, by Bank Street writers), they also espouse certain theoretical rationales and teaching practices that contradict this body of theory. In particular, the developmental-interactional marriage of theories has left relatively unintegrated a neopsychoanalytic theory of emotional develop-ment stressing progress arising from within and a practical approach to cognitive development that seems to us often close to the empiricist and cultural trans-mission views (which we criticized in Chapter 1). In our view, Bank Street's neopsychoanalytic approach to play has not yet merged fully as a true integration with a Piagetian concern for cognitive development.

Gap between Theory and Practice

We have noted, in a number of illustrations of Bank Street teaching, certain contradictions between the explicit or implicit theory underlying these practices and cognitive-developmental theory. We also observed that Bank Street does not provide a clear, coherent theoretical perspective that prevents advocacy of practices having contradictory theoretical assumptions. Furthermore, theore-tical justification of many practices is either lacking or imprecise. This loose relation between Bank Street theory and practice is due to the fact that, on the one hand, Bank Street practices are not derived principally from theory, and, on the other hand, developmental-interaction theory is not sufficiently explicitly articulated to provide a solid developmental justification for many specific practices. In part, this loose theory-practice relation results from the fact that Bank Street was developing its early practices when developmental theory itself was in its infancy. As noted in our review of Bank Street evolution, Dewey's philosophy provided the basis for definition of practices. Emerging psycho-dynamic and cognitive theories played principally a corroborating and validating role rather than leading directly to critique and revision of practices. While Bank Street presents its practices as having strong theoretical justification, a clear articulation of this justification has not been provided. In part, the loose relation between theory and practice may be due to a less intensive and less close relation between program designers and teachers than is found in the constructivist approach we advocate.

THEORY AND EDUCATIONAL PRACTICE RECONSIDERED

Our discussion of the Bank Street program raises some general theoretical issues about the relationship between constructivist theory (elaborated in earlier chapters of this book) and psychoanalytic and neopsychoanalytic theories of child development as they pertain to education. We offer some concluding thoughts on the relation between these theories and education.

The field of early education has suffered from a false division, the division between the cognitive-intellectual and the social-emotional aspects of the child's development. At its worst, this has been reflected in the view that time spent on intellectual development is time taken from social and emotional development, and vice versa. Those emphasizing the intellectual from an academic perspective tend to view as wasted time spent in peer play and teacher-child focus on wishes and feelings. Such time would be better spent, in their view, in "learning" "skills" needed in later life. Contrariwise, those emphasizing the socioemotional tended to view "cognitive activities" as taking place at the expense of expression of feelings and other experiences necessary for socioemotional growth.

Most theories of social growth such as the psychoanalytic cannot be integrated with constructivist theory because they stress the child's individuality and processes of social-emotional growth that do not relate to cognitive experience and cognitive development. In these theories social-emotional growth is seen as a matter of the maturation and regulation of new needs and the liberation of old needs from conflict and anxiety. The resulting definition of the educator's role is to provide the individual child's needs for affection, for aggression, for gratification, and for the right balance of expression and control for a healthy emotional integration.

One can hardly deny that the teacher should be sensitive to the individual child and his emotional concerns and to try to see that life in the classroom takes account in a constructive way of his individual pattern of concerns and emotional strengths and weaknesses. Such a sensitivity by the teacher, however, does not create a set of positive objectives for social development that the teacher can implement through planning and using the activities of the classroom as a whole. Sensitivity to the individual child's needs does not lead to a "curriculum" (in the broad sense) in the socioemotional area any more than it does in the intellectual area.

Another problem in trying to integrate psychoanalytic and cognitive theory results from the fact that, in practice, the psychoanalytic approach tends to focus on the pathological, the negative, or the disturbed. Both theoretical and practical considerations suggest that this is a poor focus for educational practice. It is a legitimate criticism of cognitive-developmental theory that it gives an inadequate account of the role of conflict and anxiety in human life and human development. It is an equally legitimate criticism of clinical and Freudian theories that they provide not only a distorted version of "normal" processes of growth and development but that they provide a misleading notion of the developmental significance of the negative and the disturbed. Kohlberg and Colleagues (1987) discuss the logical and empirical faults of approaches that define educational goals in mental health terms. Their review of the studies of the longitudinal or adult outcomes of traits of childhood emotional disturbance indicates that psychological and clinical ratings of childhood disturbances do not predict adult life adjustment or pathology. Many emotional "symptoms" are not symptoms at all. As an example, "shyness" or "withdrawal" is a temperamental trait of introversion combined with situational factors rather than a warning of later neurosis, schizophrenia, or autism. Many other "symptoms" are products of situational forces or of temporary developmental crises, symptoms which spontaneously disappear with time. In contrast, measures of retardation of ego development do have validity in predicting adult life adjustment. Their conclusion is that a concern for stimulating ego development is a more valid long-range concern than a concern for therapy for emotional symptoms.

These problems in integrating theories of socioemotional and cognitive development in educational practice need to be resolved, so that the socioemotional also becomes a sphere of "curriculum" with specific practical implications that go beyond teacher sensitivity to children's individual needs. As spelled out in Chapters 5 and 6 constructivist programs address this problem by including discussion of moral/social dilemmas, democratic decision making, and group games, as well as group projects (the latter, of course, not being unique to constructivist programs). These activities shift the teacher's focus from "therapeutic" concern with pathology to concern with positive aspects of development.

From a practical point of view, this focus is justified by ample documentation of the "Pygmalion" effect in the classroom though the scope or power of this effect is uncertain.[9] The problem is not only one of expectations that segregate and demean, but of weakening the positive expectations for the child's behavior and development. The expectation that all children can respond responsibly and with awareness of others is important for the development of each child and for the maintenance of a positive or fair moral or social atmosphere of the classroom as a whole.

In summary, it is realistic to say that many children do have negative emotional preoccupations and that the teacher should develop some sensitivity and skill in dealing with them. It is even more basic, however, to say that the

---

9. The Pygmalion effect refers to the self-fulfilling quality of the teacher's expectations for individual children. Teachers arbitrarily told that a child has been certified "creative" by tests tend to treat the child in a more positive, responsive way so that the child actually tends to improve in objective performance.

teacher needs positive developmental social-emotional goals and approaches to stimulating development and that this concern should dominate her basic dealings with each child and with the group as a whole.

Most early educators seek a theory of the "whole child" that will define socioemotional goals that can be integrated with stimulation of cognitive development. As we have tried to show in this chapter, while the Bank Street developmental interaction theory holds out the promise of doing this, the integration is more easily said than done. We suggest that Piagetian theory contributes to a better integration by providing a common theoretical framework for important aspects of both socioemotional and cognitive development. Such theoretical constructs as "constructivism," "decentering," "coordination of relationships," "co-operation," "empirical and reflective abstraction," and "autonomy and heteronomy" apply equally to cognitive and socioemotional growth. Piaget-derived goals and programs are conceptualized with explicit concern for how cognitive and socioemotional development are facilitated simultaneously. In particular, the psychological nature of the teacher-child relationship is specified not only in terms of warmth and trust but also in terms of the reduction of adult authority necessary for the child's exercise of full intellectual, moral, social, and emotional autonomy. Further, constructivist program advocates have tried to provide explicit description of practices in terms of detailed classroom interactions, without, however, falling into "cookbook" programming. By clearly linking specific theory and specific practices, such an approach seems to contribute to progress in the development theory of educational practice. In short, it seems to us that Piagetian cognitive-developmental and constructivist theory and practice improve upon the Bank Street effort to provide an educational program reflecting a comprehensive, integrated theoretical view of the "whole child." We believe the Bank Street approach to the socioemotional would be strengthened by the sociomoral "curriculum" described in Chapter 6 just as we also believe its approach to cognitive development would be strengthened by the cognitive "curriculum" described in Chapters 4–8.

Chapter 11

The Future of Cognitive-Developmental and Constructivist Early Education

We have tried throughout this book to call attention to the nature of the child's psychological experience in programs of early education that are broadly compatible with cognitive-developmental (and within cognitive-developmental, constructivist) assumptions about human development. Two themes presented here are:

1. The nature of the child's *psychological experience* in school affects possibilities for developmental progress—social, intellectual, affective, and moral.
2. The educational *worldviews of teachers* are implicit in classroom practices that affect the nature of the child's psychological experience in school.

These themes in relation to affective (and to some extent, social) development have been appreciated by those in the child-centered or child-development tradition in early education. However, this tradition[1] (from which current cognitive-developmental programs borrow a great deal) has had a tough time getting accepted as education. Child care, yes; education, no. In part, this attitude reflects the romantic stream of educational thought that dominated nursery school education until the 1960s when concern about cognitive development in the preschool years began to emerge. Until that time, a more or less comfortable schism existed between the romantic view in nursery school and the cultural transmission view in elementary school. Disagreement over the goals of kindergarten education may be viewed in terms of a struggle between these two worldviews, and since the 1960s, the debate has been extended to preschool.

To the extent that play and child autonomy have been accepted as educationally valid, receptivity has generally been based on recognition that before the age of about 6 years, children cannot accommodate easily to the structure of teacher-directed academic work. However, where acceptance of a

1. The Montessori Method is part of this tradition.

child-centered approach to preschool or kindergarten education has occurred, the goal has usually still reflected the cultural-transmission view. That is, the aim is to get children ready for the demands of an academic classroom—rather than to promote developmental progress in the broad domains with which constructivist education is concerned. In general, educational practices are dominated by the cultural-transmission school of thought that contradicts central assumptions of constructivist theory and philosophy. Thus, readiness training often infiltrates the child-centered tradition in the form of high priorities for listening to and obeying the teacher, and learning colors, shapes, numerals, and letters through lessons and worksheets. From a constructivist perspective, these priorities trivialize the goals of early education. We have argued throughout this book for more ambitious, longer-range objectives that nevertheless include the very academic objectives generally believed too little emphasized in traditional child-centered programs.

Cognitive-developmental and constructivist programs offer alternatives to those inspired by romantic or cultural transmission schools of thought. These alternatives preserve much of the child-centered approach while modifying and strengthening cognitive and sociomoral aims and experiences. How widespread are these cognitive-developmental programs? How well accepted are cognitive developmental and constructivist worldviews? We have sought information on these questions from other leaders connected with a variety of cognitive developmental programs. Their answers indicate increasing interest, active exploration, and acceptance. The influence of these leaders is felt through their publications;[2] films, filmstrips, and slide-cassette presentations;[3] videotapes;[4] and teaching of undergraduate and graduate students in university programs.[5]

Programs providing cognitive-developmental and constructivist education to children are scattered across the United States and elsewhere. For example, over 300 High/Scope trainers are active in the United States, Peru, Chile,

2. Many of these are published in languages other than English, including Spanish, French, Portuguese, Japanese, German, Dutch, and Greek.
3. For example, Kamii, DeVries, Ellis, and Zaritsky (1975) made a film on a physical-knowledge activity, which is available through Indiania University, and High/Scope has a number of films available from the High/Scope Foundation. Lavatelli's (1971a, 1971b) filmstrips on her program are available through Knowledge Tree Films. A set of slides and accompanying text on the Montessori Method is available through the American Montessori Society.
4. For example, Sigel (1979) has a videotape, "Educating the Young Thinker," available from the Educational Testing Service in Princeton, New Jersey, and Kamii (1986) has a videotape, "How Young Children Learn to Think," available from the National Association for the Education of Young Children.
5. All colleges and universities have courses in which cognitive-developmental and constructivist theory and research are taught, and many teacher education programs include components on constructivist education if not a major emphasis.

Ecuador, and Bolivia, with informal relationships in other countries. Sigel's program is implemented in a private school in Honolulu. The Kamii-DeVries program is currently implemented in Chicago, Houston, and Homewood, Alabama. Kamii reports the formation of a statewide consortium of about 20 school administrators who meet every six to eight weeks in School Executives' Work Conferences to study constructivist education, under the general leadership of Dr. Milly Cowles, dean of the School of Education at the University of Alabama at Birmingham. The Montessori Method is found in most major U.S. cities as well as many other countries.

Despite a good deal of progress in disseminating ideas and establishing programs, cognitive-developmental and constructivist educational ideas are far from being well integrated in mainstream education. The programs described in this book have been implemented in public schools primarily as federally funded experimental programs and have often been dropped when outside funding ceased. The friendliest reception has been from professionals in preschool education and day care (many associated with university-based preschools) who are outside mainstream public and private education. Nevertheless, cognitive developmental and constructivist views are gaining ground. Begun only in the late 1960s and early 1970s, these programs have expanded and are beginning to influence not only preschool but also primary school education.

We conclude by discussing briefly four core issues bearing on the future of constructivist education because this is the cognitive-developmental approach we know best. These issues are the development of constructivist teachers, the relation of constructivist education to the teaching of subject matter, and the development of applied constructivist theory. Finally, we discuss evaluating the effectiveness of cognitive-developmental and constructivist program effectiveness.

TEACHER DEVELOPMENT

The future of constructivist education rests on developing constructivist teachers. Becoming a constructivist teacher involves bringing to consciousness implicit beliefs about learning and child development, examining these, and constructing a new way of thinking that is different from both the cultural-transmission and romantic views discussed in Chapter 1.

Some of the romantic views to be given up include beliefs that children's intelligence is innate and simply matures with age, that the major early developmental goals are affective, that intellectual stimulation is best postponed until school age, and that the major purpose of preschool is to help children resolve emotional conflicts that have arisen in the family. Becoming a constructivist teacher does not mean giving up a commitment to promoting children's emotional development, but it means integrating this commitment with cognitive and sociomoral goals. Cognitive and sociomoral development also become appreciated in terms of early developmental roots and experience that stimulates progress.

To be more specific about some of the empiricist or cultural-transmission ideas that constructivist teachers give up and about the new ideas that replace them, consider three shifts, from: (1) *instruction to construction,* (2) *reinforcement to interest,* and (3) *obedience to autonomy* (or, *coercion to co-operation*).

From Instruction to Construction

The teacher who focuses on instruction views teaching as transmission of information. In traditional teacher training, the emphasis is on subject matter and how to present it to children. The teacher's preoccupation is with instructing through sequencing content, drilling, correcting, and testing. In contrast, for teachers informed by Piaget's theory, the preoccupation is not the teacher's *in*struction, but the child's *con*struction. Preoccupation with the child's construction presumes knowledge about the mind of the child and its development. Without this knowledge, teachers will not understand children's spontaneous efforts and may view them as a waste of time and beside the point of educational aims.

In moving away from an emphasis on didactic instruction of children, a danger exists of going off the deep end of romantic philosophy. Some teachers fall into the romantic trap of leaving children to play without adding the stimulation of special activities or asking intriguing questions children will be motivated to try to figure out. Some nursery school teachers in the child-centered tradition reflect both the romantic school of thought (for example, in leaving children to build with blocks, pretend, and so on) and the cultural-transmission school of thought (for example, in didactic lessons on colors, letters, and numerals).

Consider the preoccupation with drill in the transmission of information. The common assumption is that if children do not know something, they should practice it by reciting the right answers. However, from a constructivist perspective, when a child does not understand instruction, it is very often because he *cannot.* Therefore, perhaps the worst thing we can do is make that child do more of what he cannot do.

Another preoccupation related to instruction is teachers' commitment to eradicating children's errors. The cultural-transmission view of education leads to the conviction that the responsible teacher tells a child when she is wrong and corrects the child's mistakes. In contrast, the teacher informed by Piaget's theory has a healthy respect for errors as an important part of the constructive process. As discussed in Chapter 2, constructivist teachers' responses depend on the kind of knowledge involved in an error. If it is an error of physical knowledge that can be corrected by the child through her own observation and action, the teacher encourages the child to test out her idea. If an error is logico-mathematical in nature and depends for its correction on the child's deductive reasoning, the constructivist teacher explores and accepts the child's ideas, and finds ways to inspire continued thought.[6] If an error in arbitrary or conventional knowledge occurs, the teacher does provide correction in a friendly manner.

Preoccupation with testing leads teachers to believe that tests tell what children know. However, most tests only scratch the surface of right answers. They tell us nothing about why wrong answers make sense to children. The constructivist teacher wants to understand the child's reasoning behind wrong answers. This is information that will inform teaching. Preoccupation with testing is so entrenched in American education—and has become more so in the last few years—that not only do teachers teach for tests, but teaching itself often becomes just more testing. Consider the widespread use of worksheets. These amount to tests because a child cannot learn anything new by doing them. If he doesn't know the right answer, he can't understand why he is wrong; and if he knows it already, he doesn't need the practice.

In some ways, it is much easier to teach with a focus on behavior. With this focus, the teacher is the instructor who transmits information and tests children on whether they can give back this information. However, when children *fail* to give back correct information, it is *more* difficult to teach in this behavioristic fashion. It is more difficult because more of the methods that *already* failed continue to fail.

When traditional education fails, it is not the child's failure so much as the failure of *instruction*. Piaget's work gives us the basis for an alternative to the kind of education that has failed. This alternative requires that we revise how we think about what the child can know. This leads to revision of how we think about what we do.

From Reinforcement to Interest

Behaviorist teachers in the cultural-transmission school of educational thought believe children learn through the motivation of reinforcement. This assumption is built upon the idea of the child as basically a passive responder to environmental stimuli. From this perspective, the role of the school is to arrange environmental stimulation to modify the individual's behavior through conditioning. The teacher is concerned about reward and punishment as the essential mechanisms for changing the child's behavior. With this model of the child in mind, the teacher focuses on strengthening, weakening, extinguishing, or maintaining behavior through positive and negative reinforcement. Preoccupation with reinforcement leads to efforts aimed at artificially motivating children—for example, with gold stars or other rewards.

---

6. The teacher's role in the construction of logico-mathematical knowledge is complex, and we refer the reader to Chapter 7 for extensive discussion of number and arithmetic. We do not mean to suggest that the teacher never provides correct logico-mathematical knowledge, but that it is important to be sensitive to a child's ability to assimilate such knowledge.

In contrast, the constructivist notion is that the child learns through the motivation of interest. Piaget's emphasis on interest can be found throughout his writings (see Chapter 2). In his theory of the equilibration process by which cognitive structures change, Piaget (1975/1985) gave interest a central role. Even in infancy, interest is crucial to elaboration of cognitive structures. For example, interest in an object out of reach on a rug can lead to substitution of interest in the rug and construction of the solution by pulling the rug as a means to the end of getting the object. This is one example of how intelligence becomes more differentiated through compensations constructed when actions fail and the child integrates these perturbations into the cognitive system (Piaget, 1975/1985, p. 77).

In speaking about interest, Piaget echoed John Dewey who wrote more extensively on the importance of interest in intellectual development with reference to the educational context. Dewey's (1913/1975) book, *Interest and Effort in Education*, is an excellent presentation of his argument that effort without interest creates divided attention and a divided self when the child thinks about an uninteresting task only while external pressure is applied. As soon as it lets up, his attention turns to what interests him. Dewey cites as uneducative tasks that mean to the child only sheer strain, constraint, and the need for external motivation for persisting at them. He says such tasks are uneducative because they fail to produce in the child a clearer consciousness of their ends or a search for how to realize these. Dewey also criticizes such tasks as miseducative because they "deaden and stupefy," leading to a confused and dulled state of mind that occurs when an action is carried out without a sense of what it's all about (Dewey, 1913/1975, p. 55). Like Piaget, Dewey criticized heteronomous experiences because they lead to dependence on externals—the avoidance of punishment or attainment of reward having no connection to what the child is doing. He called attention to the problem of arrested development when "illegitimate interest" is aroused by sugar coating a basically uninteresting activity (for example, with bribes), or by coercion (for example, with threats of punishment). Divided attention brings a disintegration of intellectual and moral character because the child learns how to give just enough attention to external demands to satisfy authorities.

Dewey advocated intrinsically motivating experiences as essential for the development of a united self and real understanding of subject matter. That is, educational experiences should be based on children's interests, powers, and tendencies in action, and should aim to increase children's intellectual and moral powers as well as increase understanding of subject matter.

We have given many examples in this book of how constructivist teachers can promote development by appealing to children's interests, in contrast with cultural transmission methods that rely on reinforcement. We should, however, point out a danger of falling into the romantic school of educational thought by only considering general interest in a type of activity rather than specific interest in reasoning about particular problems within that activity. For example, we have observed teachers who provide water as an activity without much thought about materials and questions to challenge reasoning and move development forward. Dewey noted the importance of introducing at an appropriate moment an element of work (not drudgery, but production of an object of value) when children are ready for something more than play that requires reflective thought.

From Obedience to Autonomy (or, Coercion to Co-operation)

This shift in teachers thinking from obedience to autonomy (or from coercion to co-operation) involves the teacher's most basic conception of what she tries to do and how she tries to do it. Obedience is implicit in the cultural-transmission view of learning in which children must orient toward teachers as their main source of information and rules for behavior. In contrast, autonomy (self-regulation) is implicit in the constructivist view of learning in which children orient more toward their own actions and interactions with others as their main source of knowledge and reasons for behaving.

The teacher who views obedience as a high priority usually resorts to coercive methods—to the heteronomous relation with children discussed in Chapter 2. While heteronomous practices can be seen as a continuum from outright hostile and punitive methods to sugar-coated coercion, they have in common an emphasis on *obedient behavior*. The teacher is clearly the authority, and children's behavior is regulated by what the teacher wants. In contrast, the constructivist teacher is a companion and guide who expresses respect for children and practices co-operation rather than coercion (see Chapter 2). In the constructivist view, affective reciprocity in mutual affection is part of the foundation for reciprocity in reasoning.

Moving toward Constructivist Teaching

It is not easy to make these shifts in one's thinking about teaching and learning. Some people have to overcome romantic tendencies in thinking about young children. But most people have to overcome tendencies to authoritarian relations with children. This is partly because of the upbringing most have had, and partly because teacher training has given us this model of the teacher. The shifts described above are really basic shifts in attitude and way of being. It is often painful to engage in the necessary self-examination and work of changing one's self.

In order to discuss contrasting teacher orientations, we set up the polarities of instruction versus construction, reinforcement versus interest, and obedience versus autonomy (or coercion versus co-operation). However, these shifts in teachers thinking are actually shifts of emphasis. The constructivist teacher does sometimes instruct, does sometimes reinforce, and is sometimes coercive. Knowing the when, what, and why of instruction is a lot harder than simply asserting instruction and construction as thesis and antithesis. Knowing how to use reinforcement to foster children's assimilation of social-arbitrary knowledge, how to encourage experimentation in constructing physical knowledge and logico-mathematical knowledge, and how to support efforts to interact and co-operate with others is a lot harder than thinking in absolute terms about re-inforcement and interest. Similarly, knowing how to decide when it is necessary to be coercive, and how to insist on obedience without damaging the development of autonomy is harder than thinking of coercion and co-operation in either-or terms. One can imagine an emphasis on construction, interest, and autonomy that would fall into the romantic school of educational philosophy. To avoid this as well as the cultural-transmission philosophy, the constructivist teacher must make a dialectical integration that transcends these polarities.

Constructivism is not just a process for children's development. Teachers, too, construct their conception of what constructivist teaching means and their convictions about it. New questions and concerns emerge that must be worked out in the course of teaching and discussion with colleagues. In our experience, progress toward becoming a constructivist teacher is marked by a struggle having at least four aspects, discussed below.

SKEPTICISM.   The first reaction to constructivist educational ideas is often total rejection: "It won't work." Then there is the skepticism in the reaction, "I can't do it," and "These children can't do it." Another type of skepticism is concern that the teaching of content will be lost: "Reasoning and moral development are nice, but what about reading and writing?" The teacher may be concerned about whether children are wasting time. As if the teacher's own skepticism were not enough, there is the skepticism of parents and school administrators. This book tries to answer extreme forms of skepticism on these points while encouraging a critical and reflective viewpoint by the teacher.

CHANGING THE ENVIRONMENT.   This aspect of the teacher's struggle is characterized by such questions as "How do I arrange the room?" "What materials do I need?" "What activities do I write on the lesson plan?" A teacher new to constructivist teaching typically goes through a period of anxiety over not having enough for children to do. The development of a repertoire of activities is important. As the repertoire becomes richer, the teacher also becomes more flexible in planning and changing plans to follow up on children's ideas and interests.

Obstacles encountered in this struggle are both internal and external. Administrators may not be supportive. Fellow teachers may be critical, and their skepticism may increase the teacher's own self-doubts. There may be no place to *put* the desks to be removed from the classroom. The floor may be too cold for children. The budget may not be large enough to provide all the materials desired. Making materials takes a lot of time. The classroom cannot be fully equipped all at once. When a teacher is beginning constructivist teaching, it is hard to know just what to give first priority.

These difficulties can be eased by apprenticeships with teachers who have resolved them, by visiting classrooms where the program is already implemented, and by getting solidly into a social network in which difficulties can be discussed. Mutual support from colleagues cannot be too strongly emphasized. Different people will be learning different things, and everyone can be a resource for someone.

CHANGING TEACHING STYLE. Once the issue of environment is resolved, questions about the teacher's role arise. Teachers often say, "I used to *know* what to do and say to children, but suddenly I seem immobilized." In this struggle, the teacher must confront questions such as "What do I say?" "What do I do?" "*How* do I reduce my authority and not have chaos?" This struggle may be heightened by new problems that will emerge in children's behavior. In a coercive environment, children suppress a lot. In a co-operative environment, the teacher gives up a lot of control, and emotional difficulties are more freely expressed. It is sometimes small consolation to realize that these difficulties will not be overcome unless they are expressed so the teacher can work on them. Too, children who are accustomed to a coercive environment in school may react to the new freedom by testing it to see what its limits are. In trying to shift to a co-operative style, teachers sometimes have difficulty being coercive when this is necessary (for example, when they have to follow through in enforcing classroom rules). They have to learn when it is necessary to be heteronomous and in such situations how to exercise authority in a way that still preserves children's autonomy as much as possible. Seasoned constructivist teachers point out that when they must enforce rules (for example, to prevent harm to children) it is important to give reasons that children can understand. Similarly, when they must punish serious rule-breaking (for example, in cases of physical aggression), constructivist teachers emphasize the importance of explanation and use of natural consequences (for example, intentionally hurting someone is the sole occasion for being deprived for a time of the opportunity to play with others), and offering possibilities for restitution (such as helping to put a Band-Aid on a hurt child).

Giving up coercive techniques to control children is the hardest task for many teachers. Giving up personal control sometimes feels to the teacher as though she is giving up responsibility. However, if child autonomy is to be fostered, the teacher has to give the child freedom to control himself. This is scary because it is hard to know whether children can. The teacher new to constructivist teaching is skeptical with good reason. Children accustomed to being regulated by adults do not know how to take responsibility for their actions at the first opportunity for autonomy. Developing children's autonomy takes time. The teacher's development of confidence in children's ability also takes time.

Teachers struggling with their own role have difficulty following the first principle of constructivist teaching: to think about how children are thinking and feeling. This difficulty may be due to one of the following reasons.

1. Some teachers spend such a large proportion of their time in classroom organization that they give themselves little opportunity to observe children's reasoning.

2. Some teachers provide few activities that inspire children's reasoning.
3. When engaging in activities, some teachers relate to children in an authoritarian way that requires children to try to figure out what the teacher wants them to say. This cuts off or circumvents children's spontaneous reasoning.

In the Human Development Lab School at the University of Houston, the main problem for new teachers is how to talk to children—and also how not to talk too much. Experienced constructivist teachers say that one of the hardest things they had to do was to eliminate from their vocabulary "Don't," "Stop," and "Because I say so." They had to retrain themselves on how to express respect for children. This means consulting with children, asking children for solutions to problems, and giving real choices that preserve the child's control of his behavior. Teachers in the lab have found it helpful to know "words to say" as they work out their understanding of what it means to respect children, consult them, and give them choices. For example, they learned to ask new kinds of questions. They gave up asking for information, and began asking questions that appeal to action. In shadow activities, for example, teachers had to overcome a desire to get children to *tell* about shadows. Instead, they found it more productive to inspire experimentation by suggesting effects like "Could you make the shadow bigger/longer?" and asking "What would happen if . . . (you backed up, or raised your flashlight higher, etc.)?"

All this takes a lot longer than telling children what to do. At first, teachers will be skeptical of the worth of taking this time. Teachers are not *really* convinced until they see changes in children.

AUTONOMY.   Conviction about teaching based on theoretical rationale characterizes teacher autonomy. Like constructivism, autonomy is not just for children. The autonomous constructivist teacher knows not only *what* to do, but *why*. She has a solid network of convictions that are both practical and theoretical. The autonomous teacher can think about how children are thinking and at the same time think about how to intervene to promote the constructive process. Autonomy, too, is reflected in new ways of evaluating teaching effectiveness, new ways of assessing learning. The teacher becomes sensitive to subtle but profound changes in children.

Teachers in the Human Development Lab emphasize in particular that to attain autonomy meant overcoming elementary education training and their own childhood educational experiences. They report finding that once this is accomplished their growth continues to be stimulated as children keep providing new actions and reactions to which their teaching must be adapted.

Autonomous teachers do not just accept uncritically what curriculum specialists give them. They *think* about whether they agree with what is suggested. They take responsibility for the education they are offering children.

THE TEACHING OF SUBJECT MATTER

Traditional instructional orientation has generally led to subject-matter analysis with the objective of sequencing content from simple to complex. Unfortunately, this usually reflects a definition of what is simplest from the adult perspective. Seldom is this simplest for children.

Constructivist curriculum development did not start with the teaching of subject matter as a first priority. Rather, the first priority was to devise activities and a classroom atmosphere to promote reasoning and autonomy in children. However, teaching subject matter cannot be isolated from fostering reasoning and autonomy, since these are always exercised in relation to some content. Without a concern for subject matter, efforts to implement cognitive-developmental and constructivist programs may fall into the romantic stream.

Subject matter is represented in the content of constructivist activity components. Reading is embedded in many group games, in pretend play (for example, menus and signs in a "restaurant"), in cooking using specially designed teacher-made cookbboks (one book of recipes for children has been published by Chicago colleagues—University of Illinois Children's Center, 1985), and many other activities discussed in Chapter 8. Writing is embedded in pretend play (for example, writing customers' orders in the "restaurant"), in daily living in school (for example, writing an invitation to another class to take a walk), and in holiday celebrations (for example, writing invitations to parents for a Valentine lunch), in attendance checks, and many other situations. Elementary science is represented in physical-knowledge activities, as discussed in Chapter 4. Curriculum involving elementary arithmetic is perhaps best developed in group games and daily living activities, as discussed in Chapter 7.

While the constructivist approach takes seriously the goal of teaching subject matter, it begins not with subject-matter analysis, but with child analysis—with thinking about how children think about subject matter. Teaching informed by Piaget's theory must be based on knowledge of mental development within a subject-matter domain (as illustrated by the description of developmental levels in children's conceptions of shadow phenomena). Further research is needed to identify the course of developmental progress for other contents that are accessible to children's thought. However, teachers do not have to wait for researchers to tell them what content to teach. With the criteria given in this book for constructivist activities as a guide, the teacher can select likely content and experiment in the classroom to find out whether children respond with interest and productive action.

Looking over many curriculum materials in early education leads to the conclusion that it is not so easy to find appropriate content objectives and activities. Much that is recommended to teachers is too easy for preschool children, belaboring what they already know. For example, one finds lessons that are supposed to teach that you smell with your nose, many things move, cars take you places, and that airplanes fly. Other content recommended to teachers is inaccessible to children's reasoning. For example, one finds lessons to teach that fire needs air to burn, that water evaporates into the air, and that light from the sun bounces off the moon (Mallinson, Mallinson, Smallwood, & Valentino, 1985). Such ideas are inaccessible to the young child's reasoning because the interaction of elements and action of light cannot be observed. Understanding this kind of subject matter requires deductions that go beyond the observable. As pointed out in Chapter 3, most of the Genevan tasks require operational reasoning for understanding, and are thus not appropriate as educational activities. Much more practical classroom research is needed to develop recommendations to teachers about what content appeals to children's interests and stimulates constructive activity.

While the general outlines of a constructivist approach to early education are fairly clear, curriculum has not been developed in some areas (for example, music[7]). Moreover, constructivist curriculum development for primary school education is very incomplete. Much work is needed in programs of arithmetic, reading, and in physical and social sciences as well as the arts. Piagetian work is especially weak in aesthetic development (however, see Parsons, 1987, on stages in the development of appreciation of paintings).

APPLIED CONSTRUCTIVIST THEORY

Piaget's theoretical concerns were broadly epistemological with a focus on the hypothetical or epistemic subject. Piaget did not aim to provide a theory of individual development, though his theory is often useful in understanding aspects of individual development. The need remains for further research and theory building directly applicable to educational concerns.

Constructivist educational settings can provide an important context for further revision and development of constructivist theory. For example, recent revisions of Piaget's conception of childhood egocentrism may be tested and elaborated by studies in settings where teachers work specifically on helping children become less egocentric. The role of contradiction in cognitive development may be elaborated by studies of children's reactions to failures of their efforts in physical-knowledge activities and group games. The role of contradiction in sociomoral development may be elaborated by studies of children's interactions in classrooms where teachers consciously make interpersonal conflict part of the curriculum and engage children in moral discussions that confront children with diverse points of view. The theory Piaget constructed can be tested and revised through research in educational settings where its practical implications are taken seriously.

Research on developmental levels in children's construction of knowledge about subject matter (such as shadow phenomena discussed in Chapter 4) will not only be useful to teacher's practical work with children, but will contribute to

---

7. Though Bamberger (1980) has proposed a developmental account of children's construction of symbolic thought with regard to simple rhythms.

the development of a theory of educational practice. Such a theory can then guide further curriculum development.

EVALUATION OF COGNITIVE-DEVELOPMENTAL EDUCATION

Evaluation of the effects of early education has grown out of research on the effects of early experience. While we do not attempt a full review here of research on early experience, we remind the reader of the long debate on this issue. In the 1930s evidence began to accumulate that extreme lack of stimulation in infancy and early childhood resulted in serious defects in physical, cognitive, and social development (see reviews by Horowitz & Paden, 1973; Lazar & Darlington, 1982; and Clarke-Stewart, 1982). Several decades later a variety of influences converged to put the emphasis on evaluating cognitive effects of early experience, especially as represented by IQ. One of these was Hunt's (1961) review of the literature and his conclusion that intelligence is not fixed but subject to change. Another was Bloom's (1964) analyses of psychometric studies leading him to the conclusion that 50% of intellectual development occurs by age 4. Also, during the 1960s, the cumulative deficit hypothesis was proposed—that the gap between lower- and middle-class children widens over time. While still debated, all these contributed to the tide of optimistic opinion that early education could rescue disadvantaged children from a fate of failure in school and life. On the basis of collected opinion, federal programs such as Head Start, Follow Through, and Parent-Child Centers were established.

Most educational research has looked at schools as they are. Following Dewey, progressive education (the forerunner of cognitive-developmental and constructivist education) both rejects this kind of research and is a challenge to research, since the goals of developmental education are different from those of traditional education. We refer the reader to Kohlberg and Colleagues (1987) for reviews of cognitive-developmental research pointing to the validity of cognitive-developmental educational aims.

Cognitive-developmental research in education requires first the development and implementation of new programs in classrooms, then studying these with new methods that reflect cognitive-developmental aims. Where cognitive-developmental programs have been implemented, it is unfortunate that most evaluation research has not reflected cognitive-developmental aims. We give a very brief overview below of some of the major studies of the effects of early education, and then turn to studies of the effects of constructivist education.

Longitudinal Studies

Longitudinal studies of the effects of early education provide information on the difference between preschool experience versus no preschool experience, and on differences between preschool programs. Unfortunately, in these studies children experience a special program for a limited time and then are evaluated after extended experience in regular schools.

Preschool versus No Preschool Experience

COGNITIVE EFFECTS.   Most research on the effects of early education has reflected the cultural-transmission view of the cognitive aim of education—with psychometric measures of IQ and achievement dominating evaluation concerns. Although some of the programs studied were cognitive-developmental, their validation was sought in cultural-transmission terms. In general, optimism about long-range increase in psychometric intelligence due to preschool education has not been strongly supported by follow-up data. This, however, does not imply that early education does not have other positive long-range effects, a conclusion supported by recent findings.

The widely publicized results from a High/Scope study (Berruta-Clement, Schweinhart, Barnett, Epstein, and Weikart, 1984; Weikart, Schweinhart, & Barnett, 1985) show that at age 19, children from the Perry Preschool Project (out of which the High/Scope Preschool Curriculum developed) are significantly higher than a control group (without any preschool experience) in proportion of high school graduates (67% and 49%), average or above scores on a test of functional competence, enrollment in postsecondary education (38% and 21%), and classification as mentally retarded (15% and 35%). They also spent less time in special education classes (16% and 28% of school years).

In an analysis of pooled data from 12 program follow-up studies,[8] lasting effects of early education are reported by the Consortium for Longitudinal Studies (Lazar & Darlington, 1982). In comparison with control groups, children with preschool had less likelihood of later assignment to special education classes and retention in grade, greater likelihood of pride in achievement, higher self-rating of school performance, and greater maternal satisfaction with child's school performance and higher maternal aspirations for children. Lazer and Darlington reported persistence several years after preschool (but not thereafter) of higher Stanford-Binet IQ than controls, and some indication of better performance on achievement tests.

SOCIAL EFFECTS.   Several studies emphasizing psychometric performance have also included some noncognitive measures. In the High/Scope study, children with preschool experience were found at age 19 to be significantly

---

8. Programs represented in this analysis included cognitive-developmental programs (High/Scope, Bank Street, Montessori), cultural-transmission programs (Bereiter-Engelmann, Palmer's Concept Training), and programs combining characteristics of child-development programs with a cultural-transmission orientation to developing school-related skills (Gray's DARCEE). It is unclear whether Beller's program should be classified as romantic because of its psychoanalytic emphasis or cognitive-developmental because it included cognitive components. Also represented were parent education programs (Gordon's Florida Parent Education Project and Levenstein's Verbal Interaction Project). Children's age in follow-up studies varied from 10 to 14 years, and intermediate data were collected on most programs.

higher than a control group in employment (50% and 32%), and significantly lower in proportion arrested for law violations (31% and 51%), teen pregnancy (64% and 17%), and welfare dependence (18% and 32%).

We cited as a cognitive effect less time spent in special education classes of children with preschool experience in High/Scope and consortium studies. This effect may be social as well as cognitive.

No long-range studies have been made of the effects of early education on stages of cognitive or sociomoral development.

Comparison of Differences between Programs

COGNITIVE EFFECTS. The consortium longitudinal study (Lazar & Darlington, 1982) was not designed to compare the effectiveness of various preschool programs with each other, but with each one's control group. However, the results showed that for each variable studied (listed above), some programs were significantly different from their controls and some were not. No one program emerges as always significantly better than its control, but the Levenstein program that provided toys and encouraged mother-child verbal interaction from age 2 or 3 years is better on the most variables.

The effects of nine quasi-experimental planned variation Head Start projects were compared (System Development Corporation, 1972). Essentially no cognitive effects were found that differentiated programs. Except for the teacher's use of physical control and presence of large-muscle equipment (variables that may reflect greater autonomy in children's experience), few variables had clear relationships to children's gains in IQ or achievement. Children whose teachers used no physical control had higher IQ and knowledge on the Caldwell-Soule Preschool Inventory. Presence of large muscle equipment in the classroom was also positively associated with cognitive gains (Horowitz & Paden, 1973, p. 361).

Miller and Dyer (1975) studied the effects of four preschool programs— Bereiter-Engelmann, Montessori, DARCEE (Gray's Demonstration and Research Center in Early Education developed at Peabody College), and traditional Head Start, the official Head Start program sponsored by the Office of Economic Opportunity and described in the Rainbow books (Rainbow Series, 1965) published by that agency.[9] They compared immediate effects (after preschool) and long-term effects (after second grade). However, after preschool in one of the four programs, children shifted either to Behavior Analysis or Regular (public school) programs. Long-term effects are thus confounded so as to make solid generalizations impossible about differential program effects. Nevertheless, several findings should be noted.

By the end of the preschool year, children in the Bereiter-Engelmann program scored highest of all programs in arithmetic, sentence production,

9. The Head Start program was child-centered, emphasizing active free play in activities like those of Bank Street. Goals stressed social more than cognitive development, but also motivational and physical development.

vocabulary, and persistence on a difficult task. However, these gains had disappeared 3 years later (after 3 years in a non-Bereiter-Engelmann program), and the children scored low in IQ, letters, numbers, word meanings, inventiveness, and curiosity.

The DARCEE program (with a combination of structured lessons and free choice of activities) had the highest scores after 8 weeks on arithmetic, vocabulary, sentence production, and persistence, but also gained in curiosity, inventiveness, and social participation. After 3 years in a non-DARCEE program, DARCEE children were still high on IQ, inventiveness, curiosity, and verbal-social skills.

Montessori children at the end of 1 year were high in curiosity and inventiveness, and 3 years later (after 3 years of non-Montessori experience), were also high in IQ, reading, and math and were highly motivated to achieve in school.

At the end of 1 year, children in the traditional child-development nursery school were curious and socially active but also aggressive and lower in IQ than children in the other programs. Three years later, they were low on academic achievement but still high in verbal-social skills such as initiating conversations and cooperating.

Clarke-Stewart (1982) interprets these findings by concluding that programs with the combination of a moderate number of structured activities and free choice of activities have the best overall effects, in comparison with both highly structured and very open programs. We agree with this interpretation but again note that these assessments do not adequately address cognitive-developmental and constructivist objectives.

We argue in Chapter 3 that the content of most Piagetian tasks is not a good source of educational objectives or activities because understanding requires deduction beyond the competence of preschool children. However, since operational reasoning is a long-term goal, progress on Piagetian tasks might be hypothesized as differentiating programs when assessments are made beyond preschool. One study of this hypothesis was done by DeVries and Karnes (in preparation), comparing matched samples of children with 1 year of preschool, after the end of first grade. The effects of three preschool programs were compared: Bereiter-Engelmann (forerunner of DISTAR), traditional nursery school, and Karnes's Ameliorative program (forerunner of GOAL, Karnes, 1972).[10] Children in the Karnes program were more advanced than those from

---

10. Karnes' Ameliorative program (which evolved into the Game Oriented Activities for Learning) had as its aim language development, based on the assumption that success in school and life depends on language ability. It also aimed to foster social competence, positive self-concept and emotional development, creative and problem-solving ability, motor skills, and motivation to learn. The Ameliorative program was conceived in terms of the ITPA (*Illinois Test of Psycholinguistic Abilities*) model of cognitive functioning. Lessons reflect the five principal language processing areas: Reception, Association, Expression, Sequential Memory, and Closure. While the conceptual basis of the Ameliorative program reflects a sensory theory of knowing, its practical basis reflects the child-centered or child-development tradition in nursery school education. Activity content

both other programs on conservation of length and number, object sorting, and role taking in a guessing game. Both Karnes and Bereiter-Engelmann children were more advanced than traditional children on conservation of substance and class inclusion.

Thus, in summary, a child-centered program with a self-conscious cognitive emphasis appears to be more effective on the whole in promoting lasting intellectual development than either traditional nursery school (romantic) or straight didactic teaching (cultural-transmission). Also, less didactic and cognitive-developmental programs have more positive long-term effects.

SOCIAL EFFECTS.   No significant social effects were reported by Horowitz and Paden (1973) in their review of the effects of the planned variation Head Start projects. Fein and Moorin (1980), however, reported advantages in social competence for children 21 to 31 months of age who had been in an educational program longer than a comparison group in the same program. More experienced children manifested a higher level of pretend play and communication with others, more effective negotiation strategies for resolving conflicts, and fewer negative behaviors (such as grabbing toys).

Most recently, Schweinhart, Weikart, and Larner (1986) report results of a longitudinal comparison of children who attended High/Scope, DISTAR, and nursery school preschool programs, representing cognitive-developmental, cultural transmission, and romantic philosophies, respectively. It should be emphasized that the High/Scope and nursery school programs had many similarities, while both are diametric opposites to DISTAR's method of fast-paced drill and repetition. While the three groups differed little in their IQ and school achievement, at age 15 the DISTAR group, in comparison with the other

---

emphasizes traditional aims of teaching colors, shapes, and counting, but adds such aims as one-to-one correspondence and comparison of numerical sets. The program itself has some similarities with cognitive-developmental programs. For example, pretend play, puzzles, stories, and rhymes are emphasized, and some games like Lotto and guessing are included (though Karnes's definition of "game" is much broader than ours, encompassing activities and lessons as well as games with rules in which winning is possible). Activities appeal to children's interests and purposes despite didactic goals. For example, shapes are taught in the context of stories ("The Three Bears" is told as "The Three Circles," with Papa Circle, Mama Circle, and Baby Circle). Classification is taught in an active context. For example, in a Treasure Hunt, children pretend to look for treasure and find a box with many objects. The teacher models taking out her treasure—the set of things made of cloth—and then asks children to help her subdivide the set into subsets.

We view Karnes's program as an effort to make the traditional nursery school experience more cognitive, an effort shared by cognitive-developmental programs (with the exception of Montessori, whose method developed concurrently with the traditional nursery school and in a different direction). In comparison with our constructivist approach, the Ameliorative program activity content and educational objectives are different, but there is similarity in some types of activities. Both approaches appeal to children's interests, but in the constructivist experience this appeal is more organic than in the Ameliorative experience, where it becomes more didactic. The constructivist approach emphasizes sociomoral objectives that are absent in Karnes's program and places greater emphasis on autonomy and reasoning.

two groups, engaged in twice as many delinquent acts, including five times as many acts of property violence. The DISTAR group also reported "relatively poor relations with their families, less participation in sports, fewer school job appointments, and less reaching out to others for help with personal problems" (p. 15).

In summary, some evidence suggests that social development is facilitated by child-centered and cognitive-developmental programs, but may be negatively influenced by didactic programs.

Evaluation of Constructivist Programs

Having outlined a definition of constructivist education in the foregoing chapters, a final issue must be raised. Does constructivist education attain its objectives of promoting children's intellectual, personality, and sociomoral development? The educational aim of development implies the goal of progress through cognitive and sociomoral stages. It implies the goal of active curiosity and the exercise of autonomy in initiative—experimentation, discovery, and invention in relation to physical phenomena, and interpersonal engagement with peers and adults in play and community activities—including opportunities for social and moral decision making. Constructive error and conflict are important parts of the fabric of experience hypothesized to effect long-term progress.

The problem of evaluating constructivist education is threefold:

1. Program implementation is difficult to establish, since it requires intensive teacher development that takes at least a year;
2. New methods are required to assess the attainment of constructivist objectives;
3. Its developmental effects are expected to be principally long-term rather than short-term.

The first problem was discussed above. Teacher development is, of course, a problem for evaluating any educational program, but is more acute for constructivist education because of the absence of a written curriculum or detailed guidelines for daily implementation. Constructivist teachers have to construct a philosophy grounded in theory and research that guides the creation of a complex moral and intellectual atmosphere. They have to construct their own specific principles of teaching oriented to children's constructive activities and experience.

With regard to the second problem of the need for new evaluation methods, it is important to note that one of the reasons for the emphasis on psychometric tests in preschool evaluation is that these were already well developed. Further, as pointed out by Kamii (1984), the new preschool inventories emphasized the easiest things both to teach and to measure. These include naming letters, colors, and geometric shapes, counting to 10 or 20, and understanding words such as "on-off" and "over-under." Duckworth (1978) discussed the difficulty of evaluating objectives of informal education. She noted that in contrast with prominent science programs, objectives of informal education are not limited to those that can be readily evaluated. Zimiles (1968, 1970) also argued that cognition measured by most instruments is very narrow and more suited for use with product-oriented than process-oriented educational programs. The constructivist aim of development requires methods of evaluation different from those reflecting the cultural-transmission world view.

The third problem for evaluation of constructivist education (as might be said for all programs) is that it requires longitudinal measurement of long-term intervention. Piaget (1969/1970) cautioned that we should not draw conclusions about the effects of early education unless we carry out an experimental program to the end of secondary school. Comprehensive program implementation is limited by the fact that thus far, constructivist program development is fairly well defined only for preschool and, for elementary and secondary schools, only in the domain of moral development. Zimiles (1968) has also cautioned that outcomes can be studied with precision only where there is control over the experience in the period intervening between early education and the measurment of outcome years later. The longitudinal studies cited above do not meet the requirements of control of experience intervening between preschool and follow-up evaluation, and they do not measure individual developmental growth from a constructivist perspective. We review below formative research bearing directly on goals of constructivist education.

Cognitive Effects

EVALUATION OF AN AFRICAN PRIMARY SCIENCE PROGRAM. The African Primary Science Program grew out of the Elementary Science Study approach developed by the Education Development Center in Newton, Massachusetts. It took place in Kenya, developed under the auspices of the Kenya Institute of Education, and involved children from 5 to 10 years of age in the beginning of the program that extended over 3 years. Although not consciously based on Piaget's ideas, the broad goals and many activities of the African Primary Science Program are similar to those developed later by Kamii and DeVries for physical-knowledge activities.

Duckworth designed an evaluation study based on the assumption that "the important thing in any learning is to be able to use it, to go beyond it, in the direction of still further learning and activity" (Duckworth, 1978, p. 51). The first evaluation procedure was to study behavior in a situation in which children were introduced to a room with a variety of both familiar and unfamiliar materials. They were told to do whatever they wished, and for the next 35 minutes two observers followed a time-sampling procedure to record what children did. Complexity of thought in children's activities was categorized as simple, moderate, elaborate, or extraordinary. "Simple" activities included those that were the obvious and easy things to do with a given material (such as picking things up). "Moderate" activities required some determination and went beyond the obvious in any of a number of ways (such as putting objects on the balance in some systematic way). "Elaborate" activities required more planning and/or understanding of the nature of the materials (such as using a mirror to look for an image other than the child). "Extraordinary" activities went beyond these (such as making a "walking" cotton spool by passing a rubber band through the center hole and winding it on bits of stiff grass, strung with string to make a braking mechanism). Diversity was assessed by counting the number of "different" activities.

The second evaluation procedure was to study children's development of reasoning on tasks involving classification, seriation, and spatial relations.

Using these procedures, Duckworth compared children from the active African Primary Science Program with children from the regular school program who had a traditional text-oriented science program. Her analysis revealed that the classes showing the most complexity and diversity of ideas were classes from the African Primary Science Program. Classes with the fewest ideas and the least initiative were comparison classes from the regular school program. Significantly more children in the active program did work that was at least "elaborate," and significantly fewer children from these classes did work that was no higher than "simple" in complexity. All work scored as "extraordinary" was done by children from the active African Primary Science Program.

On five of the six reasoning tasks, randomly selected children from the active program classes scored significantly higher than children from comparison classes. Only on Seriation of Weights were the groups not statistically different. The one class in the active program for the longest time (3 years) did better than classes in the program less time.

This study is important because, first, it provides evidence on effects of an extended experience of 3 years in a program emphasizing objectives and activities similar to those described in Chapter 4 on physical knowledge. Second, it provides evidence in a situation having high ecological validity—an unstructured opportunity for children without adult intervention to engage with materials and each other, however their natural interests lead. Third, the evidence shows advance in structure (stage) of reasoning for African Primary Science children relative to the comparison children in the regular school program.

EVALUATION OF A CONSTRUCTIVIST KINDERGARTEN PRO-GRAM. Kamii and DeVries consulted on a regular basis for two years with teachers, psychologists, and principals involved in an experimental kindergarten program in four schools in the Evanston (Illinois) Public School System. The objective was to realize an implementation of the Kamii-DeVries approach.

Piagetian tasks of operational reasoning were rejected as assessments because no matter how good a program, virtually all 4- and 5-year-olds would be expected to remain preoperational in reasoning. Evaluation at this age must thus focus on other social and cognitive indicators. Duckworth's study of a free-activity situation was taken as a model by Golub and Kolen (1976) in their evaluation at the end of the program's second year. All 90 children in the "Piagetian" or constructivist classrooms were compared with 80 children from regular classes (having more teacher-directed activities and less emphasis on peer interaction), matched on race, sex, and socioeconomic status. Children were randomly assigned in three of the schools to either regular or constructivist groups. In the fourth school, all kindergarten children were included in the constructivist program.

In the adaptation of Duckworth's procedure, children (10 at a time from a class) spent 20 minutes in a room with three types of materials placed on tables and rugs: items typically found in kindergarten classrooms (such as scissors, paper, pencils, crayons, and blocks), commonplace items not usually associated with school (such as twigs, funnels, seeds, and buttons), and unfamiliar items including some from another culture (such as African musical instruments) and educational materials not commonly available.

Analysis of children's activities showed that mean complexity score of children from the constructivist program was significantly higher than that of children from the regular program. Moderate or extraordinary complexity was found in a significantly higher percentage of constructivist children (35%) than comparison children (27%).

Golub and Kolen also report that while achievement tests did not measure program goals, mean achievement of constructivist children at the end of first grade was at least as high as that of the comparison children. In summary, this study is important because it shows not only that the constructivist program succeeded in promoting complexity of thought, but also that the lack of emphasis on academics in a constructivist program leads to no less academic success in traditional terms.

EVALUATION OF THE CONSTRUCTIVIST APPROACH TO BEGIN- NING ARITHMETIC. Kamii (1985) has made an effort to evaluate a con- structivist approach to arithmetic (described in Chapter 7), in comparison with traditional methods (workbooks, worksheets, and flashcards). Using dice with numerals, 24 children in the constructivist program and 12 children from a traditional academic program were asked to give sums using addends up to 10. On the whole, the constructivist group did no worse than the traditional group. In addition to this product-oriented comparison, Kamii also studied children's reasoning processes. She notes qualitative differences between the two groups, commenting, "The children in the traditional group were mentally and socially passive. They only gave answers and hardly ever volunteered anything else. When asked how they got particular answers, they either redid what they had just done or responded by saying, 'I don't know,' or 'I thought it in my head'." In contrast, the children in the constructivist group spontaneously talked about many varied relationships. Following are the kinds of relationships they created:

- *Relationship between what they wanted to know and what they know*. When asked about 9 + 9, Ann said, "18. If you know that 8 + 8 = 16, you know to skip another one, and it *has to be* 18."
- *Relationship between intuitive thinking and an answer arrived at through a more precise procedure*. When asked about 5 + 7, Bob said, "5 + 5, 17, no it should be less, 12."
- *Compensation*. When asked about 5 + 7, Brad said, "If you take 1 from 7 and put it with 5, that's 6 + 6, and that's 12."
- *Commutativity*. About 2 + 8, Brad said, "You could do it backwards like 8 + 2, that's 10."
- *Relationships between one answer and another*. After 1 + 10 and 10 + 10 came 9 + 2, and the children in the constructivist group often said 9 + 2 made "11 again." (Kamii, 1985, pp. 234–235)

It should be emphasized that this study did not credit children with correct answers if they took longer than 2 seconds to respond. Children's intuitive strategies such as those quoted above often took more time than recitation of memorized sums. Constructivist evaluation calls for mastery, not timed or curve-based tests, and the results of the Kamii study are therefore a conservative estimate of the effects of a constructivist program on calculation of sums. Constructivist teaching is expected to result in slower but more solid acquisition of specific right answers than teaching based on drill and memory. Evaluation of constructivist education in number and arithmetic must include not only assessment of correct calculation and right answers, but must extend to understanding children's procedures for getting both wrong *and* right answers.

Social Effects

In the Golub and Kolen study, social interaction was assessed with four of Parten and Newhall's (1943) categories: solitary activity, parallel play, some interaction, and collaboration. Interaction with the adult observers and instances of adult intervention to maintain order were recorded, and group atmosphere was rated. Social interaction was significantly greater and more independent of adult guidance among children from the constructivist kindergartens than among children from the more academic regular kindergartens. While 61% of constructivist children were observed engaged in collaboration, this was observed in only 26% of comparison children. Conversely, while only 7% of constructivist children engaged only in solitary or parallel play, this was true for 36% of comparison children. The use of the adult also differed between the two groups. As the children went about their activities, interaction with the adult was initiated by a higher percentage of comparison children (51%) than constructivist children (25%). Comparison children made five times as many requests (20 of 80 children) for permission or direction (e.g., "What do we do with these?" or, "Can we make things with this?") as constructivist children (4 of 90 children).

Ratings of group atmosphere revealed that the quietest groups who interacted least and the noisiest groups bordering on disorder were all from comparison classes. None of the constructivist groups showed such extremes. Adult intervention was necessary to maintain order only once for constructivist groups and 4 times for comparison groups. No negative group behavior or sustained individual negative behavior was observed in constructivist groups. However, Golub and Kolen describe the following negative interactions in comparison groups.

> In three of the eight Comparison groups, several children were involved in behavior which would lead a casual observer to assume that the group was out of control. For example, in one Comparison group there seemed to be a generally unfriendly feeling. Three of these children were so intent on trying to fight with each other that at the end of the session an adult was needed to physically restrain one of them. In another Comparison group, some of the children spent a good part of the session banging the instruments and screaming at each other to "stop it" and "shut up". In a third Comparison group, a few of the children led by one child spent the latter part of their session dumping out the contents of the containers onto the floor while the other children watched passively or ignored the goings on. (p. 10)

These findings are similar in some respects to those in the study reported below.

INTERPERSONAL RELATIONS IN CHILDREN FROM CONSTRUCTIVIST AND MONTESSORI PROGRAMS.   DeVries and Goncu (in press) studied the social-cognitive competence in interpersonal negotiation strategies of children experiencing constructivist and Montessori preschool. The procedure was to teach 40 4-year-olds in pairs to play a teacher-made board game called Halloween Run (in which players take turns rolling a die to see how many spaces to move their markers toward the end picture of Trick or Treaters), then to ask them to play the game without the teacher on a subsequent day.

Social-cognitive competence was assessed using the system of scoring interpersonal negotiation strategies developed by Selman and his colleagues (Selman & Demorest, 1984; Stone, Robinson, & Taylor, 1980). A unit of behavior was scored when it fit one of 57 interpersonal negotiation strategies, each of which was ascribed to one of four developmental stages. Level 0 strategies are defined as expressing the actor's raw will in a situation, without any reflection on the other's point of view. At Level 1, strategies express a one-way understanding of negotiated interaction in that mostly they express only the actor's needs or wishes in the situation without reference or inquiry about the needs or wishes of others. In the strategies at Level 2, the actor demonstrates an awareness of other individuals as planful and having opinions, feelings, and behaviors that impact on those of the self. This includes strategies that find out what others want to do, and communicating what the self wants in a nonbinding manner. Also, this level describes ways of working together and attending to others' needs and wishes, working with others to achieve one's own objectives. Level 3 strategies include negotiations that express an awareness of the complexity of the actual interaction process and of the individual's awareness of multiple possible meanings in group processes.

Analysis of 2,208 interaction units showed that constructivist pairs had a significantly higher proportion of Stage 2 strategies, and that Montessori pairs had a significantly higher proportion of Stage 1 strategies. More specifically, constructivist pairs showed significantly higher proportions of the following Level 2 strategies:

Directing, showing and explaining (e.g., "You go 1, 2, 3," etc., showing where to move marker)
Offer (e.g., "Want me to count 'em?")
Checking out with the other to make sure the other is in agreement and feels satisfied about what is happening and to express concern with fairness and equality in decision making (e.g., "Who's first?")
Gesturing and joint gesturing to make intentions known to the other by physically coordinating movement (e.g., looking inquiringly at other, who points to space to indicate where a marker should be)
Level 2 process (e.g., proposing new rule, or saying, "We'll say 'Eenie, meenie, miney, moe' to decide who's first")

Montessori pairs showed significantly higher proportions of the following Level 1 strategies:

Negations (e.g., "No, you have to ... ," "You didn't win")
Complaining and criticizing (e.g., "You don't know how to play this game, do you?")
Threatening (e.g., angrily raising fist, or, "Do you want me to tell the teacher?" or, "I will never, ever, ever, ever, ever, ever play with you on the playground, never invite you to my house, never do what you want—never!")
Appeals to the adult and tattling (e.g., looking toward adult when a conflict arises, asking, "Am I gonna' win?" and complaining, "She doesn't want to play, and I do," and, "He's sitting on my chair.")

At a marginally significant level, Montessori pairs were higher on Level 0 *Physical grabbing and hitting* (p = .068), and *Level 1 Offer—butinski* (e.g., "I'll count it for you," counting over the other's protest). It was therefore concluded that children from the constructivist program were more advanced in their stage of interpersonal competence than children from the Montessori program.

More conflict was found in Montessori pairs than in constructivist pairs. The total number of conflict segments was 39 for constructivist pairs and 98 for Montessori pairs. In these segments, constructivist pairs resolved a significantly higher proportion of their conflicts (64%) than Montessori children (30%).

Further analysis focused on the interpersonal negotiation strategies within conflict segments. This would seem to be the real test of social-cognitive competence—when one's self-interest is threatened. The results of this analysis parallel the general finding. Montessori pairs had a significantly higher proportion of Level 0 behaviors than constructivist pairs. No significant difference in percentage of Level 1 behaviors was found. Constructivist pairs had a significantly higher proportion of Level 2 behaviors than Montessori pairs.

In addition to these results, we noticed that only in the Montessori pairs did children wait for the experimenter to give permission a second time before beginning the game in Session II, despite having been told, "This time you are going to play by yourselves. I have some work to do over here. You let me know when you are ready to go back to your room." For example, one pair expressed pleasure at the idea of playing by themselves, but did not commence play. They did discuss which color marker each would have, where to place them at Start, and the orientation of the board so both could reach Start. Then they sat and waited. The following conversation then occurred.

Child 1: Looks at E, whose back is turned to them) Can we go now? Can we start now?
Child 2: (Looks at E) Not yet.
Child 1: (Looks at E) Can we?
Child 2: I don't know.
Child 1: (Goes to E and taps arm) Can we start now?
E: (realizing for the first time they were talking to her) You can play.
Child 1: She said we can play now.
Another pair smiled at each other, took markers, then looked in silence at E's back. Their conversation went as follows.
Child 1: (Very quietly and hesitantly) Start. (Looks at Child 2, smiling).
Child 1 and 2: (Look at E)
Child 2: (Look at E) Are we gonna start?
Child 1: (Looks at E, then after a pause, looks at second E at camera)
Child 2: (Looks at E) Are we gonna start (anxious tone)?
Child 1 and 2: (Look at E and whisper)
Child 2: She won't let us do it.
Child 1 and 2: (Look at each other, then at E)
Child 2: (Looks at E) Are we gonna start (frustrated tone)? Let's start. (Looks at second E at camera) Let's *start* (insistent tone).
Child 1 and 2: (Look at each other)
Child 2: She won't let us do it (desperate tone).
E: (Finally realizes children are talking to her) You can play by yourselves this time.
Child 1 and 2: (Begin moving markers in arbitrary way simultaneously)

This kind of heteronomous dependence on adults was never manifested by children from the constructivist program. To a geat extent, Montessori children showed themselves unable to regulate their social behavior in satisfying ways in the absence of the accustomed adult regulation.

While this study is not a comprehensive evaluation of Montessori and constructivist programs and the results cannot be generalized to all programs of these types, the results indicate that the method is promising for evaluating the objectives of a constructivist program.

SUMMARY

In this chapter we reviewed the main themes of the book—that the child's psychological experience in school affects possibilities for social, intellectual, affective, and moral development, and that the teacher's educational worldview affects the nature of the child's psychological experience in school.

The romantic worldview dominated preschool education until the 1960s when it began to be challenged by the cultural-transmission view that has long dominated primary school education. Programs based on cognitive-developmental and constructivist worldviews began to emerge in the 1960s, offering an alternative both to programs oriented to a romantic philosophy and programs oriented to a cultural-transmission philosophy.

The future of constructivist education, in particular, rests on teacher development that means in part steering clear of certain romantic and cultural-transmission ideas. The teacher moving toward the constructivist worldview frequently has to shift the focus of thinking from instruction to construction, from reinforcement to interest, and from obedience to autonomy (or from coercion to co-operation). Further, the constructivist teacher integrates a commitment to cognitive, affective, and sociomoral goals. Aspects of the movement toward constructivist teaching include skepticism and considering how to change environment and teaching style. Finally, it culminates in the autonomy that comes from a solid network of convictions that are both practical and theoretical and leads to taking responsibility for the education offered to children.

While constructivist education has the child's development as its goal, this does not mean that the teaching of subject matter is eliminated. We argue for more ambitious, longer-range objectives than usually found in programs limited to the goal of school readiness. These constructivist goals include the very academic objectives generally believed too little emphasized in traditional child-centered programs, but approach these in unique ways. Constructivist academic and subject-matter goals emerge not from subject-matter analysis, but from analysis of how children think about subject matter.

Constructivist education reflects applied cognitive-developmental and constructivist theory. This theory will be elaborated further by research on children's development in classrooms where teachers are guided by the principles discussed in this book. Studies of how children think about subject matter are needed to inspire curriculum development.

Research on program effectiveness does bear out the value of preschool education. However, most research on the effects of early education has reflected the cultural transmission view of the cognitive aim of education—with psychometric measures of IQ and achievement dominating evaluation concerns. In general, optimism about long-range increase in psychometric intelligence or achievement due to preschool education has not been strongly supported by follow-up data. Some evidence suggests more promising social effects such as later employment and less arrests for law violation, teen pregnancy, and welfare dependence.

Research findings on the differential effects of various preschool programs are often inconsistent and difficult to interpret. However, a cultural-transmission emphasis on didactic teaching may have a negative effect on at least some long-term aspects of cognitive development and social behavior. In contrast, less didactic and cognitive-developmental programs seem to have positive long-term effects on some aspects of educational accomplishment and social behavior.

The problem of evaluating constructivist programs is discussed, emphasizing three aspects: (1) difficulty in establishing implementation of constructivist programs, (2) need for new methods to assess the attainment of constructivist objectives, and (3) expectation that effects of constructivist education are principally long-term rather than short-term. Results of four studies involving constructivist programs are summarized. In comparison with children in traditional programs, children in constructivist programs show a variety of cognitive and social advantages. In comparison with children from a Montessori program, constructivist children are more advanced in social-cognitive competence.

CONCLUSION

Cognitive-developmental and, especially, constructivist education have a short past. The future of these approaches to early education depends on collaboration among teachers, school administrators, parents, and researchers. In our discussion of various programs within the cognitive-developmental worldview, we have taken the position that none should be viewed as the final word on the best educational approach. We hope the future will be characterized by the kinds of collaborative exchanges and dialogue that will lead to better theoretical and empirical clarification of the implications of developmental psychology for early education. We urge teachers to join us in practical classroom research to develop curriculum, and researchers to join us in studying the effects of cognitive-developmental programs on children's psychological development. We especially advocate the kind of research that will improve our understanding of the critical aspects of the child's psychological experience in educational programs that promote development.

In reflecting in particular about the task confronting us of constructing and evaluating constructivist education, one of us is reminded of an experience from her own childhood that seems to represent the current state of affairs. At age 5, she observed her mother learning to knit, and learned along with her. For some time, she knitted a narrow fabric that got longer and longer. Finally, someone asked, "Rheta, what are you knitting?" The answer: "I don't know—I'm not finished yet!" We do not yet know fully what constructivist education should be. We invite you to join us in the constructive process.

References

Aukerman, R. (1971). *Approaches to beginning reading.* New York: Wiley.

Bamberger, J. (1980). Cognitive structuring in the apprehension and description of simple rhythms. *Archives de Psychologie, 48,* 171–199.

Barrie, J. (1911). *Peter Pan.* New York: Grosset & Dunlap.

Bereiter, C., & Engelmann, S. (1966). *Teaching disadvantaged children in the preschool.* Englewood Cliffs, N.J.: Prentice-Hall.

Berthoud-Papandropolou, I. (1976). La réflexion métalinguistique chez l'enfant. Unpublished doctoral dissertation, University of Geneva.

Berutta-Clement, J., Schweinhart, L., Barnett, W., Epstein, A., & Weikart, D. (1984). *Changed lives: The effects of the Perry Preschool Program on youths through age 19.* Ypsilanti, Mich.: High-Scope Press.

Beth, E., & Piaget, J. (1961). *Epistémologie mathématique et psychologique.* Paris: Presses Universitaires de France.

Biber, B. (1955). Schooling as an influence in developing healthy personality. In R. Kotinsky & H. Witmer (Eds.), *Community programs for mental health* (pp. 1–64). Cambridge, Mass.: Harvard University Press.

Biber, B. (1959a, March). The implications for public education of research in learning. *New directions in learning: Summary of the California Association of School Psychologists and Psychometrists.*

Biber, B. (1959b). The teacher's role in creativity: Premature structuring as a deterrent to creativity. *The American Journal of Orthopsychiatry, 29*(2).

Biber, B. (1961a). Effective learning and healthy personality. *The National Elementary Principal, 41,* 45–48.

Biber, B. (1961b). Integration of mental health principles in the school setting. In G. Caplan (Ed.), *Prevention of mental disorders in children.* New York: Basic Books.

Biber, B. (1964). Preschool education. In R. Ulich (Ed.), *Education and the idea of mankind* (pp. 1–28). New York: Harcourt Brace & World.

Biber, B. (1967a, September). Educational needs of young deprived children. *Childhood Education.*

Biber, B. (1967b, October). The impact of deprivation on young children. *Childhood Education.*

Biber, B. (1967c). A learning-teaching paradigm integrating intellectual and affective processes. In E. Bower & W. Hollister (Eds.), *Behavioral science frontiers in education.* New York: Wiley.

Biber, B. (1967d). *Young deprived children and their educational needs.* Washington, D.C.: Association for Childhood Education International.

Biber, B. (1970, January–February). Goals and methods in a preschool program for disadvantaged children. *Children.*

Biber, B. (1972). The "Whole Child," individuality, and values in education. In J. Squire (Ed.), *A new look at progressive education.* Washington, D.C.: Association for Supervision and Curriculum Development.

Biber, B. (1977). A developmental-interaction approach: Bank Street College of

Education. In M. Day & R. Parker (Eds.), *The preschool in action* (2nd ed., pp. 421–460). Boston: Allyn & Bacon.

Biber, B. (1979). Thinking and feeling. *Young Children, 35*(1), 4–16.

Biber, B. (1981). The evolution of the developmental-interaction view. In E. Shapiro & E. Weber (Eds.), *Cognitive and affective growth* (pp. 9–30). Hillsdale, N.J.: Erlbaum.

Biber, B. (1984). *Early education and psychological development.* New Haven, Conn.: Yale University Press.

Biber, B., & Franklin, M. (1967). The relevance of developmental and psychodynamic concepts to the education of the preschool child. *Journal of the American Academy of Child Psychiatry, 6*(1).

Biber, B., Gilkeson, E., & Winsor, C. (1959, April). Basic approaches to mental health: Teacher education at Bank Street College. *Personnel and Guidance Journal.*

Biber, B., Shapiro, E., & Wickens, D. (1971). *Promoting cognitive growth from a developmental-interaction point of view.* Washington, D.C.: National Association for the Education of Young Children.

Biber, B., & Snyder, A. (1948). How do we know a good teacher? *Childhood Education, 24*(6), 281–285.

Biggs, E., & MacLean, J. (1969). *Freedom to learn: An active approach to mathematics.* Don Mills, Ont.: Addison-Wesley (Canada).

Blatt, M., & Kohlberg, L. (1975). The effects of classroom moral discussion on children's levels of moral judgment. *Journal of Moral Education, 4*(147).

Bloom, B. (1964). *Stability and change in human characteristics.* New York: Wiley.

Bloom, B., Hastings, J., & Madaus, G. (1971). *Handbook on formative and summative evaluation.* New York: McGraw-Hill.

Bronfenbrenner, U. (1974). *A report on longitudinal evaluations of preschool programs.* Vol. 2: *Is early intervention effective?* (Publication No. [OHD] 74–25). Washington, D.C.: U.S. Department of Health, Education and Welfare.

Bruner, J. (1960). *The process of education.* Cambridge, Mass.: Harvard University Press.

Bruner, J. (1964). The course of cognitive growth. *American Psychologist, 19*(1), 1–15.

Canadian Council for Research in Education. (1964). *Canadian experience with the Cuisenaire method.*

Chall, J. (1983). *Stages of reading development.* New York: McGraw-Hill.

Chomsky, C. (1971). Write now, read later. *Childhood Education 47*(6).

Clarke-Stewart, A. (1982). *Daycare.* Cambridge, Mass.: Harvard University Press.

Clay, M. (1972). *Reading: The patterning of complex behavior.* Portsmouth, N.H.: Heinemann.

Clay, M. (1975). *What did I write?* Portsmouth, N.H.: Heinemann.

Clay, M. (1982). *Observing young readers: Selected papers.* Portsmouth, N.H.: Heinemann.

Colby, A., Kohlberg, L., Fenton, E., Speicher-Dubin, B., & Lieberman, M. (1977). Secondary school moral discussion programmes led by social studies teachers. *Journal of Moral Education, 6*(2), 90–117.

Copeland, R. (1970). *How Children learn mathematics: Teaching implications of Piaget's research.* London: Macmillan.

Copple, C., Sigel, I., & Saunders, R. (1979). *Educating the young thinker: Classroom strategies for cognitive growth.* New York: D. Van Nostrand.

Cuisenaire, G., & Gattegno, C. (1954). *Numbers in colour.* London: Heinemann.

Denis-Prinzhorn, M., Kamii, C., & Mounoud, P. (1972). Pedagogical applications of Piaget's theory. *People Watching, 1.*

DeVries, R. (1969). Constancy of generic identity in the years three to six. *Monographs of the society for research in child development, 34* (3, Serial No. 127).

DeVries, R. (1970). The development of role-taking in young bright, average, and retarded children as reflected in social guessing game behavior. *Child Development, 41*(3), 759–770.

DeVries, R. (1971). *Evaluation of cognitive development with Piaget-type tests: Study of young bright, average, and retarded children.* Urbana, Ill.: ERIC/ECE, ED 075 065.

DeVries, R. (1974). Theory in educational practice. In R. Colvin & E. Zaffiro (Eds.), *Preschool education: A handbook for the training of early childhood educators* (pp. 3–40). New York: Springer.

DeVries, R. (1978). Early education and Piagetian theory: Applications versus implications. In J. Gallagher & J. Easley (Eds.), *Knowledge and development* (Vol. 2). New York: Plenum.

DeVries, R. (1981). Socio-affective development in Piagetian theory. Monterrey, Mex.: *Memorias sobre encuentro nacional de grupos integrados Monterrey.*

DeVries, R. (1983). Piaget's theorie in dienste des unterrichts: Affektive, soziomoralische und kognitive aspekte ihrer praxisrelevanz. *Neue Sammlung, 2* (March/April), 150–162.

DeVries, R. (1984). Developmental stages in Piagetian theory and educational practice. *Teacher Education Quarterly, 11*(4), 78–94.

DeVries, R. (1986). *Children's conceptions of shadow phenomena.* Genetic Psychology Monographs.

DeVries, R., & Goncu, A. (In press). Interpersonal relations in four-year-old dyads from constructivist and Montessori classrooms. *Applied Developmental Psychology.*

DeVries, R., & Kamii, C. (1975) *Why group games? A Piagetian perspective.* Urbana, Ill: ERIC Publications Office.

DeVries, R., & Smith, C. (1982). Structural stages in classroom activities. *The Genetic Epistemologist, II*(1), 1–5.

Dewey, J. (1913/1975). *Interest and effort in education.* Edwardsville: Southern Illinois Press.

Dewey, J. (1916/1966). *Democracy and education.* New York: Free Press.

Dienes, Z. (1960). *Building up mathematics.* London: Hutchinson.

Dienes, Z. (1963). *An experimental study of mathematics learning.* London: Hutchinson.

Dienes, Z., & Golding, E. (1966). *Sets, numbers and powers.* New York: Herder & Herder.

Dienes, Z., & Golding, E. (1971). *Approach to modern mathematics.* New York: Herder & Herder.

Duckworth, E. (1964). Piaget rediscovered. In R. Ripple & V. Rockcastle (Eds.), *Piaget rediscovered.* Ithaca, N.Y.: Cornell University School of Education.

Duckworth, E. (1978). *The African primary science program: An evaluation and extended thoughts.* Grand Forks, N.D.: University of North Dakota Study Group on Evaluation.

Elementary Science Study. (1967a) *Gases and airs.* New York: McGraw-Hill.

Elementary Science Study. (1967b). *Small things.* New York: McGraw-Hill.

Elementary Science Study. (1968a). *Batteries and bulbs.* New York: McGraw-Hill.

Elementary Science Study. (1968b). *Microgardening.* New York: McGraw-Hill.

Elementary Science Study. (1969a). *Balancing and weighing*. New York: McGraw-Hill.

Elementary Science Study. (1969b). *Daytime astronomy*. New York: McGraw-Hill.

Elkind, D. (1961a). The development of quantitative thinking: A systematic replication of Piaget's studies. *Journal of Genetic Psychology, 98,* 37–46.

Elkind, D. (1961b). Children's discovery of the conservation of mass, weight, and volume: Piaget replication study II. *Journal of Genetic Psychology, 98,* 219–227.

Elkind, D. (1967). Piaget and Montessori. *Harvard Educational Review, 37,* 535–545.

Elkind, D. (1975a). Perceptual development in children. *American Scientist, 63*(5), 535–541.

Elkind, D. (1975b). We can teach reading better. *Today's Education, 64*(4), 34–38.

Elkind, D. (1981). Stages in the development of reading. In I. Sigel, D. Brodzinsky, & R. Golinkoff (Eds.), *New directions in Piagetian theory and practice* (pp. 267–280). Hillsdale, N.J.: Erlbaum.

Elkind, D. (1983). Montessori education: Abiding contributions and contemporary challenges. *Young Children, 38*(2), 3–10.

Erikson, E. (1963). *Childhood and society*. New York: Norton.

Erlwanger, S. (1975). Case studies of children's conceptions of mathematics, Part I. *Journal of Children's Mathematical Behavior, 1.*

Evans, R. (1973). *Jean Piaget: The man and his ideas*. New York: E. P. Dutton.

Fein, G., & Moorin, E. (1980). Group care can have good effects. *Day Care and Early Education, 7*(3), 14–17.

Fernie, D., & DeVries, R. (1984, April). *A developmental study of Tic Tac Toe*. Paper presented at the annual meeting of the American Educational Research Association, New Orleans, La.

Ferreiro, E. (1976). *Development of knowledge of linguistic representation*. Invited paper presented to the Simpósio Internacional sobre el Lenguaje Infantil, Mexico.

Ferreiro, E. (1977). Vers une théorie génétique de l'apprentissage de la lecture. *Revue Suisse de Psychologie, 36*(2), 109–130. (Ms. translated by L. Romsburg.)

Ferreiro, E. (1978). What is written in a written sentence? A developmental answer. *Journal of Education, 160*(4), 25–39.

Ferreiro, E. (1984). The underlying logic of literacy development. In H. Goelman, A. Oberg, & F. Smith (Eds.), *Awakening to literacy*. Portsmouth, N.H.: Heinemann.

Ferreiro, E. (1985a). The relationship between oral and written language: The children's viewpoints. In M. Clark (Ed.), *New directions in the study of reading*. Philadelphia: Palmer Press.

Ferreiro, E. (1985b). Literacy development: A psychogenetic perspective. In D. Olson, N. Torrance, & A. Hilliard (Eds.), *Literacy, language, and learning: The nature and consequences of reading and writing*. New York: Cambridge University Press.

Ferreiro, E. (In press). The interplay between information and assimilation in beginning literacy. In W. Teale & E. Sulzby (Eds.), *Emergent literacy*. Norwood, N.J.: Ablex.

Ferreiro, E., Gomez Palacio, M., y Colaboradores. (1982). *Analisis de las perturbaciones en el procesode aprendizaje escolar de la lectura y la escritura. Fasciculo 1: El momento inicial y el momento final del aprendizaje escolar: Comparación de las escrituras producidas por los niños en el primer año escolar*. Mexico: Dirección general de educación especial.

Ferreiro, E., & Teberosky, A. (1979/1982). *Literacy before schooling*. Portsmouth, N.H.: Heinemann.

Flavell, J. (1963). *The developmental psychology of Jean Piaget.* Princeton, N.J.: D. Van Nostrand.

Forman, G., & Hill, F. (1980). *Constructive play: Applying Piaget in the preschool.* Monterey, Calif.: Brooks/Cole.

Forman, G., & Kuschner, D. (1977). *The child's construction of knowledge: Piaget for teaching children.* Monterey, Calif.: Brooks/Cole.

Franklin, M. (1981). Perspectives on theory: Another look at the developmental-interaction point of view. In E. Shapiro & E. Weber (Eds.), *Cognitive and affective growth: Developmental interaction* (pp. 65–84). Hillsdale, N.J.: Erlbaum.

Franklin, M., & Biber, B. (1977). Psychological perspectives and early childhood education: Some relations between theory and practice. In L. Katz (Ed.), *Current topics in early childhood education* (Vol. 1, pp. 1–32), Norwood, N.J.: Ablex.

Freud, S. (1938). *An outline of psychoanalysis.* London: Hogarth.

Franklin, M. (1981). Perspectives on theory: Another look at the developmental-interaction point of view. In E. Shapiro and E. Weber (Eds.), *Cognitive and affective growth: Developmental interaction* (pp. 65–84). Hillsdale, N.J.: Erlbaum.

Gachenbach, D. (1983). *Mr. Wink and his shadow, Ned.* New York: Harper & Row.

Gans, R., Stendler, C., & Almy, M. (1952). *Teaching young children.* New York: World Book.

Gardner, H. (1982). *Developmental psychology: An introduction* (2nd ed.). Boston: Little, Brown.

Gardner, R. (1966/1968). A psychologist looks at Montessori. *Elementary School Journal.* Reprinted in J. Frost (Ed.), *Early childhood education rediscovered: Readings* (pp. 78–91). New York: Holt, Rinehart & Winston.

Gattegno, C. (1957). *Arithmetic: Introductory stage. Books 1, 2, and 3.* London: Heinemann.

Gattegno, C. (1958). *From actions to operations.* Reading, Eng.: Cuisenaire.

Gattegno, C. (1960). *A teacher's introduction to the Cuisenaire-Gattegno method of teaching arithmetic.* Reading, Eng.: Gattegno-Pollock.

Gelman, R., & Gallistel, C. (1978). *The child's understanding of number.* Cambridge, Mass.: Harvard University Press.

Gesell, A., & Ilg, F. (1949). *Child development: An introduction to the study of human growth.* New York: Harper.

Gilkeson, E. (1962). Freedom and control: Components of learning. *National Elementary Principal, 41*(7).

Ginsburg, H. (1977). *Children's arithmetic: The learning process.* New York: D. Van Nostrand.

Ginsburg, H. (1983). *The development of mathematical thinking.* New York: Academic Press.

Ginsburg, H., & Opper, S. (1979). *Piaget's theory of intellectual development.* Englewood Cliffs, N.J.: Prentice-Hall.

Golub, M., & Kolen, C. (1976, June). *Evaluation of a Piagetian kindergarten program.* Manuscript based on paper presented at Sixth Annual Symposium of The Jean Piaget Society, Philadelphia, Pa.

Goodman, K., & Goodman, Y. (1977). Learning about psycholinguistic processes by analyzing oral reading. *Harvard Educational Review, 47*(3).

Greco, P. (1962). Quantité et quotité. In P. Greco & A. Morf (Eds.) *Structures numeriques élémentaires*, Vol. 13: *Etudes d'épistémologie*. Paris: Presses Universitaires de France.

Grim, P., Kohlberg, L., & White, S. (1968). Some relationships between conscience and attentional processes. *Journal of Personality and Social Psychiatry, 8,* 239–253.

Hersch, R., Paolitto, D., & Reimer, J. (1979). *Promoting moral growth: From Piaget to Kohlberg*. White Plains, N.Y.: Longman.

Hess, R., & Croft, D. (1975). *Teachers of young children* (2nd ed.). Boston: Houghton Mifflin.

Hildebrand, V. (1971). *Introduction to early childhood education*. New York: Macmillan.

Hohmann, M., Banet, B., & Weikart, D. (1979). *Young children in action*. Ypsilanti, Mich.: High/Scope Press.

Holdaway, D. (1979). *Foundations of literacy*. Portsmouth, N.H.: Heinemann Educational Books.

Horowitz, F., & Paden, L. (1973). The effectiveness of environmental intervention programs. In B. Caldwell & H. Ricciuti (Eds.), *Review of child development research* (pp. 331–402). Chicago: University of Chicago Press.

Hunt, J. (1961). *Intelligence and experience*. New York: Ronald Press.

Hunt, J. (1964/1968). Revisiting Montessori. In *The Montessori method*. New York: Schocken Books. Reprinted in J. Frost (Ed.), *Early childhood education rediscovered: Readings* (pp. 102–127). New York: Holt, Rinehart & Winston.

Hunt, J. (1969). *The challenge of incompetence and poverty: Papers on the role of early education*. Urbana: University of Illinois Press.

Inhelder, B., & Piaget, J. (1955/1958). *The growth of logical thinking from childhood to adolescence*. New York: Basic Books.

Inhelder, B., & Piaget, J. (1959/1964). *The early growth of logic in the child*. New York: Harper & Row.

Inhelder, B., Sinclair, H., & Bovet, M. (1974). *Learning and the development of cognition*. Cambridge, Mass.: Harvard University Press.

Isaacs, S. (1930). *Intellectual growth in young children*. London: Routledge and Kegan Paul.

Jackson, P. (1967). *Life in classrooms*. New York: Holt, Rinehart & Winston.

Johns, J. (1977). Children's conceptions of a spoken word: A developmental study. *Reading World, 16,* 248–257.

Johnson, H. (1928/1972). *Children in the nursery school*. New York: Agathon Press.

Kamii, C. (1971). Evaluation of learning in preschool education: Socio-emotional, perceptual-motor, cognitive development. In B. Bloom, J. Hastings, & G. Madaus (Eds.), *Handbook on formative and summative evaluation of student learning*. New York: McGraw-Hill.

Kamii, C. (1972a). An application of Piaget's theory to the conceptualization of a preschool curriculum. In R. Parker (Ed.), *The preschool in action*. Boston: Allyn & Bacon.

Kamii, C. (1972b). A sketch of the Piaget-derived preschool curriculum developed by the Ypsilanti early education program. In S. Braun & E. Edwards, *History and theory of early childhood education*. Worthington, Ohio.: Charles A. Jones.

Kamii, C. (1973a). A sketch of the Piaget-derived preschool curriculum developed by the Ypsilanti early education program. In J. Frost (Ed.), *Revisiting early childhood education*. New York: Holt, Rinehart & Winston.

Kamii, C. (1973b). A sketch of the Piaget-derived preschool curriculum developed by the

Ypsilanti early education program. In B. Spodek (Ed.), *Early childhood education.* Englewood Cliffs, N.J.: Prentice-Hall.

Kamii, C. (1982a). Autonomy: *The aim of education envisioned by Piaget.* Unpublished manuscript.

Kamii, C. (1982b). Encouraging thinking in mathematics. *Phi Delta Kappan, 64*(4), 247–251.

Kamii, C. (1982c). *Number in preschool and kindergarten: Educational implications of theory.* Washington, D.C.: National Association for the Education of Young Children.

Kamii, C. (1984a). Autonomy: The aim of education envisioned by Piaget. *Phi Delta Kappan, 65*(6), 410–415.

Kamii, C. (1984b). Evaluation: It all depends on your theory. Paper presented at seminar Experiences in Alternative Projects in Early Childhood Education, Viña del Mar, Chile.

Kamii, C. (1985). *Young children reinvent arithmetic.* New York: Teachers College Press.

Kamii, C. (1986). *How children learn to think* [Videotape]. Washington, D.C.: National Association for the Education of Young Children.

Kamii, C., Derman, L., Sonquist, H., & Anderson, E. (1967). *The development of a Piaget-derived curriculum for use in the classroom and in a home tutoring program.* Unpublished manuscript.

Kamii, C., & DeVries, R. (1973, April). *Piaget-based curricula for early childhood education: Three different approaches.* Paper presented at the meeting of the Society for Research in Child Development, Philadelphia, Pa.

Kamii, C., & DeVries, R. (1975/1977). Piaget for early education. In M. Day & R. Parker (Eds.), *Preschool in action* (2nd ed.). Boston: Allyn & Bacon.

Kamii, C., & DeVries, R. (1976). *Piaget, children, and number.* Washington, D.C.: National Association for the Education of Young Children.

Kamii, C., & DeVries, R. (1978). *Physical knowledge in preschool education: Implications of Piaget's theory.* Englewood Cliffs, N.J.: Prentice-Hall.

Kamii, C., & DeVries, R. (1980). *Group games in early education: Implications of Piaget's theory.* Washington, D.C.: National Association for the Education of Young Children.

Kamii, C., DeVries, R., Ellis, M., & Zaritsky, R. (1975). *Playing with rollers: A preschool teacher uses Piaget's theory* [Film]. Chicago, Ill.: Office of Instructional Resources Development, University of Illinois at Chicago Circle.

Kamii, C., & Radin, N. (1967). A framework for a preschool curriculum based on some Piagetian concepts. *Journal of Creative Behavior, 1,* 314–324.

Kamii, C., & Radin, N. (1970). A framework for a preschool curriculum based on some Piagetian concepts. In I. Athey, *Educational implications of Piaget's theory.* Waltham, Mass.: Xerox College Publishers.

Kamii, C., & Randazzo, M. (1985). Social interaction and invented spelling. *Language Arts, 62*(2), 124–132.

Kamii, M. (1980, June). Place value: Children's efforts to find a correspondence between digits and numbers of objects. Paper presented at the Tenth Annual Symposium of The Jean Piaget Society, Philadelphia, Pa.

Kamii, M. (1981, June). Children's ideas about written number. Paper presented at the Eleventh Annual Symposium of The Jean Piaget Society, Philadelphia, Pa.

Karlson, A. (1970). *A naturalistic method for identifying behavioral aspects of cognitive acquisition in young children participating in preschool programs.* Unpublished doctoral dissertation, University of Chicago.

Karnes, M. (1972). *Guide to the use of the GOAL Program: Language development.* Springfield, Mass.: Milton Bradley.

Kellogg, R. (1949). *Nursery school guide.* Boston: Houghton Mifflin.

Kilpatrick, W. (1914). *The Montessori system examined.* Boston: Houghton Mifflin.

Kohl, H. (1974). *Math, writing, and games in the open classroom.* New York: The New York Review, distributed by Random House.

Kohlberg, L. (1966). *Stages in children's conceptions of physical and social objects.* Unpublished monograph.

Kohlberg, L. (1968). Montessori with the culturally disadvantaged: A cognitive-developmental interpretation and some research findings. In R. Hess & R. Bear (Eds.), *Early education* (pp. 105–118). Chicago: Aldine.

Kohlberg, L. (1979). Foreword. In R. Hersh, D. Paolitto, & J. Reimer, *Promoting moral growth from Piaget to Kohlberg* (pp. ix–xvi). White Plains, N.Y.: Longman.

Kohlberg, L. (1984). *Essays on moral development: The psychology of moral development,* Vol. 2. New York: Harper & Row.

Kohlberg, L. (1984). *The psychology of moral development.* New York: Harper & Row.

Kohlberg, L., & Colleagues. (1987). *Child psychology and childhood education.* White Plains, N.Y.: Longman.

Kohlberg, L., & Mayer, R. (1972). Development as the aim of education. *Harvard Educational Review, 42*(4), 449–496.

Kohlberg, L., Ricks, D., & Snarey, J. (1984). Childhood development as a predictor of adaptation in adulthood. *Genetic Psychology Monographs, 10,* 91–172.

Kohn, M. (1977). *Class and conformity.* Chicago: University of Chicago Press.

Kuhn, T. (1962). *The structure of scientific revolutions* (2nd ed.). Chicago: University of Chicago Press.

Labinowicz, E. (1985). *Learning from children: New beginnings for teaching numerical thinking—A Piagetian approach.* Menlo Park, Calif.: Addison-Wesley.

Lavatelli, C. (1970a/1973). *Piaget's theory applied to an early childhood curriculum.* Boston: American Science and Engineering.

Lavatelli, C. (1970b/1973). *Teacher's guide to accompany early childhood curriculum—a Piaget program.* New York: American Science and Engineering.

Lavatelli, C. (1971a). *A Piaget preschool program in action. Part I: Number, measurement, and space.* [Filmstrip]. Boston: Knowledge Tree Films, Center for Media Development.

Lavatelli, C. (1971b). *A Piaget preschool program in action. Part II: Number, measurement, and space* [Filmstrip]. Boston: Knowledge Tree Films, Center for Media Development.

Lazar, I., & Darlington, R. (1982). Lasting effects of early education. A report from the consortium for longitudinal studies. *Monographs of the Society for Research in Child Development, 47*(2–3, Serial No. 195).

Leeper, S., Witherspoon, R., & Day, B. (1984). *Good schools for young children.* New York: Macmillan.

Lickona, T. (1983). *Raising good children.* New York: Bantam Books.

Lieberman, M., & Selman, R. (1975). Moral education in the primary grades: An evaluation of a developmental curriculum. *Journal of Educational Psychology. 67(5),* 712–716.

Lockwood, A. (1978). The effects of values clarification curricula on school-age subjects: A critical review of recent research. *Review of Educational Research, 48,* 325–364.

Loevinger, J. (1976). *Ego development: Conceptions and theories.* San Francisco: Jossey-Bass.

Long, R., & Bulgarella, L. (1985). Social interaction and the writing process. *Language Arts, 62*(2), 166–172.

Lovell, K. (1961). *The growth of basic mathematical and scientific concepts in children.* London: University of London Press.

Lovell, K. (1971). *The growth of understanding in mathematics: Kindergarten through grade three.* New York: Holt, Rinehart & Winston.

Lowery, L. (1969). *Dark as a shadow.* New York: Holt, Rinehart & Winston.

Mallinson, G., Mallinson, J., Smallwood, W., & Valentino, C. (1985). *Silver Burdett Science.* Morristown, N.J.: Silver Burdett.

Mayer, R. (1973). *Describing children's experiences in theoretically different classrooms: An observational assessment of four early education curriculum models.* Unpublished doctoral dissertation, Harvard University. (University Microfilms International)

Miller, L., & Dyer, J. (1975). Four preschool programs: Their dimensions and effects. *Monographs of the Society for Research in Child Development, 40*(5–6, Serial No. 162).

Mitchell, L. (1950). *Our children and our schools.* New York: Simon and Schuster.

Montessori, M. (1909/1964). *The Montessori method.* New York: Schocken Books.

Montessori, M. (1914/1965). *Dr. Montessori's own handbook.* New York: Schocken Books.

Montessori, M. (1916/1965). *Spontaneous activity in education: The advanced Montessori method.* New York: Schocken Books.

Montessori, M. (1917/1973). *The Montessori elementary material.* New York: Schocken Books.

Montessori, M. (1936a/1956). *The child in the family.* New York: Avon Books.

Montessori, M. (1936b/1966). *The secret of childhood.* New York: Ballantine Books.

Montessori, M. (1949/1967). *The absorbent mind.* New York: Dell.

Montessori, M. (undated/1973). La maestra. *Communications, 1,* 2–11.

Mosher, R. (Ed.). (1980). *Moral education.* New York: Praeger.

Murray, F. (1979, April). *The future of Piaget's theory in education.* Paper presented at the Biennial Meeting of the Society for Research in Child Development.

Neill, A. (1960). *Summerhill: A radical approach to child rearing.* New York: Hart.

Nimnicht, G., McAfee, O., & Meier, J. (1969). *The new nursery school.* Morristown, N.J.: General Learning Press.

Nuffield Foundation. (1970). *Mathematics—The first three years.* New York: Wiley.

Nuffield Foundation. (1971). *Maths with everything.* New York: Wiley.

Parsons, M. (1987). *The development of artistic appreciation.* New York: Cambridge University Press.

Parten, M., & Newhall, S. (1943). Social behavior of preschool children. In R. Barker (Ed.), *Child behavior and development* (pp. 509–525). New York: McGraw-Hill.

Perry, C. (1980). Revitalizing the Montessori apparatus. *The Constructive Triangle, 7*(3), 7–13.

Perry, W. (1970). *Forms of intellectual and ethical development in the college years: A scheme.* New York: Holt, Rinehart & Winston.

Piaget, J. (1927/1960). *The child's conception of physical causality.* Totowa, N.J.: Littlefield, Adams.

Piaget, J. (1928a/1976). Ecrits sociologiques: I. Logique génétique et sociologie. In G.

Busino (Ed.), *Les sciences sociales avec et après Jean Piaget* (pp. 44–80). Geneva: Librairie Droz.

Piaget, J. (1928b/1964). *Judgment and reasoning in the child.* Totowa; N.J.: Littlefield, Adams.

Piaget, J. (1929/1960). *The child's conception of the world.* Totowa. N.J.: Littlefield. Adams.

Piaget, J. (1932/1965). *The moral judgment of the child.* London: Free Press.

Piaget, J. (1933/1976). Ecrits sociologiques: II. L'individualité en histoire: L'individu et la formation de la raison. In G. Busino (Ed.), *Les sciences sociales avec et après Jean Piaget.* Geneva: Librairie Droz.

Piaget, J. (1936/1952). *The origins of intelligence in children.* New York: International Universities Press.

Piaget, J. (1937/1954). *The construction of reality in the child.* New York: Basic Books.

Piaget, J. (1939a). Pédagogie de l'enfance. *Encyclopédie francaise.* Tome 15: *Education et instruction* (Chap. 26, pp. 4–16). Paris: Société de Gestion de l'Encyclopédie Française.

Piaget, J. (1939b). Examen des méthodes nouvelles. *Encyclopédie française.* Tome 15: *Education et instruction* (Chap. 28, pp. 1–13). Paris: Société de Gestion de l'Encyclopédie Française.

Piaget, J. (1945/1962). *Play, dreams, and imitation in childhood.* New York: Norton. (First published as *La formation du symbol*).

Piaget, J. (1947/1966). *Psychology of intelligence.* Totowa, N.J.: Littlefield, Adams.

Piaget, J. (1948/1973). *To understand is to invent.* New York: Grossman. (First published in *Prospects,* UNESCO Quarterly Review of Education.)

Piaget, J. (1951/1976). Pensée égocentrique et pensée sociocentrique. In G. Busino (Ed.), *Les sciences sociales avec et après Jean Piaget.* Geneva: Librairie Droz.

Piaget, J. (1953, November). How children form mathematical concepts. *Scientific American,* pp. 74–79.

Piaget, J. (1954/1981). *Les relations entre l'affectivité et l'intelligence dans le développement mental de l'enfant.* Paris: Centre de Documentation Universitaire. (Published in part in J. Piaget, *Intelligence and affectivity: Their relation during child development.* Palo Alto, Calif.: Annual Reviews.)

Piaget, J. (1961/1969). *The mechanisms of perception.* New York: Basic Books.

Piaget, J. (1963/1976). Problèmes de la psycho-sociologie de l'enfance. In G. Busino (Ed.), *Les sciences sociales avec et après Jean Piaget,* Geneva: Librairie Droz.

Piaget, J. (1964). Development and learning. In R. Ripple & V. Rockcastle (Eds.), *Piaget rediscovered: A report of the conference on cognitive studies and curriculum development* (pp. 7–20). Ithaca, N.Y.: Cornell University Press.

Piaget, J. (1965/1977). *Etudes sociologiques.* Geneva: Librairie Droz.

Piaget, J. (1967). *Six psychological studies.* New York: Random House.

Piaget, J. (1969/1970). *Science of education and the psychology of the child.* New York: Viking Compass.

Piaget, J. (1970a). *Genetic epistemology.* New York: Columbia University Press.

Piaget, J. (1970b/1973). *Main trends in psychology.* New York: Harper & Row.

Piaget, J. (1970c). Piaget's theory. In P. Mussen (Ed.), *Carmichaels' manual of child psychology* (3rd ed.) (Vol. I). New York: Wiley.

Piaget, J. (1970d/1972). *The principles of genetic psychology.* New York: Basic Books.

Piaget, J. (1970e/1972). *Psychology and epistemology.* New York: Viking Press.

Piaget, J. (1971/1974). *Understanding causality.* New York: Norton.

Piaget, J. (1972a). Problems of equilibration. In C. Nodine, J. Gallagher, & R. Humphreys (Eds.), *Piaget and Inhelder on equilibration.* Philadelphia: Piaget Society.

Piaget, J. (1972b). Some aspects of operations. In M. Piers (Ed.), *Play and development,* New York: Norton.

Piaget, J. (1974a, May 10). *The development of causal relations in children.* Lecture sponsored by the Urban Education Research Program. College of Education, University of Illinois at Chicago Circle.

Piaget, J. (1974b/1980). *Experiments in contradiction.* Chicago: University of Chicago Press.

Piaget, J. (1974c). *The grasp of consciousness: Action and concept in the young child.* Cambridge, Mass.: Harvard University Press.

Piaget, J. (1974d/1978). *Success and understanding.* Cambridge, Mass.: Harvard University Press.

Piaget, J. (1975/1985). *The equilibration of cognitive structures: The central problem of intellectual development.* Chicago, Ill.: University of Chicago Press.

Piaget, J. (1976). The affective unconscious and the cognitive unconscious. In B. Inhelder & H. Chipman (Eds.), *Piaget and his school: A reader in developmental psychology.* New York: Springer-Verlag.

Piaget, J. (1978). Preface. In C. Kamii & R. DeVries, *Physical knowledge in preschool education* (pp. vii–viii). Englewood Cliffs, N.J.: Prentice-Hall.

Piaget, J. (1980). *Les formes élémentaires de la dialectique.* Paris: Galimard.

Piaget, J., & Garcia, R. (1971/1974). Physico-geometric explanations and analysis. In J. Piaget, *Understanding causality.* New York: Norton.

Piaget, J., & Inhelder, B. (1941/1974). *The child's construction of quantities.* London: Routledge and Kegan Paul.

Piaget, J., & Inhelder, B. (1964). *The early growth of logic in the child.* London: Routledge and Kegan Paul.

Piaget, J., & Inhelder, B. (1966a/1971). *Mental imagery in the child: A study of the development of imaginal representation.* New York: Basic Books.

Piaget, J., & Inhelder, B. (1966b/1969). *The psychology of the child.* New York: Basic Books.

Piaget, J., & Szeminska, A. (1941/1952). *The child's conception of number.* London: Routledge and Kegan Paul.

Power, C., Higgins, A., Kohlberg, L., & Reimer, J. (1986). *Democracy and schooling.* New York: Columbia University Press.

Pratt, C. (1948/1970). *I learn from children.* New York: Simon and Schuster. Reprint ed., New York: Cornerstone Library.

Rainbow Series, Project Head Start. (1965). Washington, D.C.: Office of Economic Opportunity.

Rambusch, N. (1962). *Learning how to learn.* Baltimore: Helicon Press.

Read, K. (1966). *The nursery school: A human relations laboratory.* Philadelphia, Pa.: W. B. Saunders.

Reid, J. (1966). Learning to think about reading. *Educational Research, 9,* 56–62.

Reese, H., Overton, W. (1970). Models of development and theories of development. In L. Goulet & P. Baltes (Eds.), *Life-span developmental psychology: Research and theory.* New York: Academic Press.

Rest, J. (1973). The hierarchical nature of moral judgment. *Journal of Personality, 41,* 86–109.

Scharf, P. (1978). *Moral education.* Davis, Calif.: Responsible Action.

Schickedanz, J. (1981, November). Hey: This book's not working right. *Young Children,* pp. 18–27.

Schweinhart, L., Weikart, D., & Larner, M. (1986). Consequences of three preschool curriculum models through age 15. *Early Childhood Research Quarterly, 1*(1), 15–46.

Scriven, M. (1967). The methodology of evaluation. *American Educational Research Association Monograph Series on Curriculum Evaluation, 1,* 39–83.

Selman, R. (1980). *The growth of interpersonal understanding.* New York: Academic Press.

Selman, R., Byrne, D., & Kohlberg, L. (1974). *Teacher's guide: A strategy for teaching social reasoning.* Pleasantville, N.Y.: Guidance Associates.

Selman, R., & Demorest, A. (1984). Observing troubled children's interpersonal negotiation strategies: Implications of and for a developmental model. *Child Development, 55,* 288–304.

Selman, R., & Kohlberg, L. (1972a). *First things: Values.* White Plains, N.Y.: Guidance Associates.

Selman, R., & Kohlberg, L. (1972b). *A strategy for teaching values.* Pleasantville, N.Y.: Guidance Associates.

Selman, R., Kohlberg, L., & Byrne, D. (1974a). *A strategy for teaching social reasoning.* Pleasantville. N.Y.: Guidance Associates.

Selman, R., Kohlberg, L., & Byrne, D. (1974b). *First things: Social reasoning.* White Plains, N.Y.: Guidance Associates.

Selman, R., & Lieberman, M. (1975). Moral education in the primary grades: An evaluation of a developmental curriculum. *Journal of Educational Psychology, 67*(5), 712–716.

Shapiro, E., & Biber, B. (1972). The education of young children: A developmental-interaction approach. *Teachers College Record, 74*(1), 56–79.

Shapiro, E., & Wallace, D. (1981). Developmental stage theory and the individual reconsidered. In E. Shapiro & E. Weber (Eds.), *Cognitive and affective growth: Developmental interaction* (pp. 111–131). Hillsdale, N.J.: Erlbaum.

Sigel, I. (1971, January). The development of classificatory skills in young children: A training program. *Young Children,* pp. 170–184.

Sigel, I. (1979). *Educating the young thinker* [Videotape]. Princeton, N.J.: Educational Testing Service.

Sinclair, A., Siegrist, F., & Sinclair, H. (1982). *Young children's ideas about the written number system.* Paper presented at the NATO Conference on the Acquisition of Symbolic Skills, University of Keele.

Sinclair, H. (1971). Piaget's theory of development: The main stages. In M. Rosskopf, L. Steffe, & S. Taback (Eds.), *Piagetian cognitive-development research and mathematical education.* Washington, D.C.: National Council of Teachers of Mathematics.

Sinclair, H. (1979). Piaget on number. Unpublished manuscript.

Skinner, B. (1984). The shame of American education. *The American Psychologist, 39*(9), 947–954.

Smilansky, S. (1968). *The effects of sociodramatic play on disadvantaged preschool children.* New York: Wiley.

Smilansky, S. (1971). Can adults facilitate play in children? Theoretical and practical considerations. In *Play: The child strives toward self-realization* (pp. 39–50). Washington, D.C.: National Association for the Education of Young Children.

Smith, F. (1975). The relation between spoken and written language. In E. Lenneberg & E. Lenneberg (Eds.), *Foundations of language development* (Vol. 2). New York: Academic Press.

Snarey, J. (1985). A critical review of cross-cultural studies of moral development. *Psychological Bulletin*, pp. 207–226.

Sonquist, H., & Kamii, C. (1967). Applying some Piagetian concepts in the classroom for the disadvantaged. *Young Children, 22,* 231–246.

Sonquist, H., Kamii, C., & Derman, L. (1970). A Piaget-derived preschool curriculum. In I. Athey & D. Rubadeau (Eds.), *Educational implications of Piaget's theory* (pp. 101–114). Waltham, Mass.: Ginn/Blaisdell.

Spodek, B. (1972). *Teaching in the early years.* Englewood Cliffs, N.J.: Prentice-Hall.

Standing, E. (1957). *Maria Montessori: Her life and work.* New York: New American Library.

Stodolsky, S., & Jensen, J. (1969). *Final report: Ancona Montessori research project for culturally disadvantaged children.* Submitted to the Office of Economic Opportunity.

Stone, C., Robinson, S., & Taylor, S. (1980). *Negotiation of task completion: Coding manuals I, II, and III.* Unpublished manuscript.

Sund, R., Adams, D., Hachett, J., & Mayer, R. (1985). *Accent on science.* Columbus, Ohio: Charles E. Merrill.

System Development Corporation. (1972). *Effects of different Head Start program approaches on children of different characteristics: Report on analyses of data from 1968–69 national evaluation.* Prepared for Project Head Start, Office of Child Development, U.S. Department of Health, Education and Welfare.

Taylor, B. (1964). *A child goes forth.* Provo, Utah: Brigham Young University Press.

Teberosky, A. (1982). Construcción de escrituras a través de la interacción grupal. In E. Ferreiro & M. Gomez Palacio (Eds.), *Nuevas perspectivas sobre los procesos de lectura y escritura.* Mexico City: Siglo.

Teberosky, A. (1984). La intervención pedagógica y la comprehensión de la lingua escrita. *Lectura y vida, 5*(4). Unpublished translation by R. Pena-Hines.

Thier, H., Karplus, R., Knott, R., Lawson, C., & Montgomery, M. (1979). *Beginnings: Teacher's guide.* New York: Rand McNally.

Todd, V., & Heffernan, H. (1970). *The years before school.* New York: Macmillan.

Tompert, A. (1984). *Nothing sticks like a shadow.* Boston: Houghton Mifflin.

Turiel, E. (1983). *The development of social cognition: Morality and social convention.* New York: Cambridge University Press.

Turner, M. (1957). *The child within the group.* Stanford, Calif.: Stanford University Press.

University of Illinois Children's Center. (1985). *I made it myself: A cookbook for young children.* Chicago: University of Illinois at Chicago.

Vygotsky, L. (1978). *Mind in society.* Cambridge, Mass.: Harvard University Press.

Wadsworth, B. (1978). *Piaget for the classroom teacher* (2nd ed.). White Plains, N.Y.: Longman.

Weber, E. (1969). *The kindergarten: Its encounter with educational thought in America.* New York: Teachers College Press.

Weber, E. (1984). *Ideas influencing early childhood education: A theoretical analysis.* New York: Teachers College Press.

Weikart, D., Rogers, L., Adcock, C., & McClelland, D. (1971). *The cognitively oriented curriculum.* Urbana, Ill., and Washington, D.C.: Educational Resources Information Center, National Association for the Education of Young Children.

Werner, H. (1948/1961). *Comparative psychology of mental development.* New York: Science Editions.

Wheeler, D. (Ed.). (1977). *Notes on mathematics for young children.* New York: Cambridge University Press.

Willert, M., & Kamii, C. (1985). Children teach themselves to read. *Young Children, 40*(4), 3–9.

Yaden, D. (1984). Reading research in metalinguistic awareness: Findings, problems, and classroom applications. *Visible Language, 17*(1), 5–47.

Zimiles, H. (1968). An analysis of current issues in the evaluation of educational programs. In J. Hellmuth (Ed.), *Disadvantaged child.* Vol. 2: *Head Start and early intervention* (pp. 545–554). New York: Brunner/Mazel.

Zimiles, H. (1970). Has evaluation failed compensatory education? In J. Hellmuth (Ed.), *Disadvantaged child.* Vol. 3: *Compensatory education: A national debate* (pp. 238–245). New York: Brunner/Mazel.

Zimiles, H. (1981). Commentary on David Elkind: Stages in the development of reading. In I. Sigel, D. Brodzinsky, & R. Golinkoff (Eds.), *New directions in Piagetian theory and practice* (pp. 281–284). Hillsdale, N.J.: Erlbaum.

Index